THE MEMOIRS OF HERBERT HOOVER

Years of Adventure
1874–1920

THE MACMILLAN COMPANY
NEW YORK · CHICAGO
DALLAS · ATLANTA · SAN FRANCISCO
LONDON · MANILA
IN CANADA
BRETT-MACMILLAN LTD.
GALT, ONTARIO

HERBERT HOOVER AS CHAIRMAN OF THE COMMISSION
FOR RELIEF IN BELGIUM, LONDON, 1916

THE MEMOIRS

OF

Herbert Hoover

❦❦❦❦❦❦❦

Years of Adventure

1874-1920

THE MACMILLAN COMPANY: NEW YORK

PREFACE

These memoirs are not a diary but a topical relation of some events and incidents in a roughly chronological order. It has been my habit to keep notes and documents rather than daily entries—for which indeed I have found little time in life.

This volume comprises three parts: the first covers the period from my birth in 1874 to the end of my professional career in 1914; the second covers the First World War and the Armistice from mid-1914 to October, 1919; the third, my relations to the making of the Treaty of Versailles in 1919.

The first part was written at odd times during 1915–1916 when I was occupied with Belgian Relief. At that time I constantly had to journey backwards and forwards from London, crossing the English Channel two score times en route to Holland, Belgium, Germany, and often thence to Switzerland, Paris, and London again. These journeys were filled with hours of waiting. Wartime boats and trains were always late in starting or in arriving. There was also the eternal waiting in hotels for appointments with officials. Consequently, in the waits, I compiled this sort of record of my varied life for my two sons who I hoped would follow my profession as an engineer (as they did). It also served to relieve the boredom and monotony of the waits.

This portion was not originally intended for publication. Mrs. Hoover and I always believed the incidents of our family life were our sole possession. But myths sometimes good and sometimes not appear as to all persons who enter public life. Whether the myths are good or bad, they do not contribute to the store of truth.

The second and third parts, relating to my activities during World War I, were written at various times from 1920 to 1924.

The text has not been changed except to include some minor quotations from subsequent disclosures in proof of what happened in the negotiation of the peace and to condense the text by eliminating a large amount of documentation. This documentation has become generally available, and footnotes to the text indicate where it can be found. Among the available sources is the Stanford War Library, which contains probably ten million items on World War I and its aftermath.

Part of the text on peace making was published in the *Saturday Evening Post* in November, 1941.

I could have revised this volume in the light of twenty-five years after, but it has seemed to me that the value of such memoirs is to reflect views one held at the time and to clothe the documents of formal history with their background of events and personalities. I saw that war in the raw, together with some of its political and international phases, probably more intimately than any other American.

CONTENTS

Contents

ILLUSTRATIONS

xi

CHAPTER 1

⬥⬥⬥⬥⬥⬥⬥

IOWA

1874–1884

FROM ZERO TO TEN YEARS OF AGE

I prefer to think of Iowa as I saw it through the eyes of a ten-year-old boy.[1] Those were eyes filled with the wonders of Iowa's streams and woods, of the mystery of growing crops. They saw days filled with adventure and great undertakings, with participation in good and comforting things. They saw days of stern but kindly discipline.

In later years I was told that if I went back to these scenes everything would have shrunk up and become small and ordinary. For instance, there was Cook's Hill. That was a great long hill where on winters' nights, to satisfy our human craving for speed, we slid down at terrific pace with our tummies tight to home-made sleds. I've seen it several times since; it's a good hill and except for the now obsolete method of

[1] Herbert Hoover was born at West Branch, Iowa, on August 10, 1874. His elder brother Theodore was born on January 28, 1871. His youngest sister May was born September 1, 1876.

His father, Jesse Clark Hoover, was born at West Milton, Ohio, September 2, 1846, and died from typhoid fever at the age of 34 in West Branch, December 10, 1880, Herbert being then six years old. His mother, Huldah Minthorn Hoover, was born at Burgersville, Norwich Township, Ontario, Canada, on May 4, 1848, and died of pneumonia at the age of 34 on February 24, 1883, Herbert being then eight years old. His mother's forebears were Quakers who landed in New England from England at various times from 1630 on.

Herbert Hoover's grandfather Eli Hoover was born at West Milton, Ohio, in 1820. His great-grandfather Jesse Hoover was born in 1800 at Uwharrie River, Randolph County, North Carolina. His great-great-grandfather John Hoover was born at Union Bridge, Maryland, 1760. His great-great-great-grandfather Andrew Hoover was born in Ellerstadt, the Palatinate, of Swiss parents, in 1723, and migrated to Pennsylvania in 1738. Andrew Hoover was of Quaker faith as were all his descendants.

[1]

thawing out frozen toes with ice-water the operation needs no modern improvement. The swimming hole under the willows down by the railroad bridge is still operating efficiently albeit modern mothers probably use cleaning fluid to get rid of clean and healthy mud when the boys come home from swimming. The hole still needs to be deepened, however. It is hard to keep from pounding the mud with your hands and feet when you shove off for the 30 feet of a cross-channel swim.

And there were the woods down by the Burlington track. The denudation of our forests hasn't reached them even yet. And there are rabbits still being trapped in cracker boxes held open by a figure four trap. Rabbits early on a cold morning are nervous rabbits, but in the lore of boys it was better to bring them home alive. My brother Theodore, being older, had surreptitiously behind the blacksmith shop read in the *Youth's Companion* full directions for rendering live rabbits secure. I say surreptitiously, for mine was a Quaker family unwilling in those days to have youth corrupted with stronger reading than the Bible, the encyclopedia, or those great novels where the hero overcomes the demon rum. Soon after Theodore had acquired this higher learning on rabbits he proceeded to instruct me to stand still in the cold snow and to hold up the rabbit while with his not over-sharp knife he proposed to puncture holes between its sinews and back knee-joints, through which holes he proposed to tie a string and thus arrive at complete security. Upon the beginning of this operation the resistance of the rabbit was too much for me. I was not only blamed for its escape all the way home and for weeks afterwards, but continuously for many years. I thought I would write to the *Youth's Companion* and suggest that they make sure this method is altered. For I never see rabbit tracks across the snowy fields that I do not have a painful recollection of it all.

There were also at times pigeons in this forest and prairie chickens in the hedges. With the efficient instruction on the use of bows and arrows from a real live American Indian boy of a neighboring Indian school and certain experiences of my own while living in Indian territory, sometimes by volleys in battalions we did bring down a pigeon or a chicken. The Ritz has never yet provided game of such wondrous flavor as this bird plucked and half-cooked over the small-boy's campfire.

There were sun-fish and cat-fish to be had. Nor did we possess the modern equipment in artificial lures, the tackle assembled from the steel of Damascus, the bamboos of Siam, the tin of Bangkok, the lacquer of China or silver of Colorado. We were still in that rude but highly effective epoch of the willow poles with a butcher-string line and hooks ten for a dime. And the dime was hard to come by. Our compelling lure was a segment of an angleworm and our incantation was to spit on the bait. We lived in the time when a fish used to bite instead of strike and we knew it bit when the cork bobbed. And moreover we ate the fish.

And in the matter of eating, my recollections of Iowa food are of the most distinguished order. Some will say that is the appetite of youth, but I have also checked this up. At later stages in my life, I had opportunity to eat both the presumably very best food in the world, as well as the very worst. When I ate the worst, my thoughts went back to Iowa, and when I ate the best I was still sure that Aunt Millie was a better cook. Some thirty years after this time, in visiting Aunt Millie, I challenged that dear old lady, then far along in years, to cook another dinner of the kind she had provided on Sabbath days when we were both more youthful. She produced that dinner, and I am able to say now that if all the cooks of Iowa are up to Aunt Millie's standard, then the gourmets of the world should leave Paris for Iowa, at least for Cedar County.

I have mentioned the Burlington track. It was an inspiring place. It was ballasted with glacial gravels where, by hard search, you discovered gems of agate and fossil coral which could, with infinite backaches, be polished on the grindstone. Their fine points came out wonderfully when wet, and you had to lick them with your tongue before each exhibit. I suppose that engineering has long since destroyed this inspiration to young geologists by mass-production of crushed rock.

My recollection of my father is of necessity dim indeed. I retain one vivid memento from his time. Playing barefoot around the blacksmith shop, I stepped on a chip of hot iron and carry the brand of Iowa on my foot to this day. Before his death he had parted with the blacksmith shop and had established a comfortable farm implement business. With larger resources and a growing family, he then bought a larger house across the street from the little cottage now preserved by the State of Iowa as my birthplace. The new house was later destroyed but my memories are associated with it.[2]

At the implement shop he had a machine for putting barbs on wire. After the barbs were fixed, the bundles of wire were dipped in hot tar to prevent rust. While no one was looking I undertook an experiment in combustion by putting a lighted stick in the caldron. It produced a smoke that brought the town running and me speeding the other way in complete terror. Whenever I see a picture of a volcanic eruption I recall that terror. Another experiment in wood carving nearly cut a forefinger off. The scar is still there, but I had compensations among other small boys from my surgical importance.

My recollections of my mother are more vivid and are chiefly of a sweet-faced woman who for two years kept the little family of four together. She took in sewing to add to the family resources. It was only years later that I learned of her careful saving of the $1000 insurance upon my father's life in order that it might help in our education. As a help to her, an uncle, Major Laban Miles, took me to the then Indian Territory for eight or nine months, where I lived with his family. He was United States Indian Agent to the Osage Nation, a position he held with the affection of the Indians for many years. It was my first train journey and my first long buggy-drive—from Arkansas City to Pawhuska, the agency. Here with cousins of my own age, I had constant association with the little Indians at the agency school. We learned much aboriginal lore of the woods and streams, and how to make bows and arrows. We attended the Indian Sunday-school which was conducted in English. One Sunday, a visiting missionary, reviewing the service, demanded to know the subject of the day's

[2] The original one-story, three-room cottage where Mr. Hoover was born was for many years obscured by a two-story addition across the front. This is the shape of the house in Grant Wood's famous painting and is the one which appears in most illustrations. After Mr. Hoover was elected President, the place became a profitable hot-dog stand catering to inquiring visitors. In 1934 Herbert Jr. and Allan succeeded in purchasing it. On their behalf, Mrs. Hoover supervised the removal of the additions, restored the original cottage, built a caretaker's house, improved the grounds and presented the property to the village of West Branch. It is looked after by the village with an appropriation from the State.

THE BIRTHPLACE OF HERBERT HOOVER, WEST BRANCH, IOWA

lesson. At once all the little Indians piped up "Ananias set fire to his wife," this being an etymological impression of "Ananias and Sapphira, his wife."

So also I was taken for a summer to live with an Uncle Pennington Minthorn in Sioux County, Iowa, where he was breaking in a prairie farm. We lived in a sod house and I was privileged to ride the lead horse of the team which was opening the virgin soil.

Iowa, through the eyes of a ten-year-old boy, is not all adventure or high living. Nor was Iowa of those days without its tragedies. Medical science was still almost powerless against the contagious diseases which swept the countryside. My own parents were among their victims. I, however, successfully passed the requirements of mumps, measles, croup, diphtheria and chickenpox.

Iowa, in those years as in these, was filled with days of school—and who does not remember with a glow some gentle woman who with infinite patience and kindness drilled into us those foundations of all we know today? And there were days of chores and labor. I am no supporter of factory labor for children but I have never joined with those who clamor against proper chores for children outside of school hours. And I speak from the common experience of most Iowa children of my day in planting corn, hoeing gardens, learning to milk, sawing wood, and in the other proper and normal occupations for boys. It was a Montessori school in stark reality. And to more purpose I can speak for the strong and healthy bodies which came from it all.

Since my mother had been educated above most women in those days—as a school-teacher—she was in demand as a speaker at Quaker meetings. She also took a considerable part in the then vigorous prohibition campaigns. On one occasion I was parked for the day at the polls, where the women were massed in an effort to make the men vote themselves dry.

After her death our home was necessarily broken up. I have dim recollections of the councils of kindly relatives and others, not as to who should undertake the duty of raising the three orphans, but who should have the joy of adding them to their own broods. Among these contestants was my school-teacher, Mollie Brown—later Mrs. Carran—

who strove to secure me for adoption. But Mollie was then unmarried, and the others insisted that family experience was a first necessity for my control. Anyway I was taken into the family of an uncle—Allan Hoover—who worked his own farm a mile from the town. My sister May was taken in by my grandmother Minthorn, and my brother Theodore by my uncle Davis Hoover.

My mother had carefully hoarded my father's life insurance. That sum plus the realizations from his agricultural implement business and the sale of our home was by application of relatives to the courts put in charge of Laurie Tatum, a grand old gentleman living at Tipton, Iowa, as legal guardian for all the three children. The relatives wanted no taint of manipulating the "estate."

Farm life then had a different economic setting. I am not stating that I had at that time any pretension to economics or the farm problem. We did know of the mortgage upon Uncle Allan's farm which was a constant source of anxiety and a dreadful damper on youthful hopes for things that could not be bought. At that stage in agricultural history of Cedar County, a farm was not only a farm but all kinds of factories. Here the family performed all the functions of a Chicago packer, a Cincinnati soap company, a Duluth carpet factory and a California canner. They gave toll to a neighbor for the service of a Minneapolis flour mill and, by way of sorghum, they possessed a New York sugar refinery. Every fall, the cellar was filled with bins and jars and barrels. That was social security itself. The farm families were their own lawyers, labor leaders, engineers, doctors, tailors, dressmakers, and beauty parlor artists. They developed high art in feathers and wax. I know that my clothes, partly homespun and dyed with butternuts, showed no influence of Paris or London.

We cut and hauled our own fuel from the wonderful woods ten miles away on the river, and incidentally gathered walnuts and hickory nuts for the winter. These and popcorn balls cemented with sorghum molasses were our chief Christmas confections.

That economic system avoided strikes, lockouts, class conflicts, labor boards and arbitration. It absolutely denied collective bargaining to small boys. The prevailing rate for picking potato bugs was one cent a hundred and if you wanted firecrackers on the Fourth of July you took it or left it.[3]

These farm families consumed perhaps eighty percent of the product of their land. The remaining twenty percent was exchanged for the few outside essentials and to pay interest on the mortgage. When prices rose and fell on the Chicago market, they affected only twenty percent of the income of the family. Today as the result of the industrial revolution and improved methods of planting and of breeding animals and whatnot, eighty percent of the product of the farm must go to the market. When the prices of these things wobble in Chicago, it has four times the effect on the family income that it did in those days. If prices are high, they mean comfort and automobiles; if prices are low, they mean increasing debt and privation.

As gentle as are memories of those times, I am not recommending a return to the good old days. Sickness was greater and death came sooner. While the standards of living in food and clothing and shelter were high enough for anybody's health and comfort, there was but little resource left for the other purposes of living. That is probably one reason why the people of Iowa of that period put more of their time into religious devotion than most of us do now. It certainly was less expensive than modern recreation. Its recreational aspects were, however, somewhat limited.

Those who are acquainted with the Quaker faith, and who know the primitive furnishing of the Quaker meeting-house, the solemnity of the long hours of meeting awaiting the spirit to move someone, will know the intense repression upon a ten-year-old boy who might not even count his toes. All this may not have been recreation, but it was strong training in patience.

The Quakers—more properly the "Friends"—were given that sobriquet in the early 17th century, not because they quaked but because of their founder, George Fox's repetitive demand for the authorities

---

[3] If that wage still prevails, it ought now to be adjusted to the commodity dollar and is entitled to a hearing by the Labor Board. It may be that the use of arsenic on bugs has created technological unemployment in the firecracker industry. If so, the recent remedy would be to dig up the potatoes while they are young.

of his time to quake and tremble before the Lord. They were one of the many Protestant sects which sprang into being because of the repressions on religious liberty and in protest against religious formalism. Their protest against religious rote up to the recent times expressed itself in their peculiar garb of "plain clothes" and adherence to the "plain language." But as time went on, these very customs, the uniform architecture of meeting-houses, the method of conducting meetings, became a sort of formalism itself.

Moreover human nature cannot be fully repressed. The pride of my "aunts" in their Quaker bonnets and their flowing gray skirts contained grains of relieving worldliness. The religious characteristics of the faith were literal belief in the Bible, great tolerance, and a conviction that spiritual inspiration sprang from the "inward light" in each individual. Thus, being extreme religious individualists, they have no paid "ministers" and no elaborate ecclesiastical organization, "the meeting" being only roughly grouped under "quarterly" or "yearly meetings" for spiritual guidance. The reflex of religious individualism is necessarily also economic individualism. The Friends have always held strongly to education, thrift, and individual enterprise. In consequence of plain living and hard work poverty has never been their lot. So far as I know, no member has ever been in jail or on public relief. This is largely because they take care of each other. Also it may be because if members evidence failings of loose living, their elders "visit" them in time to remedy their weaknesses or else expel them from the meeting.

Individual Bible-reading was a part of the Quaker concept of education—and before I left Iowa I had read the Bible in daily stints from cover to cover. Religious training among the Quakers in fact began almost from birth. Even the babies were present at the invariable family prayers and Bible readings every morning. They were taken to meeting every Sunday, since obviously there was no other place in which to park them. Their cries and hushings thereof were often the only relief from the long silences of Quaker worship. The men and women sat divided by a low partition. The elders of the women who sat upon the high "facing-bench" were the only ones of that sex that I could see. "Aunt" Hannah occupied the first place on this bench. At one time, "moved" in meeting, she rose to denounce a proposal of the youngsters that they should have singing in Sabbath-school and use the meeting-house for recreational purposes. She was bitter in her warnings of the wrath to come, and as a peroration made the prophecy that if these things came to pass "this edifice dedicated to God will some day be transformed into a place of abomination." It might even become a "the-a-ter." "Aunt" Hannah was correct. Many years afterward, when the more prosperous community built a brick "church" and introduced singing, the old meeting-house was transformed into a movie establishment.

My earliest realization of the stir of national life was the torch-light parade in the Garfield campaign of 1880. I was not only allowed out that night but I saw the torches being filled and lighted. I was not high enough to carry one but I was permitted to walk alongside the parade. There was no great need for urging voters in our town. There was only one Democrat in the village. He occasionally fell under the influence of liquor; therefore in the opinion of our village he represented all the forces of evil. At times he relapsed to goodness in the form of a ration of a single gumdrop to the small boys who did errands at his store. He also bought the old iron from which added financial resources were provided for firecrackers on the Fourth of July. He was, therefore, tolerated and he served well and efficiently for a moral and political example.

Another touch of national life was the assassination of Garfield. The flag over the main store was placed at half-mast. All the people moved in hushed and anxious hours while his life lingered on. It was thus that I learned that some great man was at the helm of our country.

CHAPTER 2

OREGON

1884–1891

FROM TEN TO SEVENTEEN YEARS OF AGE

In 1884 I was moved to Oregon. Upon the death of their only son, a maternal uncle and aunt asked that I should be surrendered to them. This uncle—Henry John Minthorn—was a country doctor at Newberg, a Quaker settlement in the Willamette Valley.

High preparations were necessary for this journey. At that time the railways conducted a service of emigrant trains to the West. Each car was fitted with bare bunks and a kitchen stove. The passengers furnished their own bedding and food. After some search, my guardians found a family named Hammil, who were emigrating and who agreed to look after me. Aunt Millie repaired my clothes, made up a roll of bedding and cooked an enormous supply of fried chicken, ham, bread, and meat pies. I was able to help feed the whole Hammil family. The daylight scenery during the entire seven-day journey composes an independent film in my memory. I reported by letter to my teacher, Miss Mollie Brown, my disappointment that the Rocky Mountains were made mostly of dirt. Castle Rock and the Devil's Slide invariably remind me of the Hammils. These kind people turned me over to Dr. Minthorn at Portland and another new world spread before a small boy.

When I arrived at Newberg, Aunt Laura Minthorn and her three daughters, my cousins, were making the pear-butter supply for the winter in a wash-boiler over a fire in the yard. I had never eaten a pear before. I was asked to stir the butter and urged to eat as many pears as

I liked. I liked them. But after two days of almost exclusively pear diet I did not eat pears again for years.

Dr. Minthorn was a man of wide attainments who had been educated at the Universities of Iowa and Michigan. Between visits to the sick he helped conduct the newly-established Newberg College—more properly, Academy—teaching history and literature. This was a Quaker institution. Indeed the Quakers played a large part in pioneer education throughout America. Though a small sect, they established primary schools in many cities long before public education became a national policy. Today there are some ten colleges and universities which they founded.

I was at once put to school and the chores. These included feeding the doctor's team of ponies twice a day, hitching them up periodically, milking the cow and splitting the wood. All this routine, plus the abundant religious occasions, somewhat interrupted the constant call for exploration of the Oregon forests and streams. That, however, was accomplished in time. Repression of the spirits of boys is not a Quaker method and the mild routines have their values. Somehow I found time for baseball, jigsaws, building dams, swimming, fishing and exploring the woods with other village boys. As time went on I was introduced to harder tasks. Dr. Minthorn possessed a piece of fir forest, the clearing of which he boldly attacked. The view of these battalions of tall trees in the moonlight haunted me as an advancing and unconquerable army. At odd times the doctor would get a fir tree down— sometimes four feet in diameter. My job was to help burn it up. This was done by boring two holes in the stump of the logs at such angles that they would meet at about a foot deep. Into the top hole we pushed burning charcoal and by blowing into the lower hole would start an internal fire. It was sport the first few times.

One summer I got a job at weeding onions in the great bottom-lands north of Newberg, for fifty cents a day and board. The job lasted about two months and I returned with some $30. It was a great sum and I kept it or part of it for a long time.

When it did not interfere with school hours, Dr. Minthorn occasionally took me on his visits to patients. Sometimes I drove and held the team when he went in. They were profitable journeys to me. The doctor was mostly a silent, taciturn man, but still a natural teacher. He told me much of physiology, health and sickness. He did it mostly after leaving the patients by way of explosions over the neglects which made them sick. The vigor of his disgust was equaled only by his determination to take no payment from poor non-Quaker families whom he called "white trash." The Quakers always paid their bills. Dr. Minthorn had run away from home and joined the Union Army and thus was a veteran of the Civil War. As a boy in Iowa he had driven teams on the Underground Railroad. In these aspects he was to me a great romantic figure, especially his recounting of the Battle of Shiloh in which he took part. He had originally been sent to Oregon as a United States Indian agent. He was one of the many Quakers who do not hold to extreme pacifism. One of his expressions was, "Turn your other cheek once, but if he smites it, then punch him." With this background of sporadic talks from him, the long tedious drives over rough and often muddy forest roads became part of my education.

When I was about 15 years old, Dr. Minthorn started a Quaker land-settlement business at Salem with Charles Moore, Ben Cook and others and I was offered the distinguished position of office-boy. There I worked for two years, living in the doctor's home, now moved to Salem, under Aunt Laura's kindly but very efficient inspections. Sometimes I slept in the back office after night school. I drew a salary ranging from $15 to $20 a month. The bookkeeper of the firm used some of my odd time and in return I received early instruction in bookkeeping. At one time I shifted my aspirations for a life work of driving railway locomotives over to his profession. But he was a sad and dour Scotsman, and after a while he created in me a conviction that it was a cheerless calling.

My duties as office-boy were not very exacting, and in my spare time, with the aid of Miss Laura Hewitt the stenographer, I learned to run a typewriter fairly well.

A few doors down the street from our office was a sewing machine agent. His practice was to take in old machines as part payment on his new variety. He dumped the old machines in the backyard after having smashed them with a hammer. I made a partnership with the office boy at the insurance office next door and we bought the dump of broken machines from the agent for $20. We classified them according to their different makes and assembled unbroken parts into new machines that would work again. But the housewives with whom we tried to do business as low as a dollar each, were suspicious of the reliability of these machines and we lost the $20. But we learned a powerful lot about the insides of sewing machines.

At this time I managed to buy a second-hand "high" bicycle. I got the better of it with many bumps. Soon the new "safety" bicycles arrived with "cushion" tires—and one of these absorbed several months of my salary.

A business college having been opened in Salem, I enrolled for its night sessions. The teacher was a helpful fellow, interested in youngsters. He knew much of mathematics and something of Latin and, finding my predilection for mathematics, carried me thoroughly through algebra, geometry, and "higher" arithmetic. He was less successful with my Latin. At Salem a blessing came my way in the person of a lady of real understanding—Miss Jennie Gray. Her interest was in boys working in stores and offices. She took me to the small library in the town and borrowed for me a copy of *Ivanhoe*. That opening of the door to a great imaginative world led me promptly through much of Scott and Dickens, often at the cost of sleep. Years later, this reading added to the joys of exploring the towns and countryside in England and Scotland.

Adolescent impressions are not of historic importance. Oregon lives in my mind for its gleaming wheat fields, its abundant fruit, its luxuriant forest vegetation, and the fish in the mountain streams. To step into its forests with their tangles of berry bushes, their ferns, their masses of wild-flowers stirs up odors peculiar to Oregon. Within these woods are never-ending journeys of discovery, and the hunts for grouse and expeditions for trout. There was not so much water in proportion to the fish then, and legal limits had not been thought of. I—and other boys—fished with worms until a generous fisherman, whom we met during an excursion to the upper Santiam, gave four of us three artificial flies each. They proved powerfully productive in the mountain streams. It never occurred to me that they were perishable. In any event I nursed those three flies and used them until all the feathers were worn off—and still the trout rose to them. The upper Santiam has sadly degenerated since. A brand-new fly of any variety, even when carefully treated with cosmetics and attached to gut leaders and expensive rods, has nothing like the potency of that bamboo pole and the fly tied directly upon the end of a string. To climb out of a thousand-foot-deep canyon was an evening's task of no effort at all in those days.

My chief contact with public affairs was through an elderly, retired, argumentative Democrat named Hobson and his helpers who came frequently to the office in the evenings to argue matters with the Republican Quakers. The various acts of the Arthur, Cleveland and Harrison administrations, the merits of Jefferson, Lincoln, Robert E. Lee, U. S. Grant and other statesmen were argued and reargued. Free trade and protection always raised high decibels. The debate invariably ended with complete disgust of each one at the obstinacy and low intelligence of his opponent.

One of the partners in the land settlement business was Mr. Charles Moore. One of my acquaintances was Bill Hindricks, the sole reporter on the *Oregon Statesman*. Many years later, Messrs. Moore, Hindricks and Laura Hewitt, our stenographer, then grown to a woman of influence, constituted themselves an effective committee which launched the Oregon campaign for my nomination for President.

The kindly attitude of the American grown-ups toward youngsters had still another fateful consequence for me. An engineer from the East—a Mr. Robert Brown—drifted into the office on some mission and made the acquaintance of the office-boy. In the course of our talks he discussed the advantages of college training for a profession. He spoke much of engineering. For a year I mulled it over, talking to all who would listen. I haunted the little foundry, the sawmill and the repair shops of the town. I collected catalogues and information on engineering and universities. I determined to become an engineer. My leanings had been initially to the mechanical side. But I had visited a mining prospect in the Cascades with a mining engineer who persuaded me that his branch of the profession offered more choice. His study of the geology of the mine and his conclusions therefrom that the mine was no good excited my imagination.

The efforts of the family secured promise of some sort of scholarship at a Quaker college—Earlham College in Indiana. But my opposition was final when I found it had no engineering courses. About this time a notice appeared in the press to the effect that public examinations would be held for entrance to the new, free university founded by Senator Leland Stanford, shortly to be opened in California. Then came the announcement that Mathematics Professor Joseph Swain would conduct entrance examinations in Portland. Dr. Swain was a well-known Quaker, so that his association with the otherwise suspiciously godless institution served to overcome that family hurdle.

In due time I appeared in Portland and did my best with the subjects put to me. The mathematics all came easy—a fact observed by the professor. But I was sadly deficient in the other approaches to higher education. Again one of those unforgettable kindnesses toward youngsters intervened. Professor Swain called me into his room and at once overcoming my diffidence talked to me about the new University, and my previous deficient schooling due to my career as office-boy. He inquired into my financial resources which embraced a few hundred dollars in the hands of Laurie Tatum as my immediate assets. In the end he suggested that I come down to the University three months early, engage a tutor and take some of the subjects over again. He thought I could earn my way through the college. I resigned my great office and gathered up all my possessions—being $160 of savings, two suits of clothes and a bicycle (and one-third of the Tatum reserve). The Minthorn family added $50 and put me on the train with blessings, affections—and food.

CHAPTER 3

STANFORD UNIVERSITY

1891–1895

I arrived at Menlo Park—there being no station yet at Palo Alto—
with my bicycle, satchel and directions from Professor Swain to go to
Adelante Villa, where a Miss Fletcher would furnish me board and
tutoring.

Miss Fletcher did her best with charm and patience. No one knew
how many students would come to the new University. A certain
anxiety that there should be enough no doubt helped me in taking
those entrance subjects at which I had failed before. And when the
crucial day came I got by with all requirements subject to some "conditions," except that I was one subject short. I earnestly examined the
various elective alternatives for a spot where I might attack this final
citadel. My association with my doctor uncle stood me in good stead.
For by polishing a sound memory and boning all night on two text-
books on physiology, I triumphantly passed in that subject. A Salem
boy—Fred Williams—and I moved into Encina Hall, the men's dor-
mitory, the week before its opening and were proudly its first inhabitants. Also, the Encina dining room gave so many options in food that
I was able to declare my complete independence from mush and milk,
which under stiff moral pressure had been my major breakfast course
ever since I could remember.

The University opened formally on October 1, 1891. It was a great
occasion. Senator and Mrs. Stanford were present. The speeches of
Senator Stanford and Dr. David Starr Jordan, the first President, make
dry reading today but they were mightily impressive to a youngster.

Dr. John Branner, who was to preside over the Department of Geology and Mining, had not yet arrived, so with Professor Swain's guidance I undertook the preparatory subjects that would lead into that department later on. Upon Dr. Branner's arrival I came under the spell of a great scientist and a great teacher, whose friendship lasted over his lifetime.

My first need was to provide for myself a way of living. I had the $210 less Miss Fletcher's services, together with a backlog of some $600 which had grown from the treasured insurance of my father. The original sum had been safeguarded and modestly increased over the years by the devoted hands of Laurie Tatum. Professor Swain interested himself and secured me a job in the University office at $5 a week —which was enough of a supplement for the time. Soon after, Dr. Branner tendered me a job in his department because I could operate a typewriter. This increased my income to $30 a month. While dwelling on earnings I may mention that with two partners I had established a laundry agency and a newspaper route upon the campus, both of which, being sub-let, brought in constant but very small income.

The first summer vacation Dr. Branner obtained for me a job as an assistant on the Geological Survey of Arkansas where he had been State Geologist. The $60 a month and expenses for three months seemed like a fortune. During my sophomore and junior summer vacations I worked upon the United States Geological Survey in California and Nevada, where I saved all my salary. These various activities and the back-log carried me over the four years at the University. I came out with $40 in my pocket and no debts.

The work in Arkansas consisted of mapping the geologic outcrops on the north side of the Ozarks. I did my job on foot mostly alone, stopping at nights at the nearest cabin. The mountain people were hospitable but suspicious of all "government agents." Some were moonshiners and to them even a gawky boy might be a spy. There were no terms that could adequately explain my presence among them. To talk about the rocks only excited more suspicion. To say that I was making a survey was worse, for they wanted no check-up on their land-holdings. To say I was tracing the zinc- or coal-bearing formations made them fearful of some wicked corporate invasion. I finally gave up trying to explain. However, I never failed to find someone who would take the stranger in at nightfall and often would refuse any payment in the morning.

The living conditions of many of these people were just as horrible as they are today. Generations of sowbelly, sorghum molasses and corn-meal, of sleeping and living half a dozen in a room, had fatally lowered their vitality and ambitions. The remedy—then as today—is to regenerate racial vitality in the next generation through education and decent feeding of the children.[1]

My work on the United States Geological Survey in the glorious High Sierra, the deserts of Nevada, and among the mining camps where vitality and character ran strong, was a far happier job. Dr. Waldemar Lindgren headed these survey parties and I was a cub assistant. When in the high mountains we camped out with teamsters, horses and pack mules, and, of equal importance, a good camp cook.

Most of the work was done on horseback. During those two summers I did my full lifetime mileage with that mode of transportation. In these long mountain rides over trails and through the brush, I arrived finally at the conclusion that a horse was one of the original mistakes of creation. I felt he was too high off the ground for convenience and safety on mountain trails. He would have been better if he had been given a dozen legs so that he had the smooth and sure pace of a centipede. Furthermore he should have had scales as protection against flies, and a larger water-tank like a camel. All these gadgets were known to creation prior to the geologic period when the horse was evolved. Why were they not used?

We had a foreign geologist visiting our party who had never seen a rattlesnake. On one hot day a rattlesnake alarm went off near the trail. The horse notified me by shying violently. I decided to take the snake's corpse to our visitor. I dismounted and carefully hit the snake on the head with a stick, then wrapped him in a bandana handkerchief and hung him on the pommel. Some minutes later while the horse and I

---

[1] Years later, during a great Mississippi flood, I had to deal with some hundred Southern counties inhabited by many of this kind of people. I took particular satisfaction in giving them a good hygienic overhauling and at least a few months of proper sanitation and food. The continuation of this for two years more, which I arranged, did wonders in the elimination of hookworm, pellagra and malaria.

were toiling along to camp, half asleep in the sun, the rattlesnake woke up and sounded another alarm. That was too much for the horse. After I got up out of the brush I had to walk five miles to camp. It added to my prejudices against horses in general.

There was some uncertainty one summer as to whether I could get a Geological Survey job. Therefore when vacation came other students and I canvassed San Francisco for work at putting up or painting advertising signs along the roads. Our very modest rates secured a few hundred dollars of contracts, with which we bought a team and camp-outfit. We made for the Yosemite Valley, putting up eyesores, advertising coffee, tea and newspapers along the roads. We pitched our camp in the Valley intending to spend a few days looking the place over. Professor Joseph Le Conte was camped nearby, and I listened spellbound to his campfire talk on the geology of the Valley. A few days later I received a telegram advising me I could join the Survey party. There was not enough money left in the pockets of my sign-painting partners to pay my stage-fare to the railroad. I walked 80 miles in three days and arrived on time.

As the youngest member of the Geological party, I was made disbursing officer. It required a little time for me to realize this was not a distinction but a liability. I had to buy supplies and keep the accounts according to an elaborate book of regulations which provided wondrous safeguards for the public treasury. One morning high in the Sierras we discovered one of the pack-mules dead. I at once read the regulations covering such catastrophes and found that the disbursing officer and two witnesses must make a full statement of the circumstances and swear to it before a notary public. Otherwise the disbursing officer was personally responsible for the value of the animal. I was thus importantly concerned to the extent of $60. The teamsters and I held an autopsy on the mule. We discovered his neck was broken and that the caulk of one loose hind-shoe was caught in the neck-rope with which he was tied to a tree. We concluded that he had been scratching his head with his hind foot, had wedged his halter-rope in the caulk, had jerked back and broken his neck. When we reached civilization we made out an elaborate affidavit to that effect. About two months afterward I was duly advised from Washington that $60 had been deducted from my pay, since this story was too highly improbable. Apparently mules did not, according to the book, scratch their heads with their hind feet. Dr. Lindgren relieved my $60 of misery by taking over the liability, saying he would collect it from some d— bureaucrat when he got back to Washington in the winter.

For years I watched every mule I met for confirmation of my story. I can affirm that they do it. I even bought a statuette of a mule doing it. Some twelve years later I was privileged to engage Dr. Lindgren for an important job in economic geology in Australia. I met him at the steamer in Melbourne. His first words were, "Do you know that that d— bureaucrat never would pay me that $60? And do you know I have since seen a hundred mules scratch their heads with their hind feet?" He would not take the $60 from me.

Lindgren was a great engineer and scientist. Like Dr. Branner, he was also a great teacher. We spent the nights of the two long summers either around campfires in the high mountains, foothill hotels or hospitable homes of mine-managers in the mining districts. He and the other important members of the survey spent their winters in Washington. Their illuminating conversations around the fire embraced a vast amount of objective observation on government outside of the scientific bureaus. And from the conversations around the mines a great amount of engineering lore and practice seeped into my mind. Moreover these summers of hard physical exertion in the mines and the mountains blessed me with a physique equal to any subsequent strain.

Stanford in those days was a small community of intimate association between professors and students. We just "soaked up" a lot of education. The inspirations of physics, chemistry, geology, mathematics, mechanics and engineering—all came easily to me. I was therefore able to carry an unusual amount—for engineers—of instruction in history, economics, and English and French literature. As I recollect it, I failed in only one course—German. I do not recollect, however, that I ever attained A grades in any of them. I had too many other yens and occupations in non-curricular activities.

I attended many lectures on biology, evolution and the reconciliation of science and religion. The impact of the University upon fundamentalist religion of the times brought spiritual conflicts to many young-sters—with much debate. The Quaker "inner light" as the basis of faith, however, suffered less than some others. I much more easily adapted fundamental natural law into my spiritual complex than those whose early training was in the more formalistic sects and of wider doctrinal base.

I was for a short time on the baseball team as shortstop, where I was not so good. In full belief in our prowess as a team we challenged the San Francisco professional team to play us on the campus. They good-humoredly accepted, but when the score was something like 30 to 0 at the end of the fifth inning and getting dark, we called it off. In time my colleagues decided I would make a better manager than short-stop. The job of manager consisted of arranging games, collecting the gate money and otherwise finding cash for equipment and uniforms. On one occasion we played the local team at Santa Rosa. The receipts from the game were not enough to buy the tickets home. I had to can-vass the Stanford parents in the town to raise the deficit. Some of them were caustic persons.

It was this activity which brought my first contact with a great pub-lic man. Former President Benjamin Harrison had been induced by Senator Stanford to deliver a course of lectures upon some phases of government. I profited by the lectures. But then as manager of the baseball team I had a stern duty to perform. We had no enclosed field. We collected the 25 cents admission by outposts of students who de-manded the cash. One afternoon Mr. Harrison came to the game. Either he ignored the collector or the collector was overcome with shyness. Anyway that outpost reported to me that Mr. Harrison had not paid. I collected the money. Mr. Harrison was cheerful about it and bought also an advance ticket to the next week's game. He would not take the 50 cents change from a dollar. But I insisted that we were not a charitable institution and that he must take it. Justice must occa-sionally be done even to ex-Presidents and I here record that he took two more tickets. Upon this solution, he became even more cheerful.

We endowed our university with a football team. Probably because I had been able to save the money for uniforms and equipment of the baseball team, I was made the manager. We arranged a game with the

University of California to be played on the University's second Thanksgiving Day. The game was to take place at the Haight Street baseball grounds in San Francisco. We had seats for a total of 15,000 fans. We bought new uniforms for our teams from a dealer on the sales expectations. We printed seat-numbered tickets for only 10,000 as we did not expect more visitors than that number. When the game came on, two things happened to disturb the managers.

First, the attendance piled up to nearly 20,000. We had no such supply of tickets. So we set up an alley of our college boys from the box offices to the gates and sold tickets for cash—the purchasers being carefully watched so that no outsiders crowded in without having first paid their respects to the box offices. At that time few bills were in use in California. We dealt in silver and gold. The cash piled up behind our entrance selling boys to the extent it spilled on the floors; we had to rent a wash-boiler and a dishpan from nearby householders for the price of a free ticket.

And while these difficulties were being solved, the captains of the two teams turned up, demanding to know where was the football. We had overlooked that detail and had to delay the game for a half-hour while we sent downtown for two pigskins.

I did not see the game, but to our astonishment we won. After the game the California manager and I retired to a hotel with our money, now transferred to grain bags, and sat up most of the night counting it. I had never seen $30,000 before. The bank the next morning found that we had $18 more. We were well financed for the next season.

During these young days of the University the Greek-letter fraternities began their colonization among the students. The fraternities had combined to secure all student offices and elective honors. With others who lived in dormitories and diggings we resented the snobbery that accompanied the fraternity system and we suspected favoritism in handling student enterprises and their loose methods of accounting for money. We declared war for reform. Together with steadfast friends, Ray Lyman Wilbur, Will Irwin, Herbert Hicks and Lester Hinsdale, we organized the "barbarians" for a fight in the student elections. Our ticket won. The forces in it all were about the same as political elections generally. But we introduced and carried a new

HERBERT HOOVER AS A STUDENT AT STANFORD

constitution for the "Student Body" and I was elected the first financial manager—without pay. I may add that in after life all these four men rose to positions of responsibility and eminence in their fields.

As the financial manager in my senior year I set up a full system of accounts of all student enterprises and published them regularly in the college paper. All this was a natural inheritance from the Scottish bookkeeper in Oregon. Football was just coming into big money (for a university activity) and I handled many tens of thousands of dollars in game receipts and athletic and other disbursements.

Stanford is a coeducational institution, but I had little time to devote to coeds. However, a major event in my life came in my senior year. Miss Lou Henry entered Stanford and the geology laboratories, determined to pursue and teach that subject as a livelihood. As I was Dr. Branner's handy boy in the department, I felt it my duty to aid the young lady in her studies both in the laboratory and in the field. And this call to duty was stimulated by her whimsical mind, her blue eyes, and a broad grinnish smile that came from an Irish ancestor. I was not long in learning that she also was born in Iowa, the same year as myself, and that she was the daughter of a hunting-fishing country banker at Monterey who had no sons and therefore had raised his daughter in the out-of-door life of a boy. After I left college she still had three years to complete her college work. I saw her once or twice during this period. We carried on a correspondence.[2]

All of these extra-curricular matters so crowded my life that I neglected to discharge those conditions on entrance "Credits" under which I had entered as a freshman. Had it not been for the active intervention of my friends, Dr. Branner and Professor J. Perrin Smith, who insisted among other things that I could write English, those impla-

---

[2] Lou Henry was born March 29, 1874 at Waterloo, Iowa. Her father was Charles D. Henry, who was born at Wooster, Ohio, in 1842 and served in the Northern armies in the Civil War. His father was born in Connecticut in about 1807. Her mother, Florence Weed, was born in 1848 in Wooster, Ohio.

Mr. Henry obtained his experience as a country banker at Waterloo, and in 1884 moved to Whittier, California, where he and others founded a bank. Lou Henry attended the public schools at Waterloo. In 1890, Mr. Henry moved to Monterey, where he organized the Bank of Monterey and served as its president for many years. Lou Henry attended the Normal School at San Jose, and entered Stanford in 1894, graduating in 1898.

cable persons in the University office would have prevented my getting a diploma with my own class. Nevertheless it duly arrived. It has been my lot in life to be the recipient of honorary diplomas (often in exchange for Commencement addresses) but none ever had the sanctity or, in my opinion, the importance of this one.

I listened to Dr. Jordan's fine Commencement address with my mind mostly on the sinking realization that a new era was opening for me with only $40 in cash and the need of finding an immediate job. The depression of 1893 had reached the Pacific Coast in 1895. I had lived all my life in hard times. But I had never heard of depressions. No one told me that there was one afoot. So I did not need to worry about that. Nor did I have to worry about what the government was going to do about it. No one was crying over "helpless youth" for that matter.

Nor did I have the tearful farewells and the parting from "friends of my youth" and from the campus landmarks which so many writers seem to have experienced. I just assumed that I would see them again.

The faculty and students of this new university in its first years were an unusual group. The faculty consisted of young men who in other universities had given promise in their special fields. The university was thus free from the accumulation of dead wood among teachers which is inevitable with longer years. The students must have had some special streak of enterprise in that they should have chosen a new and untried institution. In any event, it produced from its first five or six classes an astonishing proportion of men and women who in later years were to take leadership in their professions and communities. And this is the more astonishing when it is considered that the institution had none of the natural attractions to fine student material which go with the more settled institutions. In after years it often seemed to me that the intimacy between the faculty and the student body at Stanford had generated more widespread and more lasting friendships than are usual in our mass-production institutions of today.

CHAPTER 4

START OF ENGINEERING LIFE IN
THE UNITED STATES

1895–1897

On leaving college, I needed at once to find some person with a profit motive who needed me to help him earn a profit. At the risk of seeming counter-revolutionary or a defender of evil, I am going to suggest that this test for a job has some advantages. It does not require qualifications as to ancestry, religion, good looks, or ability to get votes.

I went to the gold mining districts of Nevada City and Grass Valley, where I had had some experience with Lindgren the previous summer, and began the search. I did not immediately succeed in impressing any of the profit (and loss) takers with the high potentialities of my diploma or experience. At that time the mines were mostly managed by Cornishmen who had been promoted from foremen. They were good mining men but they had rooted skepticism concerning "them college educated fellers." Not that I was bidding for any top job. I would have been glad to get a start anywhere near the bottom of any mine staff.

The white-collar possibilities and the $40 being exhausted, plus some credit from a kindly hotel-keeper—Mr. Rector—I finally got a job at pushing a car in the lower levels of the Reward mine for $2 a day, on a ten-hour night shift and a seven-day week. However, I did not feel like a down-trodden wage-slave. I was confident that when I got $40 or $50 ahead again I would have the option of looking for some more open-minded economic despot.

The Cornish miners on my shift, while a little offish at first, warmed

up to teaching the tricks of the trade to the anomaly of a college graduate working at common labor. Among this instruction was how to
keep warm in a wet level while the smoke of blasting cleared. It was
done by curling up in a steel wheelbarrow heated with several candles
underneath. In two or three months the Cornish foreman appointed
me helper on a drill and I became an acknowledged and real miner. In
the meantime I had learned some Cornish dialect and listened to an
enormous amount of religious doctrinal debate. The Cornishmen were
very determined in their religious views but capable of suspending
religious discussion for a period of profanity when something went
wrong in the mine. The Cornishmen on our level celebrated the advanced degree which came to me by bringing extra Cornish "pasties"
for our midnight lunch.[1]

After a few months the Reward mine slackened down and I was out
of a job. I then learned what the bottom levels of real human despair
are paved with. That is the ceaseless tramping and ceaseless refusal at
the employment office day by day. Finally I got a job at full miner's
wages at the Mayflower mine. After some time there, I communed
with myself and the $100 in savings as to the future. It was near Christ-
mas, 1895, and seemed an appropriate time to change administrations.

My brother Theodore had been compelled to interrupt his schooling
to take care of my young sister. Grandmother Minthorn, her support,
had died. They were living in Berkeley where he worked as a linotype
operator, and I joined them. My cousin Harriet Miles, with whose
father I had lived in Indian Territory, came to us to look after our
household. She was one of the most sterling women ever born—with
a wealth of Indian dialect stories.

Dr. Lindgren had at one time casually introduced me to Louis Janin
of San Francisco, who was then the outstanding mining engineer on
the Pacific Coast. I went to Mr. Janin's office in San Francisco and
asked to see him; explained to him what my meager experience was;
told him that I wanted a tryout in his office in any capacity. Mr. Janin

[1] Thirty years later the survivors of these men formed themselves into a special campaign committee for my election as President and carried the vote of every Cornish
family in the region. With a little brushing up, I was still able to speak to them in their
own terms at a Fourth of July speech many years later.

was a kindly and convivial soul and asked me to lunch at his club. He spent enough on that lunch to keep me for a week. There he explained gently that he already had more assistants than he could keep busy and that so far as he knew none of the mines with which he was connected needed staff. And to emphasize it he said the only job vacant he knew of was a copyist in his office. With visions of that diminishing $100 and hopes that something might turn up if I kept near the throne, I revealed at once that I could run a typewriter and would like the job. Mr. Janin seemed startled, but he laughed and I was hired. I have no doubt that this episode landed on his busy mind. Some days afterward he sent for me and, saying he had a few months' work upon an extensive engineering project in northern Colorado, asked if I would go as an assistant for $150 a month and expenses. I averred that I certainly would. From that day to this I have never again asked for or looked for an engineering job of any kind. They have come of their own accord.

When I finished the work in Colorado, Mr. Janin sent me as assistant manager to a mine at Steeple Rock, New Mexico. There were some interests in that place outside of the absorbing occupations in mine and mill. It was a tough place, employing Mexican miners. They practiced a good deal of original sin, especially after pay-days, and the gambling end of the straggled canyon was full of life and stimulated cheer. Mr. McDermott, the manager, was also a deputy sheriff and when anyone went so far as to commit murder or near-murder, he felt it his duty to represent the law. He always went unarmed and brought his man out. We had no jail and McDermott, at times with staff help, lowered prisoners down a disused prospecting shaft and threw the rope after them to wait for the sheriff.

Later on Mr. Janin asked me to join his San Francisco office staff in place of a young engineer who had been promoted to a mine superintendency.

During this time Janin was the "expert" in a great mining litigation in Grass Valley. I had worked on the geology of those mines under Lindgren and therefore Janin assigned me to work up the details. It brought two blessings: a special fee and the acquaintance, with later the friendship, of Judge Curtis Lindley.

After I left Nevada City, the jobs I held gave me some spare time of afternoons and evenings. During my college years I had been so intent on preparing for my profession and so occupied with earning a living and with dabbling in extra-curricular activities that I had less general education than I felt was imperative. I began voracious reading of economics, and new continents of thought and interest opened up through more diligent study of Adam Smith, Mill and Bagehot.

I had registered in Berkeley, for my first vote, as a Republican; but I was not to have an opportunity of voting. Through the newspapers I followed the campaign, especially Mr. Bryan's. It was my first shock at intellectual dishonesty as a foundation for economics.

One day in October, 1897, a cable came to Mr. Janin from an important British mining firm—Bewick, Moreing and Company—asking him to recommend to them an engineer for Australia skilled in American gold-mining practice. Janin showed me the cable and said he did not like to lose my services, but it meant $600 a month instead of $200 and he would like to have me take it. I responded that they might be disappointed in my age—then 23—and lack of experience. He gave me both encouragement and a guarantee to fix that. With some trepidation I left for London. Five years later, when I was a partner of Bewick, Moreing and Company, I read Janin's letter to the firm. It was in keeping with his generous character and his belief in youth.

This job enabled me to free Theodore to go back to college. He was graduated in engineering and after a successful career returned to Stanford as Dean of the Engineering School.

CHAPTER 5

❧❦❧❦❧❦

ENGINEERING IN AUSTRALIA

1897–1899

My journey to London was of course the first time I had been east of the Mississippi. The White Star ship of 7,000 tons proved unable to overcome the waves to my satisfaction. But I arrived in London and in due time presented myself to Bewick, Moreing and Company's office. This firm was one of international standing in mining with large head offices in the City of London. At once I had my first experience with the pomp and circumstance of British business. The uniforms of the doormen were most impressive. They ultimately deigned to pass me in to the head of the firm, who proved much less formidable. Mr. Moreing invited me to a week-end at his country place. When I was shown to my room to prepare for dinner, the footman insisted upon assisting my preparations. The idea of having a man about while I dressed was shock enough, but on top of that I sensed deeply the scantiness of my wardrobe as Buttons dissected it piece by piece. At Mr. Janin's suggestion, I had bought dinner clothes. Otherwise his sniffs would have frightened me to flight.

Mr. Moreing was much interested in public questions, and discovering my own interest in English history he arranged for me a visit to a session of the House of Commons. I managed in the few days available to see Westminster and a host of landmarks of our British forebears, including Runnymede. I have ever since envied other Americans their first visit to England. Familiarity wears off the vivid stimulation of personal discovery of the great monuments of history, but in time the comparative poverty and the servility of the mass of people to class distinction bring disillusionment.

The firm had acquired a number of gold-mines in the newly discovered fields of central Western Australia. American machinery and technical practice in gold-mining were far ahead of those of the Australians and British. My employment was for general engineering work among a group of some ten mines and a number of prospecting ventures, and I was subordinate to a resident partner of the firm. With the journey to Western Australia came glimpses for me of further new worlds—in France, Italy, Egypt, and India. History became a reality and America a contrast.

Arrival at the then port of Western Australia, Albany, was a rude shock, because smallpox had broken out on board, and I spent my first two weeks in a quarantine station. Finally I arrived at the desert mining camp of Coolgardie, over the 300 miles of newly constructed narrow-gauge railway. The town was then at the height of a mining boom. It had all the characteristics of a Western American mining camp, with some special Australian attachments. Government was more rigid, violence was absent, but petty crime, immorality, and good cheer were as generally abundant as in the California of '49. The overriding characteristic of all mining booms is the nth degree of optimism. Everybody in Coolgardie lived in a tinted atmosphere of already estimated fortune—or one about to be estimated—and therefore drank champagne as a beverage. The mines made gorgeous surface showings, but development in depth quickly dissolved many astronomic hopes. A nearby district—Kalgoorlie—however, justified its promise in full. Coolgardie, the original discovery, faded out and Kalgoorlie took the center of the mining stage. This camp produced a flock of millionaires, not one of whom so far as I could ever learn survived his subsequent mining gambles.

I was soon engrossed with our mine managers in technical work, laying out plants, planning development work, ordering American equipment, and examining new prospects. The Kalgoorlie mines were unbelievably rich, but presented difficult metallurgical problems, made more difficult by the lack of water. Our principal fuel was the scraggly bush of the desert. Such water as we had came from shallow wells in salty depressions, and had to be distilled for domestic purposes. The wholesale price of household water was 2½ cents a gallon. Under the circumstances we were confined to shower baths and these mostly by way of a suspended bucket with a few pin-holes in their bottom.

These new conditions required great alterations in hitherto known mining practice. We must of necessity recover all the water we could from our metallurgical processes in order to use it over again. To do this I introduced for the first time the filter press, a machine copied from one used in the sugar-refining process. It has since been largely adapted by the mining industry.

I was delegated to sit upon an advisory board of the mine operators on water supply. It was finally accomplished by the government building a 400 mile pipe for fresh water from the coast. We calculated water consumption for household use upon the statistics for the average civilized city. After the water arrived, however, we found the population so trained to economy that our figures were 75 per cent too high.

At one time I tried to enrich the living at our corrugated iron staff-residence by growing a vegetable garden. It started well. But a large variety of creeping things, including several species of ants, entered into competition with each other. We managed to pull two cabbages through. The bookkeeper informed me I had used $250 worth of water for each of them. Anyway the neighbors all collected on the fence every evening to watch a green thing grow.

On one occasion I temporarily took over the manager's job on the Hannan's Brownhill mine so that he might have a vacation. During this time the Governor of Australia, an English nobleman, visited the district, and as the Brownhill was one of the show mines the local reception committee asked that we take him down in it. I had told the foreman to have the mine all spick and span for the visit. He, being an ingenious soul, had, unknown to me, plastered the walls with bright, powdered iron pyrites sprayed through a cement gun. I met the party at the shaft in the usual overall togs and did my best to make the mine interesting. And I could not bear to disappoint the foreman by explaining that all was not gold that glittered beautifully under strings of electric lights. When we came up to the surface, the Governor thanked me kindly and gave me a five shilling tip.

Coolgardie and Kalgoorlie are among the hottest and driest and dustiest places on this earth. The temperature was over 100° at midnight for days at a time. The rain was little more than an inch per year and most of it all at once. The country is unbelievably flat and uninteresting. There is not a fish in stretches of a thousand miles. In fact there are no running streams and few appearances of water courses anywhere in the great interior plain. The country is covered by a low bush eight or ten feet high with occasional eucalyptus trees so starved for water as to have only an umbrella of foliage. The roads—more properly "tracks"—that were gradually cut through the low brush extended in straight lines for a hundred miles. They added to the monotony of life by their never attainable notches in the bush on the horizon. The vegetation was in fact up to expectations considering only one inch of rainfall. It had one redeeming feature. After the sole annual rain the whole desert broke into a Persian carpet of different-colored immortelles which lasted for weeks. When rain threatened the whole town started running for home. When water was 2½ cents a gallon the whole population quit its normal occupation to collect free water from the heavens. Roofs, blankets, buckets, tubs, were all in service.

Some of our mines lay long distances away in the interior and at that time the principal means of transportation was long strings of Afghan camels. We rode them on inspection trips and I am in position to state authoritatively that a camel does not fulfil all the anticipations of romantic literature. He is even a less successful creation than a horse. He needs water oftener than the schoolbooks imply. His motion imparts aches to muscles never hitherto known. No amount of petting will inspire him with affection. His long neck enables him to bite one's leg unless he is constantly watched. We traveled in 20 to 30 mile daily stages, mostly slept on the ground under the cold stars and were awakened by swarms of flies at daybreak. We cooked our own food and I soon reduced my culinary operations to a diet of toasted bread, cocoa and sardines heated in the can. Sometimes we substituted baked beans by the same metallurgical processes. Flies, sand, and dirt generally were the chief undertones. Later on with the digging of more salt-wells and the establishment of crude distilling apparatus we were able to replace our camels with horses—mostly with two-wheeled carts driven tandem.

On one of these early jaunts 150 miles into the interior I camped over-night near a prospect called the Sons of Gwalia, which was being worked by a group of Welshmen for owners in Wales. After supper I called upon them and was taken over their "show" and their small mill. I became much impressed with the evidences of a real mine and on reaching a telegraph office the next day, I cabled to Mr. Moreing that I thought the prospect well worth examination, if he could get an option from their Welsh financial backers. This was done, and a few weeks later I completed the examination and recommended the purchase of a two-thirds interest for $250,000 and a provision for $250,000 working capital. It was my first assumption of responsibility for what seemed to me a huge sum of money. However, the mine turned out well.[1] The firm was naturally pleased with this venture. I was carried for a small percentage interest and was appointed its first manager at $10,000 a year and expenses. I built a corrugated iron residence under the shadow of Mt. Leonora—one of the highest peaks in Western Australia. It rose 160 feet above the plain. I at once undertook vigorous development of the mine and the installation of a large metallurgical plant.

The sodden conditions of life at the Gwalia were perhaps expressed by a foreman who had a habit of getting blind drunk about once a month. Good foremen were too scarce to be discharged for such sins and on one occasion when I reprimanded him violently he said, "Well, if you live in this place you just have to get good and drunk once in a while." I inquired how he knew when he was "good and drunk." He replied, "When Mt. Leonora whiskey begins to taste good, then I know."

But no one need sympathize with men engaged in constructive work at the outposts of civilization. Our staff and I enjoyed every hour of it. There were many light moments. I still recollect Ernest, the Austrian cook, serving American canned corn direct from the tin as a dessert. And the burro who ate the wax matches and had to have his internal

---

[1] Over the succeeding 50 years of continuous operation it has produced $55,000,000 of gold and paid $10,000,000 in dividends.

fire put out by a bucket of water through a funnel. But to feel great works grow under one's feet and to have more men constantly getting good jobs is to be the master of contentment. And here again I had time for reading—chiefly upon Australasia and its history and government.

One day there appeared at the mine a lanky Scots-appearing young man who gave his name as John A. Agnew. He asked for a job, explaining that his experience consisted only of graduation from the University of New Zealand in engineering and some summer work at the mines. He said that he would do any kind of job to get started. My mind harked back to my own case at Nevada City. I put him on as a miner underground. In a few weeks as we needed a shift-boss we promoted him to that job, and subsequently he rose to be mine superintendent.[2]

[2] John Agnew was associated with me in engineering work from that time until I retired at the beginning of the World War. He subsequently rose to the leadership of British mining engineers. At the time of his death in 1939, he commanded the largest group of successful mines of any engineer in the world.

CHAPTER 6

ENGINEERING IN CHINA

1899–1902

In the summer of 1898 Mr. Moreing was in Peking, China, in connection with some engineering work and financial contracts under a bond issue which had been placed in England, Belgium, France and Germany, to provide development capital for a concern called the "Chinese Engineering and Mining Company." It was a large coal-mining and cement-manufacturing business operated by a European technical staff, but in majority Chinese-owned and under Chinese business management. The Chinese Director-General, however, was selected by the government. The purpose of the new capital was to open further mines and to build an ice-free coal-loading port and connecting railway at Chinwangtao on the Gulf of Chihli.

The Director-General of this Chinese Company, Mr. Chang Yen-mao, had recently been appointed head of the Bureau of Mines, a newly created department arising among the "Young Emperor" Kwang Hsu's "reform and progress" movement. Chang consulted Moreing as to the organization of the Department, explaining that he was being buffeted by all the European governments seeking the appointment of their nationals to control the technical staff. Moreing suggested that he avoid these political pressures by appointing an American as Chief Engineer. He further explained that he had in his employ such an American who could at the same time look after the bond-holders' interest in the works to be undertaken by the Chinese Engineering and Mining Company. Upon Chang's authorization, Mr. Moreing cabled to me at the Sons of Gwalia offering me the job, stating that the aggregate salaries would be about $20,000 per annum and expenses.

What with a temperature of 100° at midnight, and the prospect of a new and romantic world, never was a message more enthusiastically received. Moreover, what was more important, I could now cable to Miss Lou Henry at Monterey, California, asking if she would agree that the time had come to be married and go to China. She thought that was possible. The uncertain and turbulent life of an engineer offered no obstacles to her.

I arrived in London in January 1899 to pick up details. I reached California on February 10th. Miss Henry, having determined to join the Quaker faith, wanted a Quaker wedding. That particular kind of ceremony was not possible as there was no Quaker meeting in that part of California and the meeting is an essential part. There was at the moment no Protestant Minister in the town, and we compromised on one of her old family friends, a Catholic Priest. He secured a special dispensation, and we were able to catch the steamer the next morning for China. We sailed with a full batch of reading of all the standard books on Chinese life and customs.

We arrived in Peking in March, 1899. After long sessions with Chang Yen-mao and his multitude of advisers, Chinese and foreign, it was decided that we should live in Tientsin, and that I should assemble the necessary engineering staff. We rented a house in the settlement and Mrs. Hoover had the excitements of trying to furnish it from Chinese availabilities and equipping it with the necessary multitude of Chinese servants.

As most of my journeys into the interior were under circumstances where reasonable comfort or privacy was impossible for any woman, she determined to fill her time learning to speak Chinese. For this, she engaged a Chinese teacher and never failed in her daily stint whenever she was at home. With a natural gift for languages she made great progress in the most difficult tongue in the world. I never absorbed more than a hundred words. But all our life afterwards she kept that hundred words in use between us by speaking Chinese to me on *sotto voce* occasions.

I sent to Australia for John Agnew, Wilfred Newberry, and Daniel

Francis of the Gwalia staff; to the United States for geologists George Wilson and John Means, and to England for a harbor engineer, a Mr. John Hughes. Despite the fact that when we went to work it was 10° below zero, we at once got the Chinese Engineering and Mining Company's new harbor works started.

The problem of building the new port at Chinwangtao with its railway connections and of opening an additional coal mine with more modern equipment constituted something concrete that I could get a hold upon. But the Bureau of Mines which was my major job was something else. It was not only intangible and impalpable but already, by Palace intrigue, the Empress Dowager had wiped Emperor Kwang Hsu and his reforms away. Western ideas were no longer so popular.

The "Young Emperor" had been dethroned and imprisoned. His tutor and adviser upon reform, Kang Yu-wei, had fled for his life. Chang Yen-mao was uncertain of the future but thought that the Empress Dowager's regime could yet be brought to realize China's interest in the development of its natural resources. Chang was not wholly a pure or a reform spirit. He had been an agent of one of the Manchu Princes and had ridden into profitable places in co-operation with the Prince. He still hoped there was progress and power ahead.

The reform period had bred a horde of foreign concession hunters demanding great mining areas with the aid of each foreign Ambassador or Minister, and, with large sums for too-easy corruption, sometimes securing results. There was no form of mining law and no concept of development and production of minerals or the employment of people as a public interest. The whole process consisted in grabbing something that could be promoted upon the European stock exchanges. In the freshness of youth it seemed to me that the beginning must be a systematic mining law requiring development and production with equal rights to all nationalities but under full control of the government. I therefore drafted a decree providing for government lease of mining areas, with provisions, after a preliminary period of prospecting, for royalties to the government, and later on a more settled title requiring conditions as to employment of workers, provision of adequate capital, reversionary rights to the government at the end of a period, and other safeguards. It was a compound of American and

Australian principles of mining law. I think it was one of the first attempts to safeguard China from foreign exploitation.

Chang said it was good; but he knew, as I did by that time, that the political situation did not favor action. He was busy moulding himself into the new political form as fast as he could and, incidentally, helping a few concession hunters.

Among Chang's many advisers was a retired Commissioner of the Maritime Customs of China, Gustav Detring. Herr Detring was a unique China Coast character of his time. On his retirement with pension from the customs, he gave himself with single-minded devotion to the progress and development of China. He sought no profit for himself and believed that by building up Chang, he could effect these purposes. He was relying upon a less than idealistic Chinaman. Detring had arranged with Moreing the foreign loans to the Chinese Engineering and Mining Company—the negotiation which brought me to China. He was most helpful to me because of his fluent Chinese and his great acquaintance with most of the top Chinese officials of the time. Also, he was extraordinarily well informed on the political currents in Peking. Mrs. Detring was a most exceptional and hospitable woman, who radiated charm and friendliness through the isolated community and raised a family of magnificent daughters.

In the meantime Chang concluded that it would be very helpful if we could discover some great, rich gold mine and show an example of making a profit. I argued that China's primary need was iron, steel, coal, lead, zinc, copper and the other industrial metals. These could be only found and developed under stable legal titles which invited venture capital from many sources. However, Chang said that he had heard of some rich gold mines in Jehol, and asked that I go up and look at them with a view to putting up American machinery to take out large amounts of gold.

It was obvious from my own contacts, chiefly with the American Minister, Mr. Conger, that the reform regime had badly crumbled and that until there was a change we might as well look at the new Golconda as do anything else.

The Chinese official assigned as my nurse at once began organization of the expedition. As the place was about 150 miles from the railway,

I suggested that saddle ponies for Wilson and myself and an inter-preter, with two or three pack-mules, a Chinese boy and a cook, would be enough equipment. One can live largely upon the food of the country in China, and shelter is found in the universal village quadrangular inns built around a court. My official guardian protested violently that our proposed outfit did not comport with the dignity of our position. After days of argument I gave up and told him to let me know on what day he would be ready to start from the particular station on the Shan-haikwan Railway.

Receiving the word, Wilson and I took the train at Tientsin. Attached to the train was the private car of Mr. Tong Shao-yi, then Director-General of the Northern Railways of China, a government system of some 600 miles of line. Tong courteously invited us to ride with him, and there began a firm friendship which was to have many curious de-velopments in after years. He was an alumnus of Columbia University, a man of great abilities, fine integrity, and high ideals for the future of China. Tong soon exploded in his antagonism to Chang Yen-mao, my minister superior, explaining him as a palace creation who had risen from a groom by well-applied corruption. He informed us that the Chinese Engineering and Mining Company had been the creation of his uncle, Tong King-sing, now dead, and that the stock was largely owned by the Tong family. Tong asserted that Chang Yen-mao at the time of Tong King-sing's death had by intrigue got himself appointed Director-General of the company through his patrons, Prince Kung and Li Hung-chang, and was now looting the company. All this had a bearing on future events.

The great quantity of our own servants' baggage, even when com-bined with Wilson's and my meager luggage, proved but a molehill to the mountain that we met at our station of departure from the rail-way. Here in the compound of an inn were a hundred mules, ten rid-ing ponies, half a dozen carts, and a company of 100 Chinese cavalry with 20 officers milling around in mounds of bags, boxes, packages and rolls of rice matting. We got started in a day or two amid vast noises and with banners flying, making a cavalcade of some 200 animals with advance heralds and rear guards.

The cavalry general rode first with two staff officers, mounted orderlies and grooms; then came our official guardian with staff and grooms; then Wilson and I also with mounted servants and grooms; then the interpreter and his staff; then a multitude of carts. The dozens of men who brought up the rear, each with his ranking place, I never did fully identify, except for the cook. The interpreter's knowledge of American terms of dismay was inadequate; when things went wrong he solemnly assured us that conditions were "really damn." Wilson and I always called him "Really Damn."

It was impossible to push this cavalcade more than 20 miles a day, so that the journey spread out interminably. Of nights we took over some inn, and initiated a cleaning operation. We soon learned that no amount of sweeping and clean mats could cure the bed-bugs. After much experimenting Wilson and I partly solved this problem by setting the legs of our cots into pans of water. I, however, developed a suspicion that the spiders collaborated with the bugs by building bridges for them. Anyway they invaded us periodically. The cook had once been employed in the French Legation. He insisted upon a full five-course meal and even after most of the "foreign" supplies gave out and the staff of life was wholly chicken and eggs he managed it—chicken soup, welsh rarebit, hot roast chicken, cold chicken salad and sweet omelet. Anything less than five courses was a loss of face and dignity. All of which he cooked over an assortment of charcoal-fired pots in the courtyard. But it was good food.

One permanent gain from such journeying was again the opportunity to read. I had armed myself with a supply of cheap paper translations of Balzac, Dumas, Zola, Victor Hugo, Rousseau, and Montaigne, so that I made at least a beginning of an education in French literature. It subsequently traveled the more solid road of Voltaire, Mirabeau, the Encyclopedists, and the other Revolutionaries.

In about a week we arrived at the mine, to be met with a mob of seeming thousands. I inquired of the interpreter if it meant violence. He said no, but admitted that word had been sent ahead that a great foreign mandarin was coming who could see through the ground and find gold. My Chinese "boy" assured all and sundry that it was because our eyes were green. The Chinese were anxious to check this up and the intimacy of their investigations was somewhat embarrassing. With this valuable special-eye equipment we surveyed the mining scene from the top of a low knoll. Spread over the valley below were hundreds of mat-shaded stone mills, each propelled by an ever-circling pony or mule. These stone mills were the same as those that humanity has used to grind its grain since the days of Ancient Egypt. Each ground up a few score pounds of hard quartz a day. The free gold was washed out over a blanket. The tailings were zealously saved, for the Chinese believed that gold grew in them. Indeed it did, for with oxidation more gold was freed, and they were worked over and over. The richly clad elderly official in charge of the mines proved to be a former shift-boss in the Hite's Cove mine celebrated in the early days of California. He racked his memory hard for English words of greeting, and finally with great dignity produced "Hello, Boss!" In reality he knew a good deal about mining. Next day, with proper dignity we went to the mine. Here clouds of steam were coming from three or four shafts sunk a few hundred feet apart. We soon learned that phenomenon was due to a multitude of leaky steam pumps. It seems that when this manager opened the mines, which had been flooded out for some centuries, he brought up a steam pump from Shanghai. As more water had to be handled with increased workings, he brought more steam pumps of the same size and make, for the original had proved to be very good. There were 30 of them and whole rows of vertical boilers. Underground there proved to be a small vein a foot wide and some 600 feet long, fairly rich. And with labor at 6 cents a day it seemed to pay, despite the multitude of workers. The miners had reached about 500 feet in depth and the manager was desperate over the increasing water. Our guardian at once demanded that we look hard and tell him where there were more profitable veins of less depth. We did look hard but told him we must report our observations only to our superior at Peking. This, at least, served to get us away without being mobbed or losing face. As a matter of fact, every inch for miles had been prospected by the Chinese themselves without consequential result. We reported with a certain amount of confidence that there were no likely possibilities. After a few days to give assurance of exhaustive examination we inquired if it were possible to get back more quickly by running the rapids of the Lanchow River. We were told that it could be done in small boats, but that it would not be proper, as only two persons and a boatman could go in one boat and we would lose face. However, Wilson and I insisted upon it and reached the railway in two days instead of seven.

I went on more expeditions of this sort, following Chang's collection of rumors about gold mines, in Shantung, the Gobi Desert, Manchuria, Shansi and Shensi provinces; always a case of chasing rainbows. However, we made many side excursions in the study of geology, hoping for some evidence of the industrial metals—iron, copper and lead. Some of these journeys required as much as two months. Hundreds of travelers have reported the interesting incidentals of travel in interior China. They are perhaps more interesting to sight-seeing travelers than to engineers who want to get there and find something worth while. One of these horseback journeys reached as far as Urga, the Mongol capital in the Gobi Desert. The Mongol camps and the ceremonies of hospitality are accurately described by Marco Polo and show no foreign influence for good since that time. The monotony of that trip was enlivened by a call on the Hutuktu Lama—a Living Buddha—through the introduction of a Swedish engineer who was building a telegraph line connecting Peking with Russia and the influence of his friend the Russian consul. The Living Buddha, when we arrived, was riding a bicycle madly around an inner court in the great Thibetan Lamasery. He entertained us with a phonograph supplied with Russian records. All of which modern mitigations of the lot of divinity had been provided by the Russian consul.

On one occasion on a return journey from Shensi I came into Kalgan, a gate to the Great Wall of China, on Christmas Eve, with snow and temperatures below zero. The caravan was tired out from my days of pushing to arrive home for Christmas with Mrs. Hoover, and that proved impossible, for our retinue had to rest.

The next morning I called upon the Tao Tai—the local governor—to thank him for our cavalry escort. He proved a distinguished-looking old man of great intellectual perceptiveness and considerable knowledge of the outside world. Someone raised the question of missionaries. He informed us that there was a large American mission in Kalgan and expressed his admiration for the missionaries' devotion in educational and medical work among the people. He said they gave no trouble, but rather wistfully remarked that it would be better if they accepted the jurisdiction of the civil government of China over their converts and did not constantly strain the questions of extra-territorial rights to guard their activities and independence. He said they were too high-minded to realize that they were sometimes imposed upon and that bad characters occasionally found shelter under them. He added that it was a small drawback, however, in proportion to the good they did. He seemed to like to talk with a foreigner and so I stayed with him for some time. At one moment he called a Chinese servant and gave an order that required elaborate explanation. Really Damn informed me that he had ordered a bottle of most precious foreign wine made from honey which a Catholic priest had given him years ago and he wanted to use it on this distinguished occasion. It came in the shape of a beer-sized foreign drinking-glass of Benedictine. Among other things, the Tao Tai told me that he had served as a young officer under General Gordon during the Taiping rebellion. He said he had corresponded with Gordon for some time but that many years ago Gordon had ceased to reply. I was able to give him the ill-tidings of Gordon's death. My story of Gordon's heroic stand at Khartoum served to lighten his real and evident grief. I asked him if he had kept any of Gordon's letters. He said he would search and went into the adjoining room to do so. I had been wondering what I could do about that tank of Benedictine so as not to evidence a lack of appreciation. I seized the opportunity to recommend it to Really Damn for his quick consumption. He went as far as he could and I got more of it down a crack in the brick-paved floor. The Tao Tai had not been able to find the letters and soon I began to note flaws in Really Damn. I withdrew as fast as the thousand polite expressions would permit. Our host had provided a mounted escort back to the inn. And we needed their aid to hold Really Damn on his pony.

Having put the interpreter to bed I made a visit to the Mission. Here I found some twelve Americans—men and women and children—under the direction of a distinguished old gentleman. The Mission was a large compound of schoolrooms, living quarters and a medical clinic. The whole place was alive with Christmas preparations and joyousness. The good doctor asked me to come to the noon Christmas dinner next day and promised turkey. It was a good dinner but the fine American faces were better fare. We talked gaily, mostly with the children, until a Chinese messenger spoke something to the missionary. He saddened visibly and explained that there had been a dreadful incident in the compound. It appeared that many years before in time of great famine the Mission had bought a large number of Chinese children, whose parents sell them in such desperation, hoping thus to save their lives. After the famine the Mission returned the children to all the families they could locate, but had some left over. These they had raised in the compound under continuous Christian influence. In time a pair of them had married. Then arrived several girl-babies in succession with no boy; and finally that morning the disgusted mother had drowned the last arrival. What would I suggest that the Mission do? Remembering the conversation of the day before, I advised them to consult the Tao Tai, for this was a crime under Chinese law. However, they could not bring themselves to do it. She might be executed. I still do not know how it came out.

I found that among the Christmas gifts from the States for the Mission Chinese children were four second-hand regulation footballs. The missionary's daughter seemed stumped on what to do with them. I suggested that, as I was experienced in that line, if they would produce the players I would instruct. She produced three hundred alert youngsters in usual Chinese dress with loose Chinese shoes—but there was snow on the ground. With the aid of the daughter I divided the youngsters into two equal squads, instructed them to get the balls to the opposite fences and put all four balls into play at once. In a minute 300 pairs of shoes were flying in the air but not even stocking feet in the snow slowed up the vitality of those kids.

These missionaries were good people of whose devotion America can be proud. Some months later under Boxer mob-violence they were driven out on to the Gobi Desert. But the Tao Tai gave them protection which saw them safely across the desert to the Russian frontier, though with much hardship. And sturdy, devoted people that they were, they returned again after the disturbances were over. Theirs was an idealism that lived on a level far above cheap treaty-port gossip.

I protested time and again to Minister Chang Yen-mao we were wasting time and money on our expeditions, and that there were far more important duties which could be performed for the Chinese people. However, I entertained the sound conviction that he was hoping to find a gold mine for himself and colleagues at government expense and that he sought therein certain standing by his evidences of ministerial vigor. I finally did get him to agree to a study of the anthracite coal fields which extended inland from west of Peking, and put Agnew, Means and Newberry to work on it.

One expedition during this period had a special interest. Mr. Pethick, an American secretary of Li Hung-chang, asked me to call at Li's *yamen* in Tientsin. I was introduced by Pethick who also interpreted. Li was, among other duties, the Minister of the Yellow River Conservancy. He said that the behavior of the river was giving him anxiety and that as I was an American engineer he wished me to visit the flood-control works and advise him. I protested that I was not that kind of engineer. But all engineers were the same to him and he would have no refusal and said he had arranged it with Chang Yen-mao. From the discussion and from what I already knew it did not seem an intricate matter, so I agreed to go. During the conversation a servant entered with a champagne bottle wrapped in a napkin, foreign style, and served it to me. I found myself faced with another trial by the fire of alcohol and the courtesy of showing appreciation through consumption. I took a swallow and choked into a spasm. I begged Pethick to make some sort of excuse to his Excellency for my inability to take it. He grinned and accepted the apology with great gravity. After we went out, I asked Pethick what was in that bottle. He explained that Li had served from that same bottle to foreigners for a long time and that when the guest departed, the leavings were poured back into the bottle. It was one of Li's variety of jokes.

The Yellow River—the "Sorrow of China"—comes down from the loess hills into the great plain of China on a gently sloping fan. The river has two possible outlets to the sea, the one north of the Shantung Peninsula into the Gulf of Chihli, the other some hundreds of miles to the south of the Peninsula. When this gigantic river decided to change its mouth, it meant the drowning of millions of people. And often enough, mere breaks without such a change resulted in fearful loss of life. Centuries ago, Chinese engineers recognized that the imperative necessity was to hold the river constantly in one channel on its way down the fan. To do this they had for a thousand years built dikes and more dikes in most complicated systems. One result has been that the river has built up its bed above the surrounding land level, thus increasing the dangers. In places they had planted forests of willows along either bank for many miles in length and width. When the river was in flood it brought down a mass of sediment from the loess hills. As the flood spread out among the willows the current was retarded and the sediment deposited. Thus the forest automatically built itself up as a dike. The job was to keep the willow forests in good condition; but beyond all this were the hundreds of miles of artificial and complicated dikes which must be kept in repair.

An important and scholarly official, Mr. Ching Wan-te, was appointed to conduct our expedition of inspection. I was glad that Mrs. Hoover was able to accompany me on this trip for we could travel in reasonable comfort by boat through the waterways—initially through the Grand Canal—and she got much joy out of the teeming life all about us. We had much conversation with Ching Wan-te on Chinese politics, history and lore. Among other things he told us was the solidly established belief of the Chinese that when the Yellow River broke out of its channel in one of its fatal and costly changes of mouth, it was an infallible portent of the fall of the dynasty. He gave corroborative instances running over a thousand years. The river had had its last disastrous break about 1870, but the dynasty had not yet fallen. After examining the works I was convinced the Chinese engineers had been capable enough and that the essential thing was to keep their works in repair. I further concluded that the river and the whole system of conservancy required an exhaustive engineering study in the hope that something could be done to increase the gradient by shortening the course of the river. That would scour the bottom and would relieve the pressure on the dikes. I reported to Li that aside from keeping up the present works there must be a competent study which would require a year of investigation.

Also I concluded that the superstition connecting the floods with the fall of a dynasty had a sound foundation. A new dynasty meant virility in government, the renewed planting of the willows and constant work on the dikes. As the dynasty became old and corrupt, the appropriations for works were grafted and the Chinese cut the willows for fuel. Indeed, according to Ching Wan-te, graft and negligence were the roots of the poor condition of the works which I found. And the grafting had apparently been in action for a long time. The dynasty fell a few years later, according to portent.

These journeyings gave me not only a unique opportunity to observe Chinese life and government, but much time for general reading. Chinese history, Confucius, Mencius, economics, sociology, fiction, Plato, Shakespeare, Schiller, Goethe—and I do not now remember what-all.

All these journeys were suddenly interrupted. There exploded in the faces of two twenty-six-year-old peaceful Americans an event that was to modify their lives, and also give them something to talk about for "the rest of their born days." But, of far greater moment than that, it was to start one of many currents which shaped the new century. The constant encroachment by the European empires—Britain, Russia, Germany, France—on the independence and sovereignty of China had at last touched off hidden mines in the Chinese soul. There swept over North China one of those blind emotional movements not unusual among Asiatic masses.

In the winter and spring of 1900 we began to hear of the new secret society directed against foreigners. It was named the I Ho Tuan—the mailed fist. The foreigners called it "The Boxers." Their avowed purpose was to expel all foreigners from China, to root out every foreign thing—houses, railways, telegraphs, mines—and they included all Christian Chinese and all Chinese who had been associated with foreign things. They believed they had supernatural protection from foreign bullets and other great powers. How far they were originally encouraged by some of the officials around the Empress is not clear. Certainly the Imperial group joined later. This, however, is not the place to recite the history of China in these times. It would take volumes and I am here concerned only with the personal contacts of two young Americans with the forces in motion.

By May 1st (1900) the danger had grown so great that I called in our geological expeditions from the interior. These men had, however, outlined a field of anthracite coal greater than all the other anthracite fields in the world put together.

In June I went to Peking to see Chang, who was in mourning for his mother and by Chinese custom confined to his home—then in his country place outside of the city. I found him greatly agitated over the general outlook and especially the Palace intrigues wherein the Dowager Empress was now encouraging the Boxer movement—in fact, the Boxers were then drilling in a neighboring village.

Mrs. Hoover had accompanied me to Peking and upon my return to the city next day I found her very ill at the hotel. There was no doctor available, so I had her carried to the station and took the first train to Tientsin where there was an able physician. That trouble proved to be a sinus stoppage and was quickly relieved.

Rumors of Boxer attacks upon missionaries and others rumbled all about us. Foreign-drilled Chinese troops were brought up to protect the foreign settlement. On Sunday morning, June 10th, however, we were rudely awakened by shells bursting over the settlement from modern artillery—the foreign-drilled army. At first we thought it was poor firing from gunners trying to reach groups of Boxers on the other side of the settlement. Soon, however, such foreign officers who were drilling the Chinese army as could escape came running into the settlement. They reported that the troops had killed several of their European comrades. The alarm bell on the town hall was rung and we expected the worst. Tientsin had no consequential defense works, but there were about 1,100 sailors and marines of various nationalities in the settlement who, during the few days previous, had been sent up from war-vessels in the Port at Taku, sixty miles away. They were on their way to Peking to protect the foreign legations. They had no artillery except two small cannon and only a dozen machine guns. It was a small force to oppose some 25,000 foreign-equipped Chinese troops. Had those troops attacked that day they could easily have overwhelmed the settlement. We learned later that, though urged by the Boxers, they had no stomach for attack and that there were great disputes as to a command because of the absence of the foreign officers.

THE COOLGARDIE (ABOVE) AND CHIN CHANG (BELOW) MINES
WHERE MR. HOOVER CARRIED ON HIS ENGINEERING OPERATIONS

Quickly the settlement pulled itself together. A Russian, Colonel Wogack, outranked the other foreign officers. All the troops, American, Japanese, German, Russian, French and Italian, accepted Wogack's command, except the British under command of a naval bully named Captain Bailey, who was his own law. Learning of my engineering staff, Wogack sent word to us to organize the Christian Chinese who had fled to the settlement for safety to build barricades. The settlement was about a quarter-mile wide and a mile long, protected by the river on one side. In hunting material for barricades, we lit upon the great godowns (warehouses) filled with sacked sugar, peanuts, rice and other grain. Soon we and other foreigners whom I enlisted had a thousand terrified Christian Chinese carrying and piling up walls of sacked grain and sugar along the exposed sides of the town and at cross streets. By morning we were in a better state. The big attack came the second day, but the marines and sailors repulsed it from behind our bags.

Our house was on the edge of the settlement and exposed to constant rifle and artillery fire. We, with other American families, joined up with Edward Drew—the Commissioner of Customs—who lived near the center of the settlement, and was, we thought, better protected, since his house was partially surrounded by godowns. Later it turned out not to be so good, because of the effort of bad artillerymen to set the godowns on fire. Practically all the Chinese servants had run away, but fortunately two of ours remained loyal and constituted the whole kitchen staff at the Drews'. On the first day one of my staff, Wilfred Newberry, climbed on the roof of our house to look about. He spied the settlement's dairy herd pasturing peacefully about a mile out. Mounting a pony, he calmly drove the herd into our yard, although exposed to fire every foot of the way. That herd became invaluable later on for hospital meat and milk.

The acute dangers came from two sources—the first, the possibility of mass attack; the second, the incessant and furious artillery fire. Some 60,000 shells were fired into the settlement from first to last. The first attacks proved to be sporadic, though sometimes there were concentrated attacks directed mostly against the spot where the settlement joined up with the Chinese city of Tientsin. Here Boxers and Chinese troops could approach under cover of the houses. If, while engaging in these attacks, they had simultaneously brought pressure upon the other sides, we could not have held out for at times we did not have a man every hundred yards on those barricades. We soon found the best protection against rifle bullets and shells was to keep in the lee of walls when moving about or trying to snatch a moment of sleep.

I soon had an additional anxiety. The Boxer movement, as I have said, was directed against Chinese who had relations with foreigners as much as against foreigners themselves. The day of the first attack Chang Yen-mao and Tong Shao-yi (the Director of Railways previously referred to) came into the settlement with their families. They found quarters in a compound across the street from our house, belonging to the Chinese Engineering and Mining Company. Here they were quickly joined by 500 or 600 other minor Chinese officials and foreign-educated Chinese in similar plight. Their first need was food and water. With the help of some of the Chinese men, I transported each morning a supply of water and rice and such other food as we could get from the godowns to their compound. In the main, however, my staff and I were preoccupied with strengthening the barricades and boiling water in the boilers of the municipal water plant for distribution to the soldiers and civilians. The waterworks was outside of the barricades and with an outpost we operated it at night and in the morning brought the boiled water back in the municipal street-sprinkling carts. The British Tommies who formed our nightly guard, being aware of the corpses floating in the nearby canal, painted large signs on the sides of the water carts "Boxeril," being reminiscent of a British beef extract, "Bovril."

An increasing number of foreigners—soldiers and civilians—were wounded. We had only one Army doctor and our settlement physician. Similarly, there was only one professional nurse. Colonel Wogack turned the settlement club into a hospital and soon all the floors were covered with wounded. Mrs. Hoover volunteered at once and I saw little of her during the first period of the siege, except when she came home occasionally to eat or catch a little sleep. She became expert in riding her bicycle close to the walls of buildings to avoid stray bullets and shells although one day she had a tire punctured by a bullet.

She found some Christian Chinese women who could milk the cows, and with the aid of Newberry and an English boy named Simpson organized the dairy herd for service. At a later stage she had great need in the hospital for soup meat. She directed young Simpson to kill one of the less productive cows. He was not an experienced butcher. He succeeded merely in grievously wounding the cow with an army revolver. When finally he got her down, he tired of trying to skin her and simply chopped her up with an axe, hide and all.

The stray bullets fired from a long distance outside came near developing a major tragedy. A number of foreign civilians already in near hysteria mood concluded they were being fired from within the settlement. They quickly picked upon the 600 Chinese of whom I had charge in the Compound across the street. The first I knew of it was when a messenger came in while we were at supper after a totally exhausting day, to say that Chang Yen-mao, Tong Shao-yi and others had been arrested and were being given a drumhead trial by Captain Bailey. I rushed to the place, to find a so-called trial going on under torch-lights with Bailey a pompous judge and various hysterical wharf-rats testifying to things that could never have taken place. I attempted to intervene and explain who these Chinese were but Bailey ordered me to get out. I was told that some Chinese had already been executed on the nearby river bank. I made for the Russian headquarters a few blocks away on my bicycle and Colonel Wogack, quickly appreciating the situation, returned with me, accompanied by a Russian platoon. He stopped the trial instantly and the Chinese were turned over to me for return to their compound.

Somewhat later in the siege Mrs. Hoover and I and our engineering staff returned to our own house for a base, as it had not been hit. Late one evening, however, a shell banged through a back window and then, exploding, blew out the front door and surroundings. Mrs. Hoover, after a long day at the hospital, was sitting in a side room playing solitaire. She never stopped the game. A few evenings later several shells came close and finally one exploded in the compound across the street where the Chinese were living. Agnew and I rushed over and found that it had landed in Tong Shao-yi's place, killing his wife and baby and slightly injuring one of his children. Tong was naturally distracted, but helped us to gather up the other children.

Agnew, Tong and I, each carrying one and leading others, brought them across to our house where Mrs. Hoover took charge of them, and Tong recovered his calm.[1]

The siege lasted about a month. It was not altogether a fight between soldiers. It was a group of civilian men, women and children fighting for very life against a horde of fanatics with modern arms, and they were fighting with their eyes open to a form of death that everyone knew but did not mention. Truly, we were fighting under the courageous protection of a few hundred soldiers of a half dozen nationalities without whom we would have been lost. But we were fighting without artillery (except the two small cannon) against tens of thousands with modern arms with only two things in our favor—inside lines and more intelligence. Most of us made it a business not to think or discuss the possibilities. We did have one dreadful person who periodically wanted to know if I intended to shoot my wife first if they closed in on us. Most of the people lifted such lumps from their minds with whatever gleam of humor was possible. In the midst of all this we did have one intermediate day of exaltation. A Chinese messenger got through in the night of about the fifteenth day with word that relief armies were on their way from Taku and would be in the next day. We were warned not to fire on them by mistake. During the morning the Chinese stopped firing on us. Soon someone said he heard cannonading in the distance. How we strained our ears! Then it came plainer and plainer. We climbed on the roof of the highest warehouse to get a glimpse. We saw them coming over the plain. They were American Marines and Welch Fusiliers. I do not remember a more satisfying musical performance than the bugles of the American Marines entering the settlement playing "There'll Be a Hot Time in the Old Town Tonight."

They proved to be only a few hundred soldiers added to our force— but they had machine guns and some artillery and we felt better for a

[1] I relate this incident because of its denouement. Some eighteen years afterward, when I was War Food Administrator in Washington, Mrs. Hoover and I received an invitation to dine at the Chinese legation. While I was taking the Minister's wife out to the dining room, Mrs. Koo said in perfect English, "I have met you before. I am Tong Shao-yi's daughter whom you carried across the street during the siege of Tientsin!" Mrs. Koo was a most attractive woman; unfortunately she died a few years later. Twenty-eight years later when I was in Shanghai I received gracious hospitality from her sister.

while. Then the Chinese closed the ring again and with even more
violent and more dangerous assaults. Late in July sufficient forces came
in to drive the Chinese back far enough for calm if not peace. Most of
the wounded, the women and children were evacuated under guard
down the river as well as many civilian men. Mrs. Hoover and six or
seven other women refused to desert their posts as there were some
wounded who could not be moved.

When sufficient forces arrived it was determined to attack the Chinese Army itself. As I was familiar with topographic details from
horseback riding about the settlement with Mrs. Hoover, I was requested by Colonel Waller, in command of the American Marines, to
accompany them as a sort of guide in their part of the attack on the
Chinese city. We came under sharp fire from the Chinese located on
its old walls. We were out in the open plains with little cover except
Chinese graves. I was completely scared, especially when some of the
Marines next to me were hit. I was unarmed and I could scarcely make
my feet move forward. I asked the officer I was accompanying if I
could have a rifle. He produced one from a wounded Marine, and at
once I experienced a curious psychological change for I was no longer
scared, although I never fired a shot. I can recommend that men carry
weapons when they go into battle—it is a great comfort.

With the final relief forces came a number of American newspaper
correspondents. Mrs. Hoover opened our house to all of them who
would forage for food. She provided floor spots to sleep upon for a
dozen or fifteen, including Joaquin Miller, the California poet, who
was representing the Hearst press. This picturesque old gentleman
finally hired a rickshaw to take him to Peking. We told him that the
foreigners there were still under siege and that there were a few armies
in between. But such arguments seemed to carry little weight with
Joaquin. Mrs. Hoover finally bribed his rickshaw boy to desert him
and he remained contentedly with us.

The foreigners in Peking had suffered a longer siege and were without the advantage of food warehouses, but there were no modern
troops against them and no modern artillery. Their losses were small.
At this time the South African War was raging and the dramatic and
much news-commented sieges of Kimberley, Mafeking and Lady-

smith had just been relieved. The total losses of defenders in all three of these put together did not equal our white losses at Tientsin, to say nothing of the losses among the Chinese refugees. But their publicity arrangements were better.

Peking being relieved, the Empress Dowager and her government fled into the interior. It seemed to me that I had been delivered a strong hint by way of artillery fire that my engineering engagement with that government was over. We prepared to return to America.

In the meantime things happened to the Chinese Engineering and Mining Company. The Russian Army seized the coal mines and the extensive shops at Tongshan. The British Navy seized the harbor works and coal stocks at Chinwangtao. The German Army seized the coal yards at Taku and Tientsin. The Japanese Army seized the company's offices at Tientsin. The American Army seized the twelve coal steamers. It was universally believed that China would be dismembered. Everybody was entering upon a grand grab.

Early in August, when we had disposed of our belongings and were about ready to leave for home, Chang Yen-mao and his adviser, Detring, sent for me and suggested that the bondholders of the Chinese Engineering and Mining Company intervene to save the property. They had a plan for Mr. Moreing to accept a deed for the property and reorganize it into a British corporation for the benefit of all concerned. Chang and Detring wished me to sign as agent for Moreing at once, so that they could better defend the property from the seizures going on. I telegraphed to Mr. Moreing and he authorized me to sign on his behalf, subject to his subsequent approval of the terms. I had no experience in high finance and Chang and Detring made the terms.

I left with Mrs. Hoover for London at once, taking along the contract, and leaving my engineering staff to await events. We left Tientsin by a tugboat down the river to Taku, taking Chang Yen-mao along. As a great red moon rose Chang remarked that it was a bad omen for China. My feeling was that it was a little late. We went to London via the Red Sea. Air-conditioning had not yet been born.

Arriving in London, I urged the great possibilities of the property if it were placed under foreign management. The bondholders and Moreing accepted Chang's and Detring's terms which, among other things, called for additional capital of some millions to clear up a multitude of creditors and restore the property.

All that end of the transaction was carried out with the co-operation of the British, Belgian, German and other bondholders. I was appointed General Manager of the company at increased salary and I was carried by Moreing for a small interest in the reorganization. As the transfer implied recovering the seized properties from five different governments and negotiations with the Chinese government for approval of the contract, Chevalier Edmond de Wouters, a member of the Belgian Foreign Office who was already in China, was appointed a special agent to take charge of the negotiation and diplomatic aspects of these affairs.

We sailed again from England for China, via the United States, taking a few days off in California en route. In January 1901, we reached Japan where Mrs. Hoover remained for the winter while I went to Shanghai in search of a method of reaching North China. The Port of Taku being frozen and there being then no railway connection between Shanghai and the north, all communication had been suspended for the winter. After some days I joined with some British and American army officers in chartering a 1,200-ton steamer to take us to Chinwangtao, where we thought the ice would be open. We ran at once into a furious storm. The second day the Norwegian captain came into the bunkhouse-like cabin where we five passengers were desperately seasick. He announced that the Chinese crew were becoming unruly and demanding that we put back to Shanghai. He said that his Norwegian mate and engineer might need help to stand the Chinese off. The British Colonel turned over with a moan and declared that so far as he was concerned he was not going to get out of bed and make any fight to keep out of smooth water. He expressed our general views. However, the sea smoothed over somewhat and we heard nothing more from the captain and on the third day arrived off Chinwangtao. The harbor was full of floating ice. The captain rammed the steamer in as far as he dared go and invited us to disembark onto the ice and walk ashore. That we did, but within twenty feet on the shallow beach the waves had churned the ice to mush. After probing, which indicated shallow water, we plunged into icewater up to the hips, each carrying a suitcase. It was not too comfortable. I had expected our harbor engineering staff who were building the new works to have returned there but our first discovery was that their buildings had been burned and that the staff had not come back. We stumbled seven miles in the dark to the railway, with the temperature below zero. The walk probably saved us from pneumonia. Arriving at the railway, we lit a bonfire and before daylight signaled a troop train.

That railway journey to Tientsin had some unsatisfactory features. There was a private car at the end of the train filled with British officers. The English Colonel who accompanied us from Shanghai disappeared into this car. As my American fellow travelers were going in the other direction, they did not board the train. After it started, I discovered there was no heat except in the private car. It was bitterly cold, and I went back to ask if I could come in. A British Colonel, whose name I later learned was Cook, was on the platform and refused me abruptly, saying that the car was reserved for British officers. I asked to see the Shanghai Colonel but Colonel Cook refused to awaken him. It was still dark, yet I expect I did shine out like a ruffian, being unshaven and covered with mud.

I went back into a car filled with sleeping Russian privates to wait for daylight and possible connection with the Shanghai Colonel. I also engaged myself, between shivers, in contemplation of what discipline in good manners I might administer to Colonel Cook. Just at daybreak the train came to a stop. On looking out, I saw a small knot of men gathered around the locomotive. To warm up, I walked up to them and found there a Russian officer who could speak some English, and that the locomotive crew was Russian. I made out that some burned-out boiler tubes were leaking into the fire box, and with its reduced power the engine could not pull so long a train up the grade and had stalled. By degrees I conveyed to the Russian officer the idea that we detach the locomotive and the first car of the train, and go quickly into Tong-shan, 150 miles away, and there arrange to send an uninjured engine back to bring in the train. He thought this was reasonable and we left Colonel Cook for a 24-hour wait. My conscience hurt me for some days until I met my Shanghai Colonel who was enthusiastic, saying, "Beastly fellow, we ran out of coal; it served him right."

During my absence large numbers of foreign troops had been poured into North China, although any real fighting was long since over. Various zones were occupied by the armies of eleven different nationalities. Each was going to have a piece of China or protect its "national interest."

The coal mines of the Chinese Engineering and Mining Company at Tongshan and Linsi were thirty miles apart. They were equipped to produce about 5,000 tons a day. There were large machine shops capable of constructing almost any sort of mining machinery. There were a coking plant and cement factories. These works were surrounded by high walls and employed about 25,000 men. The company possessed (when we recovered possession of them) coal yards at the different China ports and a fleet of coal ships—a dozen steamers.

Chevalier de Wouters had secured nominal possession of the various mines. I placed Agnew in charge at Tongshan and Newberry in charge at Linsi and at once got reorganization and operations underway. But our daily business of producing and transporting coal became involved with all these armies. The inclination of military officers to regard civilians as a nuisance even in peace becomes a fixed determination in war. However, they needed coal and cement, and we were the only producers. And they needed our aid in the reconstruction of the railways and ports.

Owing to the total disruption of business, household and food supplies were difficult to obtain in Tientsin where I made my headquarters. I solved most of the problem by inviting General Humphries, the American Quartermaster-General, to live with me, and we thus were able to purchase quartermaster's supplies. To get fresh milk and butter I bought a cow and a calf and engaged a "proper" Chinese "keeper" to look after them. Late one night the Number One Boy burst into the room with the announcement "The cow he lost." We sent for the cow's "keeper." He offered a constructive suggestion through the Number One Boy as interpreter. "His cow's pup he have stay. Cow he have go. Pup he cry. Maybe pup he walk road he cry. Cow he cry. We find cow." Chinese were not allowed on the streets at night except with a foreigner. Whereupon the General and I, with another guest, J. Bromley Eames, who was a professor of law at the Chinese Tientsin University, the Number One Boy and the "cow's keeper," taking two lantern bearers, ventured into the night in solemn parade. The "pup" he duly "cry" and the "cow he cry" from inside a German Army barracks. Thereupon Mr. Eames summoned his best German and demanded to know from the sentry if they had recently acquired a cow. The sentry listened a moment to the "pup he cry" and the "cow he cry" and solemnly inquired if that calf belonged to that cow. On being assured of the relationship he observed, "Then I take he calf." And he did. The General's temperature rose suddenly. The sentry seemed utterly immune to the General's rank, his explosive English and to Eames' legal arguments in German. Finally we retreated to reorganize our moral forces. Next morning General Humphries called upon the German General in person. I was not present. But "he cow" and "he cow's pup" came home.

One of my first acts as General Manager was to survey the depredations of the foreign armies on the property and demand reparations. The British replied that they could not entertain our claims unless they were filed in the proper forms in triplicate. After a maze of red tape, they ultimately paid the full amount. The Germans replied that they had occupied the property as an act of war and would entertain no claims for coal or other things taken. Pressure from the bondholders in Berlin obtained payment a year later. The Russians had been the worst, for they loaded several trains with machinery and supplies from the mines and ran them off on the railway into Manchuria. We sent them a bill for 700,000 Mexican dollars.[2] I heard nothing from them for some weeks but finally an agent appeared who offered to settle, subject to a commission for himself of about 150,000 Mexican dollars. That I refused, but later he came back with the full amount in silver and considerable extra. He carried away the extra. Some months afterwards the commander of the Russian forces in Manchuria offered to sell us all the machinery and stores back for about $200,000 Mexican. We bought them. I have been curious ever since as to the entries in the Imperial accounts. The Japanese ignored all communications and refused to vacate our offices. On the evening when he received our bill for damages, the American Quartermaster General stormed into me in

[2] The Mexican dollar was the chief silver circulation medium in China at this time and was valued at about 50 cents American.

great outrage over the bill he had received during the day for the use and repair of our ships. He opined that the American Army was our savior and it was a wicked proposal. His profane emphasis maintained the highest standards of the Army. My long argument ran to the effect that the American Government was demanding the cost of the expedition from the Chinese Government, so why should a private company give our government the whole sum as a profit? In the end he offered 75 per cent of the $300,000 Mexican in cash, and in the spirit of democracy we compromised on that.

In the course of the early military occupation the British had been assigned the guardianship of a sizable city about twenty miles from Tongshan. Order was maintained in the city by an Indian contingent under a Captain Strong. The Captain visited our Tongshan staff frequently and was full of his accomplishments in maintaining order, cleaning up the streets and generally teaching the Chinese the higher arts of municipal government. Among other things he had set up an advisory council of Chinese residents who had early visited him offering their cooperation. After the British withdrew from those parts I began to hear strange stories through the Chinese as to Captain Strong's conduct. Not believing them, nevertheless, I sent to the Captain who was then in Peking and suggested that for his good name he had better investigate. He did so with the aid of some of our Chinese staff.

It appeared that the "advisory council" had, from time to time, informed the Captain of bandits in the neighborhood, and the Captain would, thereupon, with a platoon of terrifying Sikhs and great clatter ride out for attack. He seldom found them. But the advisory council carried on a side enterprise by way of notifying persons that Captain Strong suspected them of being bandits and that it would require X dollars to buy him and his dreadful Indians off. When the Captain returned from his corroborative investigation, he devoted much expressive language to the futility of a foreigner trying to teach good government to a Chinaman.

It was necessary to go frequently to Peking with De Wouters to see the various Foreign Ministers—British, German, Russian, Belgian, French, and American—upon matters involved in our contracts with the occupying troops in North China. We had also to maintain constant relations with their military commands—and with it all contact with the temporary Chinese government which had been erected under the veteran statesman Li Hung-chang.

As the only hotel in Peking had been occupied by the troops I joined with some other Americans in renting a temple for residence not far from the American legation. Among these Americans were a Mr. Jamison and "Jersey" Chamberlin, who was the correspondent for the New York *Sun*. At three o'clock one morning Jamison, accompanied by a British Colonel, invaded my special temple and shook me awake. They insisted that they had a most wonderful discovery out of which huge fortunes could be gained by all. It appeared that the Colonel commanded an Indian regiment quartered at the Temple of Heaven and he had discovered that one of the buildings had a gold roof. The surgeon of the regiment, being a scientist, had estimated it to be worth two million dollars. The Colonel and his soldiers had quietly removed the roof and transported it to an empty warehouse on the other side of the city. They wanted me to join them as a partner and quietly get it to market. I expressed both skepticism and a resolution to have nothing to do with it. Jamison was alarmed at my skepticism, and urged me to look at it for his sake. Finally I agreed to go as far as that. Thereupon with half a dozen lantern bearers we trudged two miles through the deserted streets of Peking to the warehouse. There I found the floor littered with metal sheets about a yard square, moulded into the shape of tiles. Scratching the sheets with a pocket knife, I quickly determined they were copper covered with a thin gold leaf. Twenty gold dollars could be spread as thin as gold leaf over 20 square feet, and those sheets showed the leaf only on one side at that. The Colonel was upset; Jamison soon found moral reasons why the enterprise should be abandoned. But the Colonel still clung to hope. He wanted some more adequate test. I told him that if he would heat one of the sheets on a hot bed of charcoal the leaf would blister off and he could collect and, by engaging a Chinese jeweler, could get it melted into a button and weigh it. The Colonel said he had no place to do this and doubted his ability to do it anyway. Finally, while we shivered in the cold, Jamison offered to take two sheets back to the temple and try it. So we trudged back in the early dawn with the two sheets following on the heads of the coolies. When we arrived, Chamberlin was having breakfast and evidenced great interest at once. Jamison went ahead with the test and calculated the whole roof was worth about $5,000 as scrap metal. His moral resolution against looting grew even stronger; and by this time he was trying to save the Colonel from himself. The Colonel melted away but Chamberlin did not. He insisted on more details from Jamison. From it all he devised an entertaining cable to the New York *Sun* under the caption "The British Still Looting." Thereupon a sad court-martial, but so far as I knew no public announcement of the result.

The Northern Railways of China had been greatly torn up by the Boxers in their anti-foreign frenzies. The military authorities needed them to move troops for police purposes. We needed them to transport coal from the mines. The military authorities appointed a board of officers to take over reconstruction operations. At their request I co-operated and assigned some of our engineering staff—foreigners and Chinese—to their aid. The Boxers or peasants had unbolted the fish-plates, pulled the spikes over long stretches and carried every atom of this metal miles into the interior. It was distributed over a thousand villages, each rejoicing in a prudent supply of iron for its blacksmith shops for years ahead. They had also carried off the ties for building material and fuel. In considering how to recover it all, we suggested that the Chinese would soon find that the rails were not iron but steel from which they could not even chip pieces. We felt that when they realized this the villagers would be glad to sell the rails back if a price was offered, accompanied by promise of immunity and vigorous threats if they did not comply. My recollection is that we offered $5 Mexican a rail. In a few days the countryside for miles along the destroyed sections was alive with caterpillar-like processions of thirty or forty villagers bringing back one rail each.

In our reorganization of the management of the Chinese Engineering and Mining Company we quickly ran afoul of Chinese "squeeze" in huge dimensions. It was not exactly graft. According to Chinese concepts all officials were supposed to make something beyond very nominal salaries. It was typified by the plaint of the Chinese paymaster. We discovered that about 6,000 of the theoretical 25,000 names on our list of employees were fictitious. We installed the simple device of issuing to each employee a numbered brass check which he must deposit upon coming to work in the walled compound around the works. This upset the paymaster seriously. He came to my office in manifest grief. He explained that his salary of $50 Mexican a month was nothing—that he had paid a superior official $50,000 Mexican for the job and it was to last for three years. He had occupied the position for only one year. Worse still, he had organized a participating syndicate among his friends to raise the original $50,000 and they had rights in the matter. With recognition both of Chinese customs and human justice at large, we compounded with his creditors so as to save at least part of his face.

This system of numbered brass checks as the certificate of a job brought us embarrassments unique to China. For the humane and good economic reasons that our workers' pay would not buy enough to eat, I had raised wages to about 40 per cent above the levels in the surrounding towns. At once the brass check came to have a value in itself. A job seeker only had to buy one to get a job. The price of checks rose to about a month's pay. We found we were losing our rights of choice as to skill and character of men who had jobs. We could prevent the practice by skilled workmen among whom a stranger was at once known to their foreman. But in the indiscriminate gangs of common labor it was more difficult. On top of this, competent artists started making counterfeit checks. On complaint to the local magistrate, his advice was to reduce wages. However, we solved the problem by more effective identification.

"Squeeze" in China does not have exactly the same moral implications as "graft" among foreigners. It is hallowed by ages of custom, has certain recognized limitations, is, in fact, a sort of appendage of the profit system. It is difficult for a foreigner to decipher its moral permutations. For instance, after the siege, the foreign governments demanded and secured damages for losses by foreign residents and their employees. I asked Quah, our loyal No. 1 Boy, if he had lost anything, saying that I might get something back for him. He produced evidence, which the reparations authorities accepted, of about $900 of losses. I had known he was broke when I had employed him eighteen months previous for $15 (Mexican) per month. To Mrs. Hoover's playful suggestion that she would like to share the profits of running the household, he made neither facial nor vocal response.

A part of Quah's job was to see that others received the very minimum of squeeze, and he did so faithfully. Mrs. Hoover one day complained to him that our household bills were about twice those of a neighbor with about the same establishment. The reply was "Master have two times pay of Mr. Francis." Yet we could, and did, entrust all of the ten servants (whose combined salaries were about $108 Mexican per month) with the family cash and valuables without the remotest anxiety. The same No. 1 Boy, out of sheer loyalty, took all the risks of the siege to stay with us.

Another angle on this different code of morals of that period arose when a Chinese made a contract. He performed it to the letter. And in so doing he represented integrity of the highest order. He would often commit suicide if he failed. But to take squeeze or adulterate a product not specifically prohibited in the contract is legitimate. This extraordinary fidelity to agreement probably had its origins in the fact that there had up to this time been but little commercial law in China. There was little opportunity to enforce debt. Yet the Chinese conducted an intensive commercial life. The only penalty for failure to keep agreements was ostracism. Over centuries this had built up fidelity into almost a fetish. There were bad persons in China—just as there are in all races. What the relative proportions of good and bad there are depends a great deal on how much they have to eat. I doubt if Americans would average as well as the Chinese if they had so little.

It was hopeless to conduct Western industrial operations with so large a ratio of "squeeze," and we steadily decreased it. In ninety days we turned a losing business into a profit of $150,000 Mexican a month by reducing the "squeeze" alone. These surgical operations had wide after effects. Certainly Chang Yen-mao was a bad exhibit. Chang found himself with only his nominal salary of $500 Mexican a month as

Chinese Director-General and began to raise trouble for De Wouters over transfer details of various pieces of property to the British Company.[3]

De Wouters finally settled (or thought he had settled) with Chang by securing him and his advisers an allotment of stock in the company for their "squeeze" rights, and by signing with me a separate memorandum providing for Chang's face as head of a local board to represent the Chinese interest in the company at an increase of his salary. I relate all this because this "memorandum" was to make subsequent trouble.

However, we all got along amicably for some months, until the fall of 1901. The business was rapidly expanding. We had procured new equipment and completed the ice-free port at Chinwangtao far enough to begin loading coal during the ice season. We had brought in a new American staff and revised technical methods, all of which steadily increased the profits. The original Chinese shares in the company, as represented by the new stock issued, showed a 500 per cent increase in market value. I had kept Mr. Tong Shao-yi (who was the largest Chinese stockholder) fully advised and he was strong in his approval, for he had long despaired of ever securing anything as a result of Chang Yen-mao's control.[4]

In the fall of 1901 I was advised from London that the Belgians had purchased majority control of the business from other European and Chinese interests and were sending Emile Francqui, a director of the company, with a Belgian technical staff, to replace the Americans at the mines. In due time Mr. Francqui arrived. He assured me I was to remain as general manager. One of his early acts, however, was to announce that the "memorandum" was not binding and that co-operation with the Chinese Board under Chang would cease. He declared that they were still grafting. There was much reason for Francqui's complaint, as Chang had sold a port property at Hong Kong, asserting that it was his own. The books showed that the company owned it

[3] A long dispute ensued, which is of interest only because of subsequent litigation and its use for smearing purposes in my Presidential campaign of 1928.

[4] Tong was destined to twice become Premier of China and to perform for me afterward a great act of friendship.

years before Chang became connected with the enterprise. However, both De Wouters and I contended that the memorandum was not only legally but morally binding and that it was the job of the management to head off graft.

Francqui was a most able but a most arbitrary person. In the end De Wouters and I resigned, and Francqui set up a management which was largely Belgian. I did not at this time suppose Francqui had the least lingering affection for me, as our discussion over what I thought was an immoral repudiation of an agreement had been something more than plain.[5]

I notified Moreing of these events and added that I was returning to America. Within a few days I received a cable from him, asking if I would accept a junior partnership in Bewick, Moreing and Company. I was then 27 years old and delighted to get out of China into a larger engineering world. Together with Chevalier de Wouters, Mrs. Hoover and I took a tramp steamer to Nagasaki and thence to London via California.

During our time in China, Mrs. Hoover became interested in the exquisite antique Chinese porcelains. Soon she narrowed that interest to Ming (A.D. 1368–1662) and K'ang Hse (A.D. 1662–1720) blue-and-whites. Steadily she, all her life, built up her collection when pieces became available and the prices were not too high. In the course of forty years the collection became an outstanding one. During the winter of 1901, while she was in Japan, my Chinese boy produced an itinerant Chinese dealer who had twelve plates to sell. The boy urged that I buy them "for Madame" at once for about $10 Mexican each. Not trusting my judgment, I bought one and sent it to her at Tokyo. Her instant cable was to buy the other eleven at most any price. But we could not find the vender again. A plate similar to her one specimen sold at auction in London years later for over $1,000 American. Our plate remained for years the index of my judgment of porcelains. However, in time, under instruction, I improved somewhat.

The whole period of the China experience, starting from Australia, and back to America again, had extended over about three years, with

[5] I was destined to meet him again in a great undertaking—the Belgian Relief.

two trips around the globe in the meantime.[6] The incidents were but the normal reactions of mixing Occidental and Oriental civilizations, especially when engineering is thrown in as a catalyst. However vivid one's experiences may be and the light thrown upon the government or the people, no one man can appraise or make arbitrary judgments on a race of 400,000,000 people who have 3,000 years of written history. The impression I have held of the Chinese people is one of abiding admiration. Ninety per cent of the huge mass live so close to the starvation line that someone falls below it in nearly every village every year. Yet they live with patience, with tolerance. They have the deepest fidelity to family ties, and the fullest affection for their children. They work harder and more hours than any other race in the world. True, they are superstitious beyond belief, but they have a vivid sense of humor. They are courageous, as witness the armies they have created.

One's despair for them comes from the knowledge that no matter how much their productivity may be increased by science and technology, the pressures of population growth will pull down most of the possible increments to living standards. The spread of education will perhaps open the doors of opportunity to a larger and larger part of the 90 per cent and slowly perhaps the proportions of the impoverished mass will decrease.

The top 10 per cent of the literate Chinese are highly intelligent. They are able in thought; they have moral courage. Their culture is one of the oldest and most complete. In art, literature, and philosophy, they have made a magnificent contribution to civilization. This 10 per cent, excluding the Manchu officials, are in a sense democratic, for there are no barriers of class stratification to prevent rise from the mass. Indeed, for centuries they had a civil service which embraced most officials' entry into government by competitive examination. The 10 per cent are easily moved by new "isms," for they are naturally speculative-minded and theoretic.

Until recent years there was little feeling of nationalism. Indeed there was formerly no adequate word for the emotion we call patriot-

[6] These appraisals of China and the Chinese were written in the years 1915–1916, some five years after the Kuomintang rebellion and the expulsion of the Manchu Dynasty in 1910. I have thought they should stand without revision as presenting some picture of the times.

ism. The appropriate word for that sentiment is new to their language. Times moves slowly with the Chinese in great matters. We move by minutes; they by years.

As a whole the Chinese are a peaceful commercial people, temperamentally ill-adapted to compete with militaristic races. Indeed the militaristic races to the north of them have furnished nearly every dynasty over 3,000 years. And the people have absorbed every conquering northern tribe and made it Chinese. The inflexible *mores* of the race will inevitably absorb any conquest of them.

Their curious customs, their history, are a never-ending source of foreign book-making. One of the sayings on the China Coast is, "Write your book in the first ten days or you will never write it." Indeed all books on China relate to the 90 per cent fraction of the mass.[7]

Constantly, "understanders" of China dinned into American ears the opportunities of trade and development in China. There are two illusions in the picture, as it was presented to the Western world. The first is that because of four hundred million people there is a possibility of enormous trade expansion. But the standard of living of the 90 per cent is too low, and likely to remain too low, to absorb what to them are costly foreign goods. Foreign trade is with the 10 per cent. China produces comparatively few surpluses to export abroad or to exchange even among themselves. As an illustration I may cite that in my time the Northern Railways, 600 miles long, served a population of 30,000,000 people in one of the richest agricultural countries in the world. Except for coal there was comparatively no freight traffic on that line. The Chinese ate everything on the ground. There was little surplus to export from the region, and therefore no means to buy imports. The traffic was largely passengers, and that but an infinitesimal per cent of the traffic on a railway serving 30,000,000 people in America or Europe.

The second illusion is that China will develop vast metal resources. In a very rough way the heart of China is a vast agricultural plain surrounded by a half-moon of great mountain ranges, plateaus and deserts. There are some mountain islands on this plain. The core of these surrounding and island mountains is the older rocks flanked by great

[7] A great book—*The House of Exile*, by Nora Waln—has beautifully interpreted the 10 per cent. And it is a charming and inspiring picture of the best of China as I saw it.

carboniferous beds. There are a few exposed rocks above the carboniferous. With such a formation engineers and geologists would expect coal from the flank rocks and metals in the older core of the mountains. In fact, there is more coal of every variety than in all of the rest of the world combined.

Despite earnest search there is no evidence of more than comparatively local iron deposits. The possibilities of the nonferrous metals—copper, lead, zinc, gold, silver, antimony, cobalt, tin, etc.—are obscured by circumstances peculiar to China. It must not be believed that the Chinese are ignorant of the value of the metals or of methods of working them. They have used them for 2,000 or 3,000 years. They discovered the process of reducing zinc ore to metallic zinc and of using cobalt for coloring porcelains hundreds of years before the Western world knew of these processes. They were cupelling lead to separate the silver centuries ago.

Any engineer who explores the mineral-bearing cores of the mountains will be astonished by the myriads of old mine workings as evidenced by cave-ins and waste dumps. But the Chinese have mined every shred of metal down to water level. And as the farmer could work at mining in the otherwise idle months of the winter, labor cost was nothing. Thus they mined every sort and size of deposit. The trouble of the engineer is, therefore, that there is no surface evidence, like that in our virgin country, of how big the deposit was and, often enough, no evidence of what it was because every shot of metal was carefully garnered. Actual reopening of these old workings for modern prospecting is most expensive because pumps must be installed. Where such prospecting has been done it has been found that the majority of ancient miners worked deposits so small and so low grade as not to be commercial today. In the ordinary occurrence of metals there are a hundred unprofitable deposits to one profitable. Mathematically it would become necessary to open a hundred workings before a commercial one is discovered. Nor is the size of the waste dump much of an indication, for the smaller the deposit, the more the waste that must be extracted and the bigger the dump. Those concerns that have tried base metal mining in China have mostly gone broke.

No rule is universal. The great mines in North Burma were formerly in Chinese territory and were worked by the Chinese for centuries. They were easily discovered from the character of the dumps and openings. These mines were abandoned when they reached such depths that water or metallurgical difficulties became too great. Generally, however, from these obscuration handicaps the outlook for commercial development of great metal resources such as those of the Americas, Europe, Australasia, Russia or Africa will be very doubtful.

China's first resource and skill is agriculture. To have maintained the productivity of the soil of the great plain and of even the steep mountain sides over 3,000 years with its hundreds of millions of teeming people, is an astonishing performance in itself. And in weight of food produced per acre it probably exceeds any other part of the world. The greatest blessing that could come to these hardest working of all human beings would be improved seeds and plants from our experimental stations.

There is at least a further partial illusion in the concept that with such masses of cheap labor, China can be converted into a great industrial country from which there can be a lift in the standard of living and a violent competition in the sale of products to the Western world.

The first handicap is the lack of great supplies of mineral raw material, except for coal.

The second lies in some kink in the Chinese mind which does not adapt itself well to Western methods of administrative organization, whether political or industrial. Our basis is delegation of authority over departmental divisions with adequate wages and salaries. Its success requires fundamental disciplines, integrity, loyalty and a conscientious devotion to performance. The native Chinese basis of organization is subcontracting. Even in government, over thousands of years, the Viceroys of provinces contracted to pay a certain amount annually to the throne and to keep order with justice. The Viceroys subcontracted to the next stage of district Tao Tais, and they in turn to the smaller districts of the Sheins. Each provided a generous margin of tax income between stages for general purposes and private enrichment. Their native form of production and distribution was organized in the same way. To the Chinese mentality, it has many advantages; but it was not efficient in the functions introduced from the Occident. In its adaptation to the railways, they subcontracted with the railway station agents for a given sum per month or per annum, and the ticket agent had to get what he could out of the sale of tickets and the collections from freight charges.

Foreigners in my time often confused the margins at each stage of this form of organization with "squeeze" or graft. As I have said that contains only a fraction of truth. The margin comprised what would otherwise be salary or wages and compensation for taking the risk of the contract. There were elements of free enterprise in it.

However, it does not make for efficiency in Occidental industry. My experience showed that the Northern Railways, under Chinese methods of organization, never returned to the Government owners more than the bond interest of the foreign bonds secured on them. When the Allies took over the railways during the Boxer disturbances, the railways were greatly damaged. But one year of foreign administration not only paid for reconstruction but purchased more and new equipment, paid the bond interest, and left about one million dollars in their treasury. The following year, under Chinese administration, they again paid bond interest only. This difference was only in small percentage illegitimate abstractions. It was lowered efficiency in administrative methods.

Even the foreign-drilled Chinese Army was administered on a subcontractual basis. The General took a contract to feed, clothe and pay the men. He sublet it to the colonels, the colonels sublet it to the captains, and so on.

A third handicap to widespread Occidental industrialization is the fact that the Chinese are a less mechanical-minded people than the European-descended races. Our inventions and machinery came out of our racial instincts and qualities. Our people learn easily how to make them work efficiently. The consequence of the Chinese mental lack of mechanical instinct is that they require many times more men to operate our intricate machines. The cotton mills at the time of my visits required men to watch each modern loom. Our workmen can operate a dozen at one time. They required seven or eight men to operate a modern locomotive—two to watch the tracks ahead, three to fire the boilers, and two to operate the various devices, and usually one to watch the other seven to see that they kept their minds on the job. At Tong-shan we installed a very large and intricate winding engine to haul several thousand tons of coal daily from a fairly deep shaft with ten stops at different levels. It was equipped with signals, indicators, gauges and gadgets designed for one engine driver to know and do everything. Yet we were constantly killing men through the mistakes of the engine driver. We finally had to put on nine men to watch the different indicators and gadgets and one more to watch all of them. With the good humor and natural gaiety of Chinese when well-fed, they soon developed a sort of chanty which they sang to the effect:

She (the cage) is now at number ten (level). She wants to go to number nine (or any other number). She is coming to number nine to rest there. She is coming to the top—Look out.

Our general conclusion from the Tongshan experience with 25,000 healthy men in all positions was that it took about two Chinese to perform the common labor tasks of an American, about four to one to operate the machines, and about ten to one skilled in mechanical trades to assemble intricate machines. They could imitate anything if given time enough, but no world-startling mechanical invention has come out of China. That does not apply to their artistic development or architecture—but even here, their advance was slow. None of these observations must be taken as saying that China cannot be much more developed by Western ideas. They mean only that the Western world clouds its mind with thoughts of vast territory and 400,000,000 people and makes unwarrantably astronomical calculations.

Another of the illusions of the Western world concerns democracy and China. There never has been and there never will be, in another generation, truly representative government whereby the common people determine their own fate. That is impossible in the face of 90 per cent illiteracy and the low standard of living among the masses. Nevertheless, some time with the fine streak of idealism in its intellectual groups, it should be able to build up a sort of democratic oligarchy which will serve until the masses can be lifted at least to partial literacy.

Moreover, as I have said, the Chinese are not administrators from a Western point of view. Democracy is a Western concept which requires the same form of administrative machinery as we have developed for production and distribution. My fear is that any real democracy in China would fail on its administrative side. In fact, the Chinese are not good administrators. They can at times be successful dictators—but usually not even that.

With their philosophic and emotional minds, they sometimes move with great violence, as witness the Taiping, Boxer and Kuomintang rebellions.[8]

But none of this is intended to disparage a great race. It is given simply as a caution to Western minds that China is not going to be made Occidental.

[8] I could have added later on the Communist revolutions.

CHAPTER 7

⟨◇⟩⟨◇⟩⟨◇⟩

ENGINEERING OVER THE WORLD

1902–1908

London was at this time the center of the metal-mining world. The firm of Bewick, Moreing and Company was a typical British mechanism—being a partnership (not a corporation) which had operated mines for some 150 years, beginning in Cornwall and Derbyshire and gradually extending over the world. As partners grew old and retired, new men were taken in. This method of organization had come down over hundreds of years in British firms engaged in industry, shipping or merchandising. The names of such firms sometimes shifted with new partners but usually preserved some of the old names for a long period even when the owners of them were long since dead. The group of partners themselves, individually and with friends, put up the capital for each new enterprise, sometimes in corporate form, sometimes in partnership. The enterprises were managed by the firms themselves for fees and percentage of the profit.

Mrs. Hoover and I arrived in London early in November, 1901. I quickly settled the terms of partnership with Mr. Moreing and his colleagues. Two partners, Mr. Bewick (the second of that family in the firm) and Mr. Edward Hooper, were retiring and part of their interest was divided—20% to me and 10% each to two other new partners, A. S. Rowe and T. W. Wellstead. Under this arrangement, such ownership as the firm held directly in different mines was distributed among the old partners, and the new firm started practically fresh. The assets, outside of the office equipment and testing laboratories over

[73]

the world, were the good-will and the contracts for management fees which were based on an annual sum and a percentage of the profits. The good-will of the firm was valued at the past three years' net earnings, and we, the new partners, undertook to pay this amount out of future earnings. The partnership deed specifically provided that no partner could engage in stock-market speculation, a fact I mention because of a calamity which came upon us.

The firm held contracts as managers and engineers to some twenty mines in different parts of the world, together with two substantial exploration syndicates whose purpose was to discover new mines and develop them. Mr. Moreing's main interest was in finance and public matters, as he was a very active member of the Conservative Party and had been a candidate for Parliament. My job was to operate the mines —both as an engineer and administrator. Rowe, who was not an engineer, had long been Chief Accountant of the firm and continued to look after the accounts of the mines over the world. Wellstead was a sturdy Welshman of some mechanical engineering experience. He looked after the office management, the purchase of supplies for the mines, details of contracts, etc.

At the time I entered the firm, the business included coal mines in China, Wales and the Transvaal, a tin mine in Cornwall, a group of gold mines in Western Australia, New Zealand, South Africa, and West Africa, copper mines in Queensland and Canada, a lead-silver mine in Nevada, and a turquoise mine in the Sinai Peninsula of Egypt. In addition there were constant examinations of new prospects and engineering work for other concerns. The firm had branch offices in New York, Kalgoorlie, Melbourne, and Johannesburg, under local heads who participated in profits.

I was to remain a partner in this firm for about seven years, or until July, 1908.

I decided that, unlike the previous partners who sat around London and New York, I should work mostly in the field.

To discuss the technical and administrative problems of a host of mines would be tiresome. If anyone is interested, they can be found in the technical and industrial press of the time. As this is a personal account, I shall keep out of technology and in the human field as much as possible.[1]

Our problems being all over the world, I was involved in a vast amount of travel—in fact, after joining this partnership, I circled the globe five times. Mrs. Hoover went on most of these journeys, and when the babies came she brought them along in a basket. The experiences of journeyings on passenger liners, tramp steamers and tugs, or by railways, motor-cars, buggies, horses or camels, are not particularly new. For those interested, there are whole libraries of books in every geographical setting.

There were diverting and educational contacts with leaders of men, heads of governments and public officials; with snobs and crooks; with plain, good people and intellectually inspiring people, with human boll weevils. There was good food and bad food, there were good beds, bad beds, bugs, mosquitoes, dust, sand and malaria. There were the excitements of dealings with officials decent or dumb, of passenger stories pointed or dull, of glorious scenery, of soft tropic mornings at sea, of freezing northern storms, of strange peoples and customs, and finally of arrivals and customs officers. There was the daily meed of joy and sorrow.

The real interest lies in the question: What was one bothering about anyway? Most of the time I had to take along a secretary or an engineering assistant in order that I might work between ports. At each stop we received a bagful of reports; at each wirehead we sent a flock of cablegrams. There was ample time to read and at times it seemed to me that I would exhaust all the books on earth. But the supply still holds out.

Just to indicate the amount of travel in those years, I set down the following list of countries where we stopped during the time when I was a partner in Bewick, Moreing and Company:

1901 China, United States, England, France, India, Australia, New Zealand, Hawaiian Islands.

[1] During this period I made several contributions to professional journals and societies on technical phases of our work. They can be found in their indexes. They are dull reading for laymen.

1902 France, Italy, England, Australia, New Zealand, Canada, United States.

1903 United States, Canada, England, France, India, Australia, New Zealand, Hawaiian Islands.

1904 United States, Germany, Italy, England, South Africa.

1905 England, United States, Australia, New Zealand, Egypt, France, Italy.

1906 Egypt, England, United States.

1907 England, Australia, Malay States, United States, Burma, France.

1908 England, United States.

Housekeeping is always a problem for itinerants. We felt early that we should have a mooring in America. In 1902 we joined with Mrs. Hoover's father, Mr. Henry, in building a cottage in Monterey as a geographical anchor. Subsequently in 1907 we moved the anchorage to Stanford University where we acquired a six room cottage.

In the spring of 1902 Mrs. Hoover thought that we were going to settle down for a summer, so she searched out a small country house for us at Walton-on-Thames.[2] Promptly, my job called me away to the United States, but she stuck to the house. That fall it seemed necessary to have some sort of headquarters in Europe even if we were not often there. Therefore, Mrs. Hoover determined upon a flat at Hyde Park Gate in London and furnished it to her heart's desire. The furniture was so good that it still exists. Herbert, Jr., was born there on August 4, 1903. His mother's first expedition after she was up was to the American Consul's to get Herbert registered as an American born on a temporary visit abroad. In mid-September, five weeks after his appearance on earth, we started for Australia with Herbert—in a basket—and a nurse. Traveling with babies is easier than with most grown-ups.

In Australia, New Zealand, and Burma, we lived in company houses. In addition to the California anchorage, in 1907, Mrs. Hoover found a delightful old but small house with a garden in Campden Hill, London, which we could sublease—the Red House. The original lease was so old that we were required to prevent our cows from wandering in

[2] Curiously, it was called the White House.

High Street or hanging our laundry in view of the neighbors. Because of our journeys we were not in it as much as we would have liked, but in addition to California at least it was a convenient place in which to leave things, although we were eternally storing them to make way for a tenant. Allan was born at Hyde Park Gate, on July 17, 1907, while we were furnishing the Red House. He, too, after being duly registered at the American Consulate, went promptly on a journey to Burma, aged five weeks.

The largest single area of the firm's business being in Australia, our first expedition at the start, after I became a partner, was a voyage of inspection on that front. We arrived at Kalgoorlie in December, 1901, via Suez and Ceylon. It was about three years since I had left those hot precincts—and the temperature had not diminished.

Western Australia had now passed through one of the gigantic gold booms of history and was in the bitter headache of the morning after. Three major causes had brought this sadness. First was human frailty. The new goldfield had been the scene of the most unscrupulous stock-market promotion since the Mississippi Bubble. The second was a geological frailty. The geological conditions of desert erosion by which several hundreds or thousands of feet of rock had been blown or washed away over geologic ages had resulted in much secondary enrichment of the upper levels of the gold veins. As the workings extended in depth, the ore constantly proved lower grade and many originally promising mines proved only flashes in the pan. To use another miner's phrase, "They did not go down." The third cause of relapse was an engineering frailty. The technical work was not up to high standards. Australia was still in the stage of forming managerial staffs from promoted foremen instead of from trained engineers. While often capable superintendents of mines, these men lacked the technical equipment for progressive engineering in new fields with new problems. Systematic checking of ore reserves and values by detailed sampling was little known. The guide was the foreman's eye for values. In consequence of the usual optimism of foremen, there was much honest over-expansion. Added to this was stock speculation and collusion by some mine superintendents through deliberate manipulation of production.

After my departure from Australia three years before, the engineering work of the firm had largely relapsed to English and Colonial lines. It was the head office anxiety over these matters that brought me into the firm. That I might assure integrity and reliability in management, improve the equipment and the recoveries of metals and thus diminish working costs, I sent to the United States for fifteen university-trained mine managers, metallurgists, and mechanical engineers.[3] We stiffened the whole set-up by establishing stronger and more independently centralized inspection with central mechanical and metallurgical offices. We consolidated the buying of supplies through the one office at Kalgoorlie. This reformed organization in the course of time reduced the costs by 40 per cent, although we increased wages.

Of the original Australasian mines under our management when I came into the firm, four were great mines. They were the Oroya Brownhill, the Great Fingall, the Sons of Gwalia in Western Australia, and the Talisman in New Zealand. Six others, which had produced largely, were beginning to be disappointing in depth and after a few years had to be abandoned. They were the East Murchison, the Long Reef, the Vivian, the Diorite King, the Youanmi, the Menzies and the Lake Darlot. Four others which had been profitable were now down and out and had to be closed. They were the Bailey's Reward, the Bank of England, the Mercy's Reward and the Queensland mine. This surgical operation cut into the firm's income sadly, for staff was costing more and the number of fees diminishing. After this clean-up we were operating the equivalent of about 340 stamps on the various gold mines in Australasia, producing ore at the rate of about 500,000 tons per annum to a value of about 8 or 9 millions of dollars a year and employing directly or indirectly about 2,000 men.

However, a cheerful circumstance lightened this gloomy outlook. On the ship of this particular journey from Marseilles to Australia, I met a Mr. Francis Govette. He was an English investment banker who had been elected chairman of the Lake View and the Ivanhoe com-

[3] Of these, W. A. Pritchard, Arthur Diggles, Dean Mitchell and Frank Dennis were Stanford men. Others included Thomas Pomeroy, a Columbia man, William Goldstone, a University of California man, H. A. Shipman and Robert J. Grant of the Colorado School of Mines, and W. J. Loring. I recalled John Agnew and Wilfred Newberry from China.

panies, operating two of the most important mines at Kalgoorlie. The history of these companies was marked by wicked stock-market manipulation and fraud, which finally exploded in the criminal conviction and suicide of Whitaker Wright, the chief manipulator. The stockholders had chosen Mr. Govette to reorganize and salvage the business. He was a man of wide outlook and of high integrity, with all the loyalties and formalism of Englishmen of his class. He had no previous experience at all with mines. After he had been in Kalgoorlie a few days he came to me and stated that he was in a complete fog. He said it was all Greek to him. He trusted neither the honesty nor the estimates of the superintendents. He asked that our firm take complete charge of these two mines, reorganize them technically and financially. That began a most satisfactory and important expansion of the firm's connections. Over the years following, Mr. Govette, in co-operation with us, directed his and his friends' interests more and more into the industrial mining field. He and his wife remained all their lives our most faithful friends, socially as well as in business.

The demonstration afforded by our systematic improvement of the Lake View and the Ivanhoe, which had been notoriously badly managed, and the recognition of the value of an independent and trained staff, had an important bearing upon our business. Other bewildered and swindled stockholders from the wreckage of the Australian boom were looking for guidance. Many honest European boards of directors of other concerns wished to reassure their stockholders. And some directors who had themselves been wicked wanted an umbrella against the wrath that might come from stockholders. Everybody seemed to be resorting to reform and truth. Thus in time several other Western Australian groups came to us for management. The White Feather Reward, the Champion Reef, the South Kalgurli, the Cosmopolitan, the Bellview, the Boulder Main Reef, the Hannan's Star, the Oroya Links and West Fingall mines soon added themselves to our engineering group. They were all producing mines.

Subsequently two other groups which came into our fold caused us great grief. They were the Golden Horseshoe and the Perseverance groups of four mines. The London boards of directors of these concerns were under fire from their stockholders for manipulation and misrepresentation. They needed reform badly. Following the usual routine we at once put in new superintendents and systematically checked the records, the ore reserves and the engineering practice. We discovered that the reserves were greatly over-estimated, that the outputs had been maintained by picking the richer spots for stock manipulation. Our report to the directors was not welcomed as an exhibit of abstract truth. They wanted to argue. The stocks began to fall in the market and, finding that some of the directors were selling short while they withheld our reports from the stockholders on the ground that such revolutionary news must be checked over again, we flared up and resigned. This led to long and acrimonious discussions and in the end to a Parliamentary investigation by the Western Australian government. It served to teach me one fundamental lesson. That is, it does not pay to try to reform a stock-market crook. He can even make a profit out of reform.

All mines are sooner or later worked out and die, or at least they become comatose. New mines must constantly be discovered if the supply of metals is to be kept up, and engineers are to have a living. Many mines, however, have nine lives. Economic change or new discoveries in metallurgy or methods make ores which have been at one time abandoned as unprofitable worthy of new attack. Moreover, most mines, particularly when they become filled with water, gather legends of wasteful management, unexplored lodes, foremen who covered up a great discovery or something else, which periodically stimulate the imagination of new promoters. Thus fresh mining operations spring from four sources—the prospector who pioneers in the discovery of new mines, the mine operator who finds the capital with which to carry the prospector's mine from infancy to equipment with mills or smelters, the engineer who finds new methods and processes which render one-time unprofitable ores worth working, and finally the promoter.

The prospector lives a hard life, but one with stimulating dreams of what he will do when he "strikes it." And among these thousands of courageous hard-working dreamers, some few in every decade realize the dream. It keeps the thousands going. On behalf of the exploration companies and of other firms which we managed, we carried on a systematic search for possible new mines among these prospectors' finds.

It soon appeared that there was not enough intelligent prospecting and development by the prospector himself to maintain the industry in Australia. The terms on which prospectors were allowed a title by the government to their discoveries were too onerous. A prospector was required—unless by special relief—to keep two men continuously at work on each lease. Periodically he must go back to work at day's wages for a new supply of "grub," and thus could not always retain title to his "show." The Australian law, unlike the more liberal American law, starved him out. Whether a prospect be good or bad, if the prospector can keep it he will sooner or later return and do some more work on it. And occasionally he makes good. In all this, I interested my friend Walter James, the Premier of Western Australia, and he secured some important ameliorations for the prospectors.

While I am on the subject of prospectors: Mr. Agnew and I were driving along a bush track one day when we saw a new shaft being dug not far away. We went over to see what the prospector had found. He was engaged in winding up rock in a rawhide bucket with a windlass, his "mate" being at work in the bottom of a two-by-five-foot shaft some seventy feet deep. As we talked with the man at the top he made a slip in landing a bucket of rock. Rock and all, it fell into the shaft. He sprang back yelling, "I have killed my mate! I have killed my mate!" I leaned over the shaft and called down, "Are you hurt, mate?" The mate replied, "You *!*!*!*!, why don't you throw down the windlass?" I felt relieved.

A part of our business was the second-stage development from the prospector. There large capital is required for equipment. I could not recall even a fraction of the names of the prospects we tried out but did not equip. And those which we equipped and which failed us in depth are painful memories. The names of the Cue Consolidated, the Lancefield, the Walunga, the Nundydroog, the Wegemultha, rise up to demonstrate that even under most careful technical controls and despite the romantic names with which prospectors endowed their mines, gold mining is a hazardous business.

As a matter of fact, if all costs are included—prospectors and subsequent equipment and operation of the more favorable prospects—gold-mining is an unprofitable business in any country. Taking the world as a whole, the gold produced costs more than it sells for. It is certainly no business for amateurs. Nevertheless, the lure of the occasional great strike and the resultant fortune maintains a steady stream of followers for this variety of Pied Piper. As a lottery industry it surpasses even oil. Millions of people who have little hope of ever getting out of the rut except by some great fluke will always find a few dollars to put up for a gold mine. Thousands of promoters live to accommodate their wishes. And engineers earn an annual income from pronouncing funeral orations upon their defeats and managing their occasional successes.

Nevertheless, our firm's business in Western Australia developed to such a point that before the end of my partnership, in 1908, we were managing mines in that state which produced about 1,000,000 tons of ore per annum valued at some $18,000,000 and employed between 4,000 and 5,000 men. They were all white workers. Peaceably, we developed labor organization. We never had a strike on our mines in my time. Others did.

I have often listened to commiseration for men who work underground in mines. They want no pity. There is such a free-masonry, a fascination, a variety and an independence of work that men will not willingly leave it for any other trade. Going below after many years of working with the surface people I always have again the same thrills, the same feeling of separation and safety from the meanness and the handicaps of those on the top. It is a curious thing that among underground gnomes—the "little men" who were in the Middle Ages implicitly believed to live in the mines—none was malevolent, but all were helpful and good humored. There are no superstitions about devils underground.

At the end of 1902, and within 12 months after I assumed my partnership in Bewick, Moreing and Company, came the greatest disaster I was to meet. Mr. Moreing had gone to Manchuria to hunt tigers. Mr. Bewick, a wise counsellor and friend who though no longer an active partner yet had many interests with us, was hunting moose in Canada. I had returned to the London office only two months before, making my total British experience less than three months. I had not even a full acquaintance with the firm's London and New York business associates. However, as the partner senior on the job I had the temporarily major responsibility.

On Boxing Day (the day after Christmas) one of the junior partners, Mr. Rowe, asked Mrs. Hoover and me to attend a play to which they were taking their four children. During the play Rowe seemed highly nervous and filled with foreboding. At one moment he turned to me and asked if, in case anything happened to him, Mrs. Hoover would take his children and rear them. On the way home we speculated as to what was the matter with him. The firm was prospering both in reputation and in tangible results. We concluded that he must have "the liver," that being a fairly reliable diagnosis for a well-fed Englishman in the dumps.

On going to my office the next morning I found upon my desk a long letter marked "Private and confidential" in Rowe's handwriting. It consisted of a 20-page confession. He had been speculating in American railroad stock, had had huge losses, and in order to recoup had committed great defalcations not only of the firm's money but of that of several companies we managed and of certain trust funds. Any speculation was a violation of the partnership deed, a fact known to some of the brokers who took his business. While he described many transactions in detail, it proved later that his memory was inadequate and that he had omitted several of them. These omissions came as subsequent shocks for some days. The ultimate total proved to be about one million dollars. Part of his method had been to issue forged certificates of stock of the companies in our office and to sell the stock. In other cases he had simply forged checks. Taking advantage of his right to sign the firm's name, he had drawn out all our cash. He kindly listed these forgeries in his confession. He closed the document with the statement that we would not hear from him again. He heard from us, however.

Unable to believe my eyes, at once I called Mrs. Rowe on the telephone. Between bursts of hysterics she managed to say that she did not know what was the matter, but that he had gone out during the night, and in the morning she had found a letter saying that he was going to commit suicide.

I called in Wellstead, the other junior partner. Both being youngsters
—I was 28, Wellstead 32—we decided that the time had come to seek
some advice from the elders. We telephoned a few important City men
who were business allies of the firm, including Francis Govette and
Sir Frederick Hamilton. We asked them to come over quickly—saying
we were in trouble. None of them had suffered any losses from these
frauds. When they assembled an hour later I admitted my ignorance
of English business customs and asked our lawyer to read Rowe's letter
aloud. The almost unanimous colloquial reaction from the assembled
company was "I will be ——."

Some of them had known and trusted Rowe for years. We discussed
the fact that Moreing could not be reached by cable for a week. The
lawyer pointed out that the firm and the companies had no legal liability for the forgeries. After some discussion, Mr. Govette turned to
me and said approximately, "Young man, you are new in this firm and
you are new in English business. We would all like to help you. We
should first like to know if you have any ideas as to what you would
like to do." I answered that what I would *like* to do was to pay every
dime over the counter whether we were liable or not and have no
public noise about it, but that I did not have any such resources and
neither did Wellstead. But I added that Moreing and Bewick were of
course rich men. They could pay it and not feel it.

Govette relieved the tension by remarking that I should say "tup-
pence" instead of "dime." They all agreed that if that was the disposition of Wellstead and myself, with no great resources, it should be
even more the disposition of Mr. Moreing. They felt that he had selected
Rowe, that his own reputation and that of an old and established firm
were at stake. That was more particularly important for the mining
industry, as our firm was almost the only one which had emerged
from the Australian boom with clean hands. I asked the firm's lawyer,
who was also Moreing's most intimate friend, whether he thought
Moreing would put up such cash as the firm could not find. He did
think so, emphatically. Taking the risk of Moreing's disapproval, we
sent out a statement to the press announcing that forgeries and defalcations had occurred, that Rowe, the culprit, had confessed and adding
that the firm would make good all losses, although it was under no

legal obligation to do so. That ended the conference, but all of those men—some then strangers to me—remained loyal friends of the firm and myself to the end of their lives. They offered to find us cash for any pressing need.

We cabled to Moreing the story of the disaster, and an account of what we had done, and waited for his possible explosion. Then came a painful job with a needed touch of comic relief. While Wellstead was checking the books under a battalion of borrowed accountants and finding new frauds, it was my task to telephone all the firms and indi-viduals named in Rowe's confession and say something like this:

"Hello, Mr. .... I regret to tell you that your firm has certificates for ...... shares of stock in .... I also regret to tell you that those certificates are forged."

"What! What?"

Then followed the announcement that our firm would make the loss good, but that we wanted a little time to turn around; meantime, that they must hold on to the stock. Then came the universal, "Well, I'll be ——."

Or, "Hello, Mr. .... I regret to tell you that forged checks have been cashed on your account amounting to ...."

"What! What?" And in turn "be——."

Moreing answered by cable, laconically approving, directing the method for realizing any necessary cash from his personal resources. He rushed home, assumed 75% of the loss and agreed to a readjustment of interests in the firm by which I was to hold 30%, Wellstead, 15%. We had to take on 25% of the Rowe losses. We paid off the entire amount in about three years. We found in two cases that the receivers of forged documents were in collusion with Rowe, they having discov-ered earlier frauds and compounded them. We refused to pay their claims. These crooks brought suit in the courts, but lost. The firm gained in respect and volume of business. The police caught Rowe in Canada. Convicted, he received a ten-year sentence. Mrs. Hoover gave Mrs. Rowe an allowance to keep her children until Rowe came out of prison. Then she divorced him and married another man.

In 1902 we bought our first automobile—a French Panhard. It ran part of the time. Obviously, the motorcar was ideal for our Australian desert mining work, even if it did not go all the time and required a highly professional nurse. On a trip to Australia in 1903 I took a car with me. This was one of the earliest automobiles introduced into those fields. Our mines were scattered at points away from the railroads, and it took more than four hundred miles of driving by team to inspect them. We were maintaining buggy horses at the interior mines upon feed which had to be transported these long distances by camels. It cost us about $10 per week to board a horse. As our staff had to make these journeys frequently and as covering 40 miles a day required relays of horses, we were spending $5,000 to $10,000 a month for this transportation. All of which confirmed my views as to the inappropriateness of a horse. The new automobile worked by coaxing. We made an unheard-of 125 miles in a single day over bush tracks. Ultimately four automobiles replaced the driving horses.

One obstacle to automobiles in the desert was the long camel trains which followed the bush tracks. The Afghan drivers disliked halting the camels and taking them off of their well-worn pad. We established a custom of giving three large bottles of beer for this service and at a long-distance honk the road would be cleared with cheers from the Afghans.

I had received a mechanical training and thought a little gas engine on wheels was nothing. Were we not building and running tens of thousands of horsepower in steam engines and electric generators, with vast complicated machinery tied to them? Yet those early Australian automobiles got me down into the dirt almost every hour of the day. They often caught a disease called sand-in-the-carburetor and the tires finally had to be bandaged in split steam hose—and replaced every little while.

But cars improved and in later years the weekends and holidays of motoring with Mrs. Hoover through the English and Scottish counties, the forest and lake country, formed a large part of those stimulating memories which make one forget much of the objectionable conduct of the human animal.

In July–August, 1904, I visited the Transvaal to examine and negotiate some matters connected with a coal company and some gold mines which we managed. The successful coal mines had been proved to be underlaid by the East Rand extension of the gold-bearing series. After the consolidation of various interests, the coal mines became highly successful gold mines. Here I had fine hospitality from my old friend and Stanford classmate, Herbert Stark, who was the manager of the Crown Mines, one of the largest of the Transvaal enterprises.

At this time the Rand mines had begun the importation of Chinese labor. I did not believe in it and made a short statement before the Chamber of Commerce contending that cheap labor was not economical, citing our lesser costs per ton in Australia and the United States with highly paid white labor. An extract of this statement subsequently appeared in the London *Chronicle*. I continued to investigate this subject, and ultimately (1909) published a little book entitled *Principles of Mining* giving additional data.

Certain supposedly large copper mines in British Columbia and in California had been part of the scenery in the Whitaker Wright scandal-drama. It was proposed by the wretched stockholders that we should take over the managements. I personally inspected the mines, but they proved to be of little future value and we were compelled to decline. There was, however, another group of mines in this same sea of wreckage that we did try to salvage. In the state of Victoria, Australia, occur a series of buried rivers with gold-bearing bedrock gravels known geologically as the Lodden River System. At some time in geologic history a flow of lava filled the valleys and buried the streams. The placer-miners of 1850 discovered rich gravel beds dipping under the lava and followed them further and further down. Some very profitable mines had been worked in this fashion. With the slope, the gravels naturally became deeper and the thickness of the lava overburden increased as they followed down the buried stream. Finally the water in the increased depth became so heavy that mine pumps of that time could not cope with it and mining efforts were abandoned for many years. Whitaker Wright and his fellow-operators secured titles to some 20 miles of these buried streams and made them the scene of a gigantic stock speculation. He had taken about $6,000,000 from the stockholders and had spent about $2,000,000 on shafts and pumps when the whole bubble burst. In supporting his last desperate market manipulations, Wright had siphoned out the other cash from the companies' treasuries.

None of his managers had yet been able to overcome the water, and the actual knowledge as to the value of the mines was no greater than when they started. In 1903 the irate stockholders approached our firm to take over the management and carry the enterprise to completion. I engaged Dr. Waldemar Lindgren to examine the area, since he, from long study of similar buried rivers in California, was pre-eminently fitted to that task. Lindgren thought that there was a chance for the stockholders to get their money back by going ahead. I advised them that it was highly speculative, but, as they had so much money in already, if they wanted to put up more money we would try to pump the water out. They found another million dollars and we began the greatest pumping operation in mining history. But the water was too much for us, and I recommended that it be abandoned.[4]

In view of the dim outlook for lasting expansion in gold mining as an industry, I determined, early in my connection with Bewick, Moreing and Company, that it was desirable that we give more emphasis to the base metals—lead, zinc, copper, and tin. Those industries were much less romantic but less speculative than gold mining and had a sound industrial purpose. Following this policy, we turned to developing base metal prospects in various parts of Australia. Out of the usual routine of prospects that did not mature we established a successful copper mine in Queensland—the Great Fitzroy. Intent on base metals in the summer of 1905, I visited the great Australian silver-lead district at Broken Hill. It was an old district. The mining methods were obsolete and none of the companies had discovered a satisfactory method of recovering the zinc which was a large element in the ore. The mines had been operating for many years, simply concentrating out the lead (containing most of the silver) with gravity methods, and had piled up mountains of millions of tons of tailings with the zinc still in them. Several mines contained too little lead to be profitable at that time, but would be so if the zinc could be recovered. New processes for re-

---

[4] It is interesting to note that now after another thirty-five years another group is about to attack this problem again. No abandoned gold mine is ever allowed to rest in peace.

covery of sulphides by oil flotation had been recently discovered and I had previously instituted systematic research upon the subject in our laboratories.

After inspecting the district, I formed an association between our firm and W. L. Ballieu and W. S. Robinson of Melbourne, and Mr. Govette in London. With Ballieu I purchased on behalf of our clients the control of some 5,000,000 tons of tailings. We obtained contracts for future outputs, and also acquired controlling interests in the low-grade mines, and some prospective extensions of the district. We erected pilot plants to test out three different methods of flotation and finally worked out a feasible one. There were, however, all the infant diseases and griefs that come with pioneering new processes.

But out of these operations there emerged the reorganized Broken Hill North Mine, the Amalgamated Zinc Company, the Zinc Corporation and the rejuvenated Broken Hill South Block Mine, the two latter concerns being under the management of our firm, the two former under that of the Ballieu firm. These concerns have all proved highly successful. Our enterprise greatly expanded employment, living conditions and the stability of the district.[5]

The older mines in Broken Hill were at that time very reactionary in their mining methods and in their treatment of labor. Strikes and quarrels were frequent. We encouraged the unions by collective bargains with them. There were no strikes in our mines during any time, although other mines in the district were several times shut down because of labor disturbances. Our operations were a demonstration, an industrial fundamental—greater technical service, more labor-saving devices, lower costs, and larger production and higher wages.

Broken Hill was one of the dreariest places in the world at this time. It lay in the middle of the desert, was unbelievably hot in summer, had no fresh water except as hauled in or distilled. There was practically no vegetation, and the mountains of tailings blew into every crack, corner, dish and bed with every wisp of wind. It was healthful enough, however, and well supplied with drinks.

[5] Over 45 years since their founding, these concerns have never failed to pay dividends and, though somewhat changed in name and corporate structure, they are still among the world's greatest suppliers of lead and zinc.

By this time Chang Yen-mao brought a suit in the British courts to establish his "rights" under the "memorandum" previously referred to, which set up the form of management of the company. His lawyers did not press action for some years, when it finally did come into Court. The trial excited great interest, both because Chang was a picturesque character in full Mandarin costume with a top button and because he paraded as an innocent Asiatic injured by important British, French and Belgian firms. Unjustly Bewick, Moreing and Company as a firm and myself individually were embraced in the action as defendants. We were dragged in to insure our appearance as witnesses and were quickly dismissed from the action. The memorandum was found binding as the result of De Wouters' and my testimony in its favor—to the annoyance of Francqui. As usual in lawsuits, wild charges of fraud had been made on all sides but none of them was substantiated.

Chang had other motives for coming all the way to England at great expense in order to establish his right to an elective job at $500 a month. Tong Shao-yi, who subsequently was twice Prime Minister of China, and others who never forgave him for real or fancied wrongs, had charged him with fraud on several counts. The Empress Dowager ordered him to get all of the property back—or else. He and his advisers set the litigation on foot and kept it alive for six years so that he could periodically report progress in his efforts to restore his "rights." [6]

In another place I was to experience again the clash of Occidental engineering with Oriental civilization. Late in 1904, while returning on a steamer to Colombo from the examination of some tin mines in which we were interested in Penang, I became acquainted with Mr. A. C. Martin, a railway contractor in Burma. He had been building the strategic railway from Mandalay to Lashio near the Chinese border. He described to me enormous abandoned mine-workings in the jungle about 60 miles north of the railway and some 50 miles south of the Chinese frontier. He said it was a lead and copper mine. He had acquired a lease from the Indian government and had enlisted a smallish promoter in London, but wanted to interest our firm in the business. On arriving in London, I opened the subject with Smith, the promoter. I found that his company had sent out some machinery—all of the

[6] I was to hear much more of this in the Presidential campaign of 1928.

wrong kind—had some reports made by unreliable men and lacked the financial strength to carry on the business. With some of the American and English clients of our firm, including other engineers, we took an option on a controlling interest. We sent a young engineer for a scouting trip. In due time I received an ecstatic cable from him stating among other things that there was at least 500,000 tons of lead on the surface in slags piled up around old smelting operations. He described enormous but inaccessible workings. I was very skeptical that any such amounts of loose lead could exist in this world, and promptly dispatched a more mature American engineer, C. D. Clark, who had large experience with that metal. Mr. Clark's report in April 1905 was even more impressive. I resolved to look at the place myself and pending my departure I set Clark at making surveys for possible railway connections with the Burma railways.

On my arrival in Burma, Clark and I stole a day off at Rangoon to visit the Shwedaung Pagoda, and later on, a day or two at Mandalay to absorb the atmosphere of the only truly happy and cheerful race in all Asia—the Burmese. Also, for the tenth time the usual British civil official informed us that Kipling was most unreliable, as witness the fact that China was not across the bay from Rangoon as the great poet represented. Kipling's many caustic notions as to Indian officials had left a definite imprint on their minds. There is a vast literature of travelers' chatter on Burma. But to those who wish to look deeper than stories of the British and to appreciate something of the spiritual forces of Asia at that time, I recommend Fielding Hall's *Soul of a People*.

Mr. Clark and I made our way from Mandalay to Hsipaw, about 130 miles up the Lashio railway. Clark, with a reserve of humor, gave me no warning of certain comic-opera preludes in what was to become a large industrial undertaking. When we arrived at Hsipaw, the wholly bamboo capital of the Shan State of that name, we were met by a courteous gentleman with a perfect Oxford accent who was introduced as the Sawbwa (native prince). He welcomed us with obvious enthusiasm and invited us to his "palace." It was a frame building with motifs reminiscent of Long Island. We were given comfortable rooms, and at dinner I began to sense some of the intellectual climate. In the usual British colonial fashion, the Prince as a boy had been taken to England, educated, and then sent back to rule his kingdom of some 200,000 primeval Shans subject to a British superintendent, who presided over three other Shan States. The Sawbwa wanted to talk and he wanted to talk to somebody other than the British as to his personal plight. His life was clutched in the meshes of Western culture and then he was set down wholly alone to rule a barbaric state with net revenues "insufficient for the living of an English shopkeeper." He had been compelled to learn the Shan language again and there were not three English-speaking persons in the state. The total revenues of the principality appeared to be about $125,000 a year, out of which he had to contribute a quarter to the British Shan States superintendent and from the remainder pay the expenses of the state, including the police, schools, and maintenance of roads. With humorous twists he stated that his family had held the principality for a thousand years and that his accumulated blood relations had certain rights to his hospitality—that alone took a lot of money. Not only did they number some thousands, but he was compelled to marry a wife from the family of each clan head. By this time, there were some 20-odd of them. They were all ugly. Besides this, to satisfy the spiritual needs of the people and support the dignity of the state he needed a new white elephant as the old one had died. He said all this in vigorous language with some humor but a sort of hopelessness.

Here were indeed the materials of a comic opera with elements of a Greek tragedy. For here was a young man put artificially out of cultural key to the station in life in which he had to serve. He did not know what else to do, and he had genuine fealty to his people and loyalty to his job. But in our persons he saw possibilities of a complete emancipation through the creation of a great industrial concern making commerce, employing labor, increasing standards of living, paying royalties and taxes. He envisaged schools, civilization, and the resources for dignity, comfort and proper appearance at the Imperial and Indian Courts.

After dinner Clark asked if we might meet the wives. They trooped in and it developed that Clark, who had been a frequent visitor, had taught them to play "drop-the-handkerchief" and "ring-around-a-rosy."

The Sawbwa was, however, more interested in what I thought about the prospects of the mines and what we were going to do. I was able later to give him much comforting hope.

We made the trip from the railway mostly on horseback through the dripping jungle. The mines were located in a mountainous area, but the ancients had grubbed up all the roots of the trees for a few miles around for charcoal and the fumes of the old smelters had killed still more of the forest. Thus the mines were surrounded by open grassy hills with only occasional trees. The workings were enormous, one open pit being nearly a thousand feet long, five hundred feet wide, and three hundred feet deep. There were hundreds of dumps and tunnels, extending over nearly three miles. The mines had been operated by the Chinese, and the inscriptions which marked the abundant graves gave a fair chronology. Apparently the period of intense working covered 450 years, from 1400 to 1850, when the great Mohammedan Rebellion in Yunnan ended the enterprise. Later on we found Chinese historical mention of the enormous production of silver from this area. The mines were apparently so difficult of access that the ancients could not transport the lead to market. Therefore, after separating the silver, they had thrown the lead residues on the dump.

It is interesting that the Chinese used the cupellation process to separate the lead from the silver. This process was used by the ancient Greeks at the lead-silver mines of Mt. Lourian and is in principle the same we use today. It also interested me to notice that here was another abandoned mine that was not allowed to rest in peace.

It was obvious that the ancient miners could have worked only the ore which the weather had oxidized near the surface. They had been stopped in depth by the turn of the ore into sulphides or when overcome by water. Clark and I were anxious to obtain access to the old workings to see the nature of the deposits and what the sulphides were like. There were in the hillsides many low tunnels about four feet high and three feet wide, preserved fairly well by the hard rock. They had been cut by hand-tools, probably with the help of water poured on the rock after subsequent fires in the fashion of Hannibal's road-building in the Alps. We started to crawl into these tunnels one by one, but sooner or later were baffled by falls of the roof. In the last one we entered I, in advance of Clark, was crawling on one hand and my knees, carrying a candle in the other hand. By chance I looked down into a puddle of water ahead, and there, as big and plain as life, loomed the fresh track of a tiger. He had been going in. I pointed it out to Clark. To fight a Bengal tiger with a miner's candlestick made no appeal whatever to either of us. With no delay and with steadily increasing panic we made for the entrance. The tiger, fortunately, was not of an inquiring turn of mind and did not come to greet us. Anyway, we explored no more tunnels. When, later on, we came to build a great double track tunnel through which to operate the mines, I named it the Tiger Tunnel. It provided more room in case of such conflicts.

The Shans elaborated on the wickedness of this tiger, for he had killed many animals and some children. Therefore we organized a hunt for him. The method was to tie a calf to a tree near his den, at four o'clock in the morning while he was asleep, and then, with rifles, sit on a stage about thirty feet up and await his coming for breakfast. We sat up until eight o'clock and being hungry ourselves, and stiff besides, we went home. We sent out a Shan to bring in the calf and in an hour he came back breathlessly with the news, "Tiger have got calf." I decided to let my colleagues pursue the matter further.

There was sufficient lead material on the surface to warrant building a railway to the main line and erecting a smelter at Mandalay, to which point we could bring coke. During this time we would develop the old workings.

On the return from the mine we made a report that elated and encouraged the Sawbwa. We asked if he could induce his hill tribes to work at building the railway. He said he had just such powers. In cooperation with the British superintendent, we arranged wage scales with him and with the adjoining state. These wages were above any standard the jungle had ever known—and the first money thousands had ever had. We arranged to have the Sawbwa recruit the labor at a small sum per man per day. We proposed to build the line in Asiatic fashion without machinery but with picks, shovels, and baskets to carry the dirt. The Sawbwa produced more than 20,000 workers. His revenues jumped sensationally. Prior to his redemption, he confessed a financial difficulty to Clark. It seemed that an Armenian merchant had appeared in the village with a stock of clocks and lamps. The Sawbwa visited the shop on his daily walks, and each time he bought a clock or a lamp on credit. All this merely by way of relieving boredom. Finally, he had most of the Armenian's stock and was being charged 10 per cent a month interest on the bill. The creditor had become very pressing and threatened to complain to the British superintendent. Clark visited the Armenian and found he had bought his stock from a chetty in Rangoon on credit, and was paying 5 per cent a month interest himself. The Armenian, just as much worried as the Sawbwa, did not dare go back to Rangoon. For the good of the Kingdom, and our mines, Clark adjusted the affair to the satisfaction of all parties concerned.

On my return to London we arranged for the necessary capital and this time I varied my usual rule of not investing very much of my savings in any mine and took the largest chance of my career.

There was a truly Kiplingesque incident in the construction of this railway. We had to bridge the Nam Tu River, a large and turbulent mountain stream. The Shans were strong believers in spirits, called "nats." One job of the "nats" was to light the pagodas. They traveled through the jungles along the open way of the streams. The "nats" had no patience with obstructions like bridges, and evidenced it by drowning all bridge builders. The Shans were adept at suspension bridges made of vines but they left this stream alone. Therefore, they would have nothing to do with a proceeding so dangerous and sacrilegious. So we imported Chinese from the nearby border for this job. The Chinese spirits of "the wind and water" travel in straight lines and thus do not follow crooked rivers. To erect our bridges we had borrowed a young engineer from an American firm who supplied the structural steel. His recreation seemed to be by taking walks on the girders of bridges and high buildings. It was a good deal of a job to span the river in this wilderness owing to the lack of foundations for false work and of skilled men. However, the youngster got the span into place. At that stage the bridge had no floor in it but as the mark of his full triumph he climbed onto one of the top girders some 18 inches wide and proceeded to walk across in defiance of all invisible forces.

Halfway over he fell. He banged through the cross struts of the span and into the water 50 feet below. One of the staff, a former British naval officer, rushed down the stream to where it spread into wider rapids and with great difficulty and courage rescued the youngster. He was full of water, his collarbone, two ribs and a leg were broken. The officer pumped him out, set his bones in splints, telegraphed to Mandalay for a surgeon to come by special train and hoped for the best. Next day the surgeon arrived and announced that the youngster's only chance to live was not to touch his settings for fear of more shock. The young man got well. Some months afterward on a visit to the mines I asked him why, after walking girders most of his life, he fell off this time. He said, "The 'nats' got me."

More prosaically, it might have been tropical sun plus excitement. Anyway, the manager posted signs and passed the word to the effect that the sacrifice had been made to the "nats." The Shan engine drivers seemed to accept this interpretation, and have taken their locomotives across ever since.

In time we completed the railway and the smelter at Mandalay to melt the slags. We began producing lead in 1908. The subsequent history of this property belongs to the next chapter. The Sawbwa prospered. He was soon able to support all the traditions as well as the attachments that his hot-house culture required and that Oriental display demanded. This time it was engineers who made the happy ending of a colorful opera.

On the next trip to Burma, Mrs. Hoover accompanied me and brought the babies along. She added much Asiatic lore to her stock, but both of us contracted malaria which took months to get rid of.

Among the side interests of Bewick, Moreing & Company, in my time, was a turquoise mine at Mt. Sinai. The venture had its romantic aspect; for one thing, it brought the miners closer to the Ten Commandments than usual; for another, the very fact that it was a turquoise mine was a surprise. Before I entered the firm, the Egyptian Government had asked it to interest itself in reopening some ancient workings reported on the Sinai Peninsula. Copper ores were known to have been mined in that area. A Cornish foreman and a prospecting party were sent in during the rainy season to explore. They finally found a large dump and the partly buried portal of a tunnel. The portal was of impressively large stones with ancient Egyptian inscriptions on every side. That portal, three or four thousand years old, became one of my griefs. The entrance was too small and narrow to suit the Cornishmen, so they enlarged it with a little dynamite. They found extensive workings, and finally discovered that the ancient Egyptians had been mining turquoise. The stones were all greenish. That color must have been fashionable among Egyptian women 3,000 or 4,000 years ago but we could not find a jeweler in the world who wanted any of them, although we had bucketfuls.

However, the Cornishmen did make a great contribution to knowledge. They informed me that they had discovered an underground warehouse full of Egyptian "gravestones" and that there were gravestones on the hills about. I instructed the miners not to touch them and notified Dr. Flinders Petrie, the great Egyptologist at Cairo. From these discoveries he was able to revise and extend a large part of the chronology and dynastic succession in ancient Egypt. It seems that the Egyptians made periodic excursions to mine a supply of jewelry and often left a stele engraved with the date and other facts. When Dr. Petrie arrived at the place he recoiled in proper horror at the blasted portal, for precious inscriptions had been destroyed. In his absorbing book he rose to the heights of righteous vituperation over this vandalism. Carried away by his indignation, he included in the indictment much destruction for which the Cornishmen were not responsible. He did not mention Americans in that book; but gossip in Egypt associated the deed with the essential barbarity of all Americans and laid it at my door.

However, Americans must be careful not to get out of character with their essentially savage background or they will be misunderstood men. A shrewd Englishman in similar position would have peddled the stele to all the museums of the world under the guise of a patron of learning.

Another of our side-activities was a survey of the mineral resources of Abyssinia at the request of the then King of Kings and Conquering Lion of Judah. I did not visit the country but we had competent parties of geologists and engineers in the field for some time. The geology is such that the probability of substantial mineral development is remote indeed.[7] We recommended that they extend irrigation instead.

We dove into ancient history again when the authorities of Northern Italy asked the firm to report on those abandoned mines in the Alps from which the Romans extracted the iron for their munitions. For a holiday in the Alps Mrs. Hoover and I made this inspection ourselves. We had two grand weeks in a delightful place with delightful people but we confirmed the general impression that the ancient Empire had never engaged in mass production. A little iron will make a lot of short-swords.

Early in 1908 I determined to retire from Bewick, Moreing and Company. There were many reasons. We wanted to spend more time in the United States. Living less than three months in any one country in any one year was a dog's life. The boys would soon need systematic American schooling. In professional work I wanted fewer projects at any one time. There was never an hour's respite from the telephone or telegraph. I hoped to be of some service in American public life. We had saved enough to be sure of a modest living. I had an interest in the Burma mines, for which we had high hopes. The firm's business was triple what it had been when I entered. My share was yielding one of the largest engineering salaries of the period. The partners in the firm understood, but they pressed me to stay. They offered to increase my share in the business. But the term of my partnership contract was drawing to a close and I determined not to renew it. My interest was taken over by some of our staff engineers on the same terms as those on which I entered. I continued to be associated with the firm in special concerns during the following years. Despite different points of view at times, these men had been pleasant associates.[8]

---

[7] Mussolini probably was not aware of this scarcity when he orated the Italian people into that tragic aggression which ended in his downfall. It was of some interest to me when just 40 years later Herbert, Jr., was called in to advise on the same subject.

[8] Mr. Moreing lived to the age of 83, his sons rose in English public life, and we have always been good friends. Forty years later the firm was still in successful operation.

CHAPTER 8

⟨⟩⟨⟩⟨⟩⟨⟩⟨⟩

INTERNATIONAL FREE-LANCE
ENGINEERING

1908–1914

For me, the period of six years that ended with the outbreak of the World War was one of even larger engineering undertakings in many different parts of the world. Instead of relief from work, although Mrs. Hoover and I traveled less constantly than during the eight preceding years and spent more time in the United States, we certainly did move. Just to indicate how far we ranged, I give a table of countries:

1909—United States, England, Germany, Poland, Russia, China.

1910—United States, Scotland, England, France, Russia, Burma, Korea, Japan.

1911—United States, Great Britain, Belgium, Germany, Russia, Burma.

1912—United States, Great Britain, France, Italy, Russia.

1913—United States, Canada, Belgium, Germany, Russia.

1914—United States, Great Britain, France, Italy, Belgium, Holland, Germany.

For a new organization I invited a number of young engineers to join with me, guaranteeing them that they would earn a minimum annual amount in fees. I created no formal firm and had no partners in the legal sense. I opened offices in New York, San Francisco, London and subsequently in Petrograd and Paris. We worked on the theory that there were in the world many sound engineering projects which, because of incompetence or outworn methods, returned small profit or none at all. If we could take hold of them, bring their operations up to date, and manage them efficiently we deserved a fair percentage of the increased profits. In other words, we would serve as engineering doctors to sick concerns. When we restored competent management to a business the youngsters would take over the details. Mr. John Agnew became ultimately the Chief of Staff. Messrs. Gilman Brown, Dean Mitchell, Louis Chevrillon, Amor Kuehn, T. J. Jones, my brother Theodore, and several others ran the routine of the various offices and did the major technical work. Ours was a happy shop. There was the sheer joy of creating productive enterprises, of giving jobs to men and women, of fighting against the whims of nature and of correcting the perversities and the incompetence of men.

The character of my professional activities during the six years from 1908 to 1914 can be indicated by a few specimens, especially in their human and romantic aspects. Many of our inquiries into the ailments of existing companies and the prospects for new ones came to nothing. For instance, in 1910 a group of Japanese bankers approached me with an invitation to join in what they considered was a large and rich group of copper and gold mines in Korea. I journeyed both ways over the Trans-Siberian Railway. The only profit was a view of the magnificent scenery of the Yalu River and various ornamental Korean chests which I sent home. We went up the Yalu River in a junk. An English-speaking Japanese colonel came aboard for a visit at one of our night stops. He was in command of a regiment engaged in putting down Chinese bandits north of the river in Manchuria. They occasionally extended their operations over the river into Korea. He said that a few days before the head bandit had asked for an interview with him under a flag of truce and had complained bitterly at the vigor with which the Japanese were harassing him and added that he was entirely out of ammunition. He ended the interview with a flat ultimatum. Unless the Japanese supplied him with money and arms he would not go on being a bandit. The bewildered Japanese officer looked into local customs and found that the Chinese Tao Tais (local governors) in this region had been doing just that for many years in order to draw more funds— which meant more "squeeze"—from the provincial treasury. If the bandits should go out of business, the Tao Tais would suffer great financial reverses.

I had been a director of Burma Mines and was its engineering nurse through infancy while a partner of Bewick, Moreing and Company. After leaving that firm I became managing director of the concern and in 1914 the chairman of the board as well. We had got our railway and temporary smelter at Mandalay in operation and we were successfully working the old slags but we had not as yet been able to get into the old mines. We battled against caving ground, tropical conditions, untrained labor, and huge amounts of water in these endeavors to get under the old workings. We tried diamond drilling, but the ground proved so soft and shattered that we did not succeed in getting dependable cores. We drove a tunnel in 1910, "The Chinaman Tunnel," which struck the old workings above the possible ore; nevertheless, we sunk a shaft from it, which gave us a peep at the rich ore bodies. But we were drowned out.

Finally we started a deep tunnel—the "Tiger"—nearly two miles long and through it we opened the mines 700 feet below the old workings. Heavy slides made this tunnel a discouraging and expensive job that required over three years for its completion. In the end we had to support great lengths of it with arched masonry. But we were amply rewarded by opening one of the largest and richest lead-zinc-silver ore bodies ever discovered. When the lateral workings from the Tiger Tunnel were completed, over 5,000,000 tons of ore were proved above that level alone. We built large mills for concentration of the ore, hydroelectric plants for power; we opened coal-mines, we constructed houses, towns, hospitals, schools, and recreation grounds. We came into large production in 1916 during the war, and that production has been greatly expanded since.[1]

It gave a living directly and indirectly to over 100,000 Chinese, Shans and Indians of many dialects—a better living than ever before in their lives, with some of the gadgets of mechanized civilization thrown in.

The Sawbwa became rich.

In 1918 I received an offer for the American interests in the mines

---

[1] During its first 30 years this mine gave the world over 1,500,000 tons of lead, 135,000,000 ounces of silver and much zinc—all of a value of over $350,000,000. And it still had many years of possible life.

and we unwillingly sold it. Also, at that time I was so involved in Belgian Relief that I could not give it proper attention.[2]

As another example of our occupation, I joined Mr. Govette as managing director of two mining investment companies for which we purchased promising mining interests. He and I also acted as managing directors of the Zinc Corporation group at Broken Hill, which I have already mentioned.[3]

Mr. Govette and I consolidated a number of low-grade mines at Kalgoorlie, Western Australia, into the Lake View Company and thus by reducing expenses from larger output gave it a long and prosperous life.[4]

Several opportunities for an industrial doctor developed in Russia, to which I was destined to make numerous prolonged visits during the six years prior to the First World War. The most interesting was the Kyshtim estate in the Ural Mountains near Ekaterinburg. This estate contained about 1,500,000 acres, comprising agricultural land, great forests, important copper deposits, an iron, steel and chemical industry, with a population of about 100,000 peasants and workers. The property belonged to a distant branch of the Romanoff family, then headed by Baron Mellor Zakomelsky. The family had lived in great state from its earnings for several generations. But through waste and extravagance the previous generation had fallen into debt, and Mr. Leslie Urquhart, an able Scottish businessman, had undertaken to refinance the estate and to modernize the copper, iron and forest industries. Urquhart was born in Russia and had been engaged for many years in the oil business in Baku. Prior to his modernizing Kyshtim the estate had depended upon English engineers who worked on a mistaken metallurgical concept. The plants they built failed to realize expectations.

---

[2] These mines were seized by the Japanese in 1942 and this great source of lead to the United Nations was cut off. They were later seized by the Communist Government of Burma and are now closed, probably for many years to come, as large capital at great risk will be required to start production again and to provide a living for some 100,000 destitute people.

[3] This enterprise and those it absorbed produced in its first thirty years over 1,500,000 tons of metallic lead, 1,400,000 tons of metallic zinc, and 40,000,000 ounces of silver of a value over $400,000,000.

[4] In the thirty years since our original reorganization of this mine it has produced over $80,000,000.

It was clear that the English metallurgists had been on the wrong track. They had based their ideas on working the richer ores with blast furnaces. This type of treatment required large supplies of coke and fluxes which must be brought from long distances and at high costs, and every ton of ore treated lost money. The ore lent itself to the unusual possibility of "pyritic" smelting upon a large scale. The technology of that process was to take advantage of the heat values in the high sulphur content of the ores by firing them with a small percentage of charcoal which could be secured locally. As the ores were of low grade, a mass production plan with low costs was essential.

Urquhart had not been able to complete the transformation within the company's resources and, in 1910, his agent appealed to my London office for aid, both in finance and engineering. I sent one of our engineers to examine the property. I had known something of it from my prior journeys in Russia and from American engineers who had seen it.

We arranged the reorganization of the company's finances and later on I visited the property personally. Gilman Brown gave the technical direction, and we brought experienced men from Butte, Montana, where a similar ore is treated. From the moment the fires in the new furnaces were started, the company made money. Everybody benefited—the Russian owners, the peasants, the workers, the creditors, the stockholders, and not least the engineers. The property ultimately produced over 25,000,000 pounds of copper yearly and a host of other salable products, earning a net of about $2,000,000 annually.

The business was the more interesting because of its complex human relations. Here was a microcosm of all Russia. Some detail is interesting because it is a sample from the tragedy of Russia. At the top was a Russian noble family and at the bottom 100,000 peasants and workers, with nobody much in between but the priesthood and the overseers. At times in history the "family" had met its feudal obligations, and at other times not. Some generations had spent the product of the estate at Monte Carlo and Paris; others had sought to sustain and improve the lot of the peasants and workers. Baron Mellor Zakomelsky was not of feudal mind. My every contact with him indicated his devotion to the interests of his people. At one time the stock in the company rose on the Continental stock exchanges to a price which I thought was unjustified. Upon inquiring I found that the Baron was the buyer. He was of course a large original holder. I suggested that he was paying too much. He replied: "I must buy it with all my dividends for I must restore it to Russia."

The agricultural land on the estate was poor, the crops uncertain, the peasants were devastated by every famine. But under the Baron's direction the forests had been for many years the model of Russian forestry, and furnished a supplementary living for the peasants. For one hundred and fifty years a small iron industry had flourished on the estate—a sort of cottage-industry. Its principal product was Russian sheet iron. The sheets were treated by a "secret process" handed down from father to son, which rendered them unusually resistant to rust and gave them at one time a world market. The older American stove-pipes were largely made of their product. Our chemists had no difficulty in penetrating the secrets of the process. It consisted of alternately heating the sheets and sweeping them when hot with a wet pine-bough. The effect was to create a coating of FeO_4 which was rust-resistant.

An even more general cottage-industry was the casting of a multitude of iron ornamental forms which sold all over Asia and appeared in the United States in the ramping cows, horses, or warriors that once topped our household base-burners. There was no company profit in these industries. The market was very difficult to maintain in competition with more modern products, especially galvanized iron. The market for the iron ornaments was largely due to the plaque originating from the high sulphur content of the special iron ore which was used for this purpose. Russian artists were engaged to make better and more salable designs and built up quite a business for the peasants chiefly in small ornamental pots designed for Mohammedan prayer ablutions.

The Company's real business was the large mining and smelting of copper ores, and a series of satellite chemical industries. Pyritic smelting required a 3 to 4 per cent charge of charcoal. Making charcoal by modern methods developed a considerable amount of producer gas which was used for power, and a long list of by-products—acetic acid, wood alcohol, turpentine, etc. From sulphur gases out of the ore the company made sulphuric acid. The copper was refined to recover the gold and silver. The isolated location required that the company have its own railway connections and large machine shops, where it ultimately made from its own iron and steel most of its own equipment except the more elaborate machines such as locomotives, electric generators, and turbine engines.

The Company's new smelting plants had been erected some miles away from the old works, and a new town of warm log houses with schools, churches, movie theatres and hospitals had been built. They had put into them as much modern equipment as the fixed habits of the people would tolerate. They established a technical school to train mechanics in higher skills and to be foremen. They used Russian technical staff at every possible point, confining our Americans to back-room direction. They paid a wage 25 per cent above the countryside level, not as charity but to attract the most capable workmen. They sold the land to the peasants—all they wanted and on very low terms. Everyone took great pride in our progressive and happy community.

No one could sustain such intimate relations with the Russian people and their officials without becoming well aware of the hideous social and governmental backgrounds. A vivid picture of it came to me one day upon a railway station platform, where a long line of intelligent, decent people brutally chained together were marched aboard a freight car bound for Siberia. Some were the faces of despair itself, some of despondency itself, some of defiance itself. The whole scene was so revolting that I reacted to it in nightmares. Always there was a feeling among us that some day the country would blow up. The Baron believed it could be directed into the channels of democracy. But centuries of poverty and repression do not express their explosions in law and peaceful transformation.[5]

[5] This enterprise became a microcosm of later Russia. The business prospered until the Russian Revolution in 1917. I had resigned as a director early in 1915 to give my time to Belgian Relief. In 1916, the Bolsheviks began agitation in the plants. Finally with the crash of the Revolution in 1917, the Communists assembled large meetings of the workmen and ultimately passed three resolutions, the gist of which was: (1) dismissal of the ownership—the property belonged to the workers; (2) dismissal of the management—the work would be directed by committees of the workmen; (3) wages were raised 100 per cent.

A Russian committee called upon the American staff and courteously tendered them a train of sleeping cars and locomotives, with flowers, food and coal aboard, to take them out. They advised going to Vladivostok—3,000 miles. In the face of raging terror and murders our people naturally accepted. The committee expressed their appreciation

Here I need to go back a few years again in the story. This success
at Kyshtim brought important repercussions. Russian industry had
hitherto been often dominated by German and British operators. The
Russians were always suspicious of them, fearing political implications.
They resented the assumed superiority of the British and the German
officials. They had none of that feeling toward Americans. The Russian
engineers were most able technical men but lacked training on the administrative side. There was instinctive camaraderie by which the
Russians and Americans got along together.

The more progressive elements in the Czar's government watched
our relations to the people with appreciation. This applied not alone to
the Kyshtim group but to the other enterprises in Russia where I and

---

for the kindly attitude of the Americans at all times past. Our sixty Americans, with
their wives and children, reached Vladivostok without difficulty.

Then began the hideous tragedy of enthroned ignorance. The Russian technical and
administrative staff was roughly driven out, many being brutally treated and many
killed as "bourgeois."

To understand the full impact of the shift from intelligence to ignorance inherent
in Communist destruction, it must be understood that the chemical and metallurgical
operations and the mechanical equipment had to be conducted minute by minute by
highly trained technical men. Many of the operations were most delicately adjusted to
ore content, fluxes, fuel, heat, chemical and gas reactions, etc. The great mechanical
equipment was represented in warehouses full of blueprints and patterns, from which
the machinery had been designed and constructed. Every item was on card catalogue
immediately under the technicians' hands. Products had to be sold, money secured and
intricate accounting carried on, so that each worker should receive on due date his pay
check. A thunderclap surcharged by centuries of mistreatment of a race and guided by
blind stupidity shattered all this tuned intelligence in an instant.

First the metallic mixtures in one of the large furnaces were unbalanced, and the
furnace "froze." That disaster had happened to us once. The workers at that time had
observed that our remedy had been to blast out a large part of the frozen furnace and
build it over again. They could do this. The Communists were well trained in destruction. But when they searched for the blueprints and patterns with which to make the
new iron-work, they did not even know how to find them. The chemical cycles failed
likewise. In a week the works were shut down, and the 100,000 people destitute. The
very furies of ignorance were in the saddle.

All these details came to me years after when I was administering the relief of Russian
famine in 1923—a famine mostly due to ignorance. I had sent some of our former
engineers on the relief staff, as they spoke Russian and knew Russia. One of them had
charge of the famine-relief in the Urals. In Kyshtim he found that thousands had died
of destitution and starvation. The people, recognizing him, flocked around to know if
the Americans were coming back to restart the works. They even sent a petition to be
transmitted to me, saying they would be "good and obedient" if we would only give
them work again. Who knows what Golgothas humanity must surmount?

other Americans were associated. I can add that in these necessarily constant contacts of these groups with the Russian officials there was never a demand for a cent of graft.

All this led to another large mining incident. In 1912 Baron Mellor Zakomelsky and Mr. Urquhart informed me that our group had been requested to undertake the development of some of the Cabinet Mines. These were the personal property of the Czar, and embraced a considerable part of the mineral resources of Siberia. The government suggested most liberal terms and said they wanted other communities built up like Kyshtim. Not one of us knew much of where these mines were or their value. I had a nebulous memory of mines in Siberia that had been worked with political prisoners, and I knew that a spasm of reform had stopped that. Something clicked in my mind and I sent for George Kennan's book, *Siberia and the Exile System,* which in 1891 had been a world-sensation, exposing the mistreatment of political prisoners in the mines. Indeed, it was this book which had caused the spasm of reform. Having read the book again we realized that these convict mines were probably valuable. We created a small syndicate, for preliminary exploration, and sent Amor Kuehn to inspect those and other convict workings.

The most promising proved to be in the Altai Mountains on the southern border of Siberia, 750 miles up the Irtysh River above Omsk and thence 55 miles through the mountains. Kuehn reported that there had been large workings on oxidized lead-zinc-silver ores which, strangely enough, also contained copper and gold. The operations had been confined to the oxidized surface area and failed when they met with the metallurgical problems of the sulphides in depth. The workings being inaccessible, he asked for diamond drills, which we sent him. In due time he reported that the first drill hole at a depth of 1,000 feet had either struck an ore body 150 feet wide or had followed a stringer for that distance. The analyses showed almost solid copper, lead and zinc sulphides, with a large amount of gold and silver. Ore of this quality had hitherto existed only in museum specimens. Skeptical through long experience in mining, we dismissed it as a rich stringer and went about our saner business. But a month or so later Kuehn reported that a second hole at the same depth as the first one and a thousand feet away from it had passed through the same ore. Then we sat up and began to make calculations.

I shall not bother with further details. Sufficient to say it developed probably the greatest and richest single body of ore known in the world. Before the Communist Revolution the company had proved many years' supply. Our financial friends undertook to provide the working capital. The company sank shafts, built mills on the mines, a railway to the river and river steamers, erected smelters and refineries for lead, copper and zinc, gold and silver, on a site near the river and half way to Omsk. Seventy-five miles from this point they had found a convenient field of fine coking coal. The plants, much delayed by the war, finally started up in 1917, a few months before the revolution. Then the American staff under dire threats and in the face of reports of wholesale murder further north, fled for their lives. The hundred Americans with many Russian engineers and their families—men, women, and children—escaped into the interior of Mongolia. With horses and mules they made the stupendous overland journey of 4,000 miles to China—and arrived safely.

It was a long stride from the poignant scene which Kennan had witnessed to engineers, systematically turning the mines into a decent industry with decently treated labor in wholesome communities.

This group undertook drilling upon still other of the Cabinet properties, particularly the lead-silver mines at Nerchinsk so vividly described by Kennan. The Nerchinsk mines promised large industries and large returns. I had many other engineering engagements in Russia outside this particular group.[6]

Another representative specimen of industrial doctoring was the case

[6] So far as I know, none of them is today even supporting the jackals. Had it not been for the First World War, I should have had the largest engineering fees ever known to man. In later years the American Communists charged that I was endeavoring to secure the return of these properties from the Soviet Government in exchange for relief. Likewise the Moscow press explained my anti-Communist feelings on the ground that I was a rapacious capitalist whom they had put in his proper place.

It happened not to be true. I had resigned all engineering connections when I took over the Belgian Relief. My interests in Irtysh and other properties had been foreclosed upon by the bondholders. Even if they had been returned they would have gone to the British and French bondholders and never have benefited me or any other of the Americans. And I had sold my minor personal holdings in all Russian enterprises before the of Lindon Bates. He was a Yale graduate, a civil engineer and contractor, with his London offices in the same building as my own. He was an attractive man. We had been friends over some years. I had at times acted for him as a member of boards of directors of his concerns. He had undertaken a number of construction contracts, for which he was to be paid in future returns from oil production or stock in oil companies and had finally got himself deeper and deeper into the oil business. In some of these enterprises he had secured financial backing from Govette and others of my friends. By 1912 he was alarmingly overextended. At his beseeching I looked into his affairs. Like most people of indomitable optimism who become involved in tangles, he did not remember at the beginning the whole story of his liabilities. The job, which at first appeared simple, became one of those personal affairs without profit and in the end proved very difficult. Bates went to New York and stayed there to untangle his American business, leaving the whole mess in London with me. However, with Govette's assistance, we secured finance to complete a contract in Peru, where Bates was entitled to an interest in a promising oil property and then sold that interest to one of the large oil companies. We carried on a similar operation for him in Trinidad. He had contracted to build a pipe line in South Russia and had partly completed it. This proved too much of a tangle, as the oilfields to be served had given out. However, we were able to get one of the Russian oil companies to take over the remaining liabilities on the contract for the salvage in the pipe. In the end we recovered a comfortable sum for him, upon which he retired.[7]

Still another case of industrial illness arose in the Klondike. In 1911 Mr. A. C. Beatty introduced me to a Mr. A. N. C. Treadgold, a friend of his. Treadgold came originally from the English Midlands, was a self-anointed engineer, and certainly an endowed promoter. He had an off-and-on partner, J. B. ("Joe") Boyle. They had industriously pur-

---

Revolution. When this report reached the press I formally notified the Soviet Government that we had no interest in any Russian enterprise.

Perhaps there was even sardonic humor in it. I did not believe Russia could get through the war without revolution. But that is ahead of my story.

[7] He subsequently administered the Belgian Relief for me in New York, and some further history will develop therefrom.

chased or secured options on a large part of the creek-bottom gravels for 40 miles around the Klondike, much of which had been worked out of their richest parts years before in the famous gold rush. It was proposed to work the gravels over again with modern dredges. Tread-gold had promoted several companies for this purpose, and had secured large sums of money from one source or another, most of which he had wasted. However, one of the companies was managed and part-owned by capable Boyle, who had got one dredge to work. He was earning some profits. Treadgold's multitude of companies were broke and in debt; they had not solved the problem of thawing the frozen gravel cheaply, yet there was great promise of long-life industrial min-ing in the idea if it could all be put together and straightened out. I passed the matter on to Mr. Govette, who, with our investment com-panies, found some preliminary cash to examine and try to untie Tread-gold's promotion knots. I engaged an experienced dredging engineer, Mr. Newton Cleaveland of San Francisco, to examine the properties. He approved of them highly. A contract was made with Treadgold, but that was only the beginning of trouble. Contracts had little effect upon him. Moreover he was in some sort of fight with somebody everywhere and all the time. The business dragged along until the Great War, when it was laid on the shelf.[8]

Boyle was a picturesque and lovable Irishman who came near getting me into trouble. When not engaged at the Klondike—every winter, in fact—he was busy in Irish national conspiracies. One day when Irish affairs had flared up into some crises, Boyle came into my London office while I was in the United States and said that he had ordered some machinery for a friend of his in Ireland: Would the office take delivery of it and ship it to the Irish address? The staff agreed to do so. It was a rude jar that met me upon my next arrival in London. Scotland Yard men appeared and wanted to know more about some

---

[8] After the War, under the direction of Mr. Agnew and Mr. Goldthorp Hay, the mixed titles, the funny finance, the litigation and working methods were solved, although it took years and was only accomplished after the deaths of both Treadgold and Boyle. By 1935 it was one of the soundest of mining enterprises. It has produced over $25,000,000 in gold and had probably fifty years of life ahead. However, the fixing of the price of gold and rising wages over the years have about paralyzed the enterprise.

machine guns which, they said, we had purchased on the pretense that they were for Central America, whereas they were about to be shipped to Ireland. In the World War, Boyle became a Colonel in the Canadian Army and rendered good service, equipping his machine gun company from his own pocket. The guns were his Irish guns.

Still another case for business and engineering repair arose in the oil business. In 1911 a British stock market oil flotation with holdings in California went bankrupt. Some of the sorry stockholders approached our office to see if we could be of any help. As I was in California at the time I examined the property and finding that parts of it adjoined General Petroleum properties at Coalinga and elsewhere I inquired of that company if it was interested. It was, and ultimately the properties were purchased by General Petroleum for securities in the company.

The matter was not itself so important but it brought me the acquaintance of Captain John Barneson, the president of General Petroleum. Captain John was one of the choice souls in American life. Honest, courageous, frank, generous and loyal, and with a high quality of humor, he had started before the mast; risen to command a naval supply ship in the Spanish-American War; gone into the shipping business for himself; thence into oil fuel business; from there finally into oil production, where he built up the General Petroleum Company to a great industry. A little later I recommended some British and New York investment companies to provide him more capital with which to build a pipe line from Coalinga to San Pedro. I received for these services a handsome fee, and became one of Captain John's directors. In 1913 the Captain, seeking more capital, got himself tied up with a Scottish shipping group and a Mr. Arthur Grenfell, both of whom came near being too much for him. He came to London and I became his chief adviser in a fight to keep him from being wiped out. The Captain's enemies had certain Scottish characteristics illustrated by a later experience that came to one of them. The gentleman in question rose to some business importance, and it was said that an agent of the Liberal Party approached him with the information that the King wished to confer a Peerage on him. It was mentioned that the Party funds were low and the need great. They discussed the amount of the subscription; the agent of the Party suggested $100,000. That not being impossible, the conversation passed on to the title which should be conferred. They agreed that it should be Lord Blank. The pressing need of funds was referred to again. Thereupon the prospective Lord Blank made out his check for a less amount, and signed it Lord Blank. Captain John, however, won out even against such a tough opponent.

Among the professional matters which came to our New York office in the spring of 1914 was the management of a large coal enterprise in Wales. I went to look at the concern. It was a profitable business and indicated a handsome professional income for our establishment. The idea of the owners was to introduce the more modern American technology. But I was sickened at the living conditions of the work people. Real wages were only a little over a third of our American standards. No such desperate sodden poverty existed anywhere in the United States. Under competitive prices for coal there was only one hope to lift wages. That was American machinery and methods by which the output per man could easily be doubled, or perhaps trebled. I interviewed the local trades union leaders on whether they would allow such innovations under their rules. It obviously meant that we would decrease the number employed at least at the start. After it got going we might be able to get a larger share of the competitive market and give jobs to all of them. The leaders argued this would put men out of jobs in some other mines. We argued to no avail that it would enable the expansion of the export market in coal which was Britain's economic backbone. It was the same old philosophy which caused the riots against Whitney's cotton gin. Of course if the whole coal industry were reequipped and prices reduced, export and consumption in total would increase. Part of the savings could go to wages and everybody would benefit. I, however, did not see how we single-handed and a minor segment could reform British economy and therefore refused to touch it.

I may mention another sort of experience as an industrial doctor in this period. The day after Christmas 1913, I went into the Bank of California to cash a check. The President of the Bank, Frank Anderson, haled me into his office and asked if I knew anything of the interests of the Sloss and Lilienthal families of San Francisco. "Somewhat," I replied. I knew much of the General Petroleum Company in which they had large interests. I knew by public knowledge of the Natomas Gold Dredging Company, in which they had secured British capital from firms with whom I was acquainted. I also had a personal relation. Many years before, while I was employed in Janin's office, Mr. P. M. Lilienthal, since dead, who was then President of the Anglo California Bank, had been very friendly to me and had even made me a loan without security. I had also had close relations with Mr. Sloss in some matters involving the Stanford Board of Trustees and had conceived a high respect for him. Mr. Anderson told me the families were in session across the street deciding whether they would file petitions in bankruptcy, for they had become so overextended in different undertakings that failure seemed inevitable. He said they needed a coolminded friend. He telephoned to them and I went over to the meeting. I found a discouraged and disconsolate group. They welcomed me as a friendly adviser and proceeded to expose a very desperate situation. It involved large issues of personally-endorsed notes to some 400 California banks, bond issues whose interest and principal were coming due but could not be met—and generally a mess of about sixty million dollars of securities of one kind or another, involving some ten large companies in which they were interested.

Their difficulties had primarily been due to a prince of optimists, Jean De Sabla, who felt that he could transform all the world into astronomic stocks and bonds and at the same time make it a better and more profitable place in which to live. If the Slosses should go bankrupt it would mean a severe blow to the whole state, and the disappearance of one of the most constructive of families from its business life. The immediately pressing point was interest and payments upon bonds sold on these concerns in London, which were due in four or five days and could not be met. I suggested that we make a fight and that my London office might be able to get a postponement of these particular payments. This was accomplished and gave us a little time. We remained in session almost night and day over the next sixty days.

The ten concerns involved all had merit but they certainly were endowed with much paper, had little cash and much sudden debt. I spent my time not only trying to stave off creditors and to find some solution to the problems at large, but also getting some order into administration of the concerns so as to stop current operating losses. In addition to the concerns I have mentioned there were the Northern Electric Railways, Holland Farms, and West Sacramento Farms. At one moment I was elected President of a number of them. Thus for a brief space I became a railway president. I traveled over the line in a private car—which meant a street car with no paying passengers. T. T. C. Gregory, then a youngster, was one of their battery of lawyers and proved the greatest tower of strength and a blithe and cheerful soul besides.

I finally discovered a key for solution of the whole puzzle. The founder of the Sloss family, Louis Sloss, Sr., had died some years before, dividing his fortune equally among his wife and the several sons and daughters. The sons had carefully safeguarded their mother's portion, which now amounted to about $2,000,000 in gilt-edged securities. They had, out of fine feeling, been unwilling either to inform her of their difficulties or to ask for help from her. She was then, as I recall, more than ninety years of age and not very strong. Without permission I, with another friend, visited the old lady, spread the situation before her and urged that here was the opportunity to save the sons, as I believed, without loss to herself. Our proposal was to take such part of her fortune as she would not need to finish her days in comfort, and to give her in its place common stock in a securities corporation. To this we would add some other loose assets from the other persons involved. We would then use this corporation to guarantee any creditor who was willing to reduce and defer interest and extend payments for a term of years. The old lady listened with keen understanding and accepted the arrangement with only one reservation. That was whether she could finish her days and maintain her pet charities on $100,000 or on $50,000. As I remember, we settled it at $250,000.

The plan worked out successfully, no creditor lost, the Sloss family pulled through and was prosperous ever afterward. De Sabla sought other fields for higher promotion. I refused to accept any remuneration. It was a humane rather than a commercial transaction.

The night the setup was legally complete and the creditors all quiescent—March 2, 1914—Mrs. Hoover and I started back to Europe on a mission to help out the Panama-Pacific Exposition. And incidentally to look over the work of my European office. We took the boys along, now seven and ten years old, and we expected to return in August.

On my arrival in London, I found another and what proved to be my last industrial repair job. There had emerged in London a new comet in the world of mining and oil promotion, Major Arthur Grenfell. I had met him with Captain Barneson some time previously. He came of an illustrious family and had served as an officer in the Guards. Among other corporations he had secured control of the Camp Bird Company, operating mines in Colorado and Colombia; the Santa Gertrudis Company, operating mines in Mexico, and the Messena Copper Company of the Transvaal. Also—and this was of special sentimental interest to me—he had a holding in Captain Barneson's General Petroleum Company. His house of cards began to fall and the criminal courts took notice of it. The treasuries of these companies had been drained to support Grenfell's other ventures. The Directors and large stockholders requested me to examine and reorganize the mining concerns. I did not wish any further English responsibilities, and for some days refused. However, it seemed that I could save something from the wreck for the stockholders, secure further employment for my colleagues and the continued employment of many people. Therefore, just before the war, I became Chairman of these concerns, placed Govette and Hamilton on the Boards and my staff in New York and London in technical control, and started to shake them up. But when the war brought me new responsibilities, I was glad to hand their future over to new Boards and to my staff. Grenfell enlisted in the Army, gave distinguished service, and all charges were withdrawn. Under the reorganization these concerns all became prosperous.

When war came my professional career was ended. We had built up a great business.

Our engineering practice extended over the United States, Canada,

Mexico, Chile, China, Russia, Mongolia, Burma, Penang, New Zealand and Australia. The variety of our practice and their national settings gave infinite interests and in aggregate they paid us high fees. There was unending interest in our multitude of concerns and their peoples. The ending of my professional work coincided with the ending of the Golden Age of American engineers in foreign countries.

CHAPTER 9

FAMILY LIVING AND
EXTRA-CURRICULAR ACTIVITIES
1908–1914

My extra-curricular activities outside my professional work in this period of six years before the war were of variegated order. I had been asked to deliver a series of lectures on engineering at both Columbia and Stanford Universities. They were given in 1909 and were compiled into a small textbook under the title *Principles of Mining*. It came into large demand, has been reprinted several times over, and is still used in the engineering schools.

For some years I had been interested in the older literature of engineering and applied science generally. I had formed quite a collection of fifteenth and sixteenth century books on early science, engineering, metallurgy, mathematics, alchemy, etc. One of these—Agricola's *De Re Metallica*—a folio published in Latin in 1556, was the first important attempt to assemble systematically in print the world-knowledge on mining, metallurgy, and industrial chemistry. It was the great textbook of those industries for two centuries and had dominated thought and practice all that time. In many mining regions and camps, including the Spanish South American, it was chained to the church altar and translated by the priest to the miners between religious services. No one had ever succeeded in translating it into English, although several had tried. My own study of Latin had never gone beyond some elementary early schooling and a few intermittent attempts to penetrate further into that language and literature after I left college. Mrs. Hoover was a good Latinist after she brushed up a little, and we found we could work it out. The problem of the "untranslatable" Agricola fascinated us both, and finally in 1907 we resolved to translate it jointly. There were formidable difficulties; for while Agricola's Latin was scholarly enough, he was dealing with subjects the whole nomenclature and practice of which had developed hundreds of years after the Latin language ceased to grow. He did not adopt into the text the German, Italian or English terms for the operations or substances he described, but coined or adapted Latin terms for them. It was thus obvious why Latin scholars had failed in translation into English. It had been translated after a fashion into both German and French by persons unfamiliar with the arts described. For this reason, their work had failed also.

The job involved finding out—either from the context, from German, French, Italian, or other fragmentary literature of the times, or from study of the processes themselves—what he meant. Mrs. Hoover's ability to read German and some French helped greatly. Sometimes the task amounted more to scientific detective work than to translation. Material A might start as an unknown substance but in different parts of the book Agricola would state its varying reactions when treated or combined with known substances B or C. Thus I could often have the meaning of his terms worked out in our laboratories. Often enough, when we discovered the meaning of a term we found that there was no modern word to express it because that particular process had been long abandoned. In any event, we grappled with it sentence by sentence, during our spare time, month after month, for over five years. We lugged the manuscript all over the world for odd moments that would be available for work on it.

The translation was completed to our satisfaction in 1912, after four complete revisions. We desired to present it to the engineering profession, and consulted our good friend Edgar Rickard, who knew everything about technical publication. Edgar knew of a commercial printer in the north of England who had a fine sense of print—a love of old books—although no practice in such work. His name was Frost. When Frost saw the manuscript and the original his eyes glistened. He exclaimed that all his life he had been a commercial printer and had always wanted to do such a book. He offered to do it at bare out-of-pocket cost. In order to make the book as like the original as possible, he found a papermaker who could produce a sixteenth-century linen paper. He had a font of type cast in exact reproduction of the original except for the ancient letter S, which is confusing to modern readers. He printed it as a folio volume with all the old prints and illustrations in astonishing fidelity to the original. By a little juggling of the opening sentence of each chapter, we were able to include reproductions of the old illuminated initial letters. Mr. Frost bound it in white vellum as the original was bound. No more beautiful job of printing was ever turned out.

In addition to the translation, I wrote an introduction covering the times and the circumstances under which Agricola lived and worked, with a brief biography of him. We included a full statement of all the known editions. I prepared extensive footnotes describing previous processes so far as knowledge of them is preserved—including those of Roman and Greek times. The footnotes also explained the processes and methods described by Agricola in relation to our modern practice. All of this involved many pleasurable hours of research.

Three thousand copies were printed and about 1,500 were sent as gifts to engineers and institutions. So that all engineers and others who were interested could obtain it, we placed 1,000 copies on sale through Edgar Rickard's publications, at a nominal price of $5, which hardly covered the binding.[1]

In 1912 I was elected to the Board of Trustees of Stanford University. I spent some time at the institution, bringing about some long-needed changes. I joined in the promotion of Dr. Jordan, then in advanced age, to the Chancellorship of the University, and the appointment of Dr. Branner as President. Dr. Branner would agree to serve only temporarily, and I proposed to the trustees that Dr. Ray Lyman Wilbur should be his successor.

At this time I arranged for the Board to publish its accounts, including lists of all securities, income and expenditures. This had never been done before; and in consequence much misinformation had arisen, including an exaggerated idea of the University's endowment and income. We formulated the statement so that it would be intelligible to

[1] Since that time it has sold in public auctions for as high as $225.

laymen and professors. I regretfully concluded that the institution could not expand unless it abolished its old policy of free tuition. The Trustees agreed that we must impose a tuition but adapted to students who were working their way through college by allowing them to give ten-year notes without interest.

In an address to the student body in 1912, I proposed the erection of a "Union" for the centralization of student activities, for eating and other clubs and general purposes. Subsequently I gave the Trustees $100,000 for the Union on condition that they lend it an additional $150,000, to be repaid to the University out of its earnings. The students raised still more money. The debt to the Trustees has long since been repaid. The students have enlarged the Union over the years until it is today one of the most beautiful and effective of such institutions among our universities.

In order to provide better housing for professors, and to persuade them to build upon the campus, where the title based on lease was not so popular as two miles away where freeholds could be obtained, we set up long-term loans without interest. The ultimate purpose was to bring faculty and students closer together. A large part of the comfortable community on the campus has been built as a result of this arrangement.

I joined the National Republican Club in 1909. In 1912 I rooted for Theodore Roosevelt and supported him by financing others to root.

In early 1913 the representatives of the Panama-Pacific Exposition, organized in San Francisco to celebrate the opening of the Panama Canal, came to me in London to ask my aid in securing participation of British and other governments. Earlier efforts in this direction, made through diplomatic agencies and pompous delegations, had failed. I engaged a British "public relations" firm and started a campaign among industrialists. It brought results at the needed spot—the House of Commons—and the British reversed their former decision not to participate. In the winter of 1914 Mr. C. C. Moore, the President of the Exposition, asked if I would go to Europe and try to obtain participation of Continental countries who had generally refused. I took up the Exposition question with various Continental governments, enlisting commercial and industrial support in each country. We were making good progress when the assassination of the Archduke Ferdinand at Sarajevo on June 28th turned the attention of all Europe to matters more pressing for civilization than a public spectacle on the shores of the Pacific. Had it not been for this mission I should probably not have been in Europe when the war broke out.

Among the extra-curricular activities of the family was an involvement in the Woman's Suffrage movement in England. That movement consisted of a violent form of propaganda including the storming of Parliament, breaking windows, assaulting police, hunger strikes and a thousand ingenious publicity outrages. One day I received a telephone call from the Bow Street Police Station from an American lady whom I shall call Jane Brown. Jane was an old college classmate of Mrs. Hoover's. I did not know that she was within five thousand miles of Bow Street. Jane explained she had been part of a suffrage demonstration, had been arrested and remanded by the magistrate for trial. She wanted bail. I sent a lawyer's clerk up with the bail and demanded that Jane come at once to see Mrs. Hoover and myself. We had always considered her an inoffensive pedantic nonentity and awaited explanation of this volcanic complex. It appeared she had caught a sudden zeal to aid the cause of Englishwomen—not knowing the remotest thing about it—bought a ticket from western United States; landed in London in the morning; got herself a banner; bought a hammer; smashed a plate glass window on sacred Bond Street; was arrested and then hit the policeman with the hammer. The latter was about Number One crime in England. Jane hoped for martyrdom in jail and resolved to go on a hunger strike. I suggested, If that was her object, why bail? She explained that martyrdom did not begin until you were convicted and sentenced. We tried to persuade her that her mission was really in the United States. The lawyer whom I engaged persuaded the magistrate to give her the alternative of fine or jail and the lawyer at once paid her fine. Jane was thereby thwarted from martyrdom and was very indignant with me. However, she continued as a trial to our peace of mind. She got arrested again and called up at six o'clock one evening to again bail her out. I arranged to have a clerk go around to the police station the next morning after she had done a little martyrdom sitting on a bench alongside the drunks. It happened that this time the magistrate dismissed her and others with a warning. Finally the British Suffragettes persuaded her to go away to reform her own country.

Although Mrs. Hoover and I moved about with less velocity in this six year period, yet we still had complicated living and domestic problems. The central theme was to have the boys grow up in America, to make the United States the home base, for me to move about the world as my profession necessitated and for Mrs. Hoover to take part in such movements where possible. I was, of necessity, away a good deal, doctoring sick industrial concerns as far as China, Alaska, Mexico and Siberia, reading burial services over others which were past human aid, and making efforts at public service. Mrs. Hoover several times accompanied me to Burma and Russia. As I have said she had acquired a cottage on the Stanford campus in 1907 and, except for an experiment of a few months of living on Pacific Avenue in San Francisco, she held to that base. The campus children's school and the Palo Alto high school offered the best of education for small boys. With the faculty offspring, there were enough fellow conspirators for our boys, with the hills and rocks ample range for such activities. Moreover, there were a host of kindly friends to look after them when she went on journeys with me. We held onto the Red House in London, as a European lodging place during the whole period, although it was frequently sublet. In the summer she usually brought the boys to England, living at the Red House with variations. She took country cottages for a few weeks during various summers at Swanage, Dorsetshire, and at Stratford-on-Avon—at which places I spent week ends. I found Stratford intellectually rather dull after I had absorbed the very full local lore on William Shakespeare. To liven up the mental processes of the neighbors, I boned up on the Baconian theory. It took only a little of it to start a cataract of indignant refutation. Shakespeare's home town is certainly loyal to him.

In England we saw a good deal of Mr. and Mrs. Edgar Rickard.[2] He was an American engineer of wide experience who had come to London to take charge of a group of technical publications. I had known him before, but here began an intimate friendship that has lasted with-

[2] Mr. Rickard died in 1951.

out a flutter over all these years. Abby, whose nickname with us was "Abby-his-wife," was one of the sweetest and most cultivated of women. She was a glorious natural blonde. She would have preferred any other color, for she was in eternal tumult that she might be thought to be artificial. We undertook many joint expeditions with the Rickards. We established a fund called "Seeing Cairo" to cover all joint traveling expenses. Into it we paid any windfalls that came our way. Neither of us was interested in speculation, but occasionally such a chance appeared of especial merit, and we operated it in a small way for this fund. At one time its assets rose to $5,000 or $6,000. In any event, out of it we saw all the "sights," including cathedrals, museums, galleries and restaurants of most of Europe—England, Germany, France, Russia, Italy and every way station—with all the abandon of tourists. The agreed method was to resolve on a date for departure somewhere, to have no destination until a few hours before and then to choose the first stop.

In after years I had many occasions to say, "To many Americans' eyes, Europe consists of magnificent cities, historic cathedrals, art, music, literature, great universities, monuments of human heroism and progress. But under this 400,000,000 people of a score of races lie the explosive forces of nationalism, of imperialism, religious antagonism, age-old hates, memories of deep wrongs, revenges, fierce distrusts, repellent fears and dangerous poverty." I confess we were among the "many Americans" but we were not searching for explosive forces.

CHAPTER 10

LIVING WITH THE BRITISH

Pre-war England was the most comfortable place in which to live in the whole world. That is, if one had the means to take part in its upper life. The servants were the best trained and the most loyal of any nationality. The machinery for joy and for keeping busy doing nothing was the most perfect in the world. The countryside was of unending beauty, and above all, to Americans, its great background of our common history, literature and institutions was of constant inspiration. To London came the greatest music, the greatest drama, the greatest art, and the best food in the world. The polite living in city and country breathed hospitality itself. Over our years of sojourning, we became greatly attached to our house on Campden Hill and to the stream of American and British friends with whom we came in contact. We spent many happy times there.

No American could live these years among the British people without forming some appraisal of them through American eyes and ears. Intimate professional associations, loyal friendships, generous hospitalities, constant glimpses of moral sturdiness, great courage, a high sense of sportsmanship, and cultivated minds could have but one result—a high admiration for the individual British man and woman. Truly, many of their attitudes jarred on Americans. But did not many American attitudes justifiably jar the English?

The differences between America and Britain were deeper than those between the individual citizens. They were differences in approach to life and to society. We had grown three hundred years apart in a new setting. In all my twenty years of professional "traveling" to and fro, I landed from ships onto American soil from abroad at least a hundred times. To me, every homecoming was an inspiration. I found always a more spontaneous kindliness, a greater neighborliness, a greater sense of individuality, a far deeper sense of equality, a lesser poverty, a greater comfort and security, and above all, a wider spread of education, a wider freedom of spirit and a wider confidence of every parent in the unlimited future of his children than in any other country in the world.

To an American of those times the pre-World-War stratified structure of British society was a constant marvel—and grief. The British were governed, and had been governed for centuries, by a large oligarchy. Within this group were the wealth, the power and the culture of the Kingdom. This oligarchy comprised probably ten million men, women and children, the twenty per cent of the "upper class" and the "upper middle class" whom God had called to their responsibilities. The other eighty per cent were reminded once a week in their prayer book that they must respect their betters. Indeed the established church was the bulwark of power and privilege. Membership in this oligarchy came automatically by birth. But not exclusively so. The British aristocracy held its position by the periodic inclusion of flowering minds from below. It was possible for individuals to push through the barriers by special talent or by gaining wealth—at least to a tentative acceptance. But even those new arrivals who were given titles were not really accepted until seasoned by a second generation. The dividing line between the oligarchy and the mass was difficult to define. Certainly, retail tradesmen belonged in the outer darkness; professional men, wholesale merchants and "City men" were, off and on, within the sacred precincts. The pains of keeping the stout borders along the front of the dominating group were well illustrated when in the World War it was necessary to commission many officers from the ranks. They were referred to as TG's—temporary gentlemen. All this was not "snobbery"; it was just complete belief in breeding and superiority. And that superiority, no matter how politely suppressed, was felt equally over Americans, Colonials and "natives" in general.

The oligarchy was democratic within its own ranks. It believed in the essential freedoms of speech and worship tenaciously. It consisted not alone of Tories but also of Liberals, who differed at times but who

closed up when the oligarchy was in danger. It was the most intelligent
and effective governing oligarchy the world has ever seen. Their governments were free of graft; their parliamentary debates were intellectually superior to our own.

To witness their social superficialities, their social season, their fox
hunts, their shooting parties, their country clubs and their week ends
was often to believe this upper group was not worth preserving. Yet
these same men died bravely; these same women worked their fingers
to the bare bone in munition factories in the Great War.

One of the lasting misfortunes of Britain was that the first million of
Kitchener's army were volunteers—and the great bulk of them came
from this class, privates as well as officers. And in the end, it was the
slaughter of this British intelligence that would not be recovered for a
generation.

This oligarchy had one dominating cause—"the Empire." It was
solidarity and resolution of all parties on this issue that extended the
power of a few small islands to rule one quarter of the world's population. For "the Empire" there was no sacrifice too costly, and there
was no moral restraint in this area. While the oligarchy individually
held high the principles of moral conduct and sportsmanship, yet
when the interest of "the Empire" was involved often the end justified
the means. Probably the most amusing thing about the foreign policies
to an American was the unction with which the British could wrap
up any transaction for "the Empire" in moral clothes. The very expression—"the white man's burden"—was typical. Despite the false
wrappings around aggression and domination of other races, the British
as a nation held in high duty their obligations under treaties. So far as
I know they have never, in modern times at least, defaulted on such
obligations. But it required a keen foreign power to hold its own when
negotiating such documents.

I had often to sense their real attitudes toward Americans, for they
became so used to Mrs. Hoover and me in some households as to
scarcely remember that we were Americans. At times it was hard to
bear the attitude of complete condescension to anything American.
And the cynical remarks upon American women who bought titles
would be hard for those ladies to bear. It added wormwood to Ameri-

LOU HENRY HOOVER

can listeners to learn the justification of such titled gentlemen for such transactions which was that that sacrifice must be made to repair their family fortunes.

No American could fail to feel the deplorable standards of living of millions of the English "masses." In the industrial areas, such as the coal mines and the Potteries, and in the slum areas of the cities there was unmitigated squalor. Whatever bad spots there were on civilization in America, they were bright in comparison to these British black spots. A never ending pull upon one's sympathies was the thousands of hopeless people who nightly slept in the parks. The luxury and extravagance of the "upper classes" across the street made the contrast even more bitter.

The economists and sociologists had long since determined that twenty-five per cent lived below the poverty line and another thirty per cent so little above it that they were constantly falling below. And one of the yardsticks of the poverty line was undernourishment. Deducting the twenty per cent of the oligarchy, roughly about twenty-five per cent of the "lower middle class" had a standard of living hardly equal to seventy-five per cent of the American people.

There were many devoted souls who cried out against this abject poverty and this callous attitude. There were, before the war, the beginnings of an awakening of responsibility which showed itself by some real stir in the Liberal Party. But to the most upper class Briton, Tory or Liberal all this was sheer wicked radicalism designed to destroy "the Empire." Dinner conversations were unending denunciations of Lloyd George and all of his works. But even the Liberal Party of England of that time was conservative compared with the whole inheritance of the American people, except perhaps in the "Solid South."

Much has been said in America of the "liberal" progress of England in comparison with America. America never had such class divisions, such impenetrable stratifications and such misery below. Moreover, America was far in advance in many essential social actions. Free education was universal in the United States long before the "upper class" in England would permit it. To them it was dangerous. In this period— prior to the World War and many years after—there was not a single restraint in British law against monopolies or restraint of trade.

Their monopolies and cartels were not only oppressive, but by their reliance upon price manipulation they lost the values of competitive improvement in industrial processes the base of which was reduced cost of production. Therefore British industry was steadily becoming obsolete as compared to the United States. Such things as old age pensions, control of child labor, working hours for women had been pioneered by individual American states before they appeared in England. America had begun to struggle with the evils of the industrial revolution years before the British. In business practices the British were no better or worse than Americans. Wall Street and Throgmorton Street equally performed a useful and necessary economic function; they were equally no place for the unwary and equally free from concern as to public welfare. But Englishmen in vast majority held scrupulous regard for personal undertakings. I would rather have an Englishman's mere confirmation letter of a verbal agreement than the most elaborate contract with any other European national.

I can, perhaps, without over-sentimentality, give a note I wrote to Mrs. Hoover in 1938, when I revisited England after having been away nearly twenty years:

While in London I sneaked away on a visit of unalloyed sentiment. I stole out of the hotel alone, found a cab, told the driver the old formula—"Kensington, High Street, Horton Street to the Red House." On the way, my mind traveled over the thousands of times we had driven along Pall Mall, Knightsbridge and High Street, nearly every house of which was still unchanged. We came to High Street, and as always, I had to direct the cabby to take the second turning to the left beyond the church. And the church was the same as when the boys used to attend all weddings as doorstep-observers, returning to tell us if the red carpet or the awning were up—that service being five shillings extra—and how many bridesmaids or how many peals of the bells there were—those being two shillings sixpence each.

I came to the door of the Red House, flooded with memories of the months we had lived there, alternatively with our New York and California homes for nearly twenty years. How we had first come, as a couple, from stays in Australia or China or Russia or Burma, or New York or the Continent; then when we had brought the babies; then when I would return from long journeys to meet you all again.

At the door, even after twenty years, I automatically fumbled in my pocket for the key. I rang the bell, gave the very stiff butler my card, and asked if I might see the lady of the house, explaining that I was an American who had lived in this house many years ago, was in London only for a few days, and would like to walk through the rooms and the garden again. The butler seemed nonplussed, but came back after some minutes, and through the partially opened door, announced, "Her Ladyship is not in." I was prepared for this British event with a ten-shilling note, sufficiently exposed, and suggested that perhaps he would let me see any part of the house that was not in use at the moment. To the left was the oak-panelled library with its fine fireplace and its leaded glass bookcases—the same as ever. I imagined again, sitting on the opposite side of the desk from you, with the manuscripts and reference books of Agricola, piled between us, as we worked over the translation of *De Re Metallica*. Again I saw "Pete" at the little table in the corner, making marks and announcing that he was writing a book too; and "Bub" clambering into his mother's lap and demanding to know what the book said. The dining room was the same walnut-panelled room and evoked all kinds of memories of the multitude of happy gatherings which had filled it. The living room had been redecorated from its old neutral tints to modern white French and was a repellent stranger. The century-old mulberry tree, which we had nursed for years with steel I beams and which had given character to the garden, was gone and replaced by some formal bushes.

Altogether my mind was a maze of revived emotional pictures and some disappointments. But by now the butler was standing on one foot and filled with anxieties—and to finish him, I shook his hand, which I suppose no "gentleman" had ever done before.

Your old parlor-maid, grim-faced Lovell, came to Claridges [hotel]. She timidly inquired of Perrin if she might see me. She asked me to thank "Madame" for sending her a nice card every Christmas and especially for the 'elp you have given her from the White 'ouse in the unemployment times and to inquire after the 'ealth of the "Young Masters"—and her stolid old face softened at every reference to the "Young Masters." I suspect, in her memory, they were still little more than babies. I thought perhaps she came for more 'elp and not wanting to offend her I remarked that if she got in a tight place again she should write to the "Madame." She replied at once, "Oh, no, I 'ave a 'nice place' with a family in 'Ide Park, but they are not the likes of 'Madame.' Besides, when I sent the money back to 'Madame' she would not take it and told me to put it in the bank in case 'ard times come again and I 'ave it."

So you will see she has never recovered an "h" and I have discovered your secret transactions. I directed one of the boys to take her down to the afternoon tea then going on in the hotel with the fashionables of London and to treat her like the real lady she is in her heart. He reported that her major observation was "These waiters is not trained to serve tea properly." She is a part of passing England.

CHAPTER 11

THE PROFESSION OF ENGINEERING

I cannot leave my profession without some general comment upon it. Within my lifetime it had been transformed from a trade into a profession. It was the American universities that took engineering away from rule-of-thumb surveyors, mechanics, and Cornish foremen and lifted it into the realm of application of science, wider learning in the humanities with the higher ethics of a profession ranking with law, medicine and the clergy. And our American profession had brought a transformation in another direction through the inclusion of administrative work as part of the engineer's job.

The European universities did not acknowledge engineering as a profession until long after America had done so. I took part in one of the debates at Oxford as to whether engineering should be included in its instruction. The major argument put forward by our side was the need of University setting and its cultural influences on the profession. We ventured to assert that not until Oxford and Cambridge recognized engineering as a profession equal to others would engineering secure its due quota of the best English brains, because able young men would always seek the professions held in the highest public esteem. I cited the fact that while various special technical colleges had been existent in England for a long time, yet there were more than a thousand American engineers of all breeds in the British Empire, occupying top positions.

Soon after the Oxford discussions, I returned to America. At my ship's table sat an English lady of great cultivation and a happy mind, who contributed much to the evanescent conversation on government, national customs, literature, art, industry, and whatnot. We were coming up New York harbor at the final farewell breakfast, when she turned to me and said:

"I hope you will forgive my dreadful curiosity, but I should like awfully to know—what is your profession?"

I replied that I was an engineer. She emitted an involuntary exclamation, and "Why, I thought you were a gentleman!"

Hundreds of times students and parents have consulted me upon engineering compared with the other professions. My comment usually is: "Its training deals with the exact sciences. That sort of exactness makes for truth and conscience. It might be good for the world if more men had that sort of mental start in life even if they did not pursue the profession. But he who would enter these precincts as a life work must have a test taken of his imaginative faculties, for engineering without imagination sinks to a trade. And those who would enter here must for years abandon their white collars except for Sunday."

In the mining branch of the profession, those who follow the gods of engineering to that success marked by an office of one's own in a large city must be prepared to live for years on the outside borders of civilization; where beds are hard, where cold bites and heat burns, where dress-up clothes are a new pair of overalls, where there is little home life—not for weeks but for years—where often they must perform the menial labor necessary to keep soul and body together. Other branches of the profession mean years on the lower rungs of the ladder —shops, works, and power-houses—where again white collars are not a part of the engineer uniform. But the engineer learns through work with his own hands not only the mind of the worker but the multitude of true gentlemen among them. On the other hand, men who love a fight with nature, who like to build and see their building grow, men who do not hold themselves above manual labor, men who have the moral courage to do these things soundly, some day will be able to move to town, wear white collars every day, and send out the youngsters to the lower rungs and the frontiers of industry.

It is a great profession. There is the fascination of watching a figment of the imagination emerge through the aid of science to a plan on paper. Then it moves to realization in stone or metal or energy. Then it brings jobs and homes to men. Then it elevates the standards of living and adds to the comforts of life. That is the engineer's high privilege.

The great liability of the engineer compared to men of other professions is that his works are out in the open where all can see them. His acts, step by step, are in hard substance. He cannot bury his mistakes in the grave like the doctors. He cannot argue them into thin air or blame the judge like the lawyers. He cannot, like the architects, cover his failures with trees and vines. He cannot, like the politicians, screen his shortcomings by blaming his opponents and hope that the people will forget. The engineer simply cannot deny that he did it. If his works do not work, he is damned. That is the phantasmagoria that haunts his nights and dogs his days. He comes from the job at the end of the day resolved to calculate it again. He wakes in the night in a cold sweat and puts something on paper that looks silly in the morning. All day he shivers at the thought of the bugs which will inevitably appear to jolt its smooth consummation.

On the other hand, unlike the doctor his is not a life among the weak. Unlike the soldier, destruction is not his purpose. Unlike the lawyer, quarrels are not his daily bread. To the engineer falls the job of clothing the bare bones of science with life, comfort, and hope. No doubt as years go by people forget which engineer did it, even if they ever knew. Or some politician puts his name on it. Or they credit it to some promoter who used other people's money with which to finance it. But the engineer himself looks back at the unending stream of goodness which flows from his successes with satisfactions that few professions may know. And the verdict of his fellow professionals is all the accolade he wants.

With the industrial revolution and the advancement of engineers to the administration of industry as well as its technical direction, the governmental, economic and social impacts upon the engineers have steadily increased. Once, lawyers were the only professional men whose contacts with the problems of government led them on to positions of public responsibility. From the point of view of accuracy and intellectual honesty the more men of engineering background who become public officials, the better for representative government.

The engineer performs many public functions from which he gets only philosophical satisfactions. Most people do not know it, but he is an economic and social force. Every time he discovers a new application of science, thereby creating a new industry, providing new jobs, adding to the standards of living, he also disturbs everything that is. New laws and regulations have to be made and new sorts of wickedness curbed. He is also the person who really corrects monopolies and redistributes national wealth.

Four hundred years ago Georgius Agricola wrote of my branch of the profession words as true today as they were then:

"Inasmuch as the chief callings are those of the moneylender, the soldier, the merchant, the farmer, and miner, I say, inasmuch as usury is odious, while the spoil cruelly captured from the possessions of the people innocent of wrong is wicked in the sight of God and man, and inasmuch as the calling of the miner excels in honor and dignity that of the merchant trading for lucre, while it is not less noble though far more profitable than agriculture, who can fail to realize that mining is a calling of peculiar dignity?"

CHAPTER 12

THE COMING OF THE WORLD WAR

The happiest period of all humanity in the Western World in ten centuries was the twenty-five years before the First World War. It was the habit of intellectuals to disparage those times as callous, crude, dominated by bad taste and greed, with privilege to the few and poverty and squalor to the many. We have seen a continuous "debunking" of the good by the concentration upon the secondary evils.

Yet in the eyes of a professional observer, this period stands in high contrast to the quarter century that had gone before.

The world had experienced half a century of freedom from great wars. The long peace had buried the fear of war. The world believed that war, except perhaps for a sporadic outburst now and then, among the Balkans, was a thing of the past. The Four Horsemen seemed only an ancient Biblical story. The last quarter of a century especially had been one of advancing human welfare and progress. The dignity of men and women and their personal liberty were everywhere receiving wider recognition. Human slavery had long since disappeared.

Freedom of speech and worship, the right of men to choose their own callings, the security of justice were yearly spreading over wider and wider areas. Men were able to move practically without any restriction across frontiers. Of all the nations in the world, Russia and Turkey alone required passports. And above all, the long peace had developed a great growth of the human spirit—that of confidence and boundless hope. Fear had disappeared in the hearts of men. It was the era of released human spirit. There were squalor, privilege, slums, slum minds, greed, corruption and bad taste. But the transcendent fact was that these evils were recognized everywhere in the Western World.

They were being lessened year by year. The proportion of the economic middle class was rapidly increasing and in America at least was over eighty per cent of the whole. Hosts of individuals before our eyes were constantly rising from lowly surroundings to security and comfort. Parents lived frugal lives under the stimulus of preparing their children for better circumstances than their own. They were sure that these blessings would come. In the material world there was steady advance in the average standard of living and in the wealth of nations. Over the whole western world taxes were inconsequential. The growth of wealth had far outstripped the growth of bureaucracies. People were busy building railways and communications, roads and power plants, new ships, discovering new mines, erecting magnificent buildings, beautifying their cities.

Scientific research was daily unfolding new truth and breaking new frontiers of human progress. Electricity and the gas engine had given man untold additions to his command of power. A thousand gadgets and labor-saving devices had taken the sweat off the backs of men and the drudgery from the work of women. The automobile had brought widened vision and multiplied human contacts. The aeroplane was lifting him from the drag of the earth. Recreation and sport filled an increasing part of life and living.

Public education was spreading to the whole of nations and new institutions of higher education were being born everywhere. Books and magazines grew into unparalleled numbers. Technology and science were steadily lifting mankind toward more beauty, understanding and inspiration. Art and music were becoming accessible to everyone. The spirit of adventure found its opportunity not only in the exploration of the Arctic and darkest Africa, but in new fields of science and scholarship and their application to human welfare.

Then the world stumbled into the Great War and the period of Great Fear settled like a fog upon the human race—to last, perhaps, for generations. This is not the place to analyze the causes of that war. They sprang from impulses far subtler, stronger and more important than the mouthings of the Czar, the German and Austrian Emperors and their minions. The world made the sad discovery that deeper in European nations than the arts of peace and human progress were age-old hates, rivalries and imperialisms. The combative nature of man, the forces of aggressive nationalism and the human yearning of men for the adventure and glory of war were only slumbering.

In France and England a month before war came, no one except a few pessimists expected it or even believed it possible. True, every nation was increasing its arms, but there was the universal feeling in all countries that that was purely defensive. And compared with the peace-time arms of twenty years later, the armies and navies of that period were small indeed.

But with a single spark the evil spirits rose to strangle all reason. The world in a storm of emotion gave way to fear, hate and destruction.

Although I was more than ordinarily familiar with eastern European national movements, I was not one of those subsequent know-it-all citizens who saw war coming. There was not one out of a million so little confident of the future as to believe it possible.

On June 28, 1914, when news came of the assassination of the Archduke at Sarajevo, the world took it as just another of those habitual Balkan lapses into barbarism—and we went about our accustomed business with little more thought than that. Other incidents had happened before in the Balkan states and, after a week or so of threats and rumors of war, things had always quieted down. It was not until three weeks later, when Austria delivered her brutal ultimatum to Serbia—on July 22nd—that we began to take an interest. It is a curious commentary on a civilization in process of being blown up that so well informed a newspaper as the *New York Times* from July 1st to July 22nd carried no alarming European news on the front page—Austria got only a minor mention from time to time on the fourth page inside.

Even with the ultimatum, we did not take immediate alarm. But when the diplomatic lightning began flashing from capital to capital, the world began to fear. The symptoms of serious disturbance first showed in the economic pulse. At once people everywhere hurried to sell something. The markets of Europe began to slump. Two days later, when Austria, Serbia and Russia showed signs of mobilizing, the continental markets crashed—Black Saturday, July 25th. All day on Sunday, thunder came from Russia, with echoes from Germany. On Monday and Tuesday, the 27th and 28th, the markets vibrated with an excitement that was near panic. One of my associates quaintly remarked, "Some fool may touch off a European explosion." All day on Wednesday and Thursday, the 29th and 30th, we hung breathlessly on every dispatch as the thunder now reverberated from Paris and London, as well as from Berlin, St. Petersburg and Vienna. Even then we thought it would be a war limited to eastern Europe. Was not Sir Edward Grey constantly negotiating to preserve peace among the great powers? We argued to ourselves that big nations were too civilized for anything more than bluffs and face-saving apologies. No doubt Grey would arrange to localize the war if it came.

But business in Europe became more and more paralyzed. Even New York began to quake. The pound rose to five dollars,—something unheard of. Cotton began to slump, wheat to rise. By Friday, every important market in the world was closed. The pound was now six dollars.

All the week we sat about in our offices engaged in sporadic bursts of conversation and curious silences. We tried to appraise what it all meant in terms of human life and misery. What would be the effect on America? And always, what would happen to our business and all the people we employed? There had been no great war in Western civilization in our lifetimes. We argued that all Europe had not been involved in war for one hundred years. We vibrated from small hope to great fear.

Despite all of this confusion the necessary routines of life and action in emergency dominated our offices. The market for our partially perfected materials had collapsed. I found myself cabling over the world to slacken production since we could not sell the products. We telegraphed our ideas for taking care of our unemployed men if distress developed among them.

On Friday afternoon, the 31st, one of our banks telephoned that we had better send over and get some ready cash to pay our office staff, for there might be a moratorium. Still we hoped. That day Foreign Minister Grey had said that negotiations looked more promising. But the hours were fleeting. Yet again we said that the world was surely too sane to go to war. Also, had not Norman Angell and other intellectuals long since proved that on the threat of a great war the economic structure of the world would so break down as to make war impossible? The economic breakdown was certainly thundering around our ears. Late that evening the government announced the banks would be closed for Saturday and Monday.

Some weeks before this, it had been arranged that Mrs. Hoover, the boys and I should spend this weekend with Edgar Rickard and "Abbie-his-wife" at Westgate where they had taken a summer cottage. The following Monday was the usual Bank Holiday, and we were to stay there until Tuesday.

Saturday morning, August 1st, I went to the office. The outlook had become terrifying. But not being able to do anything about it, and not wanting to disappoint the children, we motored to Westgate in the afternoon. That evening we received word that Germany had declared war on Russia, and the French were mobilizing. Sunday morning we heard that the bank moratorium would be extended three days more. We also heard that Germany had sent an ultimatum to Belgium, demanding passage for her army. We all went to the village inn for lunch. Everybody was strained, apprehensive of impending disaster. Someone said no more gasoline could be bought. I asked our chauffeur if he had enough to get home. He said he had heard at one station that they had received orders not to sell but he had rushed off to others and bought a few tins extra before the word got around. We decided to go home at once instead of staying over Monday. We gave Edgar some of the extra tins of gas so that he could get up to town next day. We motored home by the way of Southampton and Portsmouth. The British fleet was mobilized off Cowes. It was dark and sinister-looking with fresh war paint.

On Monday morning, the 3rd, I went to the office to see what cables might have arrived. I was telephoned the news that Germany had declared war on France. The blows were surely coming swiftly. We walked up and down the office, wondering what would happen next. We periodically gazed out of the windows at the passing troops in the street. As we could see the enclosure of a remnant of the old Roman Wall of London a block away, Agnew inquired, "How often do you suppose the men of Britain have marched out to defend their island since the Romans built that wall?" Cables advised us that many of our men and officials in Russia were being drawn into the army; that transportation was disorganized; that they had suspended production "temporarily." The managers of our industries elsewhere asked for directions—and would we please arrange bank credits from London for them to meet the pay rolls as all banks in Australia, Burma and South Africa were also closed? We had many cargoes of zinc, lead and copper concentrates on the way from Burma and Australia, consigned to French, German, Belgian and American smelters. The government had ordered the ships into the nearest ports. We must attempt to get word to them of new destinations.

There was no smelting capacity for our ores in England—the Germans and Belgians had long since driven the British out of that business. We sent cables to American smelters: "Can you take more blister copper, lead and zinc concentrates? With war on, the metal will be needed." But before they replied other things happened.

Even yet, on Monday, we prayed desperately that England would not be involved. That seemed to mean the end of decency and civilization. In our own immediate affairs it meant that we must close many enterprises, throw thousands out of work.

All that day we were to receive more shocks. The modern, intricate, economic world had never met a total world-wide war before 1914. At the time it seemed like an earthquake. The substance and bottom seemed to go out of everything. One might get used to it later, just as the second earthquake is less frightening than the first.

Some weeks before, Mrs. Hoover and I had booked passage to return home on the *Lusitania*. I inquired by telephone of the steamship office if the ship would be sailing as scheduled. The girl at the other end said, "Sure, she will be sailing to Germany. Don't you know there is a war on?" I concluded she meant that the *Lusitania* would not sail.

CHAPTER 13

❦❦❦❦❦❦

THE AMERICAN COMMITTEE
IN LONDON

Late that Monday afternoon, while ruminating over the impossible nature of things, I received a telephone call from American Consul General Skinner. I had enjoyed Mr. Skinner's friendship for many years. The Consulate was only a block away from our London offices. He said that there was a mob of a thousand American tourists milling around within the Consulate and in the street, all of whom were penniless because they could raise no money on travelers' checks or other credit documents. In the panic even American currency was refused by London hotels. Except for old customers they could not even get food or lodgings. Could I think of anything to do?

I went over to see Mr. Skinner. He was in a mess. Staunch and emphatic Americans were pounding the counter and demanding to know if their government was going to protect its citizens. They insisted that Mr. Skinner had no right to allow solvent Americans to sleep in the parks and go hungry like that. The American government should at once demand that the American banks in London be opened. Why did the United States allow their dollars to be refused? It was a disgrace. Were German Zeppelins or airplanes going to bombard London? Why did we not have courageous officials who did their duty toward these foreigners? The Consul General ought at once to tell the British what was what.

But there was one group among them that would have melted a stone. They were the American school teachers who had pinched, saved and planned for this one trip to Europe all their lives. They had come to make themselves better teachers—now they were worried and confused by it all. They were the hardest hit of all these refugees. I could see in them the teachers of my own childhood. They were anxious but not imperious. They were also polite.

I listened a few moments to the commercial traveler from Oregon and elsewhere; surveyed Mr. Skinner's distraction and borrowed his telephone.

Our offices had that cash reserve of a few hundred pounds which we had drawn on Friday in case we should need to pay the staff salaries. I therefore asked two of our American engineers Keen and Brown to come over with all the gold and currency there was in the office. I suggested to Mr. Skinner that we would exchange British money for dollars at the usual rate or would loan the stranded ones each ten shillings to tide them over the night if they had no American currency with which to buy our sterling. Skinner asked the crowd to calm itself and to line up in an orderly manner. He stated what we would do. A faint cheer broke out. But some of them did not think that was a direct enough reprimand to Europe for bringing a war on them while they were peaceably traveling abroad. Would Uncle Sam vindicate his might?

We arranged a few tables, divided the crowd of something over a thousand into five lines, and sat down behind the tables with paper, pen, ink, money and inquiring minds. Did Miss Jones have no American currency at all? Would she say it on her word of honor? All right, Miss Jones, sign this IOU for ten shillings with your name and address. Here is English money. Come back tomorrow again. In three or four hours the Mr. and Mrs. and Miss American Citizen departed announcing that they certainly would be back tomorrow to see what "our government is going to do about it."

When the last of them had departed Mr. Skinner called up the American Ambassador, Walter Hines Page, and told him of his experience and its temporary solution. Mr. Page replied promptly that he had a mob of his own and no money. He asked me to come up to the West End to see him at once. I had known Mr. Page from dining at the Embassy on a few formal occasions. Now I learned that he was in even greater trouble than the Consul. Tens of thousands of Americans were pouring in from the Continent. All British sailings to America had been suspended. The German passenger ships had scuttled into the nearest ports. Some of the more collected American travelers—among them Oscar Straus, Theodore Hetzler and William Breed—had called a mass meeting at the Savoy Hotel for that evening to see what they could all do about getting home. Mr. Page asked if I would attend the meeting. He thought that there were probably 100,000 to 200,000 Americans in Europe, most of them in a panic to get away from the war.

At the Savoy between one and two thousand stranded Americans milled around and finally elected a committee. This group were mostly people of means, whose greatest need was to find steamer accommodations. The gist of the speeches was that the British shipping authorities could give them no encouragement and very little information. Constantly passenger ships were being taken off the Atlantic runs for troop purposes. In general, it seemed a bleak outlook.

I listened to long profitless discussions and finally suggested to the committee that as most of them would be going home at once, I would set up an organization among the more permanent American residents in London and try to introduce some order into the situation. The Straus Committee agreed and a few days later disbanded. But before dissolution they collected some thousands of dollars from fellow travelers which they handed over to us for charitable uses.

During the evening I summoned American engineers Edgar Rickard, John White, Colonel Millard Hunsiker, Robert Collins, Alfred Martin and others to meet me at the Savoy Hotel the following morning. Mrs. Hoover at the same time asked a group of American ladies. I had in the meantime secured some of the reception rooms at the Savoy for offices. The hotel had agreed to furnish us with tables and chairs and charge no rent. I went home about midnight, after informing the Ambassador and the Consul General that we would be open at nine o'clock next morning ready to take on all comers. The wreck of the past week had left me stunned and unstrung. It was hard to become accustomed to world wars. But the troubles of the American tourists served to reduce the feeling of helplessness.

In the morning my associates insisted that I direct the refugee work. The banks were still closed by government order, but I called up one of the American institutions where I had standing and asked that they send us a few thousand pounds to see us through the day—which they did.

We called a number of other American business staffs in London, principally the engineers, and quickly we were on top of our job. From among the tourists we took into our service further helpers whom we had sized up as personable and efficient, and by night we had a volunteer staff of five hundred of the most capable people in the world. With scores of trusted men and women behind scores of tables we at once improved upon the methods of the day before at the Consulate.

The Americans were forwarded in droves to us from the Embassy and the Consulate. Many of them only wanted to talk with somebody, somehow, somewhere, about the approaching end of the world. Many others needed financial help. All of them wanted transportation home. Mrs. Hoover's Women's Committee took over the job of caring for the unaccompanied women and children. A good deal of their work consisted in holding the hands of the frightened. She organized regular excursions to the London "sights," to "cathedral towns," to the Shakespeare and *Lorna Doone* country, to fill in their time pending our securing steamer space.

We set up branch American committees in the main continental cities, or Americans in other cities themselves organized committees and they all dumped the "refugees" on us. We arranged lodgings in London. We secured additional American and neutral ships for home transportation.

As the stream poured into the offices, each individual was directed to a department which could consider his needs. The "front men" in the financial department consisted of half a dozen shrewd American youngsters who sized up the applicants and divided them into three groups destined for different treatment. White cards were given to those who "looked good," red ones to those who appeared to be doubtful cases, and blue ones to the destitute. For the white-card holders one of our rooms cashed checks upon their home banks or honored other documents. We paid out pounds at the normal 4.85 exchange rate. To do this we opened an account in a London bank. Ten of us guaranteed the account up to a million dollars and arranged with the British Treasury that we should draw the cash from this bank against the paper we deposited for collection from the United States. The holders of the red cards—who were the doubtfuls—we asked to sign cablegrams to relatives requesting that money be deposited to our credit in a New York bank; and upon advice of its deposit we paid over the cash. For the destitute blue-card holders, we raised more funds, to which many Americans contributed most generously by giving us checks on their home banks.

The details of organization are not important. But some results are of interest in the study of American character. During the six weeks following we handled some 120,000 troubled Americans who streamed in from all over Europe—and among them 30,000 teachers. Altogether we paid out (outside of charity) something more than $1,500,000 and lost something less than $300. It was a monument either to the shrewd judgment of our youngsters or to the honesty of the American school teacher and traveller. Our private financial operations ended in the latter part of August.

After the first flow of tourists and teachers there came a great movement of destitute Americans. Congress had appropriated a large sum to bring such people home. These were mostly naturalized Americans fleeing from war-torn countries to which they had returned to live or they were minor American employees of American concerns over the Continent. There were some thousands of colored porters and people of similar humble and useful occupations. The Commissioner sent from Washington to manage the operation shed his job onto us. We did it for him without any costs to the Government except the actual outlay to the destitute.

After a fortnight the American Committee was so organized that I could spend part of the time at my office. The whole fabric of international finance had gone to smash. Bills of lading with acceptance of sale were the prime security of the world. As our bills for ore shipments were drawn on Continental buyers now in the war the banks demanded collateral. We soon ran out of that. However, on the 12th of August the British Government authorized the Bank of England to take up all such documents for Government account.

The routine working processes in the human animal are hard to dislocate entirely. Men habitually tend to move in their own grooves and administer their own disciplines no matter what happens. In the middle of August, I called the principal lead and zinc producers with offices in England to my office to see whether we could not resurrect the old smelters at Swansea in Wales. Great Britain had few sources of finished lead, zinc and copper, although the Empire produced large quantities of these ores, but they had for many years gone to continental smelters and refineries. Now the British would need great quantities of these metals for war use. We badly wanted to put our men to work again in different parts of the world.[1]

The entire operation with the stranded Americans was enlivened by gales of humor. A thousand comedies lingered long in our memories. There was the girl from Lansing, Michigan, whose father cabled us to find his daughter at any cost and send her home at once. We traced her over the Continent and ultimately found her taking powerful interest in the war and wholly disinclined to leave it. Father's imperious telegrams, sent through us, finally moved her to come to London. She promptly lost her five trunks en route. She cabled father to remit through us $5,000 to buy a new trousseau and pay other expenses. He responded at once. She bought the trousseau and, as she no longer trusted any kind of foreigners, had the parcels delivered to our rooms at the Savoy. The American ladies under Mrs. Hoover had established an Old Clothes Department to fit out the destitute women and children coming in from the Continent. All packages of clothes went naturally to that Department. The ladies were grateful for these splendid gifts and promptly fitted out some women of the same size better than they had been dressed in their dreams. In time the young lady appeared to gather up her week's shopping. Our ladies' committee found it hard to ride the storm. Father ungratefully cabled that he would sue for damages. We invited him by a collect cable to come and try it.

And there was the Wild West show which worked its way from Poland. It appeared in the shape of twelve American Indians and ten American cowboys in full regalia together with a manager. They had

---

[1] Although I dropped out to undertake the relief of Belgium, the result of these meetings was the erection of smelters in Australia and England, in the financing of which concerns formerly under my engineering direction participated.

abandoned everything—except their valuable costumes. The feathers and chaps made a great hit on the streets of every city. We had little worry over them, for they had resources at home; but pending the arrangement of their transportation to New York they adorned our headquarters and regaled our waiting-list with their experiences, which became daily more frightful. It seems they had a small zoo attachment. When the war struck them in Poland, there were neither customers nor transportation. The armies seized their ponies, their money ran out and they could not buy food for the animals. They said that they fed the orang-outang to the tiger and the lion. In the end the innkeeper became so threatening that they walked out without notice in the middle of the night, leaving the tent, the elephant, the lion and the tiger to the innkeeper. When they arrived in London they had with them an American twelve-year-old boy whom they had picked up in Hamburg. It appeared that he had been sent from America to visit his grandparents in Croatia. He landed in Hamburg at the crack of war, and finding no one to meet him was wandering the streets when he saw walking along this vision of real America with all its beads and feathers. He promptly attached himself to them and the Indians and cowboys adopted him. He had a little money and, observing that his hosts ate nothing, promptly tendered it to them to buy food. When they arrived in London their first concern was for a loan to repay the boy. He was in such good care that our ladies advised his mother by cable that he was being returned home under the charge of White Feather of Pawhuska, Oklahoma. He was a voluble youngster and had firmly decided that his career lay permanently in the show business, and with Indians.

There was the lady who declared a hunger strike because we would not send her home at our expense in better quarters than the steerage. Our ladies gave her an easy chair in our lunch room where the constant display of food broke her iron will within a few hours. And there was the elderly lady who demanded a written guarantee that the submarines would not sink the ship. We gave it to her.

As for the Hoover family, we successively booked homeward passages and cancelled them on five ships. On October 3rd, Mrs. Hoover and the boys sailed as she had to hurry to Palo Alto to put Herbert and Allan in school. But for reasons given in the next chapter I was again held up. When Mrs. Hoover and the boys reached New York, the cable informing me of safe arrival consisted of a statement from Herbert that he had eaten seven cream puffs in one day on the voyage. This was also his indication of exuberant triumph over his forebodings of seasickness. But to the British censor it was some deep and sinister code. I don't think even yet that this British official is satisfied with the explanation. He certainly accepted it only with emphatic suspicion and dark warnings of the dire fate that awaited spies.

I did not realize it at the moment, but on Monday, August 3rd, my engineering career was over forever. I was on the slippery road of public life.

Four Horsemen
in World War I

From this point I take up my contacts with the Four Horsemen in World War I. I give them in sections devoted to:

The Belgian Relief—1914–1920
United States Food Administration—1917–1919
The Relief and Reconstruction of Europe—1918–1920
My Participation in the Peace-Making—1919

The contribution of autobiography to history is one man's record of his acts, purposes, and views on the times in which he lived and worked. The human race may not be particularly given to profiting by experience in larger affairs, but at least such experience should be recorded.

In these memoirs I treat subjects topically within rough chronological order. It involves some overlapping of time but will, I believe, be of more use to students in this form. The portion devoted to the Relief and Reconstruction activities was written during the period 1920 to 1923. There has been little revision but some condensation. I have felt that the impressions and views fresh from the period were of more value without retrospective alterations. I have included some unpublished documents of the times or give references to others to establish that there is no subsequent rationalization of my views or actions.

The whole of the documentation can be found in the War Library at Stanford University.

There is one omission from this text that I infinitely regret. That is, space prevents adequate tribute to each of the thousands of individuals who served with me in this period, as it involves hundreds of pages. There was never a public official who received such devoted and such deep and lasting friendships as have come to me—and to those living I hope these chapters will revive their memories of great days of service.

The Belgian Relief
1914–1920

CHAPTER 14

THE BELGIAN RELIEF

On the 25th of September 1914, there arrived in London from Brussels an eminent engineer whom I had known slightly—Millard Shaler. Edgar Rickard brought him to see me. Shaler, being an American, had been able to come out through the German lines with money to buy 2,500 tons of food for the City of Brussels.

It appeared that this first step toward getting food to the Belgians had been taken by the American Refugee Committee in Brussels, formed at my instance to forward stranded Americans to London. Daniel Heineman was its chairman; William Hulse, Millard Shaler, both American engineers, together with Hugh Gibson, Secretary of the American Legation, were its chief members. They had set up a Committee for the City of Brussels and Heineman had secured from the German military verbal guarantees not to interfere with the imported food.

Shaler, being innocent of the war potential of the food blockade, already had bought his supplies from merchants in England. The British authorities at once refused to allow him to export them on the grounds that the Germans would take them and that it was the duty of the Germans to feed the peoples of occupied countries. I suggested that if it were consigned to the American Minister in Brussels and distributed by agents appointed by him, the permit might be given. With this thought, I took Mr. Shaler to American Ambassador Page to find if the Ambassador would interest himself. Mr. Page was at once sympathetic but felt that he could not intervene in such a matter without authority from the State Department. I drafted a cable explaining the matter, which he sent to Secretary of State Bryan. Without waiting for a reply from Washington, however, Mr. Page took up Shaler's problem informally with Sir Edward Grey. To allay Grey's troubled mind, the American Minister in Brussels secured from the German authorities a confirmation of the promise to Heineman. The result was that some days later Shaler received the export permits for his 2,500 tons, but the Foreign Office informed him that this was to be the end.

Upon Shaler's statement of the pitiable plight of the Belgians, I took up the matter with my friend Melville E. Stone, General Manager of the Associated Press, who was in London, suggesting that their tragic situation, and that of the Northern French, might be ventilated in America. If this were done, there would be more hope for Shaler. He responded in a most generous fashion, and also gave instructions to the AP men in London, Berlin and Brussels.

All this done, I had no thought of further responsibility in the matter. I again booked passage to America for October 25, the first I could get. The Panama-Pacific Exposition had gone by the board so far as I was concerned.

In the meantime, Belgian delegations continued to arrive in London from other cities—Liege, Charleville, Mons, and Namur—asking to be allowed to import food. Antwerp was subsequently taken by the Germans (October 9), and the representatives of that city appeared soon after. Shaler brought these Belgians to me, not knowing what else to do. I suggested that they should see Mr. Page through appointment by the Belgian Minister in London.

On October 18th, I received a telephone call from the American Ambassador asking me to come to the Embassy. There I found the Belgian Minister, Count de Lalaing, Mr. Hugh Gibson, Mr. Emile Francqui and a Baron Lambert, the latter three just arrived from Belgium.

I recognized Francqui at once as a Belgian banker with whom I had parted on less than friendly terms fourteen years before in China. In the meantime, he had become the head of the leading financial house in Belgium. These gentlemen were engaged in discussion of the complex question of desperate food needs, of blockade, purchase, shipping, and protection of supplies. Mr. Page told me that he had received word from Secretary Bryan authorizing him to use his good offices but to undertake no engagements obligating the American Government. I had said little. Suddenly Francqui turned to me and in effect said:

We must have leaders to organize and conduct this matter. They must be men of wide administrative experience and knowledge of the world. They must be neutral and must be Americans. They must have the confidence of the American Ambassadors. We in Belgium and Northern France are faced with life and death for millions of our people. You alone have the setting for this job. If you will undertake it, I will either serve under you or retire from any connection with it.

Mr. Page added his urgings as did also the Belgian Minister and Hugh Gibson.

Francqui went on to describe the bare bones of the situation. He presented the facts that Belgium produced its own food for only 30 per cent of the population, and that the cities were dependent upon imports. He stated that the Germans had seized a part of the current harvest and thousands of cattle. He described the already heart-breaking condition of the poor. In any event, all supplies would soon be at an end except what the farmers could hoard for themselves—and they were only 20 per cent of the people. He had little detailed information as to the situation in Northern France but was convinced that it was similar to that of Belgium. He continued that with the British Blockade the Germans would be short of food and would do nothing to help.

I was greatly troubled over many parts of the problem. I was not bothered over administrative matters such as the purchase and overseas shipment and internal transport of large quantities of materials. Any engineer could do that. But there were other phases for which there was no former human experience to turn for guidance. It would require that we find the major food supply for a whole nation; raise the money to pay for it; get it past navies at sea and occupying armies on land; set up an agency for distribution of supplies for everybody justly; and see that the enemy took none of it. It was not "relief" in any known sense. It was the feeding of a nation.

I asked of Francqui what resources there were that we could depend upon. He stated that the Belgian banks would make available all of their balances abroad; that the exiled Belgian Government had some resources they had brought out of Belgium; that he had a plan by which food would be sold in Belgium to those who could pay and that the currency thus received could be translated into foreign exchange to buy more food. Ambassador Page was confident that if I took the leadership, there would be an enormous response in world charity.

I replied that I must have a day to consider; that I had responsibilities to concerns which were in difficulties because of the war; that I must find out whether I could get substitutes for my various positions. I must find out also whether my colleagues would feel that I was justified in such a step, and in the uncertainties of the times I had to consider whether I could give up my professional income. I stated that if I did undertake it I must do so without any remuneration, since I could not appeal to others to sacrifice without sacrifice myself.

Will Irwin was staying at our house at the time. He was one of the most important of the American war correspondents in Europe, then representing the *Saturday Evening Post* and certain daily newspapers. Bill was a college mate at Stanford. He passionately urged me to accept. The prospect entailed considerable sacrifice as my aggregate income from professional activities in various countries probably exceeded that of any other American engineer.

During the afternoon and next day I consulted my associates, and by cable our principal clients abroad. They agreed to accept my engineering colleagues in temporary charge of these responsibilities on the understanding that I should give occasional help on major matters.

The following day I again met with Francqui and the Ambassador. I told them I would do the job, but on condition that I was to have absolute command. I insisted that one could not conduct a job like that by a knitting bee. I stated we would need to organize a great campaign for charity over the world not only to secure funds but to create a world opinion that would keep the door to Belgium open through the blockade and keep the Germans from taking food from them. I stated we must set up a central organization of Belgians that would consolidate all their various local committees and supervise details of distribution. I stated that Francqui must be chairman.

I said to Mr. Page that I must have the full support and protection of the American Ambassador in London. To all of which Page and Francqui agreed. We surveyed our immediate resources, which seemed to be at least ten million dollars without counting on the charitable response.

When we had concluded the conversation, I called a broker and gave an order to buy 10,000,000 bushels of Chicago wheat futures, as that price was bound to rise rapidly with the war and with any announcement of Belgian buying.

That evening I called Millard Hunsiker, John White, Edgar Rickard, Millard Shaler, John Lucey, all engineers, Hugh Gibson, Ben S. Allen of the Associated Press, and a banker, all Americans, to meet next morning at my office.

In a few moments the Commission for Relief in Belgium (the C.R.B. for short) was born, with hardly a sheet of paper as a birth certificate.[1] It was not a corporation and, as a partnership, meant unlimited financial responsibility. On realizing this, the banker withdrew. Lucey was assigned to open our shipping office in Rotterdam, Rickard to manage the London office, White, the shipping and purchasing. Shaler was to head the Brussels office, Gibson to be our diplomatic adviser. I arranged by cable for Lindon Bates to open an office in New York.

At this time none of us thought that the war would last longer than until the next summer. Therefore, if we could tide the Belgians over for eight months until the next harvests that would end the job. The knowledge that we would have to go on for four years, to find a billion dollars, to transport five million tons of concentrated food, to administer rationing, price controls, agricultural production, to contend with combatant governments and with world shortages of foods and ships, was mercifully hidden from us. I did not know it but this was to be not only a great charity to the destitute, but it was the first Food Administration of a whole nation in history.

Despite our ignorance of many things, we were wise enough in that first meeting to determine upon certain policies. We laid out a program for organization of charity and public opinion of the world. We set about to secure an American volunteer staff to send into Belgium. We

[1] Correspondence, documents, memoranda of official interviews and statistics will be found published in full in *Public Relations of the Commission for Relief in Belgium: Documents*, edited by G. I. Gay and H. H. Fisher (2 vols., Stanford University Press, 1929), and *Statistical Review of Relief Operations of the C.R.B.*, by George I. Gay (Stanford University, Calif., 1925).

There are numerous other volumes by members of the staff and a host of magazine articles. The whole of them and all of the original documents are in the War Library at the University.

determined that we must have not only Ambassador Page as an Honorary Chairman on our letter-head, but all the other American Ambassadors and Ministers in Europe. A little later we concluded that we must try to secure important neutral Ambassadors and Ministers as patrons in order to make clear our neutral character and to have their aid and protection in negotiations with the belligerent governments.

And finally John White remarked, "We are about to handle millions of dollars. Some day some swine will rise up and say we either made a profit out of this business or that we stole the money." On the spot we sent Edgar to see Sir John Plender of the leading British firm of auditors, to engage them not only to audit the accounts but to actually keep them with their own men, and to countersign all checks. It was an unusual job for an auditing firm. Sir John agreed not only to do it, but to do it without payment except for the bare salaries of the men whom he placed in our offices all over the world. John White's prophecy proved correct. Such swine did "rise up" afterwards. But we confronted them with not only independent auditors but the most elaborate accounting statistics ever produced.

Gathering up all the information I could from Shaler and the Belgians, I added some knowledge of my own gained in engineering visits —we smelted in Belgium a proportion of the ores from our mines throughout the world—and embodied my tentative conclusions in a memorandum for Ambassador Page. It proved to be prophetic of the need which we must meet and the organization which the job required.

The Ambassador readily agreed to back up the invitation we proposed to send to the various Ambassadors and Ministers to become honorary chairmen or patrons of our organization. To this invitation he added personal messages from himself.

Soon we had not only Ambassador Page's name on our letter-head but also those of James W. Gerard, American Ambassador in Berlin; William Sharp, American Ambassador in Paris; Henry van Dyke, American Minister at The Hague; and Brand Whitlock, American Minister in Brussels. With Mr. Page's support we secured acceptances from Dr. Johan Loudon, the Netherlands Minister of Foreign Affairs, and Señor Don Alfonso Merry del Val, Spanish Ambassador in London; the Marquis de Villalobar, Spanish Minister in Brussels; Jonkheer de

Weede, the Netherlands Minister to Belgium. These latter two were already patrons of the Brussels Committee and readily joined us also. The corresponding officials of the Swedish, Norwegian, Swiss and Danish Governments declined. No doubt their governments were frightened that we might involve them in the holocaust. However, with the faithful and efficient co-operation of the American, Dutch and Spanish officials, we maintained the neutral color of the organization throughout the war.

In pursuit of our charitable contributions and the creation of world public opinion for our support, we, by telegraph, rapidly set up Belgian Relief Committees all over the world. Melville Stone helped enormously in support of a Committee set up by our New York office. I requested the Governors of all the States to set up State Committees and over forty did so. Through an old friend, Lord Courtney, I secured the Duke of Norfolk to head a British Empire Committee and he, with the active direction of Sir William Good, in turn, erected committees in Australia, New Zealand, South Africa and Canada. We set up committees in Sweden, Norway, Denmark and Switzerland. Louis Chevrillon, an eminent engineering colleague of mine in the management of some Mexican mines in which the French were interested, set up a committee in France. By degrees, beginning with the Argentine, we set up committees in most of the Latin-American states, and later Japan. The charity organization became our effective armor against the periodic attempts of both the British and German militarists to suppress or restrict our activities.

We needed an American staff for Belgium and while Bates was recruiting some volunteer help, a young man named Perrin C. Galpin walked into the office, saying that he was a Rhodes scholar at Oxford, that he had seen word of the organization in the papers, and asked if he could volunteer. At once I asked if he thought we could get some of the other American Rhodes scholars. He thought we could get them all. In a few days fifteen of the finest and most courageous American youngsters ever born were en route to Brussels. They were filled with idealism and keen on adventure. When the supply from Oxford was exhausted, the New York office gathered us volunteers of the same type. Not only the work of these men in Belgium but their subsequent service in the American Army and their careers in after life would give restoratives to any one who was pessimistic concerning American youth and manhood. Many of them served with me for years after.

With the co-operation of Foreign Minister Loudon, we picked up 20,000 tons of wheat and other supplies in Holland, and delivered them to the larger Belgian cities by canal within a week after our organization meeting. Being Dutch-owned, they required no British permit. The blockade had not yet been perfected to control indirect supplies through neutral nations. But it was so perfected soon after. However, within six weeks, we had, in addition to the Dutch supplies, delivered some 60,000 tons of food from overseas, Sir Edward Grey having secured permits for that amount through the blockade. The cities were saved for the moment.

A few weeks after the organization was set in motion, I went to Belgium to take part in building up the machinery of distribution.

My impressions of Belgium on the first visit are still vivid. Passing through the frontier from Holland I had an indescribable feeling of entering a land of imprisonment. Possibly the rather rough search of my person by the German guards strengthened that impression. German soldiers stood at every crossroads and every street corner. The depressed, unsmiling faces of the Belgians matched the mood of the dreary winter landscape. There were no children at play. The empty streets, the gaunt destroyed houses, the ruins of the fine old church of St. Pierre and the Library at Louvain, intensified the sense of suspended animation in the life of a people.

But my personal causes for depression were more pointed. I soon realized that if we were to give a minimum of even 1800 calories daily, with supplements to children, expectant mothers and hard workers (compared to 3000 calories average normal), we would need at once to enlarge our ideas as to quantities and finance.

With our reduced basis of feeding, the people would lead a desperate existence.

CHAPTER 15

FINANCING THE RELIEF
AND INTERNATIONAL TROUBLE

Early in January, 1915, after less than two months experience, it was inevitable that we would fail unless we could solve two interrelated problems: First, more assured financial resources, and second, better relations with the British and German governments.

We were approaching bankruptcy at high speed. It was obvious that to maintain the minimum of food supply that would keep these 10,000,000 Belgians and French alive, we must spend at least $12,000,000 a month. Moreover, in order to assure regular supply we must have $10,000,000 of food afloat or in stock—"in the pipe line." By this time we had exhausted the foreign assets of the Belgian banks and the Belgian Government at Le Havre, both of which proved disappointing. Charity had been generous but up to this time amounted to less than $2,000,000. We had received altogether about $15,000,000, a large part of which had already been exhausted by deliveries into Belgium. The Allied Governments did not look with favor upon our proposed exchange of Belgian currency into foreign exchange.

In order to assure the trans-ocean stream of food for the next few weeks, I had incurred a debt of $12,000,000 over and above our assets. I had financed these purchases by personally accepted trade bills payable on the arrival of the ships at Rotterdam. This money, amounting to many times any resources of my own, was not in sight—and the vanguard of ships was on its way. However, at worst, we could resell these cargoes to the neutrals and to the British, and while forced sales losses might likely be considerable, we had decided to make the gamble.

Obviously there was no hope of saving the Belgian people unless we could get governmental support somewhere. But this problem was inextricably mixed with our British and German relations. As a matter of fact, in our official existence we were walking a tight rope, the ends of which were, at this time, anchored in the desire of the British and French on one side, and the Germans on the other, to cultivate popularity in neutral countries. Our vigorous publicity in demanding justice for the Belgians who were between the millstones of a blockade and an army of occupation met with a limited amount of enthusiasm from both the British and German governments. Neither we nor the governments concerned were dumb in these matters.

Aside from our financial problems the German Army in Belgium had developed some devilish habits and manners. They had imposed upon the Belgian provinces heavy contributions of money which were paid by a compulsory issue of a new currency jointly guaranteed by the Belgian banks and secured upon provincial bonds. While the Germans were respecting the guaranties as to imported food, they now began using this currency to pay for native food and cattle, which they began to requisition upon a considerable scale. All of which amounted to our being compelled to import more food and thus to feed the Germans. The amounts were not great in proportion but they gave ample material for complaints of the widespread British Intelligence Service in Belgium. Further, the Germans had imposed such restrictions upon the movement of our American and Belgian staff that we could not keep track of what was going on. They made difficulties over every American we wanted to send into Belgium.

Among our other troubles we had to deal not alone with Governor General von Bissing's so-called civil government in Brussels but also with the German Army of occupation in Belgium, which exerted independent control over the foreigners. And beyond the reach of the "occupied" area there were four separate areas of "operations" zones for the four German Armies in Belgium and Northern France. Therefore, we were compelled to deal with six different German authorities, each acting independently.

Added to all these troubles, we had only a tacit agreement that our ships would not be attacked by submarines. And we had to secure a pass and a route direction for every ship from the Germans. Their agents insisted on searching every ship on arrival at Dutch ports, which also created much delay.

And the British Navy bent on the food blockade had also become an uncomfortable bedfellow. We were unable to secure any settled routine with them. Every single ship was a fight for a permit. They required all ships to call at a British port and be searched. That prolonged the voyage and our costs of transportation. The British authorities were tedious and full of delays to our men coming and going from Britain. Both British and Germans were convinced there might be spies and our men were searched to the skin at every crossing over frontiers.

The British naval authorities (Winston Churchill being First Lord) at one time went so far as to file with the Foreign Office charges of corruption against me personally as a spy working for the Germans. Our staunch friend, Sir Edward Grey, had these charges referred to a King's Bench Judge for a private investigation. After tedious hearings we were exonerated and eulogized.

Generally, in view of all these matters of international relations and our financial situation, I concluded that we must have quick reforms and help or we would be put out of existence.

NEGOTIATING WITH THE BRITISH

We determined to open up with the British. With the approval of Ambassador Page and through a personal friend, I secured an appointment with British Prime Minister Herbert Asquith. I presented the general situation of the Belgians and advanced the ideas that the British Government should regularize the passage of our ships through the blockade by a definite program authorized three months in advance; that they should regularize the movement of our staff and should consider giving us financial support, conditional, of course, upon more effective undertaking from the Germans. He was courteous and sympathetic on all questions except finance.

On January 13th, I secured a meeting with Sir Edward Grey. He informed me that most of the Cabinet was opposed to the whole idea of feeding the Belgians. Lord Kitchener, then Minister of War, and especially Winston Churchill, First Lord of the Admiralty, were violently opposed to it, and that Lloyd George, Chancellor of the Exchequer, was more or less on their side. The military leaders considered that if the Belgians starved it would make trouble for the Germans and help win the war. Sir Edward said that nothing could be done unless we re-formed the conduct of the Germans. He certainly thought British Government finance impossible. With little hope for us, Sir Edward arranged a meeting for me with a Cabinet committee, consisting of Lloyd George, Lord Emmott, representing the Blockade, Lord Eustace Percy, representing the Foreign Office, and Sir John Simon, the Attorney General. The discussion covered the continuation of the relief, and if that was to be, then the necessity for an approved program months ahead in order that we might arrange shipping and purchases. I also urged their approval of our Belgian monetary exchange proposals and the acceptance of our certifications for passport visas. I raised the whole financial question and asked what further German guarantees they required.

They listened patiently to my presentation of the Belgian case. Lloyd George was not as belligerent as I had expected. The committee tentatively agreed that they would allow the Relief Commission to continue in business. They would open the blockade for a regular advance program of food shipments; they accepted the exchange proposals, and agreed to the proposals as to visas. But all this was contingent upon our securing from the Germans more effective control of food in Belgium. The committee, however, held out no hope of subsidy from the British Government even if we stopped the leaks in Belgium. The Foreign Office, however, now delegated Lord Eustace Percy to look after our affairs—and he proved to be a staunch friend.

NEGOTIATING WITH THE GERMANS

The next step was obviously into Germany. I started work in that quarter by cabling (January 27th) to Secretary of State Bryan in Washington, asking him to reveal our problems (which I stated) to the German Ambassador in Washington, believing the latter would be especially sensitive to American public opinion. To invoke this impression more effectively, on January 30th, I issued to the press a frank statement of our situation. The whole document is published elsewhere but a few sentences will indicate its tenor.

The Commission for Belgian Relief takes the gloomiest possible view of the ultimate future. The problem is rapidly growing beyond the reach of private philanthropy. . . . If all these people are to be kept alive someone has got to furnish, some way or somehow, from twelve to fifteen million dollars' worth of food every month. . . . We have now reached a point where, so far as we can see, the problem will become hopeless of solution unless the belligerent powers can come to some agreement with regard to this imprisoned population.

It is desirable that the American people should understand why both sides in this gigantic struggle have refused to accept the responsibility for the feeding of these people; . . . The Germans state that the people of Belgium have always imported their food supplies and that this population still possesses resources; and that could a gate be opened through their double wall of steel by which they could import foodstuffs and raw material and export their industrial products and thus restart credit, they could provision themselves. . . . They state further that while the German food supplies, with great economy, are sufficient to carry this war to successful fruition, if they have to take upon their backs an additional ten million people their stores would be seriously jeopardized, and that it is the duty of the Germans to feed their own people first; that as this war is a war to maintain German national integrity they do not propose to jeopardize the issues in such a manner.

The English and French affirm . . . in the traditions of international law it is the duty of the occupying army to provision the civil population, and the importation of foodstuffs into Belgium and Northern France would relieve the Germans of their moral and legal responsibilities. Broader than this, however, although the civil population alone be supplied with foodstuffs, the Germans are relieved of the drain which would otherwise have fallen upon their own stores. That in general the situation is akin to that of a siege where the succor of the population relieves the moral and physical strain on the garrison; that the ending of this war will be through economic pressure and any relaxation of this pressure assists the enemy.

We were convinced from the beginning that the fixity of opinion on both sides as to the righteousness of their respective attitudes was such that the Belgians would starve before responsibility could be settled. . . . During the three months that we have been at work we have listened daily to these arguments and it is certain that were it not for the stream of food poured in by this Commission the decimation would have already begun. . . .

On the English and French side there are many who say that their people should be prepared to abandon the military advantages and give way on contentions of moral and legal issue and come to the support of these people through this Commission; but they add with vigor that they cannot be expected to go so far so long as the Germans continue draining the resources of these wretched people by way of money levies and the continued requisition of foodstuff. . . .

Here is, then, a possible ground on which, on one side, the English and French should give us financial support to feed their allies and the French their own blood, and the Germans should cease to reduce, through levies and requisitions, the abilities of these imprisoned people to help themselves. If we cannot get an agreement of this sort we must struggle on as best we can with the support of the charitable world, to whom our country has given such a magnificent lead. We will feed as many people as we can. We will skimp a nation—we will even gamble with starvation—but stretch the food supplies as we may, we must say positively that it is impossible for us to save more than a modicum of this population unless the belligerent powers can be induced to come to an arrangement. . . .

We have stated our case bluntly and frankly. Our only court of appeal is public opinion.

Next day I started for Berlin, resolved to besiege the German Government at the top directly and on all fronts. Ambassador Gerard arranged, and was often helpfully present at, interviews with Reich Chancellor von Bethmann Hollweg, Foreign Minister von Jagow, Under Minister of State Zimmermann, Finance Minister Helfferich, Minister of the Interior Lewald, who then headed the German food organization, President of the Reichsbank Hjalmar Schacht, Chairman Ballin of the Hamburg-American Line, and others. I had the effective support of Daniel Heineman of our American staff in Brussels.

Lewald was particularly helpful. He had served on various missions to the United States and was more alive to the public relations situation than most of the others. They ultimately agreed to stop all taking of food from Belgium and Northern France; to give complete freedom of movement to our staff without search; to give definite instructions to submarine commanders to respect the markings on our ships; to give us sailing directions from time to time on mine-free sea routes to Rotterdam; to charter us German merchant ships in refuge in neutral ports; to designate one officer for us to deal with authoritatively in Belgium and another at the headquarters at Charleville to deal with all questions in the four army zones. All of this they confirmed in writing through Ambassador Gerard, and generally carried out. They promised to consider our proposals to abandon forced contributions of money from the Belgian cities and provinces (which they never did).

As to finance, we arrived with the Germans at a tentative plan by which the Reichsbank would guarantee trade bills in the United States for the Commission to the amount of from 50 to 100 million dollars. This was to be secured by Belgian provincial and municipal bonds and also to be jointly guaranteed by the Belgian banks. This device obviously was a sort of kiting of paper and, unless the war ended soon, it would break down. From our point of view, however, the Belgians would have been fed in the meantime.

This visit to Germany was my first contact with the dominant German civil officials. Unlike the British, every one of them was in a uniform of some sort. In those bright clothes they were all cogs in the military machine. Their attitudes were military. Their minds were military. The military mind is without sentiment, but at least it has common sense and usually says what it means. It took less time and argument to put points over and get decisions than with the British. The mental operations of the whole group contrasted sharply with the groping and ofttimes timid and uncertain attitudes of the Allied official mind. There was less red tape, more direct and effective action.

On the other hand, there was something indescribably automatic and inhuman about their actions and their thinking. Nowhere did I encounter any relieving sense of human interest or humor. The only laugh I heard from any of them was that of Bethmann Hollweg when I illustrated to him the need for more and better instructions to submarine commanders by reciting an old American story. That was the case of a man who demanded that a neighbor keep his bulldog in better control. The neighbor replied: "Oh, he won't bite." The man observed: "You may know he won't bite. I may know he won't bite. But does the dog know it?"

The outstanding realization which came to me on this visit, however, was something more important. The Germans had been a militant, aggressive race since Caesar's time. They were the Spartans of Europe. While for years their interest had been diverted to commercial conquest, massed regimentation was their bent. And they had revived something in this war that the world had not seen since ancient Sparta. Perhaps it was never consciously conceived in advance even by themselves. That was total war. Every man and woman was quickly mobilized into the thrust at the front. For the first time in modern history a nation was incorporating its full human power into its striking strength. The whole civilian population, women as well as men, were mobilized for the one purpose of manufacturing the instruments of war and producing food.[1]

The whole philosophy of life, the whole military, social and economic organization of the Western democracies, were just as opposite to all this as ancient Athens was to ancient Sparta. The British and French were slow to realize what they had to meet. Their fumbling with inadequate armies, inadequate industrial and social organizations of civilians, gave me grave doubt as to whether they had the capacity within themselves ever to win the war.

In any event, I came back with the complete conviction that the war would not "be over in the spring"; in fact with the belief it had not yet really begun.

THE SECOND BATTLE WITH THE BRITISH

I laid our progress in Germany before Lord Eustace Percy through whom the Foreign Office accepted our new guarantees protecting the food from appropriation by the Germans and our other arrangements except finance as good enough to go on with.

As to finance, I had of course a strong premonition that the Allied Governments would not like the exhibit before the neutral world of the Germans saving Belgians. I had, however, believed that, if I could get a German offer, it would serve to thaw out the Allied treasuries. I also rightly surmised it would produce an explosion.

Lord Eustace Percy at once arranged a conference with Mr. Lloyd George, Lord Emmott and myself on February 17, 1915. Lloyd George listened patiently as I went over the ground again and to my description of where we had arrived with the Germans. He, this time, re-

---

[1] Those students who discovered the National Socialist ideology of Germany to be a product of later years have to a large extent ignored the fact that in every essence Germany was a National Socialist state from 1914 to 1918.

sponded sympathetically to the human appeal that lay behind the whole problem. I surmised by hints from Percy that Asquith, Grey and Emmott had been working on him. He did not like the idea of Germans paying for the food and thus advertising the British starvation of their Allies by the blockade. He asked me to prepare him a memorandum for presentation to the full Cabinet next morning. I prepared it during the night and had it in his hands before the Cabinet meeting at noon. It covered the whole ground of arguments, pro and con, on the principles and political weights involved, in addition to statements of our woes.[2]

The next day (February 18th) Lloyd George asked me to come to the Treasury, together with Colonel Hunsiker (who was looking after our details with the British Government), and I found Lord Eustace Percy waiting. Percy told me they had overruled Churchill and Kitchener.[3] The Chancellor told me they had agreed to give £1,000,000 a month (about $4,820,000) to the "Hoover Fund." I told him they had taken a load from millions of hearts—to which he replied, "You deserved to win out." I asked his good services to aid us with further subsidies from the French which he said he would do.

Having settled this much of our finance, we began work on the French Government. I addressed a letter to the President of France and followed it immediately by going to Paris. There I asked the American Ambassador, William Sharp, as a first step to take me to see the French Minister of Foreign Affairs Delcassé, then, subject to what happened in this interview, to take me to see the Prime Minister and possibly the President. Sharp hemmed and hawed, finally concluding that this was an internal matter of the French Government in which it would be improper for him to act. I argued the blessing we had received from the American Secretary of State and the attitudes of Ambassadors Page and Gerard but to no avail.

[2] The full memoranda and correspondence with Lloyd George have been published in *Public Relations of the Commission for Relief in Belgium: Documents*, edited by G. I. Gay and H. H. Fisher.

[3] Twenty-five years later, when Belgium was again ground between a savage German occupation and an Allied blockade, I was requested by the Belgian Government again to organize a Relief. I give a more complete account of these matters in another volume. But Winston Churchill now together with Roosevelt refused us. And this in the face of even better agreements with the Germans, for we induced them to agree to supply half the food.

Thereupon I enlisted Louis Chevrillon who arranged the appointment with Delcassé. At this interview I emphasized again the poignant situation of the 3,000,000 people in Northern France. I pointed out that all men of military age having been drafted prior to the invasion, the population was essentially limited to children, women, and old men. They were already reduced to famine rations and disease was rampant. We had done our best and were already feeding 400,000 of them. But without unjust deprivation of the Belgians, for whom even the British subsidy was insufficient, we must stop.

Delcassé listened courteously but delivered himself violently upon the obligation of the Germans to feed the occupied populations or get out. All I could reply was that they would not do it as evidenced by the thousands already starving. I stated that the Germans justified themselves on the ground that the blockade was pinching their own women and children. They also were constantly asserting that they would feed everybody if the food blockade was taken down. The Minister finally became so abrupt in his declaration that France would never condone this gross barbarity or admit any such contention that I concluded I had been wholly inadequate in my presentation, and withdrew, not only discouraged but with a feeling of humiliation.

I returned to the Meurice Hotel, where I was stopping, and started to pack my bag to return to London on the night boat. A few moments later a bellboy presented the card of M. Maurice Homberg, President of the Banque Union Parisienne. I went down to the reception room to meet an elderly and distinguished looking Frenchman, who spoke perfect English. He said he had heard that I was in Paris endeavoring to finance food for the French and Belgians in the occupied north. He asked that I explain the matter to him. I did so, as I had now become so familiar with the political, military and humanitarian arguments that I repeated them in my sleep. He asked what I estimated as the cost. I stated that for the French population we should have a minimum of $5,000,000 of capital for food in transit and $3,000,000 a month for current use for the French for the present. I felt that this would provide no more than a scanty regimen for the people, but that we might get through the balance of the winter. I also pointed out that the British subsidy was insufficient to cover the Belgians; that the French had an equal interest in that case and should follow the British in aiding us with the Belgians. Homberg said that the matter interested him greatly and inquired when I was returning to London. I told him I was going that evening unless he thought it worth while to try some other of the French Ministers. He did not think it worth while, but said I would hear from him if the possibilities should open up. This was all cold comfort and I returned to London.

The next morning, soon after I arrived at the Relief office, an official of one of the French banks in London called on me and stated that he was authorized to say that funds would be placed at my disposal. I asked if they would come from the French Government. He handed me two initial checks amounting to about $7,000,000. I asked to whom we should account. The bank official said he did not know. I kept the checks nevertheless. And the $3,000,000 a month for the French population arrived punctually.[4] We received further sums from the same source to aid our work in Belgium. And our stream of charity was about $2,000,000 a month during the first two years.

These subsidies from Britain and France, now amounting to about $10,000,000 a month, were substantially increased from time to time as prices rose and the need became greater. In 1917, when Food Administrator, I secured that the American Government join in the support, the details of which I relate later. In the last years, the costs of the Relief rose to $25,000,000 a month.

This is perhaps as good a place as any to recapitulate the external receipts of the Commission for the whole of the war:

Subsidies from the British Government for Belgium............	$109,045,328.73
Subsidies from the French Government for Northern France and Belgium	204,862,854.21
Subsidies from the American Government for Belgium and Northern France	386,632,260.44
Subsidies from the Belgian Government	6,328,328.30
World charity to the Belgians	52,290,835.51
Sales of food to other nations and in Belgium translatable into effective exchange of Belgian Bank balances abroad, together with free ship charters and other stores...................	168,521,877.79
Total	$927,681,484.98

[4] I, of course, knew it was the French Government and although I saw their officials frequently during the war we did not mention the source of the money. They were resolute that they would not publicly recede from Delcassé's position. After the Armistice, I settled the accounts with the French treasury.

The entire overhead expenditures of the Commission for the whole of over four years were $3,908,892.24, or less than one-half of one per cent. This is perhaps as good a place as any to quote comment attached to the auditors' final certificate of vastly complicated transactions.

. . . Our firm acted as auditors of the Commission from the inception of its active operations until the termination thereof, some five years later. In addition to our duties as auditors, at Mr. Herbert Hoover's request, we arranged a method of account-keeping and selected the accountants who supervised the handling of the funds in its principal offices. Thus the records covering the expenditure by the Commission of nearly a billion dollars were under our scrutiny.

Now that those records are passing into history, we are glad to emphasize the thorough and consistent attention of the Commission's Managers to the business of the Commission, and their cooperation, which enabled the records to be so maintained that all the transactions of the Commission could be fully verified, thus preventing any charge being sustained against the integrity of the administration of the Commission's affairs.

The records are evidence of the important services rendered by the Commission's principal officials, which services were given without remuneration. In this connection, we would state that Mr. Hoover set an example by not accepting, directly or indirectly, any form of remuneration from the Commission and by refusing, throughout the period of the Commission's activities, to take from the funds of the Commission the cost of his traveling or other out-of-pocket expenses while engaged on the business of the Commission.

We consider it an honor to have been selected as auditors of the Commission and to have been able to make a contribution to so great a work. We did not charge for the time of any of our principals during the whole of the term of our service, and so far as our assistants were concerned, we added only a nominal percentage to the cost of their salaries. Therefore, no profit whatever accrued to our firm as a result of the arduous services rendered by our firm over a long term of years.

Yours very truly,
DELOITTE, PLENDER, GRIFFITHS & Co.

CHAPTER 16

PIONEERING THE FIRST FOOD ADMINISTRATION IN HISTORY

In the whole operation we met with problems in Belgium that mortal man had never met before. Certain phenomena developed instantly from invasion and famine. Industry at once collapsed. Half the population were unemployed and destitute. Before we got into action prices of food rose stupendously. The rich obtained enough. The farmers hoarded for their families. The middle class got something. The unemployed and destitute got little but soup.

People do not lie down and die of sheer starvation; they don't have a chance. They lose resistance to contagious disease, which does the rest. In practical effect, two of the Four Horsemen of the Apocalypse— FAMINE and PESTILENCE—are synonymous. However, we quickly got the worst of these disasters remedied.

During my first visit to Belgium in November 1914 we elaborated our general lines of organization. Émile Francqui as chairman and Firmin Van Bree as executive secretary—two men of extraordinary ability and devotion—had expanded the Comité National to include leading Belgians from all parts of the country. Provincial committees and local committees in municipalities and communes were set up. We set up a committee of Frenchmen for Northern France under Edmond Labbé.

Under the requirements of the British and French governments, the title of all food until it reached the consumer's mouth rested in the neutral commission. They insisted that C.R.B. men must have charge of barge and rail transportation, processing and warehouses to safeguard supplies from the Germans. Also, the Allies required that the Belgian and French committees should be considered as mandatories of the C.R.B. And the C.R.B. had to account to those governments for the money.

The final stage of distribution was in the hands of the committees under burgomasters and mayors of the communes which varied from a few hundred to a few thousand people. The Americans, ex officio, sat on all committees and as the Belgians were not allowed to move freely, our men had to be mostly the channels of communication between them.

Moreover, in most cases, the minister patrons or the C.R.B. men had to conduct relations with the Germans who imposed upon the Belgians.

Generally the C.R.B. determined external policies, usually in consultation with the Belgian and French committees, and the Belgian and French committees usually determined domestic policies in consultation with the C.R.B. The relations between the various organisms were complicated enough, but by the constant good will they worked smoothly enough. Where I use the word "we" in this text, it must not be taken as personal but simply as an easy reference to the whole machinery.

We at once opened six floors of a new office building in Brussels for the American staff and three floors for the Belgian national committee. Soon the clatter of typewriters oozed from every transom.

We quickly determined we must ration the whole population with cards. Because we were reducing normal good intake by over one-third and everybody had to fare alike, we started with bread but followed that with other commodities as the situation became more tense.

And rationing was not as simple as it sounds. Separate cards had to be issued to each detached person and to each family for each major commodity, with coupons or punch squares marked for days or weeks. The farmers had to have special settlements and so did families with a cow or chicken. Some ate at restaurants, and so there were a hundred variations.

To simplify organization and accounting, we separated the "Provisioning" of the people absolutely from the "Benevolence" to the destitute. Not only were they entirely dissimilar problems but the personnel required was a different type. "Benevolence" especially was the woman's job. The rations were sold on behalf of "Provisioning" for cash by the

communal committee at the same price to everybody. The "Benevolence" purchased the ration cards from "Provisioning" and gave them
to the destitute. "Provisioning" supplied from its cash intake the needs
of "Benevolence."

"Provisioning" ultimately took control of all food warehouses, flour
mills, slaughter houses, dairies, bakeries and restaurants. In time we
requisitioned all the farmer's production above the needs of his own
family. We guaranteed profitable prices to him for subsequent crops in
order to increase production.

The Belgian national currency had disappeared almost over night.
At the start we printed an emergency issue which was used to support
various services and it obtained its stability because it would purchase
rations—the only food-based currency of modern times. However,
the Germans quickly established their forced issues and we were
compelled to withdraw our currency.

We naturally had a price problem because we had to fix prices for
the rations and for the farmers. Initially we had what were subsequently known as black markets. As our supply was so meager people
naturally tried to get around the end. At the start we tried to establish
maximum retail prices on the few unrationed commodities and to work
back from them to prices for the producer. Finally our situation became so difficult that we took over all surplus produce from the farmer
and rationed it out with the imports. We effectively killed the black
market.

In Northern France we set up a committee under Professor Edmond
Labbé of the University of Lille. The final officer in distribution was
again the *maire* of the commune. There were 1,200 French communes,
but the draft of all able-bodied Frenchmen in advance of the invasion,
together with the fact that some *maires* went out with the refugees, left
many communes without a head. There was no authority to appoint
new ones. Therefore we assumed authority. By the end of the Relief
over 500 of them were women. They turned out to be faithful and
painstaking almost beyond belief. They accounted for the last centime
and every gramme. They had a lot of accounting. The rations had to
be sold to those who could pay. Upon a hint from the French Government we secured from the Germans permission to pay French sepa-

ration allowances to wives and widows of French soldiers and other government pensions out of our sales receipts, they in turn could buy ration cards. But French francs had disappeared and there was no money to take their place. We, therefore, issued a currency of our own. The Germans levied on some of the towns for "reparations," and thus obtaining our currency, spent it to buy services and the like. To stop this we issued for every single commune a separate currency which was good only in that particular commune. We thus had 1,200 currencies. And the *maire* had to sign every single note and make the books balance. One of my vivid pictures is calling at a still lighted *maire's* office about midnight and finding an efficient French woman still signing 50-centime notes; nor did she desist while we talked with her about the food and the commission's problems.

As our cash receipts from rations in both Belgium and France in the earlier years exceeded the needs of "Benevolence" the Relief undertook to keep the schools open and pay the teachers. We even financed some building and loan associations to prevent them from going bankrupt. We paid the minor judiciary, the police and other officials.

One result of pioneering the first Food Administration with methods of processing, distribution, rationing, price control, guarantee, requisition of crops from farmers, etc., was that when the Germans instituted food control of their own people later on, they studied our experience, and followed many of our devices. Two years later, I was called in to advise the British in installing their food control, and a few months after I was called in by the French Government.

CARE OF THE BELGIAN AND FRENCH DESTITUTE

As I have said, the care of the unemployed and the destitute was the function of "Benevolence." In addition to giving out free ration cards which "Benevolence" bought from "Provisioning" they provided to this group fuel, clothes, rent, and medical care and many other services. They looked after the hospitals, insane asylums and other public institutions for the support of which they received cash from "Provisioning."

One of our daily inspirations was the efficiency of the Belgians and French and the utter devotion they showed. In the end there were over 50,000 of them, mostly women, in the work—and the highest pay they got was free rations. The women developed a zeal that sprang from the spiritual realization that they were saving their race. They had the major responsibilities of administering "Benevolence." Among the tasks of "Benevolence" were the soup kitchens. Immediately upon the outbreak of war, by the charity of citizens and local committees, soup kitchens had been established where bread and good thick soup were issued. As we became more systematized the soup kitchens were continued as a supplement to sparse food of the ration for special cases. They were also a vehicle for economical distribution of meat, fat and vegetables. The soup was no ordinary soup. Over the years I visited hundreds of "Soups" and the devoted women who ran them insisted on my sampling all of them. They were great cooks. The soup cards issued by "Benevolence" being the credential, the daily chore of the children was to go for the soup. The emblem of Belgium during the war should have been a child carrying a soup bucket.

Another service of "Benevolence" was indeed full of sentiment. We soon learned from certain almost epidemic diseases that children must have special supplies of fats in addition to the meager rations of staple food given to adults. Gradually we built up a noon meal for them in schoolhouses and public buildings until in the end over 2,500,000 children and expectant mothers were served daily—again by the volunteer Belgian and French women. Among other devices we invented was a big and solid cracker with fats, cocoa, sugar and flour, containing every chemical needed for growing children. We ultimately manufactured it on a huge scale and served one cracker every day to the 2,500,000 children. With it as a start they were given some sort of stew and imported condensed milk—or fresh milk when it was available.

From the rebuilding of the vitality in the children came the great relieving joy in the work of Belgian Relief. The troops of healthy cheerful chattering youngsters lining up for their portions, eating at long tables, cleaning their own dishes afterwards, were a gladdening lift from the drab life of an imprisoned people. And they did become healthy. When the war ended it was found that children's mortality and morbidity were lower than ever before in Belgian and French history.

The system of child-feeding which we developed was destined to be spread over most of Europe after the war.[1]

Another of the side issues of "Benevolence" was the lace workers. For over a century Belgian women makers of hand lace had led the world. It was a cottage industry aiding in livelihood about 50,000 families. With the loss of the market, not only were they destitute but the art was likely to be greatly injured for lack of continuity. The women of "Benevolence" set up an organization by which their product was bought with ration cards and further aids—enough to live on. Each piece of lace was marked with its maker's name and books kept. It was hoped that these could be sold after the war and any further realization was to be paid to the makers. We financed the operation. When the war ended we had about $4,000,000 worth of lace. I had not expected anything to come of it but to our great surprise it found a market at prices which returned substantial dividends to each lace worker.

Still another side issue of "Benevolence" was clothing for the destitute. We imported over 55 million pounds of second-hand and new clothing, materials, buttons, thread, needles and what not. The women organized great work rooms where it was sorted, made over, repaired and from which it was distributed. One phenomenon was of special interest. Women all over the world started knitting wool garments for the Belgians. They were mostly sweaters. The Belgian women carefully unraveled them and knitted them over again into shawls—which was their idea of a knitted garment.

With the innate gaiety of the race and their sense of millinery the workroom women were able to sort from our second-hand American clothing evening gowns of every fashion period for thirty years back. They put on an exhibition of them and charged admission to see it.

The finance of "Benevolence" in the end absorbed the major part of our sales of rations. In fact our grants amounted to $615,237,147.47. But it had cared for the destitute, the children, the "soups," the lace workers, the hospitals, and other public institutions. It was a monument to the women of Belgium and France.

---

[1] And over forty nations after World War II, under the leadership of Maurice Pate and our staff who learned it in Belgium, administered it.

CHAPTER 17

TROUBLES WITH SHIPS

Throughout the Relief it was difficult to determine which were our worst troubles—governments, food, finance or ships. In any event, ships were in that category.

To charter shipping was, after the first few months, always a fierce battle. The German submarines and surface raiders were steadily sinking merchant ships and the Allies constantly needed more transport. Our program called for the constant use of about 60 cargo ships, totalling about 300,000 tons, able to deliver up to 150,000 tons a month at Rotterdam.

Early in the war I had secured that the Belgian Government requisition all suitable Belgian flag merchant ships, which gave us about 100,000 tons. The balance we had to charter from neutral countries at increasing rates.

In January 1915 I had asked the British Government for permission to charter German cargo ships then in refuge in neutral ports. The British were favorably inclined. As I have mentioned I took up the matter with the Germans. Mr. Ballin of the Hamburg-American Line agreed to the idea. The details required long and tedious negotiations, but we finally settled a charter of about 150,000 tons for the period of the war, which would have given us the backbone of a fleet. I arranged that Dutch shipping companies should operate the ships with Dutch crews. The British formally agreed to the contract. But the French Government at once objected. I have never witnessed a more stupid and insensate action. They asserted that they would never again consent to a German ship going to sea, and so on to the limits of inanity. They held us up for three months. By this time the Germans began to get wise to the fact that shipping was becoming scarce and that by using their ships we would be releasing other ships that might go into Allied service. Then they withdrew the arrangement. Later on the French urged us to take it up again with the Germans. It was too late.

One of our plagues was the insistence of the British authorities that we should not carry more than four weeks' supply of imported food in Rotterdam and Belgium. I argued that our imported food stocks for two months for 10,000,000 people could only last 70,000,000 Germans for ten days at the rate they ate, even if the supplies were seized. It would not prolong the war very much. The British mind at times was less than flexible. John White led a life of worry for years, scheduling ship charters and arrivals to meet this requirement. Moreover, it constantly disturbed our distribution in Belgium, for each warehouse, likewise, had to have its stocks scheduled on a four-week basis in face of constant German army interruptions of rail and canal movements. We shipped food from the United States, Canada, India and the Argentine—wherever we could get it the cheapest.

By degrees we established safety for our ships. We agreed with both the British and Germans that these ships would carry a big sign, stretching almost from stem to stern, "Belgian Relief Commission," which was to be readable for ten miles. They were to have a deck sign and fly a flag—C.R.B.—from the main mast. All this was supposed to protect us from being stopped by the British or attacked by German submarines and raiders. We were to carry only full cargoes of our own and no passengers. Most of the ships ultimately ceased to fly any national flag.

The Dutch, by agreement with both combatants, had secured a channel from the North Sea to Rotterdam supposed to be free from mines. But initially the British required us to put all our ships into south of England ports for inspection. For ships from Canada and the United States this added days to the voyage and the expense. However, we finally prevailed on the British to inspect our ships by their Consular staffs at the points of departure. The Germans were constantly changing their minds as to this channel free from mines, but as they kept the Dutch informed the latter were able to give directions to our Captains by wireless. We were supposed to be immune from German submarine attack. However, prior to the unlimited submarine war of

January 31, 1917, we lost 19 ships for one cause or another (mostly mines) of which we credited 3 to submarines. Where we could prove it to the German authorities, they indemnified us—but the trouble was to prove it.

The Germans in their declaration of unlimited submarine war in February 1917 notified the world that they would sink all ships entering certain boundaries. These included our Relief routes. From this moment until the American entry into the war—sixty-five days later— it was for us a period hectic to the *n*th degree. The German declaration gave ships at sea four days to reach their destinations and one day more to depart from British, French and other submarine-blockaded ports. At that moment we had in Rotterdam enough food—when added to stocks of Belgian origin such as native wheat—to keep the people going until about the end of March. Nineteen of our cargoes were at sea en route to Rotterdam. Two reached that port in time. We were compelled to order the other ships into the nearest ports since they could not comply with the dates set by the Germans. Fifteen reached British ports. Two of our ships were torpedoed. The *Euphrates* was sunk on February 3rd with only one survivor. The *Lars Kruse* was sunk on February 6th. The crew escaped.

We tried at once to get safe conduct from the Germans that the ships in England might proceed to Rotterdam and also permission for the trans-shipment of some stocks which we had in London. The Germans refused. The food in England began to deteriorate and we were compelled to sell the British about 100,000 tons. Under the submarine blockade food prices rose rapidly in England and we made a large profit on the sale. But it deprived the Belgians of about a three weeks' supply.

The torpedoing of the two ships at once raised a menace to our whole existence. In order to bring matters to a head immediately, I notified the German Government, and particularly Minister Lewald, through our Rotterdam office that the Relief would be compelled to stop. I was sure it was the only way to drive the Germans to consider the consequences. I had surmised that they would be still hoping that America would not enter the war and that they would not wish to inflame American emotions further. It worked. On February 11th, the German

Government urged us to remain, promising us protection and indemnity for our two ships which had been sunk.

Between the unlimited submarine war and the United States' declaration of war on April 6th twelve more ships were lost of which eight were sunk by submarines and four sunk by mines and accidents. Two ships were fired on by submarines in the "safe" zone, but escaped. We protested after each violation, but American protests were growing weak and ineffective as we neared the war.

It was at this moment that our Dutch and Spanish patrons performed a transcendent service to the Belgians. They protested to the Germans and somewhat substituted for the Americans as desirable neutrals to be held on to. The Dutch and Spanish Ambassadors reported that the Germans said the sinkings were a mistake and would not be repeated. In the three months from January 1, 1917 to the American declaration of war, we had lost 40,000 tons of food, and four outward bound ships in ballast. We were also unable to deliver the 100,000 tons stalled in England. It was difficult to get new charters. The result of all this was that our deliveries of overseas food fell from a normal 150,000 tons a month to an average of under 25,000 tons a month from February to May. We had to disastrously pare down the already drastic rationing of the people. Cardinal Mercier ordered a special service throughout Belgium of prayers that the Relief Commission should be sustained in its fight for the lives of the people. By June we had restored shipments to normal.

Another most dangerous moment to our transportation and thus to our life arose in May 1918 from our own government. At this time I was United States Food Administrator, conducting the Belgian Relief at the same time. Our American military authorities in Washington got the bright idea one day that as the Belgian Relief was using 300,000 tons of shipping it was an easy place to get that many ships. I woke up to the fact that they had support from British and French military officials and were about to take action. I protested to President Wilson and sent information of my protest to Prime Ministers Lloyd George and Clemenceau through the London and Paris offices of the Relief. These two Prime Ministers at once sent word to President Wilson that they did not wish the Relief interfered with.

In the four years from November 1914 until November 1919, our total overseas transport amounted to over 2000 cargoes or part cargoes, with the following supplies:

	Tons		Tons
Wheat and Rye	2,923,191	Cocoa	21,205
Flour	428,104	Meat	39,140
Bacon	151,719	Fish	21,964
Lard	226,340	Milk	81,677
Corn	451,728	Soap	39,140
Rice	339,675	Sugar	51,244
Beans and Peas	102,499	Clothing	23,769
Coffee	41,975	Sundry	230,971
Total			5,174,341

CHAPTER 18

TROUBLES
CROSSING WAR FRONTIERS

With the war every frontier became tight against spies. Passports, visas, interrogations, searches and delays reduced life to its lowest level for travelers. I was immediately introduced to the process on my initial journey to Belgium in November 1914. I had gone to Tilbury Docks where the Dutch North Sea steamer was to sail at daylight. I found some 200 people lined up for inspection and general inquisition by British Intelligence officials. All passengers were supposed to be searched to their skins and to the linings of their suitcases. I had to line up with the rest and remain standing for four hours and then be searched. In the meantime, I observed favored persons being mysteriously short-circuited around this bottleneck directly onto the steamer and thus comfortably to bed. Again I went through an equally vigorous disrobing process by the Germans at the Belgian frontier. It seemed to me some reforms were badly needed in the conduct of belligerent governments. And I wanted reform not only for myself but for our whole staff which must make frequent journeys over frontiers. Early in 1915 I arranged with the British authorities, through Sir Edward Grey, that we would issue a CRB passport for our men, which would put them automatically among the favored few. I established the same passport with the Dutch and the Germans. To do this I gave the word of honor of the organization that we would attend strictly to our own business. Our men never violated this pledge with one exception.

I was never able to get this concession from the French. Once crossing to France at the request of the French Government, I stood in line at Dieppe for three hours. In front of me was a French lady. Up at the head of the long line a lady fainted. Two men stepped out of the line, picked her up and carried her into the Passport Office. They never came out. I remarked to my colleague that this was a good way of getting by. In an instant the French lady next to us toppled over. We picked her up, carried her tenderly into the Passport Office and laid her on a bench to revive. She made instant recovery. The three of us were able to get attended to at once, went into the dining car, and off to Paris.

The North Sea crossings were made by Dutch steamers only. They always left at daylight in order to spy their way along the designated path through the minefields before night. Constantly, both sides mined and countermined this seaway. The Dutch crammed the holds of their steamers with empty barrels, so that in case of a too close association with a mine the hulk would float while passengers and crew took to the boats. Altogether I made forty crossings over the North Sea during the war. It was seldom a pleasant trip. The steamers were small, the oldest they had. And that stretch of water is nearly always rough at best. I was often seasick but that semi-comatose condition has its advantage—it makes one oblivious to danger.

The tedious and ceaseless travel over the Channel and continental railways imposed a lot of waiting about. I filled in time by writing most of a narrative of my life up to that time, intending it for the information of my sons. I also did a vast amount of reading, mostly on previous wars, revolutions and peace-makings of Europe and especially the political and economic aftermaths. At one time I set up some research at London, Paris and Berlin into previous famines in Europe to see if there had developed any ideas on handling relief and pestilence. Except for the charities of the religious bodies, of occasional municipalities and of a few princes, there had never been such a thing as relief. The greatest famine in European history—that which followed the Thirty Years War—certainly had no relief for it was recorded that one-third to one-half of the population of Europe died. I was shortly convinced that gigantic famine would follow the present war. The steady degeneration of agriculture was obvious.

I have related elsewhere that during one of these North Sea crossings I read in one of Andrew D. White's writings that most of the fugitive literature of comment during the French Revolution was lost to history because no one set any value on it at the time, and that without such material it became very difficult or impossible to reconstruct the real scene. Therein lay the origins of the Library on War, Revolution and Peace at Stanford University.

During the winter of 1916 I received word that the King of the Belgians would like to see me the next time I came to France. One day I crossed to Boulogne, having arranged to motor up to the Belgian headquarters the next morning. About midnight the Germans decided to make an air attack on Boulogne Harbor. The one little hotel still open to civilians was inconveniently close to their objective. I got out of bed and from the window was watching the searchlight streamers, listening to the drone of planes and the occasional explosions, when suddenly the window was smashed in and I received my only wound of the war. It was only a cut on the arm from flying glass. I got no wound stripe. Then a cockney English non-commissioned officer pounded on the doors yelling for everybody to "go to the bisement, go to the bisement." I wrapped a towel around my arm and groped my way in the dark down to the lobby. Under the light of a single candle our cockney was now on a chair yelling, "Into the bisement. Women and children foist. Women, children foist!" A crowd of terrorized women and children were jamming the head of a narrow staircase. The wavering light made an agonizing flash of an inferno such as only Dürer could depict. As sound accompaniment to the nightmarish scene came another crash in the streets, a scream from some child, another yell from the cockney, "Women foist, women foist!" There wasn't a man within yards of the staircase. A Frenchman standing next to me said calmly, "Shall we go over and kick him to death?" I felt like that too but instead went back to bed.

The next morning we motored to the little beach resort of La Panne where on Belgian soil the King and the Queen and their children occupied a small summer cottage. I spent the day with them. Heavy shells periodically whined over the house en route from the German Front to the French city of Dunkirk. But the King insisted upon living on Belgian soil. He was anxious to know everything about the Relief and the people in Belgium. During the day he became reminiscent concerning his life in America. When he was heir apparent, after his education at Oxford, the old King Leopold had sent him to get some American experience under the tutelage of James J. Hill of the Great Northern Railway in which Leopold had a large interest. The Prince wanted no tourist visit, so he got from Mr. Hill a job as a fireman on the railway. He told me that it was the happiest period of his life. He even made up his mind to abandon his Belgian nationality and become an American. He was sure he would be promoted to be an engine driver in a few years and possibly a railroad president sometime. He thought either of them was a better job than that of being a king. Soon after he began to evidence such yearnings, the Belgian Minister at Washington turned up at Missoula and ordered him, on behalf of the King, to stop dreaming and go straight home. So ended his independence.

Albert was a man of fine and distinguished character, of magnificent moral and physical courage and devoted to his people. He was in active command of his army. They were holding across a little triangle—all that remained of Belgium, involving some twenty or thirty miles of front protected by water. I asked him about the retreat from Antwerp and the holding of the locks at Nieuport. Here the great canal, which drains a large reclaimed tidal area stretching some 25 miles into the interior, comes to the sea; the land was below high tide level and the locks were always opened at low tide to let the drainage out and closed as the tide rose to keep the sea out.

He replied very simply about as follows: "We got back to Nieuport and opened the locks so that the sea could flood the land in advance of the Germans. We had about 40,000 men left. We held the locks against constant German attack for forty-eight hours before we had to ask for help. The French promised us reinforcements the next day. They promised them every day for eleven days. Finally, reinforcements came. That allowed us to pull out our men and re-form. We had only 20,000 unwounded men left. We rebuilt the Army and took on the job again." And there they were.

For a period in the afternoon the King had something else to do. I visited with the children. They had made a collection of fragments of shells which had exploded nearby with the dates all carefully marked.

THE COMMISSION FOR RELIEF IN BELGIUM,
LONDON, AUGUST 24, 1916

The King expressed a wish to give me some decoration, as he said, "Just to assure you of our devotion." I explained my democratic feelings about such things, and he fully understood.

At the end of September (1916), on one of my perpetual North Sea crossings, I came to the Hook of Holland from Brussels to take the Dutch boat for Harwich. The requirement was as usual to be on board in the evening as the boat left at daylight. One slept comfortably at least until then.

Late next morning I was awakened by a gruff voice telling me in German to keep still. The man wore the uniform of a German marine. As he pointed a revolver with the seeming calibre of a beer glass I had no inclination to raise a disturbance. He seemed wholly disinclined to carry on a conversation, but every little while repeated his words of little comfort. Combining feeble German with gestures, I suggested that I might ring the bell over the bunk. To this he made no ultra-violent objection. When the Dutch steward arrived, he informed me that we had been captured at daylight by the Germans and taken into Zeebrugge. So far as I was concerned it had been a most peaceable battle. With the steward as a messenger to the German officer in command I obtained the privilege of getting up and going on deck in search of breakfast. There I found that we were in Zeebrugge harbor, surrounded by four or five German destroyers. All the passengers except myself and an elderly Dutch gentleman had been crowded onto the stern deck and were being examined one by one by two German officers seated behind tables. One of the officers asked if I were Mr. Hoover. On my reply he courteously told me that we would be delayed some hours, but that when they were done with their search of the mail and passengers we would be allowed to proceed to England.

The German officer sent for me later and explained that they were going to intern some thirty English passengers—part of whom were escaped prisoners from Germany and five civilians who had wives with them. The wives were insisting upon going with their husbands. Would I persuade them not to? They would be in separate internment camps for months or perhaps years. I did my best, but the two who had children at home were the only ones who could be persuaded. But the others were forcibly left on our boat. The parting of these women from their husbands was a scene in keeping with the universal tragedy of war.

When the search was over and we were waiting for a signal to depart I was standing with the Dutch gentleman observing proceedings from the upper deck. Suddenly an explosion broke in our faces and my companion fell in a heap. It flashed through my mind that we were being fired upon from the shore. Then a Dutch sailor yelled "Aeroplane!" I looked up to see a French plane circling over us, kindly dropping a bomb each time it came around. It came around five times. The first bomb had struck the bow of a barge fifty feet away, and the Dutch passenger had been slightly hurt with splinters. My neck had a crick in it for a week from the earnestness of my interest in the next four rounds from that plane. The bombs did not strike either us or the German destroyers, but the expectation that the aim would be better next time was absorbing.

In January, 1917, on what turned out to be the last return trip I was to make from Belgium during the war, I went to the Hook of Holland to take the Dutch boat for Tilbury. The Dutch maintained only one steamer in service at one time and the price of passage and mail probably paid for a boat each trip. As each boat in rotation was sunk by mines or other accidents of war, they substituted another one. Those of the crew who survived took up their duties on the succeeding ship. In forty crossings I managed to avoid playing a role in a tragedy of the North Sea, but after several boats were lost I became less and less satisfied with the mathematical theory of chances.

I had established a procedure of paying the steward for my cabin and meals at the end of the voyage. On boarding the boat this time I congratulated the steward on his having escaped from the sinking of the steamer *Queen*, which had gone down some days before. As I ate breakfast he continued to stand around, first on one foot and then on another. Finally he blurted out, "You must pay cash." I protested in pained tones that he was an old friend of mine, that he and I had been traveling together for over two years, that I had always paid generously, and that it hurt me to feel that I had lost his confidence. His encouraging reply was, "Well, ten passengers were drowned on the *Queen*, and they owed me sixty-five guilders. I can't take any more risks."

CHAPTER 19

LIVING WITH THE GERMANS

Trying to do anything for the civilians of a belligerent nation in the midst of any army of occupation is an exacting job. And the German army had special qualities of its own. Most of them were just the human qualities which armies always exhibit to civilians. Some of them were manifestations of the inquiring turn of mind which marks that race, some of them outcroppings of their convictions that they were a master race. And some of their actions, such as the massacre of hostages at Dinant, were wicked beyond any description. And all of them were dominated by the fact that war was the business of the German army. War is not an afternoon tea party.

However, our problem with them was to live, have our being, feed the Belgians, and see that the Germans did not absorb the food.

The high German officials faithfully carried out the agreements I had made in Berlin in early 1915. One of our problems solved at that time was the designation of a German reserve liaison officer at Brussels and at the German Charleville headquarters with whom we should deal. They delegated a Colonel Marx at Brussels and two German officers—Major von Kessler and Count V. Wengersky at Charleville— to attend exclusively to our matters.

I established an "Ambassador" at Charleville, who lived with the German staff. I chose Dr. Vernon Kellogg for this uncomfortable job. He had graduated from a leading German University and was respected throughout that country as a leading American scientist. His knowledge of the German language and German life proved invaluable. One of his first arrangements was to secure the appointment of German liaison officers in each of the ten districts into which we had divided the army zones. These men were soon known to our staff as the "nurses." They proved to be good helpers, and learning of the nickname they adopted it also. They were business men in civilian life and naturally they grew interested in this work. Moreover, life in the towns with comfortable beds was far more attractive than in the front line trenches. Also, our boys kept them supplied with bacon and hams— the final word in luxury. We had stipulated that if any one of these "nurses" proved unsatisfactory to us, the Germans would remove him and send another man. That helped to keep their work up to the passing mark.

Our difficulties were with minor German officers and officials. They were often not in tune with the top officials. As to food, all soldiers have money and they were sometimes hungry. Our systematic rationing made it hard for them to get much. But when armies are in action they take everything they can use, from chickens to flour mills. If they are scrupulous armies, they pay. But even if they pay, it diminishes the food supply just so much. Therefore there were constant incidents, some little, some big, arising from irresponsible action of local officers.

And we were plagued by the bootlegging of food from Holland. True, it was an addition to the Belgian supply, but it sold for twenty times the price of our rations. Only German officers and rich Belgians got it. But this little trickle of food and occasional seizures were confused with our operations by casual observers especially the British and French spies. They gave us no end of trouble disproving their charges both of corruption and of the Germans getting our food.

Ultimately we established an agreement that Germany should replace these minor amounts of food bought or taken by their people. But it worked with groans and pains when we came to settlements. In time, however, the Germans got used to us and allowed us to make our own estimates. After all, the amounts were very small compared to the quantities which we were handling or the volume of food in Germany. A ton of flour will make a lot of sandwiches.

The pompous von Bissing, Governor of Belgium, in June, 1915, three months after my agreement in Berlin, issued orders in entire violation of this agreement by placing restrictions upon the movements of our American staff. Sir Edward Grey as the result of reports from the British Intelligence sent me a note on these von Bissing emanations, laid down in detail the British idea of freedom of action by the Relief as a part of enforcement of the guarantees, and generally expressed his views on the German Governor. I sent the correspondence to Ambassador Gerard at Berlin. As a result von Bissing promptly addressed a recantation to Mr. Whitlock and announced his full agreement to all points. This transaction did not increase his affection for me.

The delegation of German officers to our different departments served to diminish German snooping and espionage of our work. These officers—most of them—proved cooperative. Colonel Marx, who looked after our affairs in Brussels, one day mentioned to me that his son, a captain, had been either killed or captured in a certain action on the Russian front, and that they had heard nothing of him since. He added that the uncertainty was a great strain on the boy's mother, who was not in good health. At the next opportunity I telegraphed to the American Ambassador at St. Petersburg, asking him to make some inquiries. In due time I was able to report to the Colonel that his son had been wounded, hospitalized, recovered, was in such and such a prison camp; and I even conveyed a message from him to his father and we periodically remitted small sums to the boy through Americans in St. Petersburg. The old Colonel was our undying friend thereafter. Indeed, he played a part in our rescue from a very embarrassing major quandary.

We had, in our Rotterdam office, a young American whom I will call Schmultz. He sometimes brought mail and messages across the frontier to our Antwerp and Brussels offices. In Belgium he naturally gossiped a good deal with our men. One day the German General Staff at Charleville indignantly notified Dr. Kellogg that our Americans were engaged in espionage. They would give no details or names, but demanded a removal of the entire American personnel from Belgium and France. Mr. Gibson telegraphed me to come over at once to Brussels from London as disaster stared us in the face. On arrival I went to see Colonel Marx. Next day he brought me the report of the German Intelligence Service which had generated the whole storm. It appeared that Schmultz, who had German leanings, had listened to any and all off-hand anti-German remarks of our men and reported them to German Intelligence, with embroidery. I found only six out of our sixty Americans were even represented as having made offensive remarks.

With the help of Major von Kessler at the General Staff and Colonel Marx in Brussels, we reduced the general order of expulsion to the six men in question. Then Marx and von Kessler undertook to interview them and also Schmultz. Even then there was no color of espionage about the words or actions of our men—just anti-German gabble. But they had proved that they were not "safe" men for our purposes, and I sent them back to America. I directed Schmultz to come to our London office. The moment he landed in England, Scotland Yard, at our request, arrested him and ordered him deported through Liverpool. He spent an unhappy week in a British jail, with constant assurances from some of our staff that he would probably be executed in the Tower. He reached New York, but I never heard of him again.

Under our agreements we were to have all the farmers' surplus production from the Army zones in Belgium and Northern France as well as in the "occupied" area of Belgium. However, it proved quite unworkable for the Americans and our local committees to requisition and collect the native farm produce in the different army zones—which were, virtually, in the midst of battle. Dr. Kellogg and I arrived at an agreement at Charleville in respect to the 1915 crop in the areas by which the German army in those areas requisitioned the farmers' surplus and used it on the spot, they giving us from stocks in Germany an amount which we jointly agreed was fair. The British approved this agreement.

Everything went smoothly in this particular until we arrived in sight of the harvest in the summer of 1916, when a storm blew up. The problem was also complicated by the fact that the Germans had planted many abandoned farms. Our men, together with our Belgian and French committees in those areas, estimated the surplus crop. The Germans did not agree with our conclusions on the quantity that should be handed to us in compensation from Germany. The British and French Intelligence, no doubt on information of the French and Belgian Committee members, promptly reported our dispute to their home governments. In the middle of our negotiations both these governments blew off in the press as to this proposed German atrocity— which did not help.

There was a serious difference. The German army's estimate was equal to about $40,000,000 less food than we contended for. At this point I went to Charleville to join Dr. Kellogg in the discussion. We were unable to agree with General von Sauberzweig, the Quartermaster General. Believing we could do better with the top officials in Berlin we settled with the General that we would all meet in the Esplanade Hotel in Berlin a few days later—on August 4—and thrash it out at the top.

Before we left Charleville one of the German staff colonels asked us if we would like to see the big battle which was raging on the Somme. The proposal was somewhat startling but being of an inquiring mind, Dr. Kellogg and I accepted. We motored for several hours to a point near a hilltop observation post in the forest, a distance back from the forward trenches and a mile or two away from the main roads. During the last few miles an occasional shell cracked nearby but the ingenious camouflage of the road—to the extent of a false parallel—seemed to give protection to our route. At the post the constant rumble of artillery seemed to pulverize the air. Seen through powerful glasses, in the distant view lay the unending blur of trenches, of volcanic explosions of dust which filled the air where over a length of sixty miles a million and a half men were fighting and dying. Once in a while, like ants, the lines of men seemed to show through the clouds of dust. Here under the thunder and belching volcanoes of 10,000 guns, over the months of this battle, the lives of Germans and Englishmen were thrown away. On the nearby road unending lines of Germans plodded along the right side to the front, not with drums and bands, but in the silence of sodden resignation. Down the left side came the unending lines of wounded men, the "walking cases," staggering among cavalcades of ambulances. A quarter of a million men died and it was but one battle in that war.

The horror of it all did not in the least affect the German officers in the post. To them it was pure mechanics. The battle had already been raging for days. Not one of the Germans showed the slightest anxiety. They said that the British were losing two to one—butting their heads against a stone wall. And that was true. It was all a horrible, devastating reality, no romance, no glory.

Dr. Kellogg and I duly arrived at the Esplanade Hotel. There, on the following morning we met General von Sauberzweig, and Major von Kessler. There was no food shortage at the Esplanade although there could be a shortage of cash to pay the price of it. The officers informed us that they would take our matter up in conference with the ministers and other authorities and meet us at the hotel later. We were disappointed not to be allowed to present our case ourselves especially as we knew Minister Lewald would be there.

At four o'clock the General and the Major returned. Dr. Kellogg has described this meeting in his book *Fighting Starvation in Belgium*. My notes and recollection differ only on some immaterial points. The General seemed upset and promptly ordered a whisky and soda. The Major who spoke perfect English gave us the news of the conference. It was bad. The authorities had decided that they would make no compromise with our estimates. Worse still, they had discussed the whole question of abolishing the Commission. The Major said that it looked bad for us. He added that several of the generals had made violent speeches directed at us. Only Lewald spoke for us. Our espionage case and matter published at this time in the British newspapers had roiled them; most of them had determined that they had better throw out the Commission and blast the British for the blockade generally. They said it was no worse for Belgians and French to starve than for Germans to starve. We naturally disavowed any responsibility for the remarks of the British and French. We urged the whole case of the Belgians and Northern French over again. The General took his nth whisky.

Then there came one of those unforgettable episodes. After we were told that the relief was probably all over, von Kessler apologetically mentioned that the General was greatly broken up by the news he had just received that his son had been permanently blinded in a gas attack on the Western Front. I expressed sympathy for this tragedy. The General, who had still another drink, then went into a monologue about the war. He said that civilians were messing into it too much and that it was no longer a soldiers' war with manly weapons. Civilians had made these poison gases. They were engaged in many activities which they should keep out of—probably meaning us.

He grew vehement on the starving of German women and children by the blockade "and then, there was the case of that Cavell woman." He seemed to want to elaborate on that. We expressed interest. He said she had organized an espionage group of a thousand Belgian women. He said he had warned them. He had punished some of them mildly. They would not stop. He was compelled as a soldier to make an example and stop it. He had her tried, she confessed, and as a soldier he was compelled to execute her to protect the German army. He had been "painted as a monster all over the world." He said he "was called a murderer; a second Duke of Alva." The neutral peoples think "I am the most infamous of men."

I had thought von Bissing, the Governor of Belgium, was responsible for the horror of Miss Cavell's execution. But I confirmed afterward that it was this General von Sauberzweig. He was temporary military Governor at that time.

As he mumbled along I had a thought. The General obviously did not like the kind of publicity he had received in the neutral world. The Relief was apparently about to blow up. I said to Dr. Kellogg that I wanted to make a further statement to the General about the whole relief matter and asked him to translate fully. I said that the conclusion of the German authorities would mean death for millions of people, mostly children; that as he was responsible officer he would be portrayed to the world as a monster infinitely bigger and blacker than the picture they drew of him after the Cavell incident. I elaborated the theme to cover the whole German army. And as my temperature rose I emphasized this theme so strongly that Kellogg hesitated to translate my language and said so. But Major von Kessler injected that he would translate. And he did it with no reservations. It appeared that he had been fighting our battle all day and was himself in no good humor. The General made no immediate reply. Then suddenly he remarked that there might be something in what I said. Whether it was the threat, the whisky, or his grief, or the human appeal that had moved him, I do not know. He directed von Kessler to inform Minister Lewald that he thought the negotiation ought to continue. He would be obliged if the Minister would take the matter in hand and settle it.

We broke up at once and with von Kessler went to the Ministry. Lewald seemed relieved to hear von Kessler's authorization.

We settled in half an hour on a basis of a part reduction in our estimates to "save face." The Minister said that he would draft a letter and
asked us to wait. When we received the draft document it was obviously
written for publication, as two-thirds of it was a blast against the British
and the inhumane effect of the blockade on German women and children. I suggested that he change a line in the last third so as to make
clear that we were not the object of the blast. He studied the text for a
few moments and said with good humor approximately this: "Let us
cut out the whole of that part anyway—we will answer the British with
bullets." Dr. Kellogg and I hurried out of Berlin within an hour for
fear that our opponents in the Army might try to call the letter back
and change the terms.

The battle was not entirely over, for the British military authorities
growled at the acceptance of our estimate; but again our staunch friend
Lord Eustace Percy in the Foreign Office softened the lion. As a matter
of fact it turned out that we got more than the Germans were able
to collect from the French farmers.

One day during 1916 I was at Namur to straighten out some tangle
of relief, which required that I call on the German colonel who was
governor of the Province. Incidentally, he had been for years an important official in a large American manufacturing company and had been
called back to Germany for Army service. After we had disposed of our
business, he mentioned that a wounded British officer—a major—was
slowly dying at the German army hospital at that place. He said that
the officer was anxious to see someone who could give a personal message to his father in England. The colonel suggested that perhaps I
would see him. I visited him at the hospital and took notes of his
tender and personal messages.

When I returned to London I gave these messages to Edgar Rickard,
who sent for the father and transmitted them. The old gentleman was
greatly affected and expressed much appreciation of our action. When,
some weeks later, I visited Namur again, the German governor recalled
the incident and told me that the surgeons had performed an operation
of desperation on the British officer, that he had recovered and had
been sent, a few days before, to a prison camp. When I returned to
London I asked Edgar to send for the father and give him this joyous

message. The old gentleman, no doubt under shock, bristled with indignation saying: "You Yankees may think that was a good joke. Do you know that we have just had a great memorial service for my son?"

Late in 1916, I went to the German Headquarters at Charleville to join Dr. Kellogg in settling some questions of transportation in the military zones where we were held up more often than we thought necessary by army movements. While there we were invited to dine at a Staff mess. There were present General von Freytag, the new Quartermaster General, and various lesser lights. Some one of them asked us to explain what the Americans meant by German militarism. Dr. Kellogg subsequently published a little book entitled *Headquarters Nights* in which he gave the spirited dialogue on militarism and democracy.

At this visit, Count Wengersky and Major von Kessler thought it would smooth our transport troubles if the great Generals in command of armies had some personal contact with us. They arranged an invitation for us to dine with General von Rentlen at his Headquarters in Sedan. The Germans provided automobiles and on our arrival we were quartered in some Frenchman's former residence. Soon after Wengersky came in all ruffled up and said that news of President Wilson's latest sharp note had just been received by the General and his staff, and that they were violent. He thought that we ought to get ill and go back at once. I told him that the General might call off his dinner if he liked; I would not do it. The Major was greatly disturbed, as he had arranged the session and found himself in something of a hole. He feared that some hot junior officer might offer an insult to us, that we would flare back, and generally it would be a mess. However, the General was polite but very stiff, the Staff was distrait, but nothing untoward happened. We did talk of the problems of transportation of our supplies in the area of the General's command. He agreed to give orders, which he did, that except for urgent military movements our railway cars should have priority. The General suggested that we persuade the French people to move back at least ten or twelve miles from the front. They were often killed under fire. We assured him we had been trying to do that for two years but the attachment of the French peasants and villagers for their homes was such that when we did get them back they would run away and return. Out of solicitude for these people themselves, we later on simply had to refuse food to the villagers unless they would move back.

General von Rentlen struck me as a highly intellectual man. He had none of the characteristics of the popularized figure of a Prussian officer. He expressed resentment at Allied reports that his troops were shelling the Cathedral of Rheims. He said that the great cathedrals were the cultural property of the world; but that the French constantly used its towers for observation and that the German artillerymen sometimes passed them a small shell to warn them. Apparently this resolution did not hold, for two years later I found the Cathedral almost destroyed. The General looked at the war in an objective way but was nevertheless convinced that the British were trying to destroy Germany and that his race had its back to the wall. And having spent these years on both sides of the front I can say that is the sum of belief of most soldiers on both sides.

There exists a vast literature upon German atrocities in Belgium and France. It is mostly the literature of propaganda. Even Lord Bryce was drawn into it—and greatly exaggerated it. He invited me to lunch one day and urged me to give him a statement for publication. Being a reasonable man, he finally agreed that to do this would make it impossible for me to do any more relief work on territory held by the Germans. However, I never found much foundation for the stories of individual outrage or cruelty. Things were done, however, by order of superior officers which to me were far worse. The wholesale execution of civilian hostages at Dinant and Tamines, and the burning of whole villages and the library and church of St. Pierre at Louvain are examples. And it can be said for the Germans that in the horrible case of Dinant the German colonel was dismissed, and a German court of inquiry delivered a scorching denunciation of the act. It can be repeated as a generalization that armies in action are not guests at afternoon receptions. Every army has a percentage of criminally minded, and the abolition of moral restraints in war is scarcely calculated to lift their souls into the realm of idealism.

CHAPTER 20

TROUBLE IN
THE UNITED STATES SENATE

Prior to the British negotiations in February, 1915, I had taken up with Ambassador Page the whole question of our contacts and negotiations with the belligerent governments. We were a great bother to our patron Ambassadors and to their legation staffs in making appointments, attending conferences, securing of visas, ship passes, and a hundred other details, to say nothing of major negotiations with top officials. Page and the Spanish and the Netherlands Ambassadors at once agreed that I should set up my own direct relations with government officials and the Ambassadors would help when things went wrong.

In 1915, a discharged and consequently aggrieved member of the Commission lodged a formal complaint with the American State Department that I was constantly violating the Logan Act of a hundred years ago which made negotiations in governmental matters by private citizens with foreign governments a crime. He also thought that through our organization we were violating George Washington's injunction against entanglements in Europe. Knowing that our State Department knew all about it I paid no attention to the matter until Colonel House advised Mr. Page that Senator Lodge was making investigations and preparing an attack upon me and our work as a violation of the law and a dangerous "involvement" of the United States.

The maintenance of public confidence and good will in the United States and over the world was the very life-blood of our work; in this area lay the safety of the Belgians and the Northern French. I feared such stuff as Lodge had in mind might, in the hands of the sensational press, do us irreparable injury among neutrals, and give a weapon to the militarist groups in Britain and Germany to attack us. I may have been overfearful but under John White's (he was now in charge of our New York office) urging I sailed for New York (May 7, 1915). I at once consulted Melville Stone, General Manager of the Associated Press, who agreed such an attack would do great damage to our prestige and our flow of charity. He took the matter in hand and the next evening assembled at dinner every leading New York publisher or editor, and the heads of the other press agencies. I described the whole relief operation, how it grew up, and my present difficulty. Frank Cobb of the New York *World* made a few "remarks" to the effect that America for a hundred years should be proud of what we were doing and he was sure the group there before him could take care of any little matter like that by a notice of counterattack—which they all applauded. I suggested my situation was akin to Caesar's wife's and, while defense was fine, what I wanted was to stop the attack and that if somebody could let the Senator know their attitude, he might desist. Mr. Stone agreed to do this. The next morning I went to Washington to see Secretary of State Lansing. He greeted me with the remark, "Have you prepared your soul for a thousand years in jail?"

During this visit to Washington I received great encouragement from Secretary of Interior Lane and Secretary of Agriculture Houston, to whom I was introduced by Secretary Lansing as good counsellors. There began a friendship with these men which lasted as long as they lived. With their advice, I settled on a plan which required the co-operation of President Wilson. Secretary Lane took me to see him.

The President listened to my difficulties with amusement (as he hated Lodge) and showed considerable knowledge of what we had been doing in Europe. I suggested that it would lend prestige and probably head off the whole trouble if he would appoint an outstanding committee to represent us in the United States. The President responded in a most generous manner. He issued a public statement of the highest commendation for the Commission and announced the selection of a "New York Advisory Committee" of men whose background could not be challenged—such as Robert Fulton Cutting, Alexander Hemphill, Chairman of the Guaranty Trust Company, Otto T. Bannard, Chairman of the New York Trust Company, S. R. Bertron, a leading

New York Democrat, Oscar Straus, former Republican Secretary of Commerce, Melville Stone, and John White of our own staff.

Stone having informed me that Lodge was even more on the war path after the President's statement, I concluded to beard the Senator himself. I went to Boston to see him. He kept me waiting an hour after the appointed time, although no other visitor came or went. He threw out a chilly, what-do-you-mean-young-man atmosphere before I could get in a word. He said he knew all about what we were doing and asked by what right I, a private American citizen, made agreements with a belligerent government which might involve the United States in serious controversies. He continued that probably I did not know that there was a law on the statute books making any such action by an American citizen a penitentiary crime. I responded that I knew the law but that we were acting under the patronage and with the approval of the American Ambassadors, whose relation to the matter was in turn approved by our Government; that these were not agreements between a belligerent government and the United States but that they were with a purely private neutral organization; and that moreover we were acting under the approval of other great neutral governments which were also our patrons. Lodge insisted that even so, I was on very dangerous personal ground and that he did not approve of our Government's involving itself even morally in undertakings which, in effect, modified the rules of international law as applied to the blockade and to war. I suggested to him that assuming his interpretations were all valid, I was sure the American people would not be adverse to saving the lives of ten million people even by such means. I mentioned in support of this view the meeting Mr. Stone had arranged for me with the press. He inquired who were present, and I took pleasure in telling him and relating to him the particular assurance I had had from them.

The Senator had been misinformed and I came away confident that nothing would happen.

The next day I received an invitation from former President Theodore Roosevelt to come to Oyster Bay for lunch. Mr. Stone had inspired it. After my experiences with his great friend Senator Lodge, I was not expecting much from that meeting, especially as President Wilson's statement commending the Relief had been issued to the press. But the former President said that he wanted to tell me that if the Democrats made any trouble for me, he would "go at 'em." I told him of my experience with Lodge. He laughed uproariously and opined that Lodge could see "involvements" in Europe under every bush but that "I will hold his hand." He further observed that I need have no fear that Lodge would break out. "The courage of any political official is stronger in his office than in the newspapers."

Mr. Roosevelt kept me most of the afternoon—making havoc of several appointments. He continued as my warm supporter to his death.

CHAPTER 21

SOME PERSONAGES IN THE RELIEF

Our most intimate supporter was the American Ambassador in London. Almost from the beginning of the war and certainly after the *Lusitania* sinking (May, 1915), Mr. Page was ardently for American intervention on the side of the Allies. I disagreed with him about getting into the war at all, but his was a tolerant mind so that he forgave my difference of opinions. He was one of those blossoms of American life which justify our civilization. When I put down that he was a great mind, a distinguished scholar, a great editor, the soul of intellectual honesty, a man of sympathy and kindness, unbreakable in friendship, almost fanatically devoted to service of his country, I feel that I am writing the presentation paragraph for an honorary college degree. Yet this praise can be written of him with more fidelity than of any other American that I have ever known. He died six weeks after the Armistice. During the reaction from the war which came in after years he was unjustly blamed. It was not Page who took America into war; it was the Germans.

Dr. Henry van Dyke, our Minister to Holland, was one of my trials. No doubt he was a very fine poet and successful in description of the birds and the bees. He felt a great need for publicity. He often suggested that we should get his name more often into the news dispatches. Our ships all came into Holland for reloading to Belgium, and for that reason he deemed he was a vital sentinel standing guard over our life line. As he proved short of the business experience needed for routine negotiations with the Netherlands Foreign Office, we evaded him entirely by securing from Foreign Minister Loudon (one of our patrons) that the Dutch Government set up a liaison officer in our Rotterdam office. Van Dyke had an "insatiable curiosity" and was constantly demanding that our overworked personnel at Rotterdam take the tedious trip to The Hague to "report." He chiefly wanted any gossip about the Germans which they might have heard in Belgium or Northern France

One night at about midnight I landed at the Hook of Holland en route to Berlin. The direct Berlin train left the next morning. At the dock was the American Consul with an urgent message from van Dyke, demanding that I take the night train at once to The Hague as he had most important matters to discuss. I protested that I would only arrive at four o'clock in the morning and that I would need to leave The Hague at five again in order to make connections to Berlin and I would get no sleep. The Consul called the Legation on the telephone to say this and to ask how urgent the matter was. He was told that the Minister was waiting up and that it was imperative and could not be discussed on the telephone. I did not believe it—but went. When I arrived he at once demanded—"What are you going to Berlin for? I will have you know that you cannot be travelling around Holland without reporting to me. What are you doing?" It was right there that for once I proved myself a patient and polite person, for I answered courteously but without explanations. Neither any of our staff nor I ever went near him again despite his stentorian orders. It was of him that Hugh Gibson coined that famous line—"Van Dyke is the only man in the diplomatic service who can strut sitting down."

Before I met James W. Gerard, the American Ambassador to Germany, he had been painted to me as a typical Tammany lawyer, whose appointment had been imposed upon an unwilling President by a crooked political machine. Instead of a callous ogre I found a man of polished attainments, of fine intellectual insight, helpful, courageous, who at once inspired confidence in his fine integrity. When I first called at his Embassy, early in 1915, he met me at the door and said at once: "We are all for you here. What can we do?"

I have recounted elsewhere the negotiations of that period with the Germans. Gerard opened every official door in Berlin for me and did not leave me on the doorstep. He brought skill and, where necessary, real punch to our negotiations. At all times, until he was recalled from Germany at our entry into the war, he stood ready to catch the ball and run with it. Whenever he smelled danger he acted without our having to appeal to him. He sought no publicity out of our activities but did at every turn single-mindedly seek the success of our work.[1]

Our Ambassador to France, William G. Sharp, was an amiable man. He was most friendly but a timid man. Unlike Gerard, he would never take the initiative on our behalf. The cause of his unwillingness to introduce me to the French Minister of Foreign Affairs was timidity, not unfriendliness. He was a man of much horse sense. He had been a Congressman. He spoke no French: he had no French friends of any consequence. Mr. Wilson seemed to ignore him by doing all of his negotiations through the French Ambassador in Washington. He was always plaintively asking: "What's going on?" Generally, he was an example of a thoroughly good, honest American come to his reward for party service, but totally out of place as a wartime Ambassador in one of the most important capitals in the world. He was enormously pleased when the Legion d'Honneur was conferred upon him by the French. I had always had a stiff prejudice against Americans being beguiled in this fashion. When he elaborated to me on the superlative distinction that had come to him, I could not help suggesting that he deserved a higher rank in the order than the one to which he was assigned because Minister Boret, who had charge of such matters, had told me that over 800,000 had been issued in that group.

Minister Brand Whitlock in Belgium was helpful. Whitlock was, however, a poet by nature and a novelist by profession. He had dabbled in local politics and learned the value of "press." But he was really a sensitive soul and shrank from the rough stuff of dealing with the German officials. Keenly aware of the drama of events around him, he devoted many hours a day to writing and polishing his voluminous journal. Parts of it were subsequently published and it is a good piece of work. He had a great sense of word pictures. While he remained in Belgium he wrote the greater part of two novels and also some poetry. Most of the Relief men never saw him. In fact, he never really knew what the Relief Commission was doing. For over two and a half years, the Embassy and the offices of the Commission were less than a mile

[1] Our minds differed on politics after the war was over, but I am glad to say that through twenty-five years this fact has never jarred our mutual affection.

apart, yet I believe that he visited our shop only once. His journal is therefore naturally deficient in any authentic record of our doings. This is not said in criticism, but merely as an indication of his dislike of dealing with hard things; and food administration is hard stuff, involving little drama. Whitlock came to think that I was pretty rough, for at times he had to be jolted to make him act.

We found that we could make more progress with the Germans either through direct approach or through Hugh Gibson, and when we needed still more power we came to rely upon the Spanish Minister, the Marquis de Villalobar. The Marquis was in fact very much more industrious in getting relief started than Whitlock, to whom it all appeared confused and unreal. A tragic instance of Whitlock's natural sensitiveness occurred when he insisted that Gibson substitute for him in the protest at Miss Cavell's execution. The Spanish Minister did not hesitate to go in person and protest. And Gibson did everything humanly possible.

Villalobar, together with the Spanish Ambassador in London and the Dutch officials, was to become the sole reliance of the Relief after the United States declared war. Villalobar was of perpetual interest to me. He had been born of an important Spanish family but a monstrosity, with stump legs and arms, without ears or hair. The family had kept him hidden away with a tutor who must have been of unusual character. He gave a unique education to an extraordinarily intelligent crippled boy who was in time able to secure artificial parts for his deficiencies. He secured a junior position in the Spanish Foreign Office and rose on sheer ability to be an Ambassador. He was most formal, always immaculately dressed, indicated little of his disabilities—and did not much like Americans. But he was devoted to the Belgian Relief.

Hugh Gibson's energetic work not only in relief but in the other functions of our Legation stirred up a subconscious jealousy of him in Whitlock which later became evident through statements which appeared when the Minister's journal was published.

Gibson early demonstrated that courage and ability which brought him to the top of the career men in our diplomatic service. To those who knew his devotion in carrying the major burden of our Legation at Brussels, and his constant effort to protect and support his chief,

Whitlock's published journal was a painful exhibit, and left the Minister a smaller man in public esteem than he deserved to be. For Whitlock was a good American. At the Armistice he sought promotion from President Wilson to an Ambassadorship in some other country and asked me to intervene for him, which I did. But the President did not seem to want his larger services. He made Gibson an Ambassador.

The Spanish Ambassador in London was also one of our props in times of trouble. A stately man, who never wanted details, just saying "What can I do about it?" Many times he sent communications supporting us to the other Spanish Ambassadors in Europe.

Another of our strengths was Johan Loudon, Foreign Minister of the Netherlands. He was in every respect a cultivated and able man. Moreover, he was ever ready to enter any fray.

Outstanding among the Belgians in our organization were Emile Francqui and Firman van Bree. Francqui became the real leader of the Belgians of his period. He was a gruff, rather unsympathetic personality. He had a quickness and adroitness of mind equal to any sort of intellectual battle. He was a natural administrator. He was at times difficult to co-operate with. Our men in Belgium often came to grips with him and at times his temperament put a good deal of strain upon me as he usually demanded the removal of men who did not wholly agree with him. But he proved to have within himself a devotion to his countrymen seldom equaled in men. He not only brought his great talents to the Relief but in later years represented the Belgians at the Peace Conference and at every other important international negotiation until his death.

Francqui had immense courage, and the Germans were in a constant quiver as to whether he was not more valuable to them in an internment camp. He had a great sense of humor. On one occasion I needed him badly in negotiations with the French and Belgian Governments. He sought a permit to visit an invalid son in England, which was true. The Germans refused to allow him to go out of Belgium, fearing that he might do them damage if he stayed out. They finally agreed he could go if a bond of 1,500,000 francs was put up for his return in ten days. We put up the bond. Francqui facetiously complained that it was an insult as it was an undervaluation of the damage he would do them if he was outside Belgium. Anyway, he overstayed his leave for a week, with the observation that if it was worth 1,500,000 francs to have him back, they would, no doubt, welcome him any time.

At last he arrived with his automobile late one evening at the Dutch-Belgian frontier. The frontier consisted of a gate across the highway with a Dutch guard on one side and a German on the other. Francqui stopped his car on the Dutch side and went into the German commandant's office to present his passport. The Colonel promptly arrested him, and he was marched into the guard-house with half a dozen German soldiers to make sure of him. The Colonel said he would attend to his case in the morning, and Francqui was destined to spend the night on a hard bench. He lighted a cigar and then, as an afterthought, drew out two more cigars and supplied two of the guards therewith. He apologized profusely at his inability to supply each one of them but added he had a whole box in his automobile if he could go through the gate to get it. There was general approval. Passing through the gate, he secured the box, handed it to the Dutch guard with directions to hand it to the Germans, entered his automobile, and returned to Rotterdam and a comfortable bed. From that vantage point we successfully negotiated his return, subject to no arrest and no forfeiture of the bond.

The other outstanding Belgian in our work was Firman van Bree, who was secretary of the organization in Belgium. He was more than a secretary in American terms. He was the effective administrator. A man of fine personality, education and devotion, he was a favorite of all our Americans—and their friend and defender in all their troubles. Besides he was a great *bon vivant* who kept a cook who could make a banquet out of relief rations—and his rare wine cellar.

And what shall I say of our American staff? They were all volunteers with at most travelling expenses for some of the youngsters. This work was no joy ride. For men to volunteer is in itself a tribute to character and idealism. And some of them continued over the whole four years. Edgar Rickard and John White not only continued to direct one or another of our important offices over the whole four years life of the Relief, but went on as volunteers in the Food Administration. Men who presided over our important offices during the two and a half years were: Prentiss Gray, Walter Brown, William Honnold and William Poland. Of other office heads, Vernon Kellogg, Oscar Crosby, Lindon Bates, Albert Connett, Millard Shaler, Daniel Heineman, John Lucey, and Carl Young served for substantial periods. All these men were engineers, except one. I could pay a special tribute to each of them. The other staff comprised over 300 volunteers for longer or shorter periods. Among those who subsequently made a mark in the world were: Hallam Tuck, Edward Hunt, Will Irwin, Tracy Kittredge, Charles Leach, Robert McCarter, Sidney Mitchell, Maurice Pate, William Percy, Gardner Richardson, Alfred Ruddock, Edwin Shattuck, John Simpson, Dorsey Stephens, Gilchrist Stockton, Lewis Strauss, Ben Allen, Frank Angell, Foster Bain, Oliver Carmichael, Alfred Fletcher, John Gade, Joseph Green, Warren Gregory, Emil Holman, and John Glenn. But the others were no less worthy, including over thirty who rose from privates to officers in the American Army.[2]

[2] As a commentary on all these 300 men, I may mention that on the final liquidation of the Commission I set up a fund to be used for any of them who, through bad luck, might fall upon evil times. At this date—30 years later—with no additions except interest, the fund is much larger than when it started. Obviously, they were a self-supporting group.

CHAPTER 22

SOME FAMILY AND
AMERICAN DIPLOMATIC MATTERS
AND COLONEL HOUSE

Mrs. Hoover, after having taken the boys to California in October, 1914, and planting them in school under the eyes and care of our professor neighbors at Stanford, returned to London early in December. She intrepidly defied the dangers of the North Sea and went with me on my second journey to Brussels, where we arrived just before Christmas. She visited every sort of relief activity. On Christmas Day she attended the special service at the shrine of all troubled Belgians—the Cathedral of St. Gudule. The hundreds of women in the deepest of mourning, the emotional response of the great audience to the moving prayers of the priest for safety of their loved ones and for delivery from their oppressions, left her greatly affected by the spiritual tragedy which had overwhelmed the Belgian people. Her question was "Do these Germans think they can hold a people whose very souls revolt?"

Our family movements during 1915 were erratic as usual. During the winter Mrs. Hoover decided instead of returning to California to remain in London, and kept the Red House open as a general commissariat for the men coming and going on relief. She also became one of the leading organizers and manager of the American Woman's Hospital which they established at Paignton. That Hospital gave service to thousands of British wounded during the whole period of the War.

At the end of May she had to return home to look after the boys. There, she spent the next months in varied activities among the campus youngsters with camping trips to Yosemite and the mountains.

I had to go to New York in connection with the American end of the Relief operations in October, 1915. Mrs. Hoover and the boys joined me there, and we sailed for Europe on November 9. We did not like to break the American schooling of the boys, but it was difficult to be parted from them for the whole of the war and to have their mother constantly crossing the Atlantic in war times trying to do two jobs. And anyway the boys would get some remote war experience.

Late in 1915 and early in 1916, it was evident that matters relating to Belgium so required my undivided energies that I was not performing any adequate service as an engineer and executive even to the London concerns—not to mention the American, Mexican, South African and Russian mines. Under their added responsibilities, my London staff had developed ample qualities of leadership in those enterprises and my American staff had carried on most capably in New York and San Francisco.

I had struggled for some months in divided mind as to whether to give up my engineering practice completely. This would mean the final sacrifice of great connections for the future. Moreover, the war was constantly offering tremendous business opportunities in view of my familiarity with the raw material sources of the world. However, only one conclusion was possible. Therefore I resigned from every business connection except membership on the Board of the Burma Lead Mines, where I had some personal interest. My share interest in the other concerns was small—our fees were built on percentages of profits—and I cleared them all out.

During 1916, our family movements were again a good deal disjointed. Part of the year Mrs. Hoover and the boys remained in London, although I was seldom there. She had undertaken still more relief responsibilities. With other American women, she had established a knitting factory for the employment of British women who had been left without means of support because of the war. Their products were distributed to needy sailors and soldiers. The ladies also conducted a service for rehabilitation of injured men and for relief of soldiers' wives who, in many cases, did not come easily within the reach of established charities. This bore the intriguing title of the American Women's Committee for Economic Relief. Her greatest activity, however, was the hospital at

Paignton. It was supported, managed and staffed by Americans throughout the war.

The boys attended a small private school nearby and quickly acquired the Oxford accent in full.

The Germans had now begun to drop bombs on London from Zeppelins. One night during a raid, a bomb dropped nearby with a great explosion. Mrs. Hoover ran to the boys' room to gather them up, intending to go into the basement, but their beds were empty. We furiously searched the house from attic to basement, but no boys. It then occurred to me that they sometimes climbed up a ladder through a trap door from the attic onto the roof. Pushing up the trap door, we found them calmly observing the streaming searchlights and the fighting planes. We decided to join them, and behold, we witnessed a Zeppelin brought down in flames north of London. We mentally marked the direction and, as soon as it was daylight, we got out the car and went in search of the wreck. With the help of a friendly policeman, both boys came home with treasured parts of the Zeppelin which clashed with our other household gods for years.

For reasons like this, plus the fact that I had to be on the Continent about two thirds of my time, and also that the boys should wear off the Oxford accent and soak in the American way of life, Mrs. Hoover decided to return with them to California. When she left the Red House for the railway station, we remarked with some sadness that it was probably the last we would see of it—and so it was. The house with its quaint garden in the middle of a great city was a place of many affections, many happy recollections, and of many stimulating discussions.

One of the annual visitors to our home in London was Colonel Edward M. House. He came to Europe on behalf of President Wilson and always spent a good deal of time with me. I was for him a sort of outpost observer of war forces. In fact, I was one of the few Americans constantly moving from one side of the battle line to the other and in constant contact with the high officials. While it was my job to ignore military matters I could not be both dumb and blind to the political forces in motion.

President Wilson's constant purpose from 1914 on was to find some ground upon which the war could be ended. From time to time I furnished the Colonel with memoranda and other information as to peace possibilities which, together with my notes of the time, can be summarized as follows:

The Colonel, at the beginning, was totally ignorant of European politics or the forces moving among the peoples at war. Both President Wilson and the Colonel were living in a stratosphere far above the earthly ground on which the war was being fought. They were exploring negotiated peace with great phrases such as "peace without bitterness," "liberation of nations," "a just peace"; they advocated some sort of "association of nations" to preserve eternal peace. They apparently could not conceive that Europe was not horrified at the deluge of blood and that it must realize and recoil from the abyss upon the edge of which civilization was hanging. They seemed to believe that the national leaders, in their secret hearts, must know that the war was a stalemate and, if eventually, why not now? It was all unreal. The hard facts were that the leaders on both sides had no ideas of a stalemate; they wanted victory; they wanted world power, new territorial possessions. The masses in each country believed that they were fighting for defense of their firesides against monstrous enemies and were going to get full compensation and vengeance upon them.

Although President Wilson was an eminent historian, he did not seem to grasp the fact that the forces in Europe were the distillation of the mores of these widely different peoples, their centuries of dangers, ambitions, wrongs, fears and hates. This war was not just a fortuitous incident apart from the whole inheritance of Europe.

Certainly the foreign offices wanted to please the Colonel, and they were all men trained in that art. The Allied side wanted to get sympathetic aid from American resources and hoped to get the United States to join them in the war. The Germans hoped to keep America neutral and prevent it from giving aid to the Allies. They even hoped to stir up trouble between us and the Allies. Therefore, the officials on all sides listened most respectfully to the Colonel's proposals but gently deferred them.

In the middle of 1915, there sprang up an organized drive in the United States for a negotiated peace to end the war, and great pressures were placed upon the President to "mediate." Many traveling Americans with these views called upon me and seemed to think I was benighted because I was not crying "Peace! Peace!" These emotions finally culminated in Henry Ford's "peace ship" whose passengers were to "get the boys out of the trenches by Christmas." I saw these well-meaning people in Holland and found them sadly crest-fallen at the hilarity with which their "dove of peace" had been received by the "boys."

In 1916, Colonel House had developed the idea that the President should propose definite terms of peace and throw our weight in the war on the side which accepted them, if the other side refused. Mr. Wilson did not appear to accept this notion fully, but in any event House came to Europe again to explore. He arrived in January, and engaged in discussions both in London and Berlin. He suggested definite terms as to freedom of Belgium, return of Alsace-Lorraine to France, cession of the Dardanelles to Russia, etc., together with a "League of Nations" and general disarmament. The Colonel informed Sir Edward Grey that the United States would "probably" come into the war on the Allied side if Germany proved obdurate.

Again, both the President and House were too high above realities. The Allies were sure the United States would never come in on the side of Germany; they believed that with the prospect of Roumania joining their side, and their carefully planned summer offensives on both the east and west fronts, they would have victory in 1916. So they gently pushed the Colonel's ideas away.

In my discussions with him I presented to him a new phenomenon of total war which seemed to me the overriding reason why his plans could not succeed. As this war wore on with its increasing death rolls and its unspeakable brutalities to the civilian populations, there was a growth of hate among civilians hitherto never equaled in war. Total war had proved to produce total hate. Previous great wars had been fought by soldiers, but this war was to a large degree a war against civilians. In "civilized" wars before, brave men had fought against other brave men. There were certain elements of chivalry and sportsmanship. In the large sense civilians had not been attacked. Now the Allied food blockade of Germany by surface craft stretched hate into every home three times a day. The German blockade of England by submarines not only threatened the food; the sinking of seamen and passengers without a chance and the air bombing of women and children in British towns had raised their hates to a degree never before known in Englishmen.

I insisted that hate had risen to such heat in the people on both sides that no statesman could persuade them to adopt the compromises which his negotiated peace implied.

The continued agitation in the United States for a negotiated peace and the pressures put upon the Ambassadors of the belligerent countries in the United States led, in September (1916), to a violent explosion by leaders in Europe on both sides. Lloyd George, Briand, Asquith and Bethmann Hollweg and all their subordinates broke out with turgid statements denouncing any form of negotiated peace. They received great acclaim from their press. However, the President was not discouraged from further effort.

I may mention that among our acquaintances (and friends) during this period were Lord Courtney and Ramsay MacDonald. They had both opposed the British entry into the war and were, of course, out of public life and damned on every street corner. I brought these men into contact with Colonel House at our home, but they could do no more than throw up their hands.

After the war, the British began to realize its futility and to realize MacDonald's qualities. He rose to be Prime Minister and I had many associations with him in after years. He was a brilliant orator, a man of great conscience, large capacities in negotiation, and did not pretend to be much of an administrator. There, he read himself aright.

Late in December, 1916, it was evident that neither side had gotten anywhere with the year's military effort. The President had hopes that there would be more reason and less emotion about. Moreover, the dangers of American involvement in the war were constantly increasing. To stop the war was obviously the only certain way to assure that we would keep out. On December 14th the Germans put up a peace balloon intended for propaganda in the United States. On December 18th, Mr. Wilson sent an eloquent message to the belligerents asking each of them to define to him its terms. He again had hopes that he might find enough common ground for a negotiated peace. The British and Germans both burst with anger. In the following month each did reply, but there was precious little common ground.

CHAPTER 23

AMERICA GOES TO WAR AND
THE C.R.B. SHIFTS
ITS BASE

Financial difficulties for the Relief began to loom up again early in 1917. The British and French Governments were desperate for foreign exchange and the $20,000,000 a month we were spending was a distinct burden. They notified me they could go on but a few months longer.

I arrived in New York on January 13th to further some preliminary negotiations which I had initiated for a loan of $150,000,000 on certain Belgian assets to be guaranteed by the British and French. In support of this idea, I made an address to the New York Chamber of Commerce on February 1st. It was the first public address I ever made and the audience listened with patience. It has no historical significance except as a general review of our whole work and needs.[1]

But other forces were now moving which brought my negotiations to an end. America was drifting or being forced into war. When I arrived in New York it was obvious at once that American temper had changed greatly from that of the year before. The forces in the war itself and the rain of skillful British and French propaganda over the year had raised a formidable war party in the United States. Financial circles were deeply involved in Allied loans where they might lose everything by an Allied defeat. But more potent were the millions who believed in the Allied cause as the cause of freedom against despotism.

[1] The text can be found in *Public Relations of the Commission for Relief in Belgium*, Stanford University Press, 1929. It is perhaps significant that I never received an invitation to again address that body for 32 years.

Especially along the Atlantic seaboard emotion had replaced all reason. New York City had reached a stage where there could be no objective discussion of America's position.

The thesis that this war was a war "to save democracy" was accepted despite the incongruity that victory would cement the Czarist regime upon the Russian people. America was moving steadily into the psychological rapids which lead to war. The President was again making a heroic effort to bring a negotiated peace. I fervently hoped that he would succeed although I saw little prospect.

I called upon Colonel House as he had always been helpful in our problems. I formed the impression that he was now for joining in the war. The Colonel again asked what I thought of the possibilities of the President's current renewed peace drive. From my memorandum at the time the following is a summary of the views I gave him. I said that during my contacts with the Germans in the previous two months I had observed a great rise of optimism. They had held the Western Front during 1916 against the maximum effort of the Allies on the Somme; they had held it with smaller forces than the Allies; they believed that they had Russia on the way to disintegration; they had smashed Roumania; they had utter contempt for Italy's military importance. The Allies also were optimistic; they were still counting greatly on Italy; they got great comfort from holding Verdun; they still believed that the blockade would bring Germany down; they were confident that America must in the end give them the financial resources with which to continue to buy food and munitions; otherwise our war boom would collapse.

But a more important wall against peace was arising from the privations and sufferings of the civil populations on both sides. There was an even further increase in mass hate. I reminded him that when we had in Europe discussed the peace drive in previous years I had said that in this furnace of hate statesmen were no longer free agents. They were imprisoned by the emotions of their people. I did not believe the leaders on either side could carry the compromises that were necessary to a negotiated peace such as the President envisaged, even if they wanted to. I was even stronger than the year before in the belief that the war would continue until one side or the other was exhausted, and in that race the victor would be only one lap behind the vanquished. In fact, European civilization was busy committing suicide.

Despite all this pessimism I advised that the President should persevere in his efforts. On January 22nd, he delivered to Congress a powerful address on peace, endeavoring to appeal over the heads of states to their peoples. It made no dent in the peoples. I made Colonel House a suggestion as to further clarifying the aims of the belligerents which he transmitted to the President.[2]

With the German declaration of unlimited submarine warfare at the end of January, 1917, the whole picture changed. This violation of specific undertakings to the United States, and the increased barbarity in the submarine war, came as a terrific shock to the American people. There was no other course for the American Government than to break off diplomatic relations with Germany (February 3rd).

The President obviously (and I also) still hoped the Germans did not intend to commit actual overt attacks upon American ships. When they began sinking Belgian relief ships in the next two days my hopes grew thin.

I had been deeply opposed to America's entering the war on many grounds—among them were my familiarity with European power politics and my little faith in our ability to change those forces and, in consequence, to make a lasting peace. Moreover, I believed that whichever way the war ended our moral, economic and military strength would make us potent in the peace-making.

The Zimmermann note, stirring Mexico against the United States, was published on February 25th. It compelled another step and the President on the 26th asked Congress for authority to arm our merchant ships.

At the time I badly needed to get back to Europe—to be on the ground if anything else broke loose and to prepare our Belgian operations for the possibility of the United States' being involved in the war. Also there was no hope of the completion of the loan for the moment. But all passenger traffic from North America to North Europe was suspended. The only passage possible was a Spanish steamer for Cadiz on March 13th.

[2] *Intimate Papers of Colonel House*, Vol. II, page 419.

During this delay of finding a passage, I was called into conference by Secretary of the Interior Franklin Lane, Secretary of Agriculture David Houston, Secretary of War Newton D. Baker, and especially Colonel House. These interviews concerned problems of war organization. Early in March, I called upon the President at his request.

The President's mind was full of the anxieties and probabilities of our joining the war. I told him that I still was hoping against hope that the Germans would commit no overt acts and that some other solution could be found which would not plunge America into the war. He said he also hoped that this last straw would not be loaded on the American back. Because of the Czar's partnership, he did not yet accept the popular European propaganda thesis that this was a crusade, a holy war for democracy.

He asked many questions about the kind of aid that America could give to the Allies in case of war, and indicated his view that industrial, financial and naval backing were all that we would need to supply should we be dragged in. He stated that the Allies had indicated that they did not need manpower. Knowing something of the diminishing manpower of the Allies, I disagreed with this view.

He made many inquiries as to the part food would play in the war. I told him that second only to military action it was the dominant factor. I sketched to him the actual food situation at the time on both sides and the part which America played in it. He showed anxiety lest our entry into war might end the Belgian Relief. I said that such would not necessarily be the case as I hoped we could transfer our guardianship to the Dutch and Spanish, provided the Germans still wished to hold the neutrality of these forces and we could finance the Relief. I stated that we had already started to explore these possibilities by cable.

He questioned me narrowly on war organization upon the economic side in the various countries and suggested that when I returned to Europe I should study these methods informally in case our situation became more acute. Secretary Lane had given me a hint that I would be wanted in Washington if we went to war.

As no other possible passage had turned up, I took the Spanish boat on the 13th. Will Irwin and his wife, Inez, fortunately offered to go also. Will had labors to perform as a correspondent for the *Saturday*

Evening Post. The *Antonio López* proved to be a 4100-ton jaloppy some 40 years of age, a cross between a full-rigged sailing ship and a steamboat. Mrs. Hoover had come to New York to see me off. She and friends, concerned over our food supplies, sent a host of packages of butter, eggs, baskets of fresh vegetables, boxes of fresh meat and what not. When we asked the steward to put them into cold storage, we learned (a) that there was none, (b) that there was not a steward on the boat who spoke any language but Spanish, (c) that the supply of beef, mutton and pork was on its four feet in pens on the forward deck, together with chickens and ducks. Later, experience taught us that from time to time as long as their lives continued, the livestock served as orchestra at uncertain periods of the day and night; they also served to mix with the other odors of the boat. By storing our food resources in my cabin, I also learned that we carried a full cargo of rats and cockroaches.

We had three excitements besides a rough sea which put Mrs. Irwin out of action for the first few days. A radio bulletin stated that the Germans were in retreat on the Western Front and that the French had retaken Noyon. That was one of our distribution centers in north-ern France. I became objectionable to some of the passengers, as I dampened their enthusiasm with the suggestion that this was only a strategic retreat to a new line which was a shorter and stronger one. Other bulletins stated that (on March 14th) the American merchant ships *Algonquin, Illinois, Memphis* and *Vigilancia* had been sunk by German submarines without warning.

There was also a radio bulletin announcing the revolution in Russia and the abdication of the Czar. Bill records in his diary something like the following observation from me:

This revolution will be difficult to stabilize. There have been centuries of oppression. There is no large middle class. There is almost total illiteracy in the people. There is no general experience in government. Russia cannot maintain a wholly liberal republic yet. Revolutions always go further than their creators expect. And in its swing, this one is more likely to go to the left than to the right.

These two events—the Russian Revolution and the sinking of American ships—made it seem inevitable that the United States would soon enter the war. The Revolution would ease the American mind as to whether this was really a fight for democracy instead of a fight to sustain the Czar, and the sinking of our ships was a direct attack by Germany upon the United States. I began making my plans accordingly.

We roamed around the Atlantic on the *Antonio López* for a long while. After twelve days we arrived at Cadiz on March 25th.

At Cadiz I was met by an official who asked me to stop at Madrid to confer with the Spanish Minister of Foreign Affairs. Our landing being on Sunday, we made a thorough examination of Cadiz, although I was in no humor for sight seeing. The city was the emblem of the vanished glory of Spain. From here had radiated the great trade of the Conquest and the Spanish colonies. The entrancing white houses with their luxurious grounds, their beautiful grilles and their minarets spoke of a greater day. And the obvious present poverty confirmed the idea that nothing is very stable in civilization.

On arrival at Madrid next day, I parted with Bill and Inez who went about their war-correspondent duties. I went at once to find out what the Minister of Foreign Affairs had in mind. It happened that he had been apprised, through the Spanish Ambassador in London, of the possibility of our asking the Dutch and Spanish to take the place of Americans for the inside work in Belgium. After discussing that possibility, his next question was, "What is your salary?" And his next, "What salary will our nationals receive if the situation develops to require them?" He seemed stunned at the idea of no pay or only expenses.

I felt he still suspected that no Yankee ever worked for nothing or ever told the truth. The major importance of the interview, however, was his agreement that the Spanish Government would do its best to see that the Relief continued. The neutrality of the Spanish and the Dutch was still important to the Germans.

I finally reached Paris with no more inconvenience than sleeping five in a compartment built for four.

As the wireless to the *Antonio López* had indicated, the Germans had drawn the Hindenburg Line some miles back to a better prepared and more strategically located defense. The result was the recovery by France of some 50 communes out of the 1200 occupied by the German Army. The recovered soil included the municipality of Noyon. We were thus relieved of relieving by so much.

The French had arranged to celebrate this victory and the recovery of French soil on March 31st. There was to be a service in the partially-destroyed *hôtel de ville* at Noyon—the great cathedral had been too far destroyed for use. I was urged by the Government to attend. A great number of notables were assembled, including Cabinet Ministers, Senators, the Cardinal, the Prefect of the Oise, the generals of that sector and other public officials.

A platform for the notables had been erected at one end of the great hall. The *maires* of the recovered communes were seated in front rows facing us. Fully half of them were women, most of whom I recognized.

It was a colorful and moving occasion. The *hôtel de ville* is an ancient mark of Gothic magnificence. The tempered light from the few stained-glass windows which remained was shot through by a streamer of sunshine from a shell hole in the roof. The magnificent music of the massed military bands, and the solemn and affecting sermon from the Cardinal stirred one's emotions to the depths. Senator Noel paid a touching tribute to the Relief, and the Prefect spoke of his amazement at finding the efficiency of the Relief and the good health of the children.

Just as we were rising at the end, still under the spell of the great spiritual expression of a great people, a raucous voice called out from fifty feet away, "Monsieur Hoover, où est l'argent pour les sacs?" (Where is the money for the sacks?) Most of those in my neighborhood looked at the grizzled old *maire* who was speaking, and then at myself. I was the only soul, aside from the *maires,* who knew what the unseemly remark was all about. I fear I broke the spell with a laugh. However, I gave the necessary assurances to the *maire* and evaded further inquiries.

Some time before, the British had discovered on captured German trenches sandbags made from C.R.B. floursacks. The British indignation was only a little less violent than when they found our condensed milk tins were being used for hand grenades. The French Committees for their "Benevolence" had been making a little money for their charities by selling the empty tins and sacks to dealers who, in turn, sold them to the Germans. After the discovery of this practice I had stopped it by requiring every *maire* to deposit 10 francs for each sack or tin, to be repaid when the empties were returned. We put the sacks into the clothing workrooms at Lille and Brussels and saw to it that they were turned into children's clothes, although the indelible words "Belgian Commission" appeared on many a youngster's front or back. The tins we shipped to Holland to be melted in the presence of British agents. Anyway, the old *maire* had a deposit of 500 francs with us. Despite his joy at being returned to France, his economic soul came to the surface.

But I can still hear the final words of the Cardinal's thanksgiving to the Almighty and his blessing on us all—then the mighty burst of La Marseillaise.

I had arranged on arrival in London next day to meet our principal Relief staff from Rotterdam and Brussels. It now seemed inevitable that the United States would be in the war and we set up the possibilities accordingly.

(a) That the Netherlands and Spanish officials might be able to keep the sea lane open to Dutch ports.

(b) If so, the Commission (as before) would deliver the food to the Belgian frontier.

(c) That the Dutch and Spanish take over the guarantees in Belgium.

(d) That we ask the British and French to continue to finance the work, with the hope the United States would help in case it joined the war.

Meantime the Belgians were having a dreadful time from the interruption in our deliveries. Rations had to be cut below any long-survival level. Cardinal Mercier called for special service and prayers throughout Belgium, that the C.R.B. be sustained in its continued fight for Belgian lives. We had 7 more inward bound ships sunk with 40,000 tons of food and 4 more sunk outward bound in ballast. The Germans apologized to Ambassador Villalobar each time.

On April 6th, on the American declaration of war, I received through Hugh Gibson a message from Colonel House saying that the President wanted me to return to the United States to take charge of food organization. I replied I would need a few days to get the Relief and other matters in hand.

We installed the Dutch and Spanish inside Belgium and withdrew our American staff, but continued the Commission as before outside Belgium. I was confident that as United States Food Administrator, I could solve the finances, the food supply and the shipping for the Belgians.

I arrived in New York from Europe on May 3, 1917, and in Washington the next morning. On reporting to the President he confirmed that he wished me to organize the food for war. I, of course, agreed to serve but stipulated that I should also conduct the Belgian Relief and that I have no salary. I believed the position would carry more moral leadership if I were a volunteer alongside of my countrymen in war.

Before I left London my good friend, Admiral Sims, came to see me. He told me that the submarine sinkings of merchant vessels amounted to a far greater tonnage than the published figures showed. The Germans were sinking 800,000 tons a month. He said at that rate Allied merchant shipping would be done for by December. He gave me two urgent messages to deliver upon seeing the President. He wanted more destroyers sent over and many more built to oppose the submarine; his other message was that the President should demand that the British adopt a convoying system across the Atlantic. They had refused to install convoys, clinging to the idea that it would slow the ships up too much. I was to impress on the President and Secretary Daniels with all my might that this must be done or we would lose the war. He was right. So deep was his conviction that he asserted that the British had probably lost, unnecessarily, two million tons of shipping by not adopting convoys sooner. The Admiral was endowed by nature with strong sailor "language." He applied it with emotional extras to these messages and in his expressions over British opposition. I expurgated the Admiral's message in delivering it to the President.

Although it overlaps in time with other jobs—Food Administrator and Director of European Relief and Reconstruction—I will here complete the Belgian Relief account.

As Food Administrator, I was able to secure finance of food to Belgium from the United States Treasury, with the British and French paying for transport. The Commission continued to deliver until after the peace of Versailles.

CHAPTER 24

❧❦❧❦❧❦❧

THE BELGIAN RELIEF PICTURE
CHANGES AGAIN
WITH THE ARMISTICE

A few days after the Armistice in November, 1918, I returned to Europe and combined my duties as United States Food Administrator with the new duties of administering the economic rehabilitation of Europe on behalf of some twenty-two governments. I continued the Belgian Relief as a department of these larger activities.

Immediately with the Armistice the Belgian and French governments resumed the political administration of the German occupied parts of their countries. The C.R.B. organizations during the whole four years of the war not only had fed the Belgians and the occupied French, but had cared for the destitute and performed many other economic and semi-governmental functions in those areas.

Soon after my arrival, I visited Brussels with Mr. Poland, who had been our Director in Europe after my return to the United States in 1917. We had naturally expected to liquidate this tiresome and anxious task at the Armistice. We went to Brussels intending to wind it up. It quickly developed, however, that some time would be required to reestablish commercial imports and distribution of supplies. Therefore, at the urgent request of the Belgian and French governments we consented to continue the Commission for a few months ultimately to July 1, 1919.

We were destined to have some surprises. We had expected a large amount of unemployment during the transition period from war to peace. In the last months of the war, the destitute had risen to more than six million out of the Belgian and French population of ten million—an unemployment rate of about 60 per cent. Within ninety days after the Armistice, practically every Belgian and Frenchman had gone back to work. The destitute decreased at once to a few hundred thousand. We reduced "Benevolence" to small dimensions. We no longer needed protection from the Germans. Nor did we need to continue drastic rationing. We abandoned our whole agricultural control. We were in no difficulties about ships or supplies. But we soon found ourselves transformed into a gigantic grocery business, having a practical monopoly over ten million customers.

Our next surprise was in respect to prices, ours being an organization buying in bulk and mostly with volunteer committees conducting all processing and distribution of food. It at once developed that the prices of our food were below those in adjoining France. The French population west of the former Hindenburg Line promptly and bitterly complained to the French Government that prices of bread and fats were lower in the formerly occupied territory than in their own areas. The French Government's solution was to ask us to raise prices to equate the situation. The Belgian Government, then fearful of the effect of probable rise in prices when we withdrew, asked us to do likewise. We were thus taking in huge sums of local currency for sale of food for which we had no need to expend on "Benevolence." We were making huge profits.

Added to these sums were others. In order to expedite the relief of Germany, Finland and others, I had caused the Commission to lay in some $45,000,000 in extra stocks. It seemed to me only just that the prices to the Germans should be the same as those charged to the Belgian public. We were paid in gold by the Germans. From this we had a great profit in gold in the hands of the Commission.

At the time of the unlimited submarine war which preceded the entry of the United States, we had sold the 100,000 tons of food aboard ships marooned in England. As prices were higher at the time of the sale than when we bought this stock, we again had a large profit in sterling.

Out of all these profits and some remainders of charity gifts, we found we possessed, after we had settled all our accounts with the

British, French, Belgian and American governments, a variety of currencies. We of the Commission did not own them personally—to whom did they belong?

At the then exchange rates, we had about $34,000,000 in the Belgian account. As a quick method of resolving the quandary, in July I proposed to the Belgian Ministry that they appoint Belgians to all the jobs of the Relief organization—from mine down to the last office boy. They could wind it up at their leisure, and dispose of the money balances as they saw fit. We would simply take our hats and pipes and walk out.

The Belgian ministry was appalled at the job of winding up accounts with the governments and the large amount of shipping, insurance and other tedious claims. Moreover, they had a genuine sentiment to which they wished to give expression. Therefore, they set up the theory that these balances were the property of the Commission and requested that I dispose of them in such fashion as I deemed wise in the interest of the Belgian people and as might result in a living memorial to the Commission.

Therefore, on the 28th of August, 1919, I submitted to the Belgian Ministry a memorandum of a plan, the documents as to which will be found in the "Public Relations of the Commission for Relief in Belgium."

We made a preliminary allocation of the money as follows:

To University of Brussels	$ 3,818,897.64
To University of Ghent	3,818,897.64
To University of Liège	3,818,897.64
To University of Louvain	3,818,897.64
To School of Mines, Mons	954,724.39
To Colonial School, Antwerp	1,909,448.84
To Ecole de Carillonneurs, Malines	3,000.00
To Fondation Universitaire à Bruxelles	6,846,080.88
To C.R.B. Educational Foundation in New York	7,686,065.17
Total	$32,674,909.84

The Fondation Universitaire undertook scholarships, scientific research and general promotion of education in Belgium. The C.R.B. Educational foundation arranged for intellectual exchanges between Belgium and the United States and other services. At this point we still retained about $1,100,000 to cover liquidation claims, and we realized still more in their settlement.

Out of these funds we were able to complete the rebuilding of the Louvain Library. Dr. Nicholas Murray Butler, in an explosion of high powered generosity after the Armistice, promised the rebuilding of this library by contributions of American school children and college students. He received many honorary degrees from Belgian universities. He hired a publicity firm to organize the givers. His agency collected some two or three hundred thousand dollars at 40 per cent for expenses. He hired an architect and started construction on the $700,000 project. It collapsed, to the mortification of every American. Therefore, to preserve our national face and restore the library, the C.R.B. took it over and completed it.

We took a special interest in the University of Brussels. It was an institution organized on somewhat medieval lines—by which students paid fees to part-time professors, many of whom were otherwise engaged in the practice of medicine, law, engineering, and the other professions. The University itself examined the students and conferred the degrees. It had some 4,000 students but not much equipment outside of its administration building.

In the fall of 1919 I invited its Chancellor and other representatives to visit the United States at the expense of our foundation in order that they might study our suburban type of universities. Their enthusiasm upon their return led to the securing of an ample campus near Brussels. With their own funds, together with allocations from us and returns from a public drive in Belgium "American fashion," they built a whole new University. It has the regular American equipment of libraries, laboratories, classrooms and dormitories — with full-time teaching staff.

In cooperation with the University trustees, we held an architectural competition for the designs of the new buildings among Belgian architects, the final award being made by a committee of American architects. The result was a beautiful development of Flemish architecture, in itself an inspiration to students.

One of those curious kinks of memory by which serious matters fade and immaterial moments remain arises in this visit of the Chancellor of the University to the United States. During his visit Mrs. Hoover and I, as a part of his education in American university expression, took him to the Princeton-Yale football game. He had never seen the American game and was greatly interested in the rules. He spoke no English and Mrs. Hoover undertook to translate the technology into French. There were no equivalents. The Chancellor became more and more confused. The crowd around became intensely interested and a score entered into the attempts at translation. They failed. The Chancellor, however, persisted and, taking notes, he subsequently tried to introduce our game to the Belgians. But games are evolved, not made, so he failed.

THE NORTHERN FRANCE SOLUTION

There were profits accumulated from the Relief of Northern France similar to those in Belgium. With the approval of the French Government we formed a committee through which these profits would be expended upon the children of the liberated area. We paid over to them more than $1,500,000. Another problem we solved soon after the Armistice as part of French Relief was that of the French refugees from the north of France who had fled to Belgium and to Southern France during the war. They immediately poured back to their homes—more than half a million of them—but many of their homes had been destroyed. Shelter soon began to be as important as food. To provide for this, in December, 1918, Admiral Benson granted my request that our Navy do this job for us. He gave us all of the wooden navy barracks which were being abandoned by the withdrawal of our sailors and those which had been shipped over from the United States but not yet erected. His gift included much of the furniture—especially kitchens. He assigned to me 15 officers and 500 men to move and superintend the erection of these buildings, transforming them into hospitals, kitchens and temporary shelters while the people rebuilt their homes. We thus erected whole villages at strategic points using German prisoners for workmen under the direction of our sailors. The naval officers and men did the job magnificently and got a great thrill out of it.

PARTING WITH THE BELGIANS

In August (1919) before leaving Europe for home I paid a visit to Belgium. The Belgians again raised the question of some public mark of their appreciation. They wanted to put on receptions and parades in every Belgian city. They raised again the idea of conferring their greatest orders of distinction and nobility, for all of which I had no liking.

This question of European decorations rose periodically to plague me. In 1916, the Belgian King had proposed it. In November, 1917, Minister Brand Whitlock (then attached to the Exiled Belgian Government at Le Havre) wrote to me saying:

. . . that the Belgians would feel a little bit more comfortable if the decorations could be given.

I replied:

As to European decorations, I have a complete abhorrence of all such toys. I do not want any distinctions of this kind whatever and have often expressed myself to this end.

My attitude toward decorations from foreign governments for our men was different, as many of them felt these made interesting evidences of service. Therefore, when the subject was broached to me by various governments, I stated that I would appreciate such attentions to our staff.

King Albert however evolved an idea of his own of creating a new order in Belgium with only one member—and one that no man would not be proud of, "The Friend of Belgium and Honorary Citizen of Belgium." The King proposed the necessary legislation to the Belgian Parliament at a special session. I was required to be present and witness the law passed without opposition. Returning from this ceremony in company with the Belgian Foreign Minister, I jokingly asked him if the Honorary Citizen was entitled to a passport. He said in similar humor that it might be a good idea to keep the frontiers of Belgium always open to me in case I ever needed a sanctuary for any misdeed. Next morning he sent a passport marked "perpetual." Therefore I am probably the only person in the world holding legitimate passports from two countries.

I did accept degrees from the various Belgian universities and the "freedom" of many Belgian cities. In ancient customs these freedoms entitled the rare recipient to freedom from hotel bills and the right to appropriate anything in a shop. This latter part of the custom seemed to have died out. However, the City of Antwerp, in order to add more than usual distinction, printed the certificate upon the original Plantin Press now in the museum and enclosed the certificate in a treasure box from their museum as a token.

In subsequent years we published all the important documents of the Commission and volumes of statistics showing every shipload, its detailed contents, its cost, the destination and distribution of its cargo— all down to the last cent and the last grain. They may be found in most public libraries.

The question as to whether the Germans got the food of the Belgians during our regime has seemingly been an eternal theme of sensationalists' genius. They rose to a crescendo when we proposed renewing the relief to Belgium for World War II. These charges were made by British officials and even by pro-British ministers of the gospel in the United States. At this time we published some evidence in the matter.

The broad answers to all these charges aside from the emphatic assurances of 300 Americans who had been on the ground were: (a) The relief was supported financially by the British and French governments. They had espionage agents in every part of the territory all the time. They were not likely to put up money to feed Germans. (b) When the war ended the Belgian population was found to be well nourished while the German population over the border was found to be greatly undernourished. If they had taken the food, the situation would have been in reverse. (c) In all the 25 years since there has never appeared a single statement by the people in Northern France or Belgium that the Germans got their food after the Relief was organized. With their proclivity to proclaiming German atrocities, they would scarcely have missed any such charge. On the contrary, they have proclaimed at all times their own zeal in preventing it.

In our answers to an outbreak of these false charges twenty-five years later we quoted many statements of the highest Allied officials at various times. They included Prime Ministers Asquith, Lloyd George, Foreign Ministers Grey and Briand, the Spanish and Dutch officials.

A final answer to assertions that the Germans benefited by the Relief would seem to be in the fact that, upon a proposal to stop the Relief in the spring of 1918 because of shipping shortage, Prime Ministers Lloyd George and Clemenceau directly intervened to demand its continuance. They can scarcely be accused of wishing to aid the Germans.

It remained for Americans—and ministers of the gospel at that— conducting British propaganda by foul lies to defame one of the greatest expressions of American humanism in our history; and for the purpose of defeating relief to the children of Belgium in the Second World War. But I deal with them in another part of these memoirs which might be entitled "The Four Horsemen in World War II."

CHAPTER 25

INTERLUDE TWENTY YEARS AFTER

I will again jump a few years to complete the Belgian story.

For thirty years the Foundations established by the Relief Commission had functioned with great benefits to Belgium and the United States.

The Belgian American Educational Foundation had been directed at all times by former C.R.B. men under my chairmanship, with Edgar Rickard, Hallam Tuck, Millard Shaler, John White, Sidney Mitchell, Lewis Strauss and that fine product of American life, Perrin Galpin, as its active heads. The Belgian Scientific Research Foundation has produced most valuable additions to knowledge. The Fondation Universitaire has poured out scholarships to Belgian youth and support to their institutions of higher learning. Our Belgian American Educational Foundation has brought a constant stream of Belgian youth to America for graduate work, and Belgian professors to lecture in our American universities. Likewise, we have sent a constant stream of American students to Belgian universities for graduate work, and our best American professors to lecture at their institutions. So careful has been the selection of Belgian students that, at one time, five of the members of the Belgian Ministry and nearly one-half of the major faculty members of Belgian universities had done postgraduate work in the United States under our auspices.

In 1938 I responded to many urgings by the Belgian King and Belgian Government to revisit their country. I deal with other matters connected with this visit of twenty years after in another place, but I may well include here a part that touches upon Relief days.

The first of these reminders of days past came early in that visit when

I was tendered an official reception at the *hôtel de ville,* presided over by my old friend, Burgomaster Max. I had had much to do with him when he was Burgomaster after the Germans occupied Brussels in 1914. A year later a German General and his aides, discontented with the Burgomaster's conduct, had come to the City Hall and sent for Max. The General unbuckled his two revolvers and laid them on the council table either to be relieved of their weight or as a preliminary to negotiation. Max solemnly opened his fountain pen and laid it beside the revolvers. Soon after he was taken to a German prison—but had been Burgomaster again ever since his release in 1918 by the German surrender.

Most deeply affecting was the meeting called of our old Comité National, which had coordinated the relief work inside Belgium.

The Comité had been composed of the leading Americans in the Commission, together with myself when in Belgium, of over 90 leading Belgians representative of every political, religious, economic and geographic group. In those days of desperation this committee sustained the greatest unity the Belgians had ever attained. Aside from its practical job in distribution, it furnished a great spiritual and moral rallying point for the people. The American members, standing between the Comité and the Germans, had shielded the Belgians from a thousand tragedies.

The full Comité met once a month over the four years of war. The meeting place was the board room of one of the large banks. The chairs at a great table, with Belgian meticulousness, had been marked for each member. After our final meeting dissolving the Relief in August, 1919, the Comité had never met again, even for social purposes. In the meantime Emile Francqui, the Chairman, had passed away. But with the exact old protocol at its former hour and place, the Vice Chairman Emile Janssen and the Secretary van Bree had summoned this special meeting of the Comité. Of the Americans Hallam Tuck, Perrin Galpin, Millard Shaler and myself were present. We all occupied our old seats. The Chairman, with a formality that for the moment covered his emotion, declared that the agenda for the day had but three items—to call the roll, to honor the dead, to renew friendships built in time of trial. I have seldom been more affected than by that roll-call and the frequent reply "Mort." More than one-third of the chairs were empty. Many of the chairs were occupied by men obviously feeble with age, all of them under great emotion at so vivid a reminder of those who had passed on. It was then I realized that while I was in my early forties during that war our Belgian colleagues had been composed of the old and tried men who then were mostly twenty years my senior.

Every article in the room and every word revived memories of men who had risen to great acts and great days. Some way a great spirit flowing with human devotion flooded the room.

We all had difficulty in completing our sentences.[1]

---

[1] Soon thereafter another great war and a second German occupation were to envelop Belgium. But the British would not permit a Relief Commission. The Belgians suffered dreadfully and had no protection from German outrages.

United States
Food Administration
1917–1919

CHAPTER 26

POLICIES AND ORGANIZATION[1]

I arrived in Washington on May 5, 1917. President Wilson, on the same day, formally requested me to join his war team. Four days later, the Food Administration was launched.

There was little humor or romance in this job. We were greatly handicapped by the large failure of our crops in both the 1916 and 1917 harvests from which we had no "statistical" surplus to export during the first fifteen months of our part in the war. I first describe the policies we determined upon before discussing our organization as the latter flowed naturally out of the former. While all detailed policies were not formulated in advance, the major principles were firmly rooted within a few weeks.

I was already convinced that the American problem was entirely different from that of Europe, and that the American scene was not adapted to many of the methods which we had pioneered or experimented with in Belgium and other Allied countries. However, familiarity with the trials and errors in food administration by most European governments was a great advantage to us—chiefly the errors.

The North American continent and the West Indies produced in all years enough food for our own needs and some surplus. While some food was available from the Southern Hemisphere and from India for the Allies, they did not control enough ships to carry on the war and, at the same time, to make voyages which required two or three times as many days as those from Europe to North America. Moreover, these longer routes could not be adequately protected from German sub-

[1] This text was written fifteen years before our entry into World War II. As food problems were handled during the two wars upon entirely different concepts of organization, I have concluded that it is desirable to retain some otherwise uninteresting detail because of its possible usefulness to economic students.

marines. Roughly speaking, 5000 ship tons would deliver as much from North America as 15,000 tons of shipping from Australia and 10,000 tons from the Argentine. Our problem was to squeeze out enough exports from the United States, the West Indies and Canada to make up the large deficits of our Allies and certain neutrals, and to do this with a minimum of disturbance to our economy.

The first policy question arose out of President Wilson's predilection to create boards and commissions for the new war agencies. The President, like every true democrat, wished to avoid anything that smacked of the building of dictatorial powers. But with this idea, he was headed for the old rock of divided responsibility which had caused many of the Allied wrecks at the beginning of the war and which, when installed in other American departments, resulted in delay and held up effective action for many months. From observation of the host of such Allied failures in organization, I felt there must be a single head to the food problem and that his authority must cover every phase of food administration from the soil to the stomach. That included direct or indirect control over production, farm policies, conservation, exports, imports, buying for our military forces and those of the Allies, prices, rationing, processors, distributors and consumers.

The President proposed to set up a board which would avoid the appearance of one-man rule and yet, at the same time, coordinate the various departments and civilian agencies. His mind was influenced, no doubt, by the newspaper headlines of "Food Dictator" and "Food Czar" which had greeted my arrival. He was also disturbed lest my desire to control the war policies of agriculture would bring conflict with the Department of Agriculture. To this I replied, first, that I knew Secretary David F. Houston would agree and, second, that just such division of authority had created friction, waste and great failure in every country at war in Europe.

I urged strongly that an individual could secure a wealth of voluntary action in America which no impersonal board could command, and that in this voluntary action lay our guard against Prussianizing the country. I emphasized the European failures of boards and commissions due to inevitable frictions, indecision and delays. I suggested that the whole genius of American business, and even governmental administration, prescribed a single responsible executive with boards only in advisory, legislative or judicial functions.

Finally I managed to argue him out of the board idea as applied to food. Possibly his mind was won over by my proposal of a new term, that is "administrator" for the head of an "administration." I urged that this term itself would connote not dictatorship but the ideas both of coordination and executive leadership. This was, I believe, the first time this title had been used for a public function. The President finally agreed, but with a troubled mind, as he had set up all the other war agencies under boards or commissions.

The second of our policies concerned the method of internal organization. One of the preliminary mental exercises of some of our Food Administration people, habitual in all Washington departments, was the making of "organization charts" with circles, squares and converging lines showing precisely where everything belonged. Some felt that we could not know where we were going without such a chart. Finally, at one of our early meetings, I remarked that, if this kept on, we would spend every morning revising charts. I stated:

This is an emergency organization and a new operation. Every day we must meet new problems. Therefore, my notion of organization is to size up the problem, send for the best man or woman in the country who has the "know how," give him a room, table, chair, pencil, paper and wastepaper basket—and the injunction to get other people to help and then solve it. When that problem is out of the way, we shall find plenty more.

Thereafter we recruited the men and women, outlined the problem, and gave them the "go sign."

The third policy determination was to stimulate farm production by every device, for our ultimate success would depend as much upon the farmer as upon reduction of consumption. Our pre-war export surplus was less than one-third of the prospective needs of the Allies and neutrals. To stimulate production, we decided to maintain incentive prices in critical farm products which influenced the prices of all others, such as breadstuffs, meats and fats. And we would reduce the farmer's risks by giving guarantees for a period long enough ahead to allow him to market his production. We further endeavored to protect the farmer's labor and machinery supplies. Above all, we appealed to his patriotic efforts.

In working out this problem, we had to settle the relations of the Food Administration with the Department of Agriculture. This was not difficult. The Department, at that time, had little interest in economic activities. It was, in fact, a great scientific research and statistical institution, and Secretary David Houston was anxious not to have it entangled in economic problems of war production and price control. He feared the farmers' inevitable antagonism to these programs would injure the Department. At my request, the Secretary selected for us an Agricultural Advisory Committee of which former Governor Henry C. Stuart of Virginia was made Chairman. It was popularly known as the "Farmers' War Committee." I selected for the President's appointment an Advisory Committee of consumers under the Chairmanship of Dr. Harry Garfield, President of Williams College. Our two committees agreed upon $2.20 per bushel for wheat to extend from crop to crop. By stabilizing wheat we gave a stimulant to the production of other grains, because in a large measure grains substitute for each other if the prices are more favorable to one than another. We gave originally a guarantee of $15.50 (later $17.50) per hundred pounds for hogs as a method of stimulating production of meats and fats. This fixed price contributed to stabilizing the price of other animals and further stabilized the price of corn. At a later date we gave a guarantee on beans and peas. To stabilize the price of sugar, we ultimately bought the entire American and Cuban crops at prices agreed upon with committees of the sugar producers.

Early in the war I became greatly concerned as to the effect of the soldiers' draft upon the farm labor situation. I called upon General Enoch Crowder, a grand soldier (and statesman), who had been put in charge of the draft. And I began to explain to him that agriculture was really a munitions industry; that the outcome of the war and the peace afterwards might depend upon what we could produce, as well as what we could save. I had hardly finished half a dozen sentences when he interrupted with a statement to this effect:

My boy, I know all that; I would even put it stronger than you do. You must have every needed boy on the farms. Leave it to me, and we will do better if there is no public discussion.

As the result of the General's arrangements, together with the old folks' working harder, we had little reason to complain because of lack of manpower on the farms.

The fourth policy was to eliminate waste and reduce consumption of food. The question at once arose: Should we put the people on ration tickets as we had done in Belgium, and as was being done all over Europe, or should we attempt organization on a voluntary basis?

I was opposed to rationing Americans for several reasons. The American farmers and the farmers' intimate village neighbors composed 40 per cent of the population. I was well aware that every farmer in the world believed it was his family's divine right to consume any of the food he produced. Moreover, he needed no ticket to secure essential food unless we requisitioned his whole production, as we had done in Belgium. General requisition not only was the antithesis of American character, but in a country as large as ours was a practical impossibility without a hundred thousand bureaucratic snoopers. Because the rationing of farmers would in our view produce no consequential savings, the actual reduction of consumption by this method would need to be taken out of the town and city people alone. On the other hand, if we could enlist the farmer's wife to save food around the farm and stimulate the farmer to produce, we would gain far more than by irritating him with tickets.

We had a further lesson from our European experience. To issue ration cards to a hundred million Americans for bread, meats, dairy products, fats, sugar, and other staples would involve a stupendous bureaucracy with enormous expense. Above all, we knew that, although Americans can be led to make great sacrifices, they do not like to be driven.

We determined, therefore, to organize the farmers, the housewives, the public eating-places and the distribution trades on a voluntary basis for conservation as a national service.

A fifth major policy was the method of restraining prices, preventing profiteering and avoiding what were later known as black markets. Due to Allied competition in our markets with no governmental restraints, in the two and one-half years before we declared war, food prices had risen over 82 per cent. These price rises already weighed heavily upon labor and "white collar" workers and their continued rise threatened all economic stability. The apparently easy device of fixing maximum prices ("ceiling prices") by law at the retail outlets had been attempted in every European country and there was much demand, particularly from Congress, for its immediate enactment in the United States. My experience in Europe convinced me that this method utterly failed to restrain prices and was a universal stimulant to waste, black markets and violation of law. I believed that we should adopt a new method by "stabilizing" prices of the raw materials of food at the nearest market point to the farmer through the major buyers and the processors. Then we should define the "mark up," or margin for each step of processing and distribution. This avoided "ceiling retail prices" and gave us latitude for constant change. Its enforcement was greatly simplified.

Our sixth major policy was to implement this stabilization of prices at the farm level. As our first tool we secured from the Congress $150,000,000 working capital with which to buy and sell food. We created the Food Administration Grain Corporation, of which Julius H. Barnes was President and I was Chairman. This organization had the sole right to purchase wheat (later beans and peas also) in the primary markets, selling in turn to processors and exporters. As a second implement, we created the Sugar Equalization Board under my chairmanship and the presidency first of George Rolfe and later of George Zabriskie. The Board bought successively entire crops of the United States, the Philippines and the West Indies at prices accepted by the producers and sold them to the processors and exporters at a fixed price.

It was characteristic of Mr. Wilson's indifference to detail that, when I presented him the sugar plan on a single sheet of paper, he read it, said nothing, initialed it, "Approved W. W.," and handed it back. I suggested that the White House should have a copy, since it involved billions of dollars. He grinned and said: "Would that get any more sugar?"

As a third implement of stabilizing prices we centralized the purchase of all Army, Navy and Allied food supplies through, or with the approval of, the Food Administrator. For this purpose, I appointed Frederic Snyder and later Herbert Gutterson my deputy.

There was considerable competition among the Allies and our military buying agencies, and each had a consuming desire to be sure of future supplies. By so doing, they were hoarding food, producing local famines, and forcing up prices by competition with civilians. We ultimately satisfied the military that by a general pool of supplies we could better assure that the stocks of food in the country at all times would meet Allied needs and permit a priority to the military forces. As these supplies passed directly or indirectly through the Food Administration, I determined that we would never be involved in the "embalmed beef" scandals that disgraced the Spanish-American War. The Department of Agriculture conducted its usual inspection of a part of food processing under the Pure Food and Packing House regulation. But to be doubly sure, I extended our own inspection service into every other item of military and domestic food. We never had a complaint. The American soldiers and sailors were the best fed fighting men in the world.

We made use of a fourth implement of stabilization of prices by the control of export and import licenses—which applied to neutrals as well as Allies. At times we made use of a fifth instrument of stabilization. That was control of the food commodity exchanges to prevent speculation which was in fact hoarding. We made a sharp distinction between these practices and what is called "hedging."

Our seventh major policy determination was how to use restraints on those who would not cooperate in our price and distribution controls. To effect the major solution, we at once called meetings of the representatives of the different trade groups concerned. At our request each group appointed its own War Committees of five or seven men upon whom they could rely and with whom we could work. To every initial meeting we said that, while we would need cooperation in measures which would alter the usual commercial practices, yet we were determined to organize those measures so that when the war was over they could be dissolved without lasting changes in the trades. We assured them that our purpose was to win a war, not a mission to bring about social or economic reforms. I secured a ruling from the Attorney General that so long as our "War Committees" were carrying out our wishes, any collective action would not be regarded as a violation of the Anti-Trust Acts.

There were a multitude of these committees covering processing, wholesaling, retailing in different commodities. We agreed with them on definitions of fair margins or "mark-ups" beginning at the farm prices. The processor committees knew if each wholesaler and each retailer was sticking to the rules. The retailer knew if the wholesaler or processor worked honestly. The great majority of trades were jealous for honor of the trade and almost fanatically so in war—especially when responsibility was placed upon them.

Their sons were also in the war. They were to report to us any violations they themselves could not cure. They did an amazing job.

Our State and local Food Administration and our Washington enforcement division kept check on these matters, but our prime purpose was to give responsibility to the trades and avoid a huge bureaucracy of unskilled persons. It succeeded. I could cite many instances of great sacrifices made by the trades to carry out our national purposes. These committees were at times even more severe on evil persons than our office would have been. Ofttimes we had to intervene to soften their stern measures which would have put a violator out of business for the duration by cutting off his supplies.

There were some exasperating cases of processors or distributors who could not believe that war required re-orientation of our economy or that the Bill of Rights did not override any such illusions of government officials. However, personal contacts between our lawyers and theirs usually changed their minds.

On one such occasion of conflicting concepts I made a public statement as follows:

Do not be under an illusion. . . . We wish for co-operation. . . . Compared with the sacrifice of our sons and brothers, it is but little to ask. And it is a service which, if given now, will not be without interest returns for the future. . . .

One looming shadow of this war is its drift toward social disruption. We shall surely drift to that rocky coast unless we can prove the economic soundness and willingness to public service of our commercial institutions. With the gigantic sacrifice of life the world is demanding sacrifice in service.

We had some difficulties with a client of Senator James Reed of Missouri. He had received wrong advice from the Senator. The Senator attacked me in the Senate. One of his charges was the assertion that I and others had grafted money from the Belgian Relief. John White smashed out a reply in the press, pointing out that we had from the beginning appointed an independent firm of auditors to check the money and the accounts. He further quoted from those minutes: "Some swine some day will charge us with graft." White further opined that the swine had now appeared. The Senator turned his hose of slime onto poor John. Among other things he declared that John was an Englishman. John assembled his ancestral heritage over seven generations in reply, and proved he was more solidly rooted in America than Senator Reed.

The eighth major policy determination was how much legal power we would need from the Congress if our voluntary system of price and distribution control should break at any point. The bare idea of anybody interfering with the food rights of the people, especially in a land overflowing with milk and honey, came as a shock to many members of the Congress. Some violently opposed us and I spent a vast amount of time and breath both on individual Senators and Congressmen and on their various committees making clear the need of action and the methods we proposed. It was my first intimate contact with a legislative body. I learned that even in such an august institution there was the same minority of malicious and dumb that there was in the rest of the world, and their opportunity was greater. When I ran up against Senator Reed and a few others, I concluded some were also expert in the practice of malice beyond the average.

One of our major difficulties in legislation was to head off mandatory fixing of prices. My knowledge of its futility in Europe enabled us to avoid such foolish ideas. I was able to make a good case for our whole program out of the ominous Communist collapse in Russia. One of the chief causes for this disaster was the incompetence of their food administration. Every city was filled with mobs crying for food. Yet Russia possessed ample food resources. In fact, as the Germans had blockaded her outlets to Western Europe through the Baltic and the Black Sea, she had large dammed-back surpluses of wheat and fats. But the people in Moscow, St. Petersburg, and Rostov were starving and the Russian armies along the Front were hungry.

Under the leadership of Congressman Asbury F. Lever and Senator Furnifold Simmons, we finally nursed our legislation through. It included powers to give guarantees to the farmers; to suspend exchange trading; to prevent speculation and hoarding; to fix trade margins; to eliminate waste in manufacture and distribution; to organize the trades; and to buy and sell food.

As a matter of fact, we seldom used the punitive powers included in this legislation. The penalties in the act were too great. I had asked Congress for powers to enforce by way of fines for misdemeanors through the Courts, but they decided for constitutional reasons that every food handler must be licensed and that the penalty should be cancellation of the license. This penalty put a dealer out of business for the duration and would likely destroy his livelihood for long after. We applied this measure in some instances of repeated wilfulness—but those instances amounted to fewer than 100. Of some 8000 reported violations, most were mistakes or the result of ignorance, or were mild offenses, and our legal staff left them alone if they made a contribution to the Red Cross.

Our ninth major policy determination was the methods we should apply to conservation and the elimination of waste. Aside from the legal authority to eliminate waste in processing and to prevent vicious hoarding, we again determined to rely upon voluntary response. We did stipulate the percentage of wheat which could be milled into cattle feed, some requirements as to milk and the use of sugar, and the amount of grain that could be used in beer. We abolished its use in distilled liquor. There were stocks of hard liquor ample for an abstemious population for years to come.

Our major method was to enlist the housewives, public eating places, processors, wholesalers and retailers to become "members" of the Food Administration. We gave each of them a certificate and asked each to sign a pledge to follow the rules. Each received a button and a card to put in the window, indicating membership. From the number of cards distributed we knew that some 20 million members signed up. The rules were simple and directed toward eliminating waste by reducing unnecessary consumption and encouraging the use of substitutes. The footnote to the rules was:

Go back to simple food, simple clothes, simple pleasures. Pray hard, work hard, sleep hard and play hard. Do it all courageously and cheerfully. We have a victory to win.

We found in the American people exactly what we expected—a wealth of co-operation. Saving food became a sort of game. Parents took advantage of it to impose upon their children the disciplines which had been the griefs of their own youth—and blamed it on me.

There were indeed great woes, trials, and disappointments, usually known only to us on the inside. But our system did the required job and avoided rationing and the other pitfalls into which European food administrators had fallen. Sometimes the public did too much. In one emergency I asked for a special saving of fats and butter. The people saved so much that the trades were demoralized, we flooded the Allies, and I had to retreat.

The tenth major policy determination was to limit our interest in food to the score of staples which comprise 90 per cent of the necessary national diet, and to allow luxuries to "go hang!"

The eleventh policy determination was decentralization versus centralization. With a country so great and so diverse and so used to local government, and with a problem which needed local co-operation, we decided on intense decentralization. We set up state, county, and municipal food administrators with wide delegation of authority. The state administrators were appointed in cooperation with the Governors, and the State administrators in turn co-operated in the appointment of the county and municipal administrators. They were leading men or women in the communities and they were all volunteers. They had the duties of promoting conservation, production, and reporting to Washington any local shortages and major infractions of price or distribution. We decentralized the Washington administration into the "problems" of each major commodity and/or other activity, which in time became "divisions." Ultimately, jointly with the War Industries Board, we also regulated tin-containers, binder twine, and the procurement of all hemp generally. My responsibilities originally involved joint action with the Secretary of the Interior in regulation of coal, oil and gas. I later describe the divorce of this set-up into a separate war activity.

European food controllers and ministers with their drastic measures of compulsion and their inability to secure co-operation from their people had always been the most unpopular of war officials. I told the reporters on one occasion that not one of these officials had lasted in office more than nine months and I expected nothing better. But with our methods, there was little personal dissatisfaction, and I weathered the storms of the whole war. We were never "investigated" by the Congress.

The following public statements indicate our explanation of policies. On May 19th, the President said:

It is very desirable, in order to prevent misunderstandings or alarms and to assure co-operation in a vital matter, that the country should understand exactly the scope and purpose of the very great powers which I have thought it necessary in the circumstances to ask the Congress to put in my hands with regard to our food supplies. Those powers are very great, indeed, but they are no greater than it has proved necessary to lodge in the other Governments which are conducting this momentous war, and their object is stimulation and conservation, not arbitrary restraint or injurious interference with the normal processes of production. They are intended to benefit and assist the farmer and all those who play a legitimate part in the preparation, distribution, and marketing of foodstuffs.

It is proposed to draw a sharp line of distinction between the normal activities of the Government represented in the Department of Agriculture in reference to food production, conservation, and marketing, on the one hand, and the emergency activities necessitated by the war in reference to the regulation of food distribution and consumption on the other. . . .

I have asked Mr. Herbert Hoover to undertake this all-important task of food administration. He has expressed his willingness to do so on condition that he is to receive no payment for his services and that the whole of the force under him, exclusive of clerical assistance, shall be employed, so far as possible, upon the same volunteer basis. . . .

Although it is absolutely necessary that unquestionable powers shall be placed in my hands in order to insure the success of this administration of the food supplies of the country, I am confident that the exercise of those powers will be necessary only in the few cases where some small and selfish minority proves unwilling to put the Nation's interests above personal advantage, and that the whole country will heartily support Mr. Hoover's efforts by supplying the necessary volunteer agencies throughout the country. . . .

The proposed food administration is intended, of course, only to meet a manifest emergency and to continue only while the war lasts. Since it will be composed, for the most part, of volunteers, there need be no fear of the possibility of a permanent bureaucracy arising out of it. All control of consumption will disappear when the emergency has passed. . . .

The last thing that any American could contemplate with equanimity would be the introduction of anything resembling Prussian autocracy into the food control in this country.

It is of vital interest and importance to every man who produces food and to every man who takes part in its distribution that these policies thus liberally administered should succeed and succeed altogether. It is only in that way that we can prove it to be absolutely unnecessary to resort to the rigorous and drastic measures which have proved to be necessary in some of the European countries.

WOODROW WILSON

I made a press statement amplifying the President and an explanation of why we were opposed to the demands from some quarters for rationing and fixed retail prices.

I concluded:

. . . The whole foundation of democracy lies in the individual initiative of its people and their willingness to serve the interests of the Nation with complete self-effacement in the time of emergency. I hold that Democracy can yield to discipline and that we can solve this food problem for our own people and for our allies largely by voluntary action. To have done so will have been a greater service than our immediate objective, for we have demonstrated the rightness of our faith and our ability to defend ourselves without being Prussianized.

ORGANIZATION

Within a few days after my arrival in Washington we had recruited the foundations of our personnel.

On the administrative side we secured Edgar Rickard, John B. White, John F. Lucey, Mark L. Requa, Duncan McDuffie, Frederic C. Walcott, Everett Colby, later with Lewis L. Strauss as my secretary.

On the legal staff we secured Judge Curtis H. Lindley, Judge William A. Glasgow, Robert A. Taft, Harvey Bundy, William C. Mullendore, Joseph P. Cotton, Roland W. Boyden and Lawrence Richey.

On the nutritional and statistical staff we enlisted Vernon Kellogg, Alonzo E. Taylor, Frank Surface and Raymond Pearl.

On the educational side we secured Gertrude B. Lane, Sarah Field Splint, Katherine Blunt, Edith Guerrier, Flora Rose, Ben S. Allen, and Martha Van Rensselaer.

On the conservation side we secured University President Ray Lyman Wilbur, Harry A. Garfield, aided on the public-eating places side by Fred Harvey and John M. Bowman.

For the administration of commodity controls we originally enlisted Julius H. Barnes, James F. Bell, Edward M. Flesh, Theodore F. Whitmarsh, Joseph P. Cotton, Frederic S. Snyder, Gardner Poole, George M. Rolfe, George W. Lawrence, G. Harold Powell, Charles H. Bentley, and Charles W. Merrill.

For the agricultural phases, as I have stated, Secretary of Agriculture David F. Houston set up for us a committee of twenty nation-wide farm representatives under former Governor Henry C. Stuart of Virginia.

For rail transportation we secured Edward Chambers, Vice President of the Sante Fe, later C. E. Spens, Vice President of the Burlington, and for shipping Prentiss N. Gray and J. D. Fletcher.

For our State relations we secured John W. Hallowell, Huntley N. Spaulding of New Hampshire and John M. Parker of Louisiana.

We were all volunteers. As time went on we expanded this personnel with the necessary staff of clerks, secretaries, stenographers and accountants.

With America at war, Washington at once was jammed by the new agencies of government. We started at the Willard Hotel, thence into a few rooms in the Interior Department, then to the complete occupancy of an old hotel, the Gordon. It was an impossible place. John R. Kilpatrick (later General) designed for us and erected a two-story wallboard building which would accommodate an office force of two or three thousand employees. By the efforts of Mr. Kilpatrick, the building was completed in 90 days. It was the first large building of its kind, and its general lines were subsequently followed for most of the war agencies. These buildings were abominably cold in winter and hot in summer. But enthusiasm is little dulled by temperature.[1]

Details of our organization, its personnel and its current undertakings are of interest to students but not particularly romantic reading. For students, there are a multitude of books, reports, statistics, documents and other items of which the largest collection is in the War Library at Stanford University. The records of the Food Administration are in the National Archives at Washington.

---

[1] I had thought that this building might last three or four years but the job was so well done that it was still in use 33 years later.

CHAPTER 27

FOOD AND MILITARY STRATEGY—
THE FOOD BLOCKADE—THE GREAT
FOOD CRISIS WHICH NEVER CAME

During the last half of 1917 and the early part of 1918, the Allied Governments were in constant turmoil of indecision on major military strategy. It also involved food. The question was, Should we send a large American Army to Europe? In the early stages the British and French military authorities opposed a large American Army, believing that they could handle the situation with the aid of our fleet, some special services, such as air forces, engineers, together with ample food and munitions.

General Pershing and our military leaders did not believe we could quickly end the war without large ground troops and were insistent that they be sent. But this could not be done without positive assurance of British and French ships for troop transport and supplies. But for them to furnish the ships they must abandon their long voyages to the Southern Hemisphere, China, and the Indies for supplies, and depend upon Canada and the United States. This in turn involved sacrifice of their foreign trade in many parts of the world. They greatly feared we could not produce the supplies. There was some reason for this trepidation in view of our prewar record of exports and the fact that we had two partial crop failures in 1916 and 1917.

Also, in the background was the specter of German submarine sinkings. In April, 1917, the month we entered the war, more than 850,000 tons of merchant ships were sunk. The losses exceeded 500,000 tons a month until August. Prior to that time, the British had been loath to accept Admiral Sims' demand for an Atlantic convoy system as an answer to the submarine. They had finally accepted it, however, and by November the losses from these sinkings were reduced to under 300,000 tons a month.

I had repeatedly advised President Wilson, Colonel House and General Pershing that unless the British and French would make these changes it would be dangerous to undertake sending a huge army to Europe. I stated that from the response of the American people to our conservation measures, and the energies of our farmers, I was confident we could furnish the food needed by the Allies from even our meagre 1917 production, and I was further confident we would greatly increase our surplus with the 1918 crops. The British, however, would not accept our assurances on the food side. General Pershing urged the Allies to make the changes which I suggested and thus give him the ships, but ultimately, the British Cabinet flatly closed the discussion in a dispatch (October 11th) that they would furnish no considerable tonnage to transport American troops.

However, events intervened to shift the whole British point of view. The Germans had compelled Bolshevist Russia to make peace (March 3, 1918), and then concentrated their armies, and late in March smashed the British Fifth Army. Among the minor results was the loss of 100,000 tons of food. By extra exertion we replaced it within thirty days. But the major result was a realization by the British and French that the large American Expeditionary Force upon which General Pershing had insisted, was necessary.

At the time we had fewer than 200,000 combat troops in the European theater. Admiral Sims' program had diminished the fear of the submarine. The Food Administration's steady performance in producing large shipments from a statistically empty barrel had vital weight in these decisions. Seven months later we had 2,000,000 men in France.

It was my contribution to this strategy, by assurance of food to the Allies, that caused General Pershing to inscribe a note to me later which I may be permitted the vanity of reproducing:

For Herbert Hoover, whose contribution to the success of the Allied cause can hardly be overestimated.[1]

THE FOOD BLOCKADE

To lower the morale of the enemy by reducing his food supply was one of the major strategies of the war. I did not myself believe in the food blockade. I did not believe that it was the effective weapon of which the Allies were so confident. I did not believe in starving women and children. And above all, I did not believe that stunted bodies and deformed minds in the next generation were secure foundations upon which to rebuild civilization.

The facts were that soldiers, government officials, munitions workers and farmers in enemy countries would always be fed; that the impact of blockade was upon the weak and the women and children. Moreover, because of the food blockade, Germany had no need to spend money abroad and she would have long since gone broke if she could have bought what her public would have demanded. I insisted that the war would not be won by the blockade on food for women and children, but by the blockade on military supplies and by military action. There were important Englishmen who agreed with me.

I knew well enough that such revolutionary ideas would not prevail when we came into the war, but nevertheless I presented a plan to

[1] During World War II, I made a protest that men were being drawn from the farms faster than they could be trained or transported abroad, thus needlessly endangering our food production.

In answer the Roosevelt Administration staged Senator Theodore F. Green of Rhode Island to make a smear speech, saying I had opposed sending an Army to Europe in 1917. His text was founded upon some sentences out of their context and only partially representing several discussions with Colonel House over the dangers of sending large armies to Europe unless the convoy system was adopted, unless the British and French would withdraw their shipping from foreign trade, and unless reliance was placed on the short haul from North America for food instead of the long voyages to the Indies and the Southern Hemisphere.

President Charles Seymour of Yale University had furnished the War Department officials with these partial quotations from the House papers in Seymour's keeping. Professor Ralph H. Lutz of Stanford War Library made a spirited reply. I demanded and received written apologies from both President Seymour and Secretary of War Henry Stimson. Those interested in the subject can find ample corroboration and discussion of this situation in Ralph Haswell Lutz, *A Typical New Deal Smear and Distortion* (17 April 1943).

President Wilson by which we could give supplementary food, under proper neutral controls, to German children and weaker women through soup kitchens and school feeding, without essentially weakening our war effort. Through our control of world shipping we could see that such minor tonnage of food was carried by neutrals from the Southern Hemisphere. The President was sympathetic, but the Allies would not hear of such a thing.

However, one secondary phase of the food blockade was handed to me for administration—controlling the food supplies sold to Germany by the surrounding neutrals. These consisted mostly of animal products created by imported feed grains and used almost exclusively by enemy armies and officials.

The Allies had two means for bringing pressure upon the neutrals in Europe. The first was the control of all the bunker coal in the world; the second was the naval blockade generally. The Allies had been trying for a long time through control of neutral imports to prevent leaks to Germany. The British had pursued an attitude of carping harassment. The six small neutral nations all depended upon imports of certain commodities, mainly breadstuffs and feed. They never knew from day to day whether they would have food for their own people or not. They hated the Allies almost as much as they feared the Germans. I therefore concluded to try a reversal of this attitude. I insisted we must use food to make friends by feeding neutral people the commodities they essentially lacked, not starving them. I sent for their representatives ,in Washington and informed them that we intended that they should have their needed food; that we would include them in our world food program; that we did not wish to force them into the war; that we wanted them to get supplies from the Southern Hemisphere for which they had ships; that we could get them bunker coal for that purpose; that we would expect them to stop sales of meats and fats to the Germans; that we wanted co-operation from them by giving us the use of their surplus ships and otherwise. I told them also that since they had raised rates 1000 per cent on ships which we chartered from them as against our increase in food prices of under 100 per cent, I thought it only right that they should pay a reasonable service charge to the Food Administration on food we sold to them. They agreed to this program.

This policy greatly improved American relations with the neutral world. Incidentally, the profits of the Grain and Sugar Corporations from these and other sources were sufficient to return the entire capital and a substantial surplus.

OUR GREATEST CRISIS—WHICH NEVER CAME

Probably my lowest spiritual point in the three years of war was when the news came of the German break through the British Front in March, 1918. We knew from that date that our job was cut out. With daily anxiety I pored over the Agriculture Department's special information to me on the progress of our expanded farm production and our own statistics of food conservation.

With the summer of 1918, relief came to us in the form of an abundant crop and the enormous savings of the spiritually mobilized people. Our main problem now was ships. On July 11, 1918, I sailed with Dr. Alonzo Taylor and Lewis Strauss on the *Olympic* for London and Paris to confer with the Prime Ministers and the Food Administrators of Britain, France and Italy together with the military authorities. The *Olympic* was then a troopship carrying 6,000 American soldiers a trip. The precautions against submarines manifested themselves in requirements to wear an uncomfortable life belt all day and to have no lights.[2]

At once we set up the Allied Food Council of which I acted as Chairman. We quickly completed a resurvey of British, French, Italian, Belgian and neutral food needs for the forthcoming year, the sources of available food supply and the available shipping to transport it. Our minimum estimate for the allied civilians was 2,000,000 tons a month of food, clothing and medical supplies. I believed that together with the Canadians we could do it if we had the ships.

But here General Pershing intervened. He had determined upon a general assault on the front for September and concluded that we could not have more than 1,200,000 tons of ships per month for the next four months. We food people agreed that the Allies could overdraw on the summer crops and their animals but that it would create a dangerous

[2] We sat thirteen at the table every meal, and at least fifteen years afterward when I last checked up, the whole company was still alive.

vacuum during the spring months. Worse, however, when the General got into battle, our shipping space was cut to 700,000 tons per month. He was confident, but had he failed we would have had a debacle.

I could only ruminate that the military would learn something very sad indeed about the morale and conduct of civilian populations short of food if they failed in the fall attack. I had a sinking feeling that food might lose the war, instead of, as represented in all our posters—"Food Will Win the War."

Our salvation came from a quarter which we had hardly dared to consider. That was the American victories followed by the Armistice in November, 1918, after which ships were available.

CHAPTER 28

WASHINGTON WAR ORGANIZATION—
THE WAR COUNCIL—AND
VARIOUS MATTERS

My original insistence that food should have a single-headed administrator instead of a committee and that the Food Administration should
have control of every aspect of its problem had proved sound. That
principle of organization for other agencies, however, was slow of
adoption in the early stages of the war. During the first six months the
government broke out with a rash of boards, commissions, and committees for every conceivable administrative purpose.

When one of these bodies fell sick from conflicting policies and
ambitions, the administration had several standard cures. The favorite
included changing the membership, changing the name or appointing
another board, committee or commission with the same powers as the
ailing one or setting up a new "co-ordinator." None of these bodies
was complete without a resurrected colonel of the Spanish-American
War. And many of the civilian members were in army or navy uniforms as high in rank as the wearer could exact. These men were
easily distinguishable from real officers by their attempts to salute. In
full session, with all the papers in front of them, these boards were
truly impressive. The Food Administration for months stood alone as
the only war agency encumbered by neither bells nor costume jewelry.
A multitude of good men worked in these other establishments. I spent
much of my time listening to them while they wept over the hopeless
set-ups in their organizations. Democracy has to learn all of its lessons
with tears—or laughter.

In August, 1917, the President asked me to see him about the coal and oil mess which the Food Administration, together with the committees of the Department of the Interior, was hopelessly attempting to straighten out with "co-ordinators." He opened the interview by remarking that I was *also* a mining engineer. I emphasized again the need of a single-headed administration to succeed the multitude of fumbling committees and the conflicting departmental action by which he had attempted to handle this problem. Knowing his fear of delegating power to business men whom he did not know, I suggested he appoint his old friend, Dr. Harry Garfield, as Fuel Administrator. Dr. Garfield was with me in the Food Administration and I had already employed him to "co-operate" with the Interior Department committees to solve the coal and oil problems. I assured the President that we could provide Dr. Garfield with an adequate technical and business staff. Finally, he sacrificed the board idea on the altar of progress.

I secured for Dr. Garfield, Walter Hope, a lawyer, and Mark Requa, an engineer, skilled in oil, from the Food Administration, and Henry Taylor, a coal operator, as his right-hand men. They quickly built up an efficient organization on the same lines as the Food Administration. Except for complaints over drastic—yet necessary—conservation measures, the President never had to worry again about coal and oil.

The other boards and commissions fell one by one into inevitable disputes and muddled action. The Shipping Board scandal was straightened out only by the President's personally firing two leading members, accepting the resignations of the others and appointing Mr. Edward N. Hurley Chairman of the Board. It still remained a board, but Hurley exacted the right to hire and fire the other members of the board and those of all its subsidiary committees.

The War Trade Board did not function properly until Vance McCormick was placed in full control (October 15th).

The railways almost broke down under a board and were only pulled together when W. G. McAdoo was made Director General (December 26th). Because of McAdoo's lack of railway experience, it was not well done.

The Council of National Defense, supposed to be devoted to munitions, was reorganized at least four times with different names or personnel. Finally the whole munitions question blew up in a congressional investigation and a spasm of public agitation. It was not until March 4, 1918, that the President gave Bernard M. Baruch full control of what was then called the "War Industries Board." From that time on it began to function.

Building up teamwork between all these necessarily different agencies of war administration was another pressing problem. We used the words co-ordination and co-operation until they were worn out. We surrounded ourselves with "co-ordinators" and we spent hours in endless discussions with no court of appeal for final decisions. The pre-war departments of government were as usual mostly dominated by the political leaders who had helped to elect the President. Some of them were jealous of the mushroom war agencies, and considerable friction developed. They were panting for publicity. Daily, one saw a department grab a piece of war work and run to the press with the glad tidings. But after the prize faded from the front page, usually some upstart war organization had to take it on in order to kill it or to make it function.

Finally, in February, 1918, out of my experience with every European government at war, and our own muddle, I furnished Dr. Garfield with a memorandum recommending a sort of War Cabinet composed of the heads of the regular Departments which dealt with war questions. That was the Secretaries of State, War, Navy, and Treasury, together with the heads of the Munitions, Food, Fuel, Shipping, Railways and War Trade Administrations. I felt that Dr. Garfield possibly could convert the President where I had failed. He succeeded. The President called the first meeting on March 20, 1918, and we met with him regularly thereafter. It became known to the press as the War Council. Not only did the Council deal with co-ordination and economic strategy, such as labor, manpower and transport, but the President brought up to it more and more major military and international policies.

The dispute over General Pershing and his independent command, the terms of the Armistice and other critical questions were threshed out and real aid developed for the President. Mr. Hurley gave a graphic account of one of its sittings in his book, *The Bridge to France,* saying, "In the thirty years of my business career I have never been associated.

with a group who worked so harmoniously and effectively." Mr. McCormick described it as "a clearing-house of facts and policy."

As an example of such co-ordination Shipping Administrator Hurley and Secretary of War Baker in a meeting stated their need to secure some sixty-eight ships then lying in American waters which the Dutch under German pressure refused to charter to the Allies. I suggested that I might ask the director of the Belgian Relief at Rotterdam to negotiate quietly for the consent of the Dutch owners to seizure and to a generous price for charters. If that were settled we might seize the ships for the duration without moral turpitude. This was done. The Netherlands Government, to keep its face, protested. The price of the stock in the Dutch companies at once rose several hundred per cent and everybody was happy.

I was constantly sorry for the President having to spend so much time listening to much argument within his War Council while we developed agreement on matters of conflict or needed co-ordination. Nevertheless, it served to educate him, and his ability to make the final decisions on the spot greatly expedited the whole war work. There were questions, such as transportation, rail, ships and labor, where there were simply not enough for each of our activities. He alone could divide them. Once he decided such questions, this body of men carried on.

SOME WAR OFFICIALS

The quality of men in leading war positions was eventually of a very high order.

Secretary of War Newton D. Baker was modest, courageous, methodical and helpful. He surrounded himself with able men, irrespective of party, and left a name high in the annals of American public service. Secretary of the Navy Josephus Daniels was an honest, considerate man. He had no great abilities as an administrator but the Admirals took care of that.

We, naturally, had daily problems with the War Industries Board under Mr. Baruch. He had great capacity in the choice of men. The industrial success of the Board was due to Alexander Legge, and its success in conservation of materials was due to Arch W. Shaw. Its other problems were in the able hands of Daniel Willard, Julius Rosenwald and Judge Lovett. These men did not wear uniforms. Aside from Baruch's ability to select men, he possessed a fine mind and fine probity of character. He had two other qualities: a capacity for friendship and loyalty and an ability to listen patiently to complicated discussions and in the end produce a penetrating and successful solution of the problem. It seemed, at times, to be almost a sixth sense.

Another outstanding war administrator was Vance McCormick, Chairman of the War Trade Board, which controlled imports and exports. He was so co-operative as to set up a branch of the Food Administration in his office with John Beaver White as its head and accepted our views as final in our field.

David Houston, Secretary of Agriculture, and Franklin K. Lane, the Secretary of the Interior, were my most helpful colleagues in the Cabinet. Houston was an able, austere man of fine co-operative sense. Lane was what even men called a sweet character; lovable, loyal and able. Robert Lansing, the Secretary of State, was always considerate and helpful to me.

THE EXCESS PROFITS TAX

Early in July, 1918, I urged upon President Wilson the necessity for broad tax actions by the Congress in order to prevent excessive profits by low-cost manufacturers of food and other war supplies. The difficulty arose from the fact that we had to make prices and set margins such as would bring high-cost producers into production and thus the low-cost producers were making inordinate profits out of the war. Mr. Wilson requested Senator Simmons to go into the question with me with a view to appropriate legislation. As the idea was then new in the United States, I gave the Senator, at his request, on July 18, 1918, a memorandum setting forth my ideas in detail for use to educate his colleagues. The memorandum seemed to carry conviction, for such a law was enacted. Students will find it in the Senate Committee records and the Stanford War Library.

A NOTE ON RUSSIA

There was great dissension between the Allies as to what should be done about Bolshevist Russia. Mr. Wilson, knowing of my experience in that country, requested my views on an Allied proposal that Japan should be asked to move into Siberia. I told him that in view of Russian racial hatred toward the Japanese such a policy would consolidate many Russian elements behind Lenin and Trotsky. Moreover, I was confident that if the Japanese moved in they would never get out. Certainly if Japan made any such effort she would demand Eastern Siberia as a reward. However, Mr. Wilson yielded—though reluctantly—to British and French pressures and as a compromise determined to send American troops in order not to give the Japanese a monopoly. The whole business proved futile and disastrous.

Out of these discussions, however, there came up to the President from Colonel House a plan (June, 1918) that I should head some sort of food mission to Bolshevist Russia to tell them how to relieve their famine, to restore their agriculture and to reorganize their food distribution. I informed the President that I would serve anywhere, any time, but that to send an army to attack the Bolshevists' Eastern Front while extending kindness on their Western Front was not quite logical. In any event, our ideas of industrial organization would scarcely fit into the philosophy of Messrs. Lenin and Trotsky, even if they did not reject the plan utterly as an Allied Trojan horse. I heard nothing more of the matter.

A FORAY INTO POLITICS

My only participation in politics during the war got me into some hot water. Although I was a registered Republican and had been a member of the National Republican Club for years, I considered it my duty in the 1918 election, to support the Congressmen who were loyal to Wilson's objectives whether Republicans or Democrats. I made a public statement on the subject which brought much abuse from Republican politicians. As I stated at that time, an adverse vote in this election would greatly weaken Mr. Wilson's hand in making peace. It did.

CHAPTER 29

SOME RESULTS OF
THE FOOD ADMINISTRATION

A few statistics will illustrate the success of the national effort in food. The result of our policies of stimulating production is visible in the following Department of Agriculture figures of the harvested acreage of the 17 principal ground crops.

	Acres
1914 (pre-war)	314,432,000
1917	328,924,000
1918	341,196,000
1919	342,588,000

That is, our farmers increased by over 28,000,000 the harvested acres. The vital ground crop production for those years was as follows:

	Wheat	Corn	Oats	Potatoes	Rice
1916	634,572,000	2,425,000	1,138,000	270,388,000	39,544,000
1917	619,790,000	2,908,000	1,442,000	398,653,000	34,714,000
1918	904,130,000	2,441,000	1,428,000	346,114,000	39,998,000

In reading these statistics it must be understood that they refer to crop years. Thus when we entered the war in April, 1917, we still lived upon the 1916 crop until the 1917 harvest in August. We were afflicted with a drought and short crops both in 1916 and 1917, and therefore these subnormal crops entered heavily into the problem of war supplies. But the abundant crops of 1918 and 1919 eased our problems.

The following tables show our exports (mostly to the Allies) and are given in fiscal years ending June 30th as more nearly approximating the "harvest" years.

NET BREADSTUFFS EXPORTED
(Wheat, Flour, Corn Products—Rice and Cereals)

	Tons
Three-year pre-war average	3,720,000
1917	8,580,000
1918	11,762,000
1919	10,210,000

NET FEED GRAINS EXPORTED
(Barley, Oats, Corn for Feed)

	Tons
Three-year pre-war average	1,045,000
1917	2,445,000
1918	2,126,000
1919	1,100,000

The drop in 1919 was due to the use of shipping for human food and to the decrease in European animals.

NET SUGAR EXPORTED
(From the United States and West Indies)

	Tons
Three-year pre-war average	679,800
1917	1,672,000
1918	1,874,400
1919	1,200,000

After the Armistice, in 1919, the Java and Indian crops became available to Europe.

ANIMAL PRODUCTS

The following tables indicate the progress in increasing the food animals. These figures become the more impressive if we consider the decreasing tide when we began in the spring of 1917.

Our special attention was devoted to hogs and sheep, as cattle increase was too slow.

HOGS

	Total Number	Number Slaughtered (Calendar Yr.)	Pork & Lard Produced Lbs.
July 1, 1917	53,000,000	56,500,000	8,490,000,000
Jan. 1, 1918	62,931,000	65,100,000	10,230,000,000
Jan. 1, 1919	64,000,000	65,795,000	10,381,000,000

SHEEP

	Number	Number Slaughtered (Calendar Yr.)	Lamb & Mutton Produced Lbs.
July 1, 1917.............	38,000,000	12,128,000	463,000,000
Jan. 1, 1918.............	39,664,000	13,220,000	506,000,000
Jan. 1, 1919.............	41,875,000	15,784,000	590,000,000

CATTLE AND CALVES

	Number	Number Slaughtered (Calendar Yr.)	Beef and Veal Produced Lbs.
July 1, 1917.............	70,000,000	15,741,000	7,983,000,000
Jan. 1, 1918.............	73,040,000	17,093,000	8,486,000,000
Jan. 1, 1919.............	72,094,000	15,029,000	7,575,000,000

The amounts given below are the estimates of net exports in tons of 2000 pounds and for the fiscal years beginning on July 1st.

MEATS AND FATS
(Animal and edible vegetable oil products)

	Tons
Three-year pre-war average	769,500
1917	2,042,500
1918	2,400,500
1919	1,641,000

DRIED FRUIT

	Tons
Three-year pre-war average..............	95,000
1917	50,500
1918	103,500
1919	146,300

There were also large increases in canned fruits and other food commodities.

TOTAL RESULTS

The increased surplus which we provided for the Allies in the war and for the relief of famine after the war is indicated by the following table of actual net exports. Three-quarters of the exports in the fiscal year ending July 1, 1919, and about one-third of the exports during the year ending July 1, 1920, came under the heading of postwar relief.

NET EXPORTS OF FOOD AND FEED
WAR AND RELIEF YEARS

	3-Year Pre-war Average	1917–1918	1918–1919	1919–1920
Breadstuffs	3,720,000	8,580,000	11,762,000	10,210,000
Meats and Fats	769,500	2,242,500	2,600,500	1,741,000
Sugar (U. S. and West Indies)	679,800	1,672,000	1,874,400	1,200,000
Sundries (Dried and Canned Fruits, etc.)..	140,200	210,000	240,400	346,800
Feed Grains	1,045,000	2,445,000	2,126,000	1,100,000
Total	6,354,500	15,149,500	18,603,300	14,597,800*

* Approximately two-thirds of this was used for relief in the last half of 1919.

PRICE CONTROL

Considering the inflationary processes of currency and credit issues and high wages inherent in war, our price controls worked out very well. Taking prices at 100 in April 1917, when we entered the war, compared with 19 months later, when we dissolved the Food Administration, the Department of Labor figures showed that farm prices had risen to 125.9, wholesale prices to 124.2, and retail prices to 124.8. But these figures included luxury foods. The rise in staples was considerably less. We had no local famines and no black markets due to our control methods.

COST OF ADMINISTRATION

The total administrative expenditures of the Food Administration were $7,862,669, including the erection of temporary buildings; this included also the entire overhead of the relief and rehabilitation of Europe which I conducted in various capacities including United States Food Administrator. As I have stated, we secured $150,000,000 as working capital from the Congress. The Grain and Sugar Corporations returned to the Treasury our entire working capital and a total of over $60,000,000 in profits, much of which had been earned outside the

United States. Thus the Food and Reconstruction Administrations cost the government $50,000,000 less than nothing.

OUR PUBLIC RECORD

It may be recorded here that the Food Administration was about the only government agency never investigated by Congress. It was never charged with malfeasance at any time although we handled over 7 billion dollars in transactions.

This agency represented the first assumption by the American Government of great economic powers. They were a necessity of war, but we avoided evil consequences to American life by the voluntary character of our staff and the building of our control measures through co-operation of the trades together with our quick dissolution of them after the war.

I would be remiss if I did not express my obligation for the loyalty and magnificent capacity of the men and women who composed the Food Administration. They are too great a host for me to include individual tribute to their service. My gratitude indeed extends much further. These men and women became my lifelong friends. Their steadfastness remained in time of defeat and grief. Their quality as Americans is shown by the numbers of them who later became leaders in their communities and in the nation.

CHAPTER 30

❧❧❧❧❧

FAMILY LIFE IN WASHINGTON
DURING THE WAR

Altogether during the three years from the beginning of the war until after the family came to Washington to live during the Food Administration, I had seen my boys less than a total of six months. Their upbringing at this critical period of their lives was the exclusive work of Mrs. Hoover.

She met me in New York on my arrival from Europe to take on the Food Administration in May 1917. At once she went on a hunt for a furnished house in Washington where our leading staff could live until they settled into other quarters. She found one to her liking on Sixteenth Street. The lady who had built it seemed to have thought of accommodations for six or eight people. Gradually we piled up inhabitants until every nook and corner was filled. We made it shelter some forty men. Its intimate associations served to weld the whole directing staff into an enthusiastic and devoted team.

After starting us in Washington life, Mrs. Hoover looked for a more permanent place for the family and secured for the winter the Adams residence on Massachusetts Avenue. After this beneficent service, she returned to the boys who were in the public school in Palo Alto, and brought them on to Washington when the Adams house was available.

If social activity, with a big S, existed in Washington during the war, we saw little of it. True, there were guests at our table almost every night, but they were mostly our own staff or the members of the other agencies with whom we shared common problems. It was also my duty to offer hospitality to visiting delegations from abroad. Arthur Balfour, Marshal Joffre, Jan Paderewski, Thomas Masaryk, Lord Reading,

Fridtjof Nansen, and many others here met other officials at our table where we could discuss affairs off-the-record.

Herbert was then 14 and Allan 11 years old. Mrs. Hoover placed them in the Friends' School and herself welded together the irregular joints of their somewhat disconnected education. The boys were busy discovering the world and their roguish accounts of their adventures and their incessant questions were vastly entertaining. At times I wondered if their mental processes were not composed wholly of an interrogation point.

During the summer of 1918 Louis Chevrillon, a French associate in engineering and in Belgian Relief work, came over on a mission for the French Government, bringing his niece and a friend, Mademoiselle Nottingier. The three of them stopped with us. Allan, from observations and deductions of his own, and to the embarrassment of the whole household, announced firmly and loudly that Mr. Chevrillon and Mademoiselle Nottingier were going to be married. He proved right, but he was in advance of the usual formalities. And a glorious lady she was.

In summer, to gain more association with the boys and a relief from war strains we, the Rickards, the Hallowells, and other families in the Food Administration searched out appropriate brooks around Washington where we held regular Sunday picnics. There we cooked our lunches over camp fires and joined with the children to build dams and canals in the streams from which sprung waterfalls, and pools with waterwheels and boats. These wet and muddy engineering employments resulted in permanent changes in the landscape. In winter on Sundays, we motored the children to good snow fields or good skating ponds and built bonfires to warm ourselves meantime.

The City of Washington was totally unprepared for the great influx of war employees and the visiting citizens. At first regular beds and regular meals for all the new people did not seem to exist. However, everybody accepted the situation in good humor and gradually we improved things.

Under the leadership of Mrs. Hoover, Mrs. Rickard, Mrs. Whitmarsh, Mrs. Hallowell and the other wives, great aids were organized for our women employees. They established the Food Administration Girls'

Club with temporary, decent living quarters for many; and they made systematic provision of outside rooms and board for the remainder. They insisted that we put a large cafeteria in the new Food Administration building. They looked after it so well that we came near being overwhelmed with employees from the other departments looking for good and cheap food. They served thousands of meals daily—and made a profit on it. They devoted the profit to their other activities on behalf of the women employees with a grim determination that the men employees must thereby contribute to their resources.

The fall of 1918 was memorable not alone for the war, but for a world-wide virulent influenza epidemic. This affliction probably killed more people than all the battles of the World War and found its parallel in the epidemics of disease which had accompanied previous great world disasters of war or famine. It struck the Food Administration with great violence. One-half of our staff was stricken and a good many died. Mrs. Hoover and the other ladies, in addition to doing their bit for the city in this crisis, organized a special service for the Food Administration employees. There was nothing that could be done for our people that they did not do. One of the sweetest services ever performed by women was the tenderness and sympathy they displayed, not alone to the sick, but to the families of those who died.

CHAPTER 31

TRANSFORMING
THE FOOD ADMINISTRATION
INTO A NEW MISSION

In September, 1918, from the internal situation and other causes—chiefly the successes of the American Army—the German military leaders had begun to revise their views of the future. The turn came with the Battle of St. Mihiel on September 12th. On September 16th, the Austrians sent a note asking for a negotiated peace. On the same day the Bulgarians asked for an armistice. On September 29th, they surrendered. On that day the American Army launched the great battle of the Argonne. We later learned that on this day Hindenburg informed the German Government that they must seek an armistice in which to negotiate peace. The German Emperor ran out, deserted his people, and the new government asked for an armistice on October 6th. The Emperor might have left the Hohenzollerns a little blaze of glory if he had mounted his white horse and charged the trenches. But he was not a Teutonic Knight. In his humiliating descent to chopping wood in Holland he made a sorry figure.

In any event, from that moment we began to adjust our food policies on a postwar basis.

These events had to be faced by me in the capacity of a member of the War Council. From the above dates until the Armistice was finally signed the President convened the Council several times. His problem was to force the kind of armistice terms which would end the war for good. We were all agreed that the terms must end the fighting once for all by demobilization of the German armies and the instant

[275]

surrender of their arms. We agreed there could be no peace negotiated between standing armies. Some of our Council members, however, wanted to rub the noses of the Germans in the dirt with the demand of "unconditional surrender" and a triumphal march down Unter den Linden. I was one of those who felt that we wanted to save American lives by making the German Army impotent, and with that done phrases counted little. Also, there was imperative need to maintain a responsible government in Germany. There was substance in the democratic elements of the country upon which a stable government and a new world might be built instead of mortgaging the future with a shattered nation. The President offered the Germans his Fourteen Points and his "subsequent addresses" as a basis. His armistice phrase finally was "an Armistice that makes the renewal of hostilities impossible." The Germans accepted. The Armistice terms certainly denatured the German Army for it began streaming home at once without its arms.

The first effect of the Armistice of November 11th on the Food Administration was temporarily to dispose of our worries over assignment of ships to carry food to Europe. Of much more importance was the immediate shift in our whole outlook from a war administration of food, to relief of the famine over the continent of Europe and its economic rehabilitation. That such a famine was inevitable had long been certain, and our American food strategy was prepared for it. We had created gigantic surpluses either to be used to carry the Allies through the war until the summer of 1919 or, alternatively, to be used to fight this inevitable famine.

OUR SECOND INTERVENTION IN EUROPE

At the Armistice the world was indeed confronted with a new and gigantic food problem. All of Europe—300,000,000 or 400,000,000 people —Allies, neutrals, enemies—twenty-six nations—were faced with some shortage of food. Many of them were starving and some were destitute of money and credit with which to buy abroad.

America had intervened with its immense military power and had brought the war to an end. She now was called upon to intervene a second time—to save Europe from the flames of starvation, pestilence, revolution, and to start the rebuilding of industry and life. If the furnace of famine continued to burn, no peace could be made. And from its aftermath no hope of a better world could come. As President Wilson phrased it: "This service is second only to the mission of our army in Europe."

Early in October, 1918, anticipating the end of the war, I instituted a survey of the food resources of the world available from overseas to meet the European situation.

The result showed a need of about 31,000,000 tons of human food for the following twelve months, and a supply of about 32,000,000 tons, of which about 18,000,000 tons could come from the United States with the remainder mostly from Canada and the dammed-back supplies in the Indies and the Southern Hemisphere. These estimates subsequently proved singularly accurate. It was obvious that the greatest burden would fall upon the United States, more particularly as we were the only country likely to extend credits to exhausted peoples with which to buy it.

During the pre-Armistice negotiations, I proposed that an assurance of food supplies to the enemy should be expressed in the Armistice terms. I feared that the French and British hate fever would continue the food blockade unless it was thus agreed. This idea was weakly incorporated into the Armistice terms as follows:

Article 26 . . . The Allies and the United States contemplate the provisioning of Germany during the Armistice as shall be necessary. . . .

Our problem, however, was not alone to organize the whole world's food reserves to save hundreds of millions of human beings from famine and pestilence; but also to bridge over the European economic transition until they could resume production and secure credit or resources to support themselves thereafter. And we had a special problem to avoid a break in our guaranteed farm prices which would ruin our farmers and the country banks which had extended credit to carry our surplus. If our prices suddenly collapsed, our arm in redemption of Europe and making peace would be paralyzed by panic at home.

On November 7th, Mr. Wilson requested me to undertake the transformation of the Food Administration into the new agency of relief and reconstruction. On November 8th Colonel House, thinking independently, cabled from Europe recommending that I head up the economic reconstruction of Europe during the Armistice. The President replied that I would be leaving for Europe as quickly as possible.

A number of meetings of Allied and American officials had been held in London immediately prior to the Armistice. They devised complete world controls of the economic life of the earth to continue for some years. These measures included control of prices, of shipping through bunker coal, the pooling of credit, food supplies and raw materials, all to be imposed on the world under a board of Allied representatives. In reply to their urging that we at once agree to such a program, I sent them the following cable on November 13th, with the approval of the President:

We consider ourselves the trustees for our surplus production of all kinds for the benefit of the most necessitous and the most deserving. We feel that we must ourselves execute this trusteeship . . . we cannot undertake any . . . arrangements that look to the control of our exports after peace and furthermore . . . the Inter-Allied councils hitherto set up in Europe were entirely for the purpose of guiding Inter-Allied relations during the period of the war and any extension of their functions either by way of their control of our relations to other nations at present or the extension of their present functions beyond peace, cannot be entertained by us. . . .

But even that did not kill the project. The subject continued to be argued. One of our European staff, Mr. George McFadden, however, vigorously objected to the whole process. Finally, with Mr. Wilson's approval, on November 16th, I again cabled that we of course would maintain our co-operation in the existing Inter-Allied economic bodies and I continued:

Particular great care must be exercised lest these bodies assume the role of permanent organizations for rationing and reconstruction of the world after peace. At the Peace Conference the economic power of the United States must be entirely unrestricted as this force in our hands may be a powerful assistance in enabling us to secure acceptance of our view . . . economic control . . . after [the peace] will . . . be decided at the Conference. We must not even by implication be committed to it now.

Even that silenced the movement only until I arrived in Europe.

Under the President's authority I made various arrangements to assure speedy arrivals of food in Europe in large quantities. The War Department's freight movement was now reversed as they would be sending ships to Europe empty to bring back troops. At once with the Armistice I had arranged with that Department to load some 160,000 tons of flour and fats and to consign them to me in Europe. I also secured that the large surplus of army food and clothing supplies in France, which had been stored as insurance against submarines, should be handed over to me.

We secured an Executive Order from the President that the Food Administration Grain Corporation enlarge its functions beyond the borders of the United States and undertake the purchase of any sort of American supplies and their transportation to European destinations. I directed the Grain Corporation to open a European office in London under Edward Flesh. We set up the Grain Corporation to do the great task of our accounting with the twenty-odd governments with whom we must deal. I secured the co-operation of the Navy for the establishment of port organizations at the points where they might be needed.

In an address to the Food Administration employees, many of whom had come to a final meeting from the interior, I reviewed our work, and concluded:

. . . As the result of this war there are large masses of people actually starving today. There are enormous populations suffering . . . privation. . . . In the midst of this the wheat loaf has ascended in imagination of men, women and children as the emblem of national survival and national tranquillity. . . .

There is a story yet incomplete and yet to be written around wheat. You will recollect that Frank Norris planned three novels, two of which were completed in his lifetime, the third of which he had outlined. The first of these, *The Octopus,* represented the hardship of the producer and the scantiness and dreariness of his life and the imposition under which he suffered. The second represented the Chicago wheat pit, the manipulation, the violence and horrible avarice which grew out of the rampant speculation with the world's bread. The third, I understand, was planned to represent the privation, suffering and even starvation imposed upon the consumer by our gigantic failure in honest distribution. . . . But when this war is over it will be possible to write this third volume, not in Norris' despondent and despairing tones of tragedy, but if we do our duty it can be written in terms of triumph. For today if we do that duty it will represent the honest and fair treatment of the farmer, the lifting of his level of life, the abolition of speculation, the honest and economic distribution of our daily bread. We will have managed the scantiness in supply of this almost famine year of 1917, not by the privation of the poor, but by the self-denial of the better-to-do and its royal sharing into the hands, on one side, of those of the Allies and, on the other, given as charity to that mass of liberty-loving people who have been oppressed and strangled by the enemy.

If Norris could have lived he would have found this—"The Song of the Wheat"—as a theme in the world's regeneration.

With the general approval of our organization, I appointed Edgar Rickard as Assistant Food Administrator to take full charge in Washington, with instructions (which were immediately carried out) to dissolve all of our regulations and control measures and to demobilize our staff, excepting those which affected our guarantees to the farmers. These were mainly the Grain Corporation, the Sugar Equalization Board, the hog and dairy guarantees, the control of processing these products, the control of imports, exports and foreign buying. Mr. Rickard, within sixty days, had reduced our other staff from some 3,000 then in the Washington office to about 400. Equally rapidly were the State and local organizations liquidated.

On November 17, 1918, six days after the Armistice, accompanied by Alonzo Taylor as nutritional adviser, Robert Taft as legal adviser, Julius Barnes, President of the Grain Corporation, and Lewis Strauss, my jewel of a secretary, I sailed for Europe aboard the *Olympic*.

The Relief and
Reconstruction of Europe
1918–1920

CHAPTER 32

AT THE DAWN OF THE ARMISTICE

1918

The Armistice brought a lift to the spirit of the Allied world. Americans believed they had won the greatest crusade for liberty of men in all history. Fear vanished. Hope swept in as a desert sunrise. The men on the front emerged from the dugouts into the sunlight. They scraped off the trench mud and the lice for the last time. They sang and shouted. They surveyed No Man's Land and the enemy trenches curiously. They talked with the enemy and gave him a smoke. Soldiers respect good soldiers. Victory had come to a billion people. Sons, husbands, brothers were coming home. Youths began again to plan their lives. Good cheer, smiles and laughter met at every crossroads, every street corner. The rebound from fear and despair was somewhat raucous and wet in spots.

Inspiring visions of justice and peace rose in men's minds. It was to be the last great war. The burdens of fear and arms would be lifted. Liberty, freedom, democracy were the watchwords of the day, and peace, lasting peace, was to come. President Wilson had proclaimed the redemption of mankind in his Fourteen Points and eleven more "points" from the "subsequent addresses." He was greeted by the world as little short of the Second Messiah. The leaders of nations had only to meet and fix these great aspirations in a covenant that would give humanity its greatest forward impulse since the Sermon on the Mount.

Within a month revolutions in the liberated and enemy countries threw off the old oppressions, expelled the old leaders, and adopted constitutional governments with guaranties of personal liberty. Their people felt the lift of release and hope. Even the German people, repressed over decades, looked forward to a peace under which they could prosper and take their proper place in the progress of men. Did not the Fourteen Points assure all these?

But after a few days the world began to survey the wreckage. Ten million men were dead or maimed. Ten million men, women and children had died of starvation and disease. Towns, cities, ships, railways were destroyed. Governments had gone $250 billion into debt which, in Europe, they could never pay. Currencies, credit and prices were inflated. There were no jobs ready in industry for the soldiers and munition workers.

Then the world began to lick its wounds. It recalled that Germany, Austria and Russia were the causes of its suffering. The recollection of their outrages, atrocities and terrorization surged back. Hate crawled in with demands for punishment, revenge, indemnities and reparations.

Then new fears came into the world. The Two Horsemen of War and Death had passed on, but now came Famine and Pestilence and their camp followers with even more violence. History might repeat itself again; for after the Thirty Years' War, a third of the population of Europe died.

This fear was sharpened by the possibility that the pressure of starvation would break down the weak revolutionary governments of Central and Eastern Europe into anarchy. After the Armistice, there began to loom up a greater fear from a more potent enemy of freedom than anarchy, which after all is an unorganized force. Communism, which had captured Russia, was a new form of organized destruction of Liberty. And it was vengeance itself. The Communists had captured the Czarist gold reserves. Their agents spread over Europe, subsidizing a new revolution. Soon we began to realize that its infectious poison was spreading alarmingly among all starving peoples. Here loomed up a defeat of all we had fought for—to establish liberty.

HIGH HOPES

On the voyage across the Atlantic, Taft, Taylor, Barnes, Strauss and myself had a chance to think and plan the solution of the problems confronting us. In our appraisal of the problems we divided the 400,-

000,000 people of Europe into groups. As a result of the war and the revolutions immediately following, there were twenty-eight nations to deal with.

There were the three major Allies—Britain, France and Italy—and the two little Allies—Portugal and Greece—with a total of about 135,000,000 people. These people could obtain some supplies from the Southern Hemisphere and India where they could exchange goods or secure credit; they required large supplies from the United States for which credit must be provided, but they did have ships and could transport their own materials.

Then there were the six neutrals—Holland, Denmark, Norway, Sweden, Switzerland and Spain—with a total of about 42,000,000 people. They had made money out of the war and had ships and credit, and they could go to distant sources for supplies.

There were the thirteen liberated countries—Belgium, Poland, Yugoslavia, Albania, Czechoslovakia, Roumania, Finland, Estonia, Latvia, Lithuania, Armenia, Georgia, and Azerbaijan, a total of over 110,000,000 people. They were destitute of everything—credit, food, raw materials and ships. They had established representative governments led by revolutionaries wholly inexperienced in public administration. They were struggling to hold their governments against the infiltration and assaults of the Communists and the Czarist gold.

There were the five enemy countries—Germany, Austria, Hungary, Bulgaria and Turkey—about 110,000,000 people. Except in Turkey they had established representative governments, but again they were in the hands of revolutionaries, inexperienced in government. These countries had some gold resources, but their ships were to be taken away from them. Their governments were threatened by the spread of Communism and unemployment.

And there was Soviet Russia, with 170,000,000 people, starving, yet her agents were everywhere stirring up trouble.

There were other problems which affected the eighteen "liberated" and "enemy" countries. The new set-up of Europe, with ten wholly new nations and five truncated enemy nations, made new boundaries; new flows of commerce, disconnected railways; stopped the movement of coal and of such small food surpluses as there were. The new nations must create the whole machinery of government, must create new systems of food distribution; they must open ports, canals, rehabilitate railways, restore communications, create currencies and do a thousand other revivifying things.

We knew from the Belgian Relief experience that there were legions of starving waifs and subnormal children throughout Europe who must have special care at once if they were not to become a generation of incompetents and criminals.

The Allies were still maintaining their blockade of food and other supplies against the twenty-three neutral, liberated, and enemy countries and Russia.

Above all, peace had to be made.

The starving "liberated" and "enemy" nations must have it quickly, for people were dying. And relief had to be brought fast if we were to maintain the order and stability upon which peace and freedom of men could be built. But we knew that food could arrive only after long voyages of ships, the finding of credits, taking down blockades, building up internal transportation, distribution and restoring employment. And it was not only the finding of the food, the credit and the ships.

Beyond all this, there were other internal political and religious conflicts in all these countries from which we must keep rigidly free. In religious aspects, the total with whom we must deal, outside Russia, something like 45% were Roman Catholics; 13% Orthodox Catholics; 34% Protestants; 6% Moslems; and 2% Jews—and they were mixed in various percentages in different countries.

To cope with this demoralized and divided Europe and the world's scarcity of supplies there must be rapid, decisive organization and executive authority. With his usual understatement, Mr. Taft opined that it was a mess.

It was with a mind filled with these problems that I arrived in London. The first evening I was warmly welcomed by old friends— British and American. We had worked together over the whole four years of war. Now that it was over, there was a release of humor and spirit. Our discussions were mostly on the peace to come. Idealism burned brightly. We felt greater by being part of a generation which had won for the earth the end of mass murder, freedom of men, the independence and safety of nations.

We discussed the economic and social reforms that must follow. We talked of abolishing want, through increased productivity, care of the aged, better homes, and wider doors of opportunity. We talked of the greater future for children of all men. We were sure that humanity, having passed through the furnace of the last four years, would be less greedy, less selfish. We discussed far into the night the measures that must be taken to get the world back to work. There would be a period of great difficulties and readjustments but the new spirit of men that had carried the war would carry the peace and reconstruction. The purification of men, the triumph of democracy would bring a new golden age. We were indeed proud that we had had a part in this rebirth of mankind.

CHAPTER 33

SOME DISAGREEABLE SURPRISES

I was still under that evening's spell the next morning when I met with the Allied Ministers for discussion of programs and organization. I had a rude awakening.[1]

This morning session was at once an enlightenment in national intrigue, selfishness, nationalism, heartlessness, rivalry and suspicion, which seemed to ooze from every pore—but with polished politeness. In analyzing it afterwards, the confusion of forces became more clear. There was here a dual mind. The Englishman, Frenchman, and Italian genuinely thought idealistically—as individuals. But when each viewed the problems of his own people, the impoverishment, the unemployment, the debt, and when he thought of national prestige and power, he was a different man.

[1] Lest anyone think subsequent intergovernmental actions are improbable, I refer to the complete documentary proof now available to students. It is mostly found in:

The Organization of American Relief in Europe, 1918–19, (documents), Suda L. Bane and Ralph H. Lutz, Stanford University Press, 1943.

The Blockade of Germany After the Armistice, 1918–19, (documents), Suda L. Bane and Ralph H. Lutz, Stanford University Press, 1942.

The Grain Trade During the World War, Frank M. Surface, The Macmillan Company, 1928.

American Pork Production in the World War, Frank M. Surface, A. W. Shaw Company, Chicago, 1926.

These publications of documents (which exceed 1,000,000 words) enabled great condensation of this manuscript. Some documents not available in the above publications are given in the text. To make some passages clear, I have skeletonized some paragraphs in the published documents, the full content of which can be found in these publications. References to them are given in the footnotes.

A host of other books and magazine articles of the period will be found in the War Library at Stanford University.

These nations in reality, always had class government. These classes survived and dominated because each served solely the nationalist interest of its own country. And that was a selfish and greedy interest. There were thus morals and idealism in individual men, but there were no morals nor idealism in the State. It was mostly America that held to such ideas. Ours was the only nation since the time of the Crusades that had fought other peoples' wars for ideals. Individually, Europeans are generous to suffering, but ours is the only Government which has poured out billions in compassion. The other nations knew this and traded on it.

It was something of a shock to realize that the war and all its elevation of spirit had not changed the collective minds of the British, French or Italians. It was still Empire First—and against all comers, including the other two. Each of the three had built their greatness on adherence to this principle. Their bureaucracies thought only in these terms.

The officials I sat with were delightful men. They believed the welfare of their Empires was the welfare of the world. As much as I am devoted to the English people, when they take on the mantle of government they have one most irritating quality. They are the masters of the world at wrapping every national action in words of sanctity which makes one really ashamed not to support it all. Perhaps the greatest of all their phrases is "the White Man's burden."

I have, however, never been disposed to be over-critical of the confusion, indirection, selfishness, materialism in the Allies and all other countries which began to emerge at once with the Armistice. Every nation—England, France, Italy, and all the rest—was faced with stupendous difficulties. Each of them certainly looked for solution of its own problems first. And they regarded America as having suffered much less than they and felt that therefore she could be liberal. But some phases of this attitude had to be resisted.

Within a few hours I found that the greatest famine since the Thirty Years' War did not seem to be of any great immediate concern. Nor was there much concern that it must be stemmed at once if Europe were to make recovery in a generation and if that social stability, out of which peace could be made, was to be maintained. Instead, I found myself projected immediately into battles of power politics on four fronts.

And incidentally I discovered that the Allied governments' suspicion of each other was greater than their suspicion of us.

First. The British, French and Italian Governments were still determined upon the pooling of all Allied and American economic power, to continue for a long period after the peace. They had not retreated from the proposals that we had already abruptly refused from Washington. The general idea was through the power of bunker-coal, food, shipping and credit they could force all nations to accept their dictates. This power was to be used for political purposes and, through favor of the Allies, they would compel all the neutral world to contribute to the rehabilitation of the Allies themselves. Had they not saved the neutrals from the German menace?

They had it all precisely worked out. It was to be managed by the unanimous decisions of a council with four members and a chairman without a vote. The United States, with all its resources, was to be one of the four. It quickly appeared that they feared President Wilson might take independent action and use American resources to effect his political ideas.

If they could not secure the extension of this arrangement over years after peace, they wanted it until peace was made. They wanted no single American command at the top even of America's own food, credit or ships. In some ways, it was the same fight they had made against the independent command of the American Army by General Pershing.

Second. They were determined to reduce the prices of American foodstuffs, or otherwise they would repudiate their purchase contracts with us, under which we were supporting the guarantees we had given to our farmers and to Cuba.

Third. There was a determination to keep the food blockade not only on Germany and the enemy states but also on the neutrals and the liberated areas. One of the reasons for this action was to bring pressure upon us to accept the reduction in prices by closing the outlet for our surpluses until we gave way. Part of this idea was to use the blockade of enemy countries until they accepted the peace terms of the Allies. But this did not answer my question of what to do about the neutrals and the liberated countries who badly needed food and other supplies.

To bring these ideas about, Lord Reading had been placed in command of the British forces with Sir Arthur Salter in the background; Clémentel, Minister of Commerce, in charge of French forces; and Crespi, Minister of Food, in charge of the Italian forces. At our first session they opened with a display of unity that indicated much prior collaboration.

After this first meeting, where I mostly listened, my old friend, Lord Eustace Percy, came to see me, stating that Lord Reading and M. Clémentel had authorized him to offer me the chairmanship of the Council to control the economic world if I would support its set-up. I was to resign my American official positions and to operate the organization from London as a neutral chairman—"It would make you the economic Foch of the world."

The same day the British Food Administrator came to me with an offer, if we would consent to a reduction of American food prices, they would ease up the blockade measures. This I stated we could not do out of justice to our farmers, to which commitment the British had heartily agreed at one time. He said they could obtain food for 50 per cent less in the Southern Hemisphere. They considered it was not fair to their people to buy the higher priced American food. I suggested that, except for the contracts they had already made with us, they go ahead and buy in these markets, let the blockade down, and we would supply other nations.

The obvious fact was that they were striving for three conflicting objectives. As they were themselves dependent upon the United States for food and reconstruction credits, they did not want the President to use these pressures against them in the Peace Conference. They also knew full well the powerful political use to which food and credits could be applied in forcing the conduct of twenty nations in Europe and they wanted to participate in the use of this power. And finally they wanted the glory and influence and prestige in those countries, of rehabilitation in their joint names. Throughout they could not but believe that the United States had deep ulterior motives.

It was obvious that we must have some sort of co-ordination of economic activities with the Allies during the Armistice. I wanted to co-operate and collaborate but not to enter any pool. I resolved, therefore, not to make an issue but merely gently to whittle these ideas down to the desired dimensions. We argued for days. We made the American position clear but did not get anywhere.

Through Colonel House the situation was transmitted to President Wilson. He came back, on the advice of House, with a clear and simple plan of a single-headed administration of rehabilitation, with an advisory committee of the Allies, but maintaining the identity of the United States and control of its own resources. The President had long since been cured of boards and commissions and he had no idea of surrendering American independence. Through the war he had insisted that the United States was only "an associated power." His message produced an explosion.

Lord Reading came to see me and insisted that the President's plan was no good. I then suggested that, before we discussed any plan of organization, we examine what financial support, what supplies, and what amount of shipping each of the four governments would contribute either to relief or to the pool, and that in these proportions each should participate in the management. We went over the organization ground each day. My constant question was what supplies and services would they contribute? It was all very wearing.

In my separate contacts with the British, French and Italian leaders, the usual sub-currents of their conflicting relations with each other became obvious.

The fight against the President's plan of organization was mostly a British affair. The French were put forward by the British to do the talking, but the French assured us privately that they were for our method. They said frankly that they had neither money nor credit, food nor ships to contribute. They also wanted to make sure they had a priority on American supplies and on credit for themselves. The Italians were interested in two aspects of the problem. They hankered to have, through the great economic pool, a partnership in toll gates over the world's commerce after the peace as the most realistic method of collecting reparations. They estimated that we could make the rest of the world pay by a tax on coal alone a billion a year. But they also wanted to make sure that they would have continuous supplies from the United States until the next harvest on credit.

My assurances that the President meant what he said on our purely humanitarian mission and its organization did not convince them— motives of international humanitarianism had not dominated European governments historically.

We realized fully the situation and the temper in the Allied countries. They had suffered indescribably in the war. Every family mourned its dead. The economic problems were staggering. Hate for the Germans still burned at every fireside. I should have been glad to be loved by the Allies for giving in to their every demand. However, despite our earnest desire to co-operate and co-ordinate our efforts with everybody, we got nowhere. Finally, Lord Reading and Minister Clémentel settled a "plan" in writing which the French informed us was drafted by the British. Lord Reading transmitted it to me and said:

As soon as you have had time to consider the document I sent you through the good offices of M. Clémentel, I should like to know whether you accept its terms or in what respects you disagree with it. . . . Until I hear from you I fear no progress can be made.

This letter had an ultimatum flavor of the Viceroy of India. Instead of further argument, I sent a note to Colonel House for him to transmit to the Prime Ministers if he wished. In summary, the "Clémentel plan" amounted again to Allied control of American resources, with no pledges from themselves. I concluded my advice to the Colonel by saying:

. . . Rather than to attempt an immediate solution of these . . . differences in fundamental principle, the President should propose that the American Government will take action independently to remedy immediate critical situations and suggest to the Allies that they co-operate. . . . This will give ample time for consideration and development of common view.

CHAPTER 34

SETTING UP ORGANIZATION

As starvation does not await the outcome of power politics, I decided to attend to the famine and reconstruction and let the power politicians work all by themselves. Having emphasized in a hundred ways our desire to co-operate in the fullest manner, we would let it go at that. The American people did not require the permission of anybody to undertake this second intervention in Europe.

I left London on December 10th and on the 12th I opened our offices in Paris. My real authority consisted of representing America in this matter. Technically I acted under several authorities. President Wilson had appointed me to do the job. I was United States Food Administrator, Chairman of the United States Grain Corporation, the Sugar Equalization Board, and the Belgian Relief Commission. I had the services of our War and Navy Departments in Washington and Europe. Secretary of the Treasury Carter Glass had agreed to establish individual credits to the various liberated countries with which to enable them to pay me for supplies and transportation. I was also authorized by General Pershing and Admiral Benson to command at any time the services of the American Army and Navy and any of their personnel or their surplus supplies. Altogether, it seemed ample authority. It gave me command of credit, food, and some ships. It did not occur to the hungry nations to ask whether my activities had been visaed by the other Allied Governments.

By the opening of operations, I had done away with the pool and Allied control of American resources in one act.

Under the arrangements I had set in motion before leaving Washington, we had—by the middle of December, thirty days after the

Armistice—more than one hundred cargoes arriving or on the seas. Admiral Benson agreed with me that we should ignore the blockade of the liberated countries—and even neutrals—with American-flag ships. He stated simply, "Let me know if anybody tries to stop an American ship on these missions." By the careful assignment of these en route cargoes the "liberated" countries were able to tide over until the whole purchase, finance, shipping and internal organization was operating. We could do little in the neutral countries and nothing in the "enemy" countries until the blockade was removed, although I did move considerable emergency supplies into Austria in spite of the blockade.

Thus "power politics" had not succeeded in delaying food to the hungry except in the enemy territory where we were blockaded for four months, and in the neutral countries who could get along temporarily on the sparse "rations" already allotted to them through the blockade.

I had determined before leaving Washington to avoid bringing a large staff from the United States, and except for some twenty key men, I was able to call our former Belgian Relief men, who were serving in the Army and Navy. Beyond that I determined to depend upon securing our new personnel from our armed forces in Europe. Those organizations, being formed of every variety of experienced civilians temporarily in uniform, furnished the greatest recruiting ground on earth. I found that almost the whole of them were ready to volunteer in order to get out of the deadly routine of French village billets or European ports. General Pershing, as always, was wonderfully co-operative. He readily undertook to detail all the personnel we wanted. In the end we drew about 2,500 officers and men from the Army and Navy.

On December 12, 1918, he wrote to me that the other top military men had inquired of him what my functions were. To them he had replied:

"Mr. Hoover is the food regulator of the world." By this I mean to express my very complete appreciation of the enormous task that has fallen to you. . . . I shall always be ready to assist in any way possible.

Our next step was to secure the delegation of Mr. Hugh Gibson, then

CHILDREN'S FEEDING OF THE AMERICAN RELIEF ADMINISTRATION

POLAND
RUSSIA

FINLAND
VIENNA

First Secretary of the London Embassy, to act as my Paris liaison officer with all the Allied foreign offices with whom I had to deal.

We finally secured an apartment house at 51 Avenue Montaigne for offices where we had some fifty rooms, and there we "holed-in" for the duration.

In setting up organization we had the usual plague of theorists making charts with squares and circles showing the relation of each job with descriptions of its particular functions and authorities. Having spent my life in administration, nothing could raise my temperature faster than to be presented with these charts. As in my previous war organizations, the job consisted of choosing men to solve each specific problem and building the organization around them. I mention this here because in later years I have received repeated demands for the "Chart of Organization" of this enterprise. We had none. We did have men and women to whom pay, titles and definitions of authority were immaterial, and the opportunity to save life and get the world going again was everything. All others got short shrift. As we built up the office with men, the organization gradually resolved itself one by one into major divisions of the work. Robert Taft directed the Paris office; Lewis Strauss ran my private office; Colonel James Logan was chief of staff; Colonel A. B. Barber was distributor of supplies; Dr. Alonzo Taylor and Dr. Vernon Kellogg determined the needs of various countries. The purchasing, transportation and accounting were done by the Grain Corporation under Edward Flesh.

In the course of organization we dispatched American mission specialists into all the eighteen liberated and enemy countries. In addition, I dispatched representatives to each of the six neutrals. Each mission embraced members who spoke the language of the country to which they were dispatched. Their job was to set up the machinery of economic rehabilitation. They were to explain what we were trying to do—that we were interested only in our work. We were not engaged in power politics. I still glow with the satisfaction of their reception. It was more than a welcome to Santa Claus, for we required that all who had resources must pay.

Never did we make a request that was not instantly law (except in some Balkan states). I deal with each country separately later on.

Many of these Americans were men who in their civil life had not dealt with governmental problems yet they showed an adaptability, a grasp, and common sense that won respect and personal affection wherever they went. Many of them determined the fate of millions and did it always to their benefit. Never was there such an exhibit of the power of the American way of life as these 2,500 inexperienced men presented. And withal they got a kick and humor out of it as they went along.

Beyond the food problems in each of the eighteen liberated and enemy countries there were problems of currency, finance, railways, coal supplies, and renewed industry. It followed that one of our first necessities was to stiffen or set up economic departments in each of these new governments. We had to furnish to many of them experienced Americans as advisers. Their new Food Administrations took control of agriculture, requisitioned all domestic food stocks, added the imports which we furnished, and therefrom rationed their populations anew. We set up machinery to constantly see that food reached the people equitably and sufficiently.

CHAPTER 35

MORE EFFORTS TO CO-OPERATE

President Wilson arrived in Paris on December 15th. Colonel House and I immediately presented our political situation to him, and with his approval I drafted a note for the Colonel to send to the Prime Ministers on the President's behalf, notifying them that we were in action.

In this note I suggested an Advisory Council *in Paris* of representatives of each of the departments concerned from each of the five governments, Belgium now being included. We would thus have their foreign offices, military, shipping, food blockade, supplies, and credit departments, all in one room—if we could find one big enough. I proposed we just co-operate on the problems as they arose without any protocols or agreements.

The President took up the question personally with Prime Ministers Clemenceau, Lloyd George and Orlando. They readily agreed that I should be appointed sole Director of Relief and Rehabilitation, directly responsible to the "Big Four."[1] They agreed to my advisory council proposal.

My additional title was of little consequence, and I continued to do my major work under the more effective title of United States Food Administrator.

We convened the "Advisory Council." At its first meeting we determined upon a name—"The Supreme Council of Supply and Relief." At once the British proposed the Clémentel plan of pooling all over

[1] There were a maze of committees and "councils" about. To avoid confusion we usually referred to the President, Prime Ministers Clemenceau, Lloyd George and Orlando as the "Big Four." They constituted what had been hitherto the "Supreme Council." There was a "Council of Foreign Ministers," a military council of the top generals and admirals of the Four Powers. There was a Shipping Council and a Block-

again. This time it was written out as an international agreement of controls of everything, including prices and defining authority, obligations, duties, and procedures in a multitude of words. I took it under "advisement" and promptly conferred separately with the French and Italian officials. I found their chief desire was to bind the British. I stated we had no objection to their executing this agreement among themselves, but (with the President's approval) we would not sign its commitment. We would co-operate. On this basis, we got ahead. Subsequently, they consumed much time in wearying discussions among themselves as to the force, effect and interpretation of their agreement.

At these meetings a multitude of functionaries—sometimes one hundred—each with a portfolio, sat in rows of chairs around the walls pushing papers to their numerous superiors at the center table and vigorously taking notes. We Americans carried our documents in our pockets. The many dull and ineffective sessions interfered with the grinding work we had to do. Therefore we arranged shifts among the Americans by which one of our members attended the meeting each day and the others carried on their work.

This organization proved to be so futile a chatterbox that on February 7, 1919, I went to the "Big Four" and proposed its abolition and the substitution of a purely co-ordinating organization where top officials only would be in one room in the shape of men of Ministerial stature. On the spot I wrote in long-hand a simple resolution of less than fifty words establishing the Supreme Economic Council to co-ordinate all economic intergovernmental action during the Armistice—food, shipping, blockade, transportation and finance—without any commitment from anybody. I was supported by Lord Robert Cecil of the British group, who was a sensible man. Its chairmanship was to rotate.

The Supreme Economic Council served as a clearing house for some questions and performed some useful services, but its minutes are filled

---

ade Council in which all four governments were represented. The buying of food for the European Allies had long been established in two "councils" known as the "Wheat Executive" and the "Fats Executive." There were subsequently created the "Council on Supplies," which died, and the "Supreme Economic Council" which was of some purpose—at least for letting off steam.

with many words and reports that had no practical effect in action. Many of the words spoken or written were for the benefit of historians. Later on when we came to see the published volumes of its proceedings we realized how great a case had been made for history by our colleagues. But we never worried because the American people would never read it.

As I reported direct to the Big Four, I only used the Supreme Economic Council in secondary matters and where we wanted to line up the bureaucrats—if possible.

As an example of the intense and justified suspicion by the European Allies of each other, Vance McCormick on one occasion dropped a bomb in the Economic Council by reporting that there was a heavy movement of textiles from France into Germany despite the supposed absolute prohibitions of the blockade. After French denials and demands for proof, he gave the actual number of cars and the contents, with dates and destinations. The British blew up. We had another such explosion on a report from myself of the sale of some millions of dollars of arms by Italian Army officers to the Bela Kun Communist government in Hungary for gold. I was able to state the details and where the gold was. The Italians on the Council were, however, men of high integrity. They had the gold seized and ultimately we used it to pay for food to Hungary from Serbia and elsewhere.

In a full desire to co-operate, I had early in the Council of Relief and Rehabilitation proposed that the British, French, and Italians appoint "Missions" to the countries in which they were especially interested. However, most countries were suspicious of their political and economic objectives and therefore leaned on the Americans. Our representatives were always courteous to the "missionaries" when they appeared and kept them fully informed. But they had little or nothing to do. Living was much more pleasant in Paris than in the outside capitals, and also, political chatter was concentrated at this point. Most of these Missions faded away from the back country into the multitude of advisers who swarmed over Paris. Their official consciences were satisfied by occasional visits to our offices to inquire how things were going.

CHAPTER 36

SOME DOWN–TO–EARTH PROBLEMS: WORLD SUPPLIES, FINANCE, ACCOUNTING, COMMUNICATIONS, PASSPORTS, GOVERNMENT CONTRACTS

Our use of the words "relief" and "rehabilitation" has always misled the American people. They suggest the city charities' methods of case workers. But our gigantic problem involved finding supplies, ships, cash or credit, rebuilding ports, railways, communications, coal supplies, and doing all in the face of political chaos. It also involved the stiffening of weak governments and the rebuilding of employment.

A survey of the economic situation in Europe (outside of Russia), which we compiled as we went along, showed what war can do to food supplies. Europe as a whole in modern peacetimes never produced enough food or raw materials to live on. She always imported large quantities. Moreover, 95 per cent of the people lived meagerly, and a part of these were never fully fed in the American sense. There was never the margin of waste to fall back upon, a margin such as America enjoys.

Some inevitable effects of war were a shortage of agricultural labor as farmers turned to fighting and to making munitions, deterioration of agricultural machinery, diversion of fertilizers to explosives, all of which had decreased the ground crops despite the heroic labor of the women of every race. We estimated that the 1918 ground crops of the Continent as a whole had been 60 per cent of pre-war normal.

On the animal products side, there was a net decrease from pre-war of 18,400,000 horned cattle from 93,300,000. But the cattle were on an average about one year younger owing to killing of the older animals. The remaining cattle were almost everywhere underfed and therefore yielded less meat and milk. The dairy and beef production was down over 50 per cent. The swine had decreased from 69,300,000 to 39,500,000 and the remainder were younger and of less weight. The fat and meat production as a whole was probably not 40 per cent of normal.

The shortages were of course not equal in different places. Some areas had an actual surplus, some had two-thirds enough, some had nothing. Moreover, the resolute determination of every farmer in Europe, just as in America, was to feed his own family first and in full. This universal instinct of farmers threw almost the whole burden of the shortage onto the town populations.

Prior to the Armistice, the 220,000,000 people under enemy domination, "liberated" as well as "enemy," were rigidly rationed. The officials in the eighteen new revolutionary governments were without technical experience and their minds were fixed upon political and ideological ideas rather than the hard toil of government housekeeping. The governments themselves were not very stable. In fact, Hungary went through four revolutions while we were trying to feed her.

In these revolutions the disciplines, such as food rationing, either collapsed or near-collapsed. Everyone who could, grabbed for food and hoarded it. There was at the beginning some rioting and pillaging of the countryside. And the major populations of towns and cities were for a time much worse off than they had been before the Armistice when there were rigid controls.

Added to all the other growing pains of these new representative governments were the Communists. They found so receptive an audience in hungry people that Communist revolutions at one time or another seized a dozen large cities and one whole country—Hungary.

We sought diligently to sustain the feeble plants of parliamentary government which had sprung up in all of these countries. A weak government possessed of the weapon of food and supplies for starving people can preserve and strengthen itself more effectively than by arms.

Although it is somewhat ahead of my story, the magnitude of the job is indicated by the fact that the total amount of overseas food brought into Europe during the period of co-ordination amounted to more than 27,000,000 tons. In addition we moved over 840,000,000 pounds of clothing, medical and miscellaneous supplies.

Of this tonnage, about 18,700,000 came from the United States, the balance from other countries. It is of interest to note how closely these figures checked with the estimates I had furnished President Wilson before the Armistice.

We financed the supplies outside the neutrals by loans from the United States, in round numbers about $2,700,000,000. We received in cash or goods $305,000,000 and gave in direct charity over $325,000,000 (which included operations over 1920–1922). The very large majority of the loans turned out to be charity also. The neutrals in addition paid in cash and goods.

The British Empire furnished for relief purposes to the Continent about 560,000 tons of food and clothing for which it received about $75,000,000 in cash and about $82,000,000 in credit which it mostly collected.

The French furnished about 85,000 tons of food and clothing for which they extended credit amounting to $46,000,000 and they collected most of it.

The Italians furnished about 140,000 tons of supplies and received full payment in goods or gold.

Other countries furnished about 425,000 tons of food and clothing, receiving $52,000,000 cash and gave $2,500,000 on credit.

It will be seen, therefore, that the combined contribution of the Allies was a little over 4% of the tonnage and about 5% of the credits, most of which they subsequently collected. We collected very little. All of this confirmed my view from the beginning that they would or could do little in rehabilitation.

In addition to these overseas supplies, our organization moved within Europe 30,000,000 tons of coal, and about 1,000,000 tons of food from surplus areas to deficient ones.

All these matters will be described in the succeeding chapters.

CO-ORDINATION OF WORLD SUPPLIES

One major problem underlying the whole rehabilitation of Europe was sources of supply in a world of shortages.

We had a constantly shifting picture puzzle to solve in securing supplies, credits, ships and preventing overlaps which involved not only the liberated and enemy supplies but the Allies' and neutrals' as well. It was necessary that there should not be competition or hoarding which would force prices any higher. It was essential that there be some order, and we had to find the "order."

However, the British, French and Italians insisted on conducting many of their operations without prior clearing with us or with the advisory committees. We met this problem by having our American consular staff over the world report daily on any shipments to these governments. As they were also partly dependent upon American supplies, I was able, as United States Food Administrator, to regulate their shipments from the United States so as to prevent them from accumulating any undue quantities.

We had no difficulty with the neutrals. They all responded most loyally to the situation. They accepted our suggestions as to sources and they reported to our agents all their purchases and shipments. A word outlining a situation was sufficient to shift their sources and ships. And often they loaned me supplies for emergencies against future replacements to them.

The problems of the eighteen liberated and enemy countries were entirely in our hands.

FINANCE

All the movement of supplies, of course, had to be financed in some way. The three Allies financed their own purchases outside those from the United States. The neutrals all paid cash or foreign exchange for American and other supplies. In the twenty-three other countries we handled the problems in three categories: first, the five enemy countries except Austria were required to pay gold or goods; second, from the thirteen liberated countries we took cash or goods to the full extent that they could pay; third, when they could not pay in cash or goods, we took their obligations to pay in the future.

The liberated countries fell into two financial categories. Most of them could borrow from the United States Treasury under the existing law and the Treasury extended the credits needed.

In the other category were the minority of liberated countries which did not have exiled governments in existence when the law was passed, so they could not be financed from the Treasury. To cover these, the President at my request secured a special appropriation of $100,000,000 in February, 1919, which we could use in charity if we wished. Senator Lodge put an amendment into this bill the effect of which was that no enemy child or adult could have food from it. However, with this appropriation we covered the needs of the other liberated countries and we managed, with non-earmarked charitable funds contributed to us, the special feeding of children in enemy countries.

The problem of whether to give the food outright from the $100,-000,000 appropriation as a gift to the liberated countries or to take obligations of governments to pay for it in the future raised many questions. I never had illusions that the European credits, in the long run, would be repaid. I had hoped that some of them would be honored. But collective political morals are so constituted that candidates for elective office will not refrain from obtaining public acclaim by squirming out of debts to other governments. Nevertheless, by requiring governments to sign such obligations, we secured a certain moderation of demands that would not have been observed had it been a gift. And we secured more economy and efficiency in distribution than would have been possible on a gift basis. Also it "saved the face" of these governments to be treated as sound debtors wanting no charity.

The extension of credits to the liberated governments with which to buy supplies set in motion another force of strength, in addition to their power over food distribution. Each of these governments sold supplies to those of its people who could pay. The governments thus received their local currency. And with this currency they could conduct the government with that much less taxation. We required them to pay the incidental expenses of our staff and offices within their countries from this currency.

Austria was a special case. She was starving and almost penniless, the peace-makers having given away most of her agricultural areas to the surrounding states, thereby creating a helpless poorhouse.[1] As we were prohibited by the Lodge amendment from using the $100,000,000

[1] In twenty years Austria never became really self-supporting and never had anything near a decent standard of living except for the upper classes.

appropriation, I secured $5,000,000 from the President's "private fund" and set up an arrangement whereby Britain, France and Italy would pay for supplies to Austria with $48,000,000 of the money advanced to them by the United States. As this worked out, it was really a gift from the United States, for the Allies never paid the loan.

ACCOUNTING

To simplify accounting, I set up a uniform contract with all eighteen liberated and enemy governments. Under this contract, they agreed to accept our auditors' statements as final. Inasmuch as we bought supplies in America and elsewhere at all sorts of prices, we fixed uniform prices on our deliveries and made them high enough to cover all eventualities. In order that there should be no profit to our Government in relief, the contract provided that, if we had a margin of profit after the operation was over, it would be rebated to charity for European children. The usefulness of this last provision was proved later on.

EXCHANGE

Owing to the fluctuations, speculation, and general uncertainty of currencies over a large part of Europe, during the Armistice, the Federal Reserve Board placed stiff restrictions upon exchange transactions from the United States. We were at once flooded with requests from American citizens to pay money to relatives and friends living all over central, northern and eastern Europe. We transformed this into a kind of relief. I placed Major F. H. McKnight in charge, and he made an arrangement with the Federal Reserve Board by which American banks were allowed to accept such remittances in dollars and to turn them over to our organization in New York with the names of the persons for whom they were intended. We arranged with each of the European governments concerned to pay these remittances to the citizens from the currency they received from the sale of food. We then used the money in New York to buy more food and to transport it. We thus set up payment in American money for some of our food. The person who received the remittance could if he wished buy rations with the currency received. We handled 17,216 of such remittances but the aggregate was only $8,900,676. It was disappointing as an addition to our food supply. The plan was very troublesome in its details, as many recipients could not be found and the money had to go back through a vast amount of protective red tape. With the signing of the peace, we ceased taking remittances. However, from this experience we learned a better method called "Food Drafts"—initiated six months later with great success—which I will describe later on.

ADMINISTRATIVE EXPENSES

All our overhead and traveling expenses were paid from funds of the United States Food Administration. I drew no salary and paid my own expenses. Most of our civilian staff drew no salaries and had very modest expense accounts. The Army and Navy men drew their modest pay from those services, and we paid their traveling expenses. The office expenses of our special missions to many countries were paid by those countries, as I have noted above.

It is impossible to state accurately the exact overhead of the operations in Europe, owing to the difficulty of separating the European from the American expenses of the Food Administration. In any event, the total expense of the Food Administration from the time the United States came into the war in 1917 until the end of the work in Europe was under $8,000,000. Of this about $1,500,000 was applicable to the period after the Armistice.

COMMUNICATIONS

Telegraph and telephone connection between former enemy areas and Allied areas was not really re-established until after the peace. During the Armistice telegraph messages, if at all possible, had to be sent to a border and, in many cases, to be walked across, paid for and relayed to the next frontier. It sometimes took a week to get a message from Paris to Warsaw—if it arrived at all. Each government was suspicious of the others and maintained a host of censors.

Soon after establishing our Paris office, I appealed to Admiral Benson for help in this matter. Under his direction, an American destroyer or cruiser equipped with wireless was placed in every important port in Europe. In addition, they established wireless offices for us at Berlin,

Vienna and other points. Through them we were placed in instant communication with most ports and all capitals in Europe. They also handled all our cables and telegrams to the United States.

In February 1919 the Navy wished to withdraw most of its vessels and staff and we were compelled to devise another system of communication. I then secured Major Frank H. Fay from the Army Signal Corps as superintendent of a telegraph system of our own. Major Fay drew into his service Captain Paul S. Clapp (who ultimately succeeded him) and six other officers who were sent into different quarters of Europe as district superintendents.

I asked the twenty-six Allied neutral, liberated and enemy governments to assign telegraph circuits between capitals, ports and other major points, to be operated by American "doughboys." As suspicion and censorship were still fully alive I pledged that all our telegrams would be *en clair* and that their officials could read the whole lot at their leisure. Every Government responded at once except the French. They insisted that our communications must go to and from the French frontier through their regular system including censorship. As that system was slower than the mail, we were stumped until General Pershing as usual solved our problem by using his own men to build a line connection from our offices in Paris to his French headquarters, which had its own line to Cologne, Germany. At Cologne we connected with all our Continental circuits. Thus we could reach every important city from Helsingfors to Constantinople in a few minutes. We also dodged the French censor.

This *en clair* provision was quickly to raise a cloud of deep trouble. Our men needed to transmit to me confidential material from governmental officials all over Europe and to express their own candid opinions of such officials generally. The wires from Helsingfors, for instance, went through seven countries where the authorities could read everything. To avoid trouble our men spontaneously resorted to American slang and to descriptive phrases for the names of individuals. Slang that had been dead for fifty years came to life. Slang of armies, baseball, football, colleges, stock markets and service clubs spread over the wires. One American Minister became Casey, being reminiscent of his usefulness at the bat. Another lives in the record as "The Cocktail Eater." Two European statesmen figured as "Mutt and Jeff." The most celebrated case was Captain Gregory's report on the decline and fall of the Grand Duke Joseph, the last of the Hapsburgs, which I give later.

Soon the Peace Delegations, our State Department and the American press awoke to the possibilities of our telegraph system. I finally arranged with the various governments that the official agencies of all governments could use our system to communicate to their delegations in Paris in code. We handled the press material *en clair* and thus avoided censorship. To do these outside services we opened a telegraph office in Paris and charged rates of our own making. Our receipts ran as high as $5,000 a month, all of which we turned into the Children's Relief Fund. If any historian had a penchant for breaking codes he could have uncovered a wealth of intrigue, human hopes and diplomatic woe by decoding the messages of the Peace Delegations to their home governments which at one time were in our files.

For mail purposes, I secured through General Pershing the establishment of a regular courier service daily or tri-weekly all over Europe. These messengers also served the American embassies and legations. The couriers were shrewd doughboys, and soon found that they could make money in a small way by trading in currencies between countries. One of them went home with a $2,000 nest egg. Owing to the railway disintegration, however, the service was slow and uncertain.

PASSPORTS

Passports were also a grief. The need to get visas for every frontier with the red tape and obstruction made great delays for our staff. Therefore, I proposed to all the twenty-six governments that it would help us greatly if I could issue personally signed passports for our own American staff in addition to their American passports. My passports were to free them from visas and give immunity to delay and search at all frontiers. Every government except the British and French agreed. These passports became a token of confidence that no race has ever equalled. Our men had the malicious joy of watching other officials struggling hours at passport offices all over the Continent while our men slipped almost instantly past the guards.

CONTRACTS WITH GOVERNMENTS

Other than accounting, internal transport, communication and transport questions, we entered into no agreements with the various governments except those of enemy countries. We wanted a free hand. We stated clearly and simply that we would do the best we could to serve their people; that so long as they co-operated in solving the common problems, we would go along; but that, if we did not continue to receive their co-operation, we simply would quit. We thus retained control of the distribution of our supplies.

CHAPTER 37

MORE DOWN-TO-EARTH PROBLEMS: SHIPS, RAILWAYS, PORTS AND CANALS, COAL, BARTER OF INTERNAL SUPPLIES

The problem of sea transportation of supplies was a continuous grief. If we had not had so many phantasmagorias from other directions to divert our minds, we would have wept hourly on what came to us from this source alone.

There had been enormous destruction of shipping in the war. With the Armistice every one of the victorious nations was determined at once to recapture its foreign trade. All after dinner orations to the contrary—and the records are full of them—every government, including the American, sought to evade assigning shipping to our service. And they evaded it every hour of the day.

Anticipating trouble in securing ships, before leaving the United States I asked the Allied authorities through Colonel House if we could not secure the German and Austrian ships which had been held during the war in their own ports and in refuge in neutral ports. I proposed that we should use them to carry supplies to the "liberated" and "enemy" countries. The idea was presented by Marshal Foch to the Germans as an American proposal and the Germans agreed in principle in December, and it was incorporated in the revised Armistice terms of January 16, 1919.

I had originated the idea and its whole spirit was that the ships were to be handed directly to me. I started negotiations with leading shipping firms in the United States, Britain, France, Italy, Norway and

Holland for their services to man and operate the cargo ships for my account. And I proposed to the Allied armies that I assign the passenger ships to them for repatriation of troops in return for equivalent cargo tonnage. I proposed to credit the Germans on their supply account at the pre-war charter rate. The final disposition of the ships was, of course, to be determined by the Peace Treaty. The Germans and Austrians had a certain hold on their ships as only they could give orders to neutrals that would release their ships in those countries. The vessels in their own harbors, no doubt, could have been seized, but this would not secure the ships in refuge, and they were an important part. There were about 2,300,000 tons of German and 700,000 tons of Austrian ships. Some were too small and others had been damaged, but there was 2,697,000 tons of useful shipping. If we could have obtained it immediately, it would have solved 75 per cent of our problems.

However, the Allied Maritime Council woke up to my proposals and insisted that they operate these ships and assign them to carrying specific cargoes for us. I objected fiercely, as I knew that, with the inter-Allied jealousies and red tape, the arrangement would be long-delayed. And I knew that I would never get more than a part of the ships, as they would be put into foreign trade. However, my American shipping colleagues sided against me and the worst came true.

When negotiations with the Germans were taken up, they demanded that as the ships were to be handed over for supply transport, they should have an agreement that they would get a definite supply program (for which they would pay in gold). I favored this, but the blockade fetish and desire to control my department delayed settlement.

It was six months before I secured a single cargo on these ships. My other worst fears were realized. Out of the total of 2,697,000 tons, the Maritime Council assigned 596,000 tons to the Italians to operate, 486,000 to the French, 1,153,000 to the British, 452,000 to the United States and 8,000 to Belgium. Despite the fact that I was theoretically to have the use of this tonnage or its equivalent, we secured the use of ships totaling only 910,000 tons, or about one third, and that only after long battles. The British kept part of them and the French and the Italians kept all their tonnage for their own use. I, of course, had all of the tonnage assigned to the United States.

Up to the end of February 80 per cent of our cargoes were transported by American ships and 10 per cent by chartered neutrals and only 10 per cent by Allied ships. The tonnage situation threatened a total debacle.

After long arguments and running in circles around a half dozen committees and shipping departments I resolved to go on the warpath. Mr. Henry M. Robinson was a member of the American Peace Mission and at the same time represented the United States on the Allied Maritime Council. He was not only able, energetic and diplomatic, but when necessary pugnacious. This was my first acquaintance with him, and from our association in this battle came a deep friendship. The nature of our private war is indicated by the documents of the time.[1]

On the American side, President Wilson cabled mandatory orders to our Shipping Board to assign to me at once 1,000,000 tons of ships, in addition to the German ships, being only a part of those they were using in foreign trade. Chairman Hurley tried to escape by assigning under 500,000 tons. But the President again intervened and I got these ships. In the meantime, Robinson had obtained about 300,000 tons from the British. With the truncated assignment of German ships and of neutral charters, we managed to get through.

RAILWAYS

One consequence of total war was an aftermath of total railway disorganization, especially for the vanquished. The railways over the whole area of Germany, Poland, Latvia, Lithuania, Estonia, Czechoslovakia, Austria, Hungary, Roumania, Yugoslavia, Bulgaria, Georgia, Azerbaijan and Armenia were in chaos. And the disorganization was made worse by the new boundaries of all of these countries. The Central European railways had been built as consolidated government-owned systems within the old Austrian, German and Russian Empires. Now they were chopped up into eighteen systems under eighteen different governments. Immediately at the birth of the new states with the Armistice, each government had created a Minister of Railways. His highest mission was to grab all the rolling stock he could lay hands

[1] In the War Library at Stanford University.

on. No government would allow cars and locomotives to go over frontiers for fear they would never come back. Some states had too big a share, some too little. Some cities in a given country could not be reached from other parts of the same country without passing over new foreign boundaries, and so were isolated. All the tracks and rolling stock were run down and in bad order. There was much war destruction. Revolution had of course brought new and inexperienced men into control.

We tackled this problem early in January (1919), by organizing a Railway Section under Colonel W. G. Atwood and drew from the Army other men who in their private lives were experienced railway men, such as Lieutenant Colonel William B. Causey and Colonel W. B. Ryan.

We had some resources. About 1500 German locomotives and 5000 cars had been assigned to the American military authorities by the Armistice. There was some surplus of the rolling stock of the American Army in France. It was useless to send the former and much of the latter back to the United States, so General Pershing made most of it available to us.

We sent an American railway man to each of the eighteen liberated and enemy governments to work with their Ministers of Railways. We requested each of the governments principally concerned to co-operate by allowing cars, and in some cases locomotives, to move over frontiers to the destination of their loads. I undertook to guarantee that the rolling stock would be returned. They all accepted this guarantee, and to assure the returns, we placed at each frontier crossing an American officer who checked the cars passing in each direction. We also erected a clearing house for distribution of freight payments. However, almost nobody paid the interstate freight. Or the money was no good when it came in.

Our next move was to get surplus cars and locomotives in one country sold to those who were short. Some of these trades were carried out, but the quality of rolling stock delivered, and the reliability of the undertakings to pay, were equally doubtful. Where there was no credit, and currency was no good, our men arranged payment in commodities.

One day I received a telegram from Vienna: "Have arranged sell Galicia ten locomotives for eggs. How many eggs go to a locomotive?" Our Communications Section replied laconically, "Does not matter. We have no confidence in the age of either."

At the initiation of our work in the old Austrian Empire, our men called a meeting of Railway Ministers and managers of the five Succession States, four in addition to the Austrian, all of whom spoke German. It was the first time in a century that four of their languages had enjoyed equal dignity with German and they all insisted on speaking their own tongues and having the replies translated back into it. Colonel W. B. Ryan, who was in charge, probably overstated his troubles when he reported that it took an hour to say good morning— and that in offensive tones.

Despite the efforts of these men, our supplies began to pile up in the ports. Cities were starving. Coal movements had so slowed down that municipal services were being suspended. The people were not only hungry but cold and in the dark. Colonel Ryan, after some acute experiences, sent in word that the new governments were using transportation as a weapon of political pressures against each other. He continued,

I have about come to the conclusion that the only way to handle Central Europe is a military dictatorship. These new nations cannot be made to work together by anything like moral suasion. They do not proceed on those tracks. The people in Paris don't know the hates in this territory.

I knew the hates. They were taking everything they could lay hands on from each other.

One of our worst jams occurred northward from the port of Trieste. In January I sent Colonel W. B. Causey to disentangle this special mess. Causey had at one time been the president of an uncertain, wobbly Midwest railway system which we may call the C. & G. Z. He was a profane man. He had been about a week in Vienna and freight was still tied up. He did not respond to urgent telegrams. Finally I sent a telegram to Captain T. T. C. Gregory, Chief of our Mission, asking him to find Causey and ascertain what he was doing and why he did not reply. A few hours later I received this telegram over our wires,

Saw Causey. He says . . ., he also says he has been . . . busy. He says further these . . . railways are in worse shape than the . . . C. & G. Z.

Finally we had 170,000 tons of food piled up in Trieste ready to spoil and people starving.

On March 5th I went before the Big Four with our woes, stating that the problem of maintaining human life and preserving order revolved not only on supplies but on the rehabilitation of internal transportation and the organization of some sort of economic unity in these states for exchange and distribution of whatever local supplies there were, including coal and everything else. I proposed as a first try-out that all the states in Central and Eastern Europe should contribute to me definite amounts of rolling stock. We would add to this from General Pershing's supplies, all to be marked as belonging to my organization and used solely for our purposes. We would then establish regular freight services over every railway; trains would move irrespective of boundaries and would have priority over all other railway services. We wanted railway employees of each nationality to be placed under my direction to conduct this new system with my American officers in immediate command. I asked that a certain part of every port be placed likewise at our exclusive disposal. This plan was adopted and the necessary orders were issued.

The Allies, however, wanted to have a part in these railway matters also, so we set up in Paris the usual advisory board with missions which traveled around a lot and called on all prime ministers. Our American Colonels supported our Allies on these missions with American food. However, they ultimately came back to the Paris cafes for more palatable supplies—and to tell us how to do it.

Our men did a great job. They soon had traffic moving and gradually became the motivating power in the management of all these railways. When the peace was signed, I informed the different nations concerned that our job was over and ordered our men to come back with their staffs and go home. Colonels Causey, Barber and Atwood had done so well that the Council of Railway Ministers of the Central European States protested at their leaving and asked them and their staffs to remain in their joint employ. They offered to allow me to set the salaries. I put those of the leaders at $25,000 per annum and of the subordinates at lesser sums. When they left some years later, it was with fine expressions of regret and gratitude.

At the Peace we thought that we had called in all the American officers who were engaged upon this service, except those who had been hired to remain. But months afterwards I received a plaintive letter from a lieutenant at Bentschen, a German-Polish railway crossing, asking if he could not be relieved. He was still taking the numbers of all the cars that went each way and reporting them to our empty offices in Paris. He was undoubtedly the forgotten man.

PORTS AND CANALS

The transportation problems were also partly port, canal and inland river problems. We quickly arranged with the Dutch, Belgians, Germans, Italians and Baltic States for their co-operation in securing use of port facilities. Admiral Benson had responded instantly to my request, placing a naval officer in each of some twenty ports to take general charge of our discharges and reloading by rail or canal for the interior. The naval men knew all about this job and went at it with a zest. We had no difficulty in arranging the opening of barge transport from ports into the interior, via the Rhine, the Elbe and the Vistula.

But the Danube presented the same sort of problem as the railways. It is a major transportation artery, serving seven states. At the start every government seized barges and would not let them go outside its boundaries. I secured through the "Big Four" that a temporary Danube Commission should be set up with Mr. Henry James as the American member. As usual with inter-Allied bodies it was very slow, and finally I set up control of our own barge service in the same way we had in the railways. The barges under our name moved without restrictions. This solved the problem for a while but had to be suspended during the Communist Revolution in Hungary. However, the river performed its proper humane service for some time.

COAL

Coal was just as essential as food. Aside from warming human beings we had to have it to operate railways and municipal services.

The division of the old Central European Empires into fourteen states was as bad for coal as it was for the railways. Not only were states separated from their former sources of supply but those without coal fields had no money to buy it. In the coal mines the miners were inefficient from hunger, and Communism was making great progress. Under-cover wars by the various states to get possession of important fields were going on. The "Big Four" was undecided as to who would get certain coal fields, and the political rivals were trying the old game of *fait accompli* by occasional seizures. Agents of contending governments were sent in to start strikes, riots and murder. One case in particular was the Duchy of Teschen, where Czechoslovakia and Poland were the antagonists for possession, with Germany hoping on the sidelines that it might come to her. Germany and Poland were also contestants in Upper Silesia. The much truncated state of Austria was fervently hated by surrounding states, and as she had no consequential coal of her own, they took it out on her by failures to make coal deliveries. We tried to solve the problem by getting up agreements between the coal areas and the non-coal areas for specific shipments. We tried to set up exchanges of commodities to pay for it. But production and deliveries constantly fell off. A typical report from one of the Prime Ministers involved in the Teschen dispute indicates the situation:

You know the whole district is in an uproar. About eighty per cent of the miners are on strike and the situation is getting worse every day. As our government has no authority and as the authority of the Miners' Organization is annihilated, it is necessary that a new authority step in and take the reins. As far as I can see the only authority in which any part of our people have any confidence is the authority of the American Commission. They are the men who can bring us back to good order again, if they have the power to interfere. . . .

I did not want to take personal possession of the whole of Central Europe. I hoped to return to America some day. It was proposed by the Allies that we set up an Allied Coal Commission. I had learned by this time that these commissions were a liability. They added further varieties of hates which each carried over from the war. The British were hated in one country, the French in another, the Italians somewhere else. They were all suspected of having some ulterior motive. Finally I arranged with the "Big Four" that I would receive a "mandate" on all Central European coal. I set up a Coal Section in our Administration. I asked General Pershing "for the best coal man in the world, who is in the Army." He assigned Colonel Anson C. Goodyear, who in civil life was both a railway man and a coal operator.

Colonel Goodyear was a cheery person and on his coming into my office the conversation ran something like this. Introducing himself, the Colonel said, "Thank goodness, somebody dug me out of this dead Army and gave me to you. So what can I do?" I replied, "For one thing, I have appointed you Duke of Teschen." "Where is the Duchy? However, I accept the Dukedom, wherever it is." I told him he had the general job of getting coal in motion all over Central Europe with as many American officers as he needed. The Colonel wanted to know, "What are the Duke's powers?" "A letter from me to the Prime Minister of each country, asking for full co-operation of their government officials and everybody else." He seemed a little unconvinced as to the potency of these powers. I suggested that if they did not co-operate their food supply could be stopped on a telegram from him. Or it could be increased if needed. He brightened up at once. He opined that the Duchy might be worth having.

Goodyear was so charming and genuine a soul that all the governments proved anxious to co-operate with him. While he had no troubles with governments, he had plenty of others. He went into Teschen with his assistants to find the whole district not only on strike but waging internecine war between the three races. With firmness, food and fair treatment he got this district quickly into action. And he was equally successful over the other fields which included: Kattowitz, Upper Silesia, Dabrowa and Galicia in Poland; Dux-Teplitz-Komotau, Falkenau, Kladno-Rakonitz, and Pilsen in Czechoslovakia; Leoben and Koflach in Austria; Trifail in Serbia; Dorog and Salgotarján in Hungary. In one month the Colonel and his men had doubled the coal production.

Our coal men found themselves involved in other jobs. Early in August (1919) a local war broke out in the Silesian coal districts between Poles and Germans. The streets were filled with rioters. Troops came into action. Many people were killed, thousands of refugees were driven onto the roads, many persons were executed in cold blood. But despite all this bloody business Colonel Goodyear, single-handed, with courage, patience and tact, raced from one side to the other and finally stopped it.

One day I received a telegram from the Colonel: "Sending $25,000. Send me that much tobacco." Both sending real money out of Central Europe and expecting tobacco from us were new departures in relief. So I asked for more details. It appeared the Colonel had found $25,000 of American gold certificates in banks of the coal region, which they had held since before the war. He replied, "These poor devils haven't had a genuine smoke for a year and you know a miner cannot work unless he gets a smoke." My mining sympathies rose at once. We got the tobacco from army stocks and the Colonel issued a tobacco ration, conditional upon increased coal output. The banks received local currency from the sale of the tobacco ration in exchange for their American money. Goodyear got the coal.

So much did Goodyear's officers endear themselves to the people that many of them were engaged to continue as co-ordinators of the many conflicting racial and labor elements after the Peace. The combination of American disinterestedness, intelligence and technical skill was the thing needed amid these seething hates. The people realized it and held to it as long as they could.

Finally, before leaving Europe, I recommended that the Allies set up a European Coal Council with every coal-producing state represented for purposes of co-ordination. It was mainly in hopes that they would recognize that an impossible situation in coal ownership had been created by the Treaty of Versailles and amend it.

BARTER OF INTERNAL SUPPLIES

Having secured independent movement of trains across frontiers under our control, we started at once to secure exchanges of vital commodities between states, in addition to coal. Condensation of one of Captain T. T. C. Gregory's monthly reports illustrates what was done. "Lubricating oils being exhausted, Colonel Jones was sent to the Polish oil fields where he loaded 92 cars with petroleum products. While he was doing this, the Ukrainian and Polish troops were fighting for possession of the fields. He succeeded in getting his cars out to Prague and Vienna." We also brought, under American escort, several trains of oil products from Roumania. We shipped 200 carloads of tannin from Serbia to Poland in exchange for 200 carloads of oil products, escorted again by American corporals. A trainload of manufactured goods was sent from Vienna to Galicia in exchange for 42 cars of eggs and other food. Altogether in Gregory's territory we exchanged over 150,000 tons of food and other commodities besides coal under American escorts. In addition we negotiated the purchase of 42,000 tons of grain in the Banat and shipped it to Austria and Hungary. These are only specimens of the job.

We did not bother to incorporate these transactions into our accounts or statistics as no American money was involved, but it ran into many hundred thousand tons and great money value.

CHAPTER 38

CHILD FEEDING—PESTILENCE—
PRISONERS OF WAR—
THE STANFORD WAR LIBRARY

There was a mass of waif, orphan, undernourished, diseased and stunted children in every town and city of the liberated and enemy areas. There were literally millions of them. They were not only pitiable little persons, but they were a menace to their nations. Unless remedied, their distorted minds were a menace to all mankind.

Our experience in Belgium had proved that quick physical recovery of children could be obtained by furnishing proper food if they were not too far gone. We had found that if in addition to the meager family rations we gave the children one hot supplemental meal daily in schoolhouses and special canteens, they made marvelous improvement —and quickly.[1] The greatest deficiencies were fats and minerals.

Our surveys had shown about ten or twelve million children already in deplorable condition in the eighteen liberated and enemy areas. We in addition were conducting this service of the C.R.B. for two million in Belgium and Northern France.

Initially, I had requested the American Red Cross to undertake the service, we to furnish the food, but they considered the responsibility too great. We therefore took on the job. We determined to make it a free gift of the American people.

Love of children is a biological trait common to all races. And it is about equally strong among them. It therefore seemed to me that around this devotion there could be built a renaissance of unity and

[1] It was true there were many beyond full repair and these were one of the origins of the brutes who made the Second World War.

of hope among their distracted elders. I hoped that in this evidence of someone's concern for their children there might be a lessening of the consuming hates that burned in the hearts of women because their own children or millions of the children of their nation had come to this condition.

The method was that as fast as children were restored to health, and if there was reasonable assurance they would be looked after, they were discharged, and others who had fallen by the wayside were picked up. This "discharge" was somewhat a theory, for the women canteen managers could not bear to turn them away even if they were fat.

We set up the Children's Feeding Section in our Paris office under the name of the "American Relief Administration." The first director was A. E. Peden, who had been Federal Food Administrator in Texas. Soon afterwards, as Mr. Peden was called home, Colonel A. J. Carlson was put in charge with Mr. R. H. Simpson, an old C.R.B. man, as chief assistant. Later on, as Colonel Carlson had to go home, I placed Walter L. Brown in charge with Parmer Fuller and Maurice Pate, all former C.R.B. men, as chief assistants. Alonzo Taylor was as usual the nutritional adviser.

The method of organization in each nation was to create a committee of leading citizens and especially women, with decentralized committees in each important town and city. These committees with American aid co-ordinated all of the existing charitable, medical and governmental agencies for children into the system.

Waifs and orphans were gathered up into established institutions or temporary orphanages created for the purpose, where we would supply food for three meals. Infant children and their mothers came under the system. We confined our work to organizing and furnishing the food, clothing, and medical supplies. The local committees, by local gifts and volunteers, found the quarters, equipment, transportation, and service. As it worked out, our supplies represented about one-half of the expense. Thus hundreds of thousands of men and women in each of these countries became partners with us.

It was not expensive to rehabilitate an individual child in this way. With this wealth of local service the cost of each meal to us could be measured by a few cents. A pound of concentrated food, in rich soup, stews, milk, porridge, cocoa, sugar, minerals and cod liver oil daily, is like water to a wilting plant.

The only exception to our routine method was in Germany. The Friends Service Committee (Quakers) had applied to me for some mission which they could perform. I was glad to secure so able a staff and assigned to them the organization of the children's work in Germany. I arranged their relations with the German government and sent experts to teach them how the job was to be done. We furnished most of the food and other supplies. The Quakers performed a magnificent service.

With the arrival of the harvest of 1919, we would have completed our major American battle against the famine. But it became obvious that to complete this health program for children would require still another year. I decided, therefore, that we would transform our governmental agencies into a private organization of Americans and carry on until the harvest of 1920.

I reviewed the whole operation in a letter (6th of June) to President Wilson and obtained his approval.

Dear Mr. President:

As you are aware, under your approval I set up . . . an organization for special feeding of subnormal children; that is, those showing the dangerous effects of undernourishment. It has been demonstrated, that the furnishing of rough staples to large massed populations under the difficulties of distribution through weak governments was more or less a hit or miss as to whether the children, especially of the poor, would receive sufficiency. Furthermore, in order to bring them back to normal they required special types of food which no available finance would provide for the population as a whole.

I have undertaken to give this service . . . as a matter of charity from the American people and have not demanded governmental obligations of repayment. . . .

The reaction which I receive from all over Europe indicates that we have touched the heart of the populations at large as much by this child feeding department as in any form of American intervention in Europe. Its continuation for some months will, in my mind, contribute to smooth out these ruffled feelings which are bound to arise from the political settlements. It is obvious that no single country in Europe is going to obtain what its politicians want, and that there will be, until they awaken to more rational sense than most of them display at the moment, a tendency for them to blame the United States for failure to secure each and every one of his objectives.

Beyond all this, of course, is the infinitely more important, intrinsic question of the saving of child life by such widely organized and wholesale methods as will meet the necessities of Europe at the present time.

Faithfully yours,
HERBERT HOOVER.

[Note in the President's handwriting]
My dear Hoover:
  I entirely approve.

WOODROW WILSON.

While I relate the story of this continued effort later on, I may say here that we passed some 14,000,000 to 16,000,000 children through the process from undernourishment to health. The whole enterprise was an American charity, for which from one source or another we provided over $325,000,000, the large part from charitable contributions.

These millions of children set upon the road to health represented only part of the benefits. This voluntary organization of nations in these fourteen countries gave to many of their people a new purpose. It gave hope and inspiration.

PESTILENCE

Then came the Fourth Horseman of the Apocalypse—Pestilence.[2] Early in April (1919) the "Big Four" received a multitude of telegrams from different Eastern European governments, depicting the

---

[2] The expression "The Four Horsemen" has been incorporated into every language of Christian peoples as the great symbol of war and its aftermaths. The riders are, in literature, universally designated as WAR, FAMINE, PESTILENCE, and DEATH. It occurred to me one day to look into the 6th chapter of Revelation to see how far it applied to modern world war.

A re-reading of the chapter with the new background suggests a re-appraisal of who these Horsemen are now.

The pertinent words of the text are as follows:

  Verse 2. And I saw . . . a white horse: and he that sat on him had a bow . . . and he went forth conquering, and to conquer.

We can accept this rider as WAR.

  Verse 4. And there went out another horse that was red: and power was given to him that sat thereon to take peace from the earth . . . that they should kill one another: and there was given unto him a great sword.

alarming spread of typhus along the old Russian front from the Baltic to the Black Sea. Lithuania, Poland, Roumania, Serbia, and the Ukraine were particularly affected. My organization had already been bombarding our Paris Office for help.

Typhus was a louse-carried infection; the people got lice mostly because of the scarcity of soap, as they ate all the fats. It was of course contributed to by the general short rations, debilitation and filth due to destruction of their homes, and consequent overcrowding in hovels.

The "Big Four" referred the matter to me for advice. It was not my job. I recommended that the American Red Cross undertake it. But that organization replied to the "Big Four" that it was just too big a job for them.

The pestilence had begun to move westward like a prairie fire. The people were trying to flee before it. Finally, I concluded that we would have to take it on. The "Big Four" thought so also—and felt relieved. I asked the Ministers of Health of these countries to come to Paris for

---

It would today appear from "kill one another" and especially from his riding a red horse that the modern name of this rider might well be REVOLUTION.

Verses 5 and 6. . . . And I beheld, and lo a black horse; and he that sat on him had a pair of balances in his hand. And I heard a voice . . . say, A measure of wheat for a penny, and three measures of barley for a penny . . .

I am not sure this rider was FAMINE. He indicates FAMINE, but his occupation seems to have been either PROFITEER or FOOD ADMINISTRATOR. That depends on whether he was raising prices or simply rationing what food there was with his balances and fixing prices in the usual shortage of war.

Verse 8. And I looked, and behold a pale horse; and his name that sat on him was Death, and Hell followed with him. And power was given . . . to kill with sword, and with hunger, and with death . . .

This rider's equipment certainly embraced FAMINE.

However, as Hell followed with him, he was at least an intimation of further aftermaths and wrath to come. The text does not specifically mention PESTILENCE as part of his equipment, but this rider certainly had a variety of methods of killing. If St. John was symbolizing human experience we could no doubt include PESTILENCE as it was a universal aftermath even in his time.

I suggest the Prophet indicated five and not four horsemen; that is, WAR, FAMINE, PESTILENCE, DEATH, and REVOLUTION.

But if the Prophet was forecasting human wickedness in total war as we experienced it nineteen hundred years after, we could add to his cavalry.

If he had lived another two thousand years he would have added seven more to his troop—IMPERIALISM, MILITARISM, TOTALITARIANISM, INFLATION, ATHEISM, FEAR, and HATE.

organization purposes. Their reports were alarming enough. They indicated that there were possibly 1,000,000 cases. The disease ran its individual course in about three weeks. The mortality was about 25 per cent, or more than 100,000 deaths a week. Many of those who recovered were not much good afterwards. The whole of Europe had become alarmed.

I secured the delousing equipment of the American Army, together with large quantities of hospital beds, supplies, soap and discarded clothing. At my request, on July 2nd, General Pershing delegated Colonel H. L. Gilchrist, twenty officers and, ultimately, 1,000 men of the Army Medical Corps to the service. The American Army as a first installment gave us 1,500,000 suits of underclothes, 3,000 beds, 10,000 hair clippers, 250 tons of soap, 500 portable baths. I also secured as a gift the British Army delousing equipment and medical supplies. I then secured, also as a gift, the delousing equipment and medical supplies of the former German Army.

We drew a line of battle in front of the typhus area hundreds of miles long—a "sanitary cordon." With the aid of local police, we stopped all traffic over this line except to persons with "deloused" certificates; then with the aid of all health authorities, we gradually deloused, disinfected and reclad the people, village by village, in a general movement eastward. Soon we had extinguished most of the fire. Colonel Gilchrist devotedly remained on the job for a few months after the rest of us left Europe to make sure that the local authorities could deal with the winter situation.

Once, Dr. Vernon Kellogg got on the wrong side of the "cordon," and in spite of his expostulations was deloused by the efficient American doughboys. For many years he proudly exhibited his certificate.

PRISONERS OF WAR

The prisoners in Germany [3]—mostly Russians—and the prisoners in Russia—mostly Germans and Austrians—presented a problem. There were six or seven hundred thousand in each place. On December 21

[3] There is in the War Library a very exhaustive manuscript on this question by Edward F. Willis.

(1918), I was informed by the American Army authorities that "the prisoners in Germany are dying wholesale from neglect." It again seemed to me a job for the Red Cross. But they did not wish to undertake it. Therefore, I took the matter up with the French and British military leaders whose armies were occupying most of the camps. We did not make much headway until I prevailed upon President Wilson to lay it before the "Big Four." They directed the military authorities to take the job in hand. But the armies passed it back to me. Finally I arranged to provide the food through the President's "Personal Fund" as we had no other applicable resources. General Pershing delegated American officers to distribute it. Later on, the French Army got the notion that the Russian prisoners should be held in Germany to prevent them from joining the Communist Armies in Russia. With that political aspect, I insisted that the French should furnish about half the food. They did so until the peace, when they lost interest and the prisoners were gradually repatriated. I mention this subject only because it appears interminably in the documents of the times.

THE STANFORD WAR LIBRARY

This appears as good a place as any to introduce another side issue which I pursued during this period. I have already mentioned the origins of the War Library at Stanford University in my account of the Belgian Relief.

I had during that time established the collection of material upon the war, particularly the fugitive material, in the principal centers of Europe. I had engaged professional collectors in the capitals of all belligerents and instructed them to hold the material until peace. With the Armistice I sent for Professor E. D. Adams, the head of the History Department of Stanford, to come to Europe and gave him a credit of $50,000 for the work. General Pershing was greatly impressed with the importance of the project, and with his co-operation we secured the assignment of some fifteen former assistant professors or instructors of history from the army and sent them all over Europe on the mission of collecting material. They were overjoyed to get out of billets and went at it with a vim. Not only did I ask our economic missions to help, but

we requested aid from the heads of the liberated and enemy governments as well. They did so in an extraordinary fashion. As these were
all revolutionary governments, none of them regarded the records of
their predecessors as sacred, and we secured confidential documents
from many of them. As the carloads of material arrived in ports, I
loaded them on our returning food ships.

CHAPTER 39

BREAKING AMERICAN FOOD PRICE GUARANTEES—THE CONTINUING BLOCKADE OF EUROPE

I have delayed recounting two inter-related troubles until I presented a general picture of our operations. They were a battle over American food prices and the continued blockade of the twenty-two neutral, liberated, and enemy countries.

Continuously during the four months from mid-November to mid-March I was compelled to carry on these two battles, in addition to those already related. We, however, did not allow it to interfere with our relief operations.

BREAKING AMERICAN GUARANTEED FARM PRICES [1]

I have mentioned the premonitory signs of the British desire to break world food prices, which would have been disastrous to our American farmers. As I have said, they wanted American prices down to the levels of the dammed-back supplies in the Indies and the Southern Hemisphere and naturally feared the rise of those prices to our levels. Originally I did not take this talk very seriously, for it would have represented a gigantic breach of good faith between men and governments.

---

[1] The complete documentation of all these matters has been published in full and thus far condensation of this text has been simply referred to, or skeletonized. They contain ample proof of transactions otherwise difficult to believe.

Especially, see *American Pork Production in the World War*, by Frank M. Surface (Chicago, 1926).

But the situation became very serious. This shrill note ran through all of our negotiations over organization and removal of the blockade. Early in December an obviously inspired attack upon American food prices appeared in the British press and was promptly echoed in the French press. I answered this attack with a press release, but the censors let very little of it get by. In any event, their food officials understood it.

My statement explained the reductions in prices brought about by the Food Administration from the levels prior to American entry into the war, the reasons for our guarantees of prices, and the moral and legal obligations we were under to farmers. It recounted that, in order to provide the breadstuffs and fats urged by the Allies as a means to carry them through 1917–1919, we had given, with their full approval, these guarantees to our farmers on wheat, hogs and some dairy products, and were supporting other prices. Further, we had bought all the sugar crops in the Western world. The Allies had at that time insisted they must have food from us to win the war. I stated in this press release that we had no need to give such guarantees to feed the American people; that the Allied governments prior to the Armistice had expressed the greatest gratitude for the extent and success of the American food effort.

In this dispute our most dangerous situation was the pork and dairy products. They were perishable. They were produced every day. They had to be processed and placed in cold storage. With our increased production the storage capacity in the United States was limited to under sixty days.

In 1918 we had assured the American farmer an increase to $17.50 per hundred pounds for hogs from that winter and spring farrowing. His stupendous response began to come to market in September (1918), and the guarantee continued until March (1919). The pigs were coming in numbers never known before in human history. The valiant farmer, in response to patriotic appeal, and assured price, produced and sent to the market 26,000,000 hogs in this period. From it we had 400,000,000 pounds a month of pork products beyond our domestic needs. The only answer was a steady movement into Europe.

The moment our storage was filled the packers must stop buying hogs and not only would the price of hogs crack but cattle prices would come down with them, then animal feeds and every other product except wheat (provided we could find storage for it). Ten thousand country banks had made loans to the farmers and merchants to produce and handle these products upon the basis of our prices. They would crash also. And the immorality of breaking faith with the farmer was unbearable.

In the preliminary conversations (in November 1918), I had suggested that if the blockaded markets of Europe were opened to us then the Allies, having the available shipping, could go to the Southern Hemisphere for the cheaper food. They contended, however, in view of the world shortage before the next harvest that prices in those quarters would quickly rise to the American level and that our prices must be reduced first. To this, I replied that if they would co-operate with me, we could regulate competitive buying in these other markets so as not to have this effect.

Precisely when they determined to take violent action against us, I do not know. As late as December 15th, more than a month after the Armistice, the "Inter-Allied (British, French and Italian) Meat and Fats Executive," which was the buying agency of these governments, had confirmed the pre-Armistice orders by which they would take about 240,000,000 pounds of pork and dairy products for each of the months of January, February and March. Then the marketing of the guaranteed fat supplies would be over. I had depended upon the operation of relief to take up the balance.

In order to ease the situation and at the same time get food started into the famine areas, I had proposed to the Allied Blockade Committee on December 22nd (1918) that the blockade on food to the neutrals and liberated countries be let down at once. I proposed that the neutrals be allowed to re-export food to Germany and import non-competitive commodities from Germany to pay for it, mainly dyestuffs and potash which all the world needed. This proposal was put into action the next day; and I proceeded at once to make contracts for delivery of fats to the neutrals. However, without my being informed, the blockade agreement was reversed on December 31st. Neutrals were notified by the blockade authorities that they could not import the orders which I had in the meantime accepted. That same day the

"Fats Executive" met and cancelled all their American orders. Nor did the "Fats Executive" inform me of this action—I learned it next day from New York and Chicago. Included in these cancellations was 200,000,000 pounds of bacon, which had been already packed on British orders in cures used only by the British.

The Allied "Wheat Executive" also notified me at the end of December that they had cancelled their written contract with us to take 100,000,000 bushels from January to March. They contended that morally the contracts were based upon the continuation of the war, although it was not in the deed. As wheat was not so perishable, our only difficulty with it was to find a place to put our huge surplus.

I at once sent Joseph Cotton over to London to see these "Executives." He wired me that they were "deaf to arguments and commitments." They claimed large stocks were on hand. I checked this and found that the stocks were below normal. I was quickly notified by the Grain Corporation that storage for fats and meat was being crowded, and by the packers that they must soon stop buying hogs.

I will not cumber this text with the vigorous telegrams, letters, and memoranda which passed between myself and the Allied Food officials, nor the constant reports to President Wilson on what was taking place.[2]

But we were not so helpless as our Allied Food Ministers must have supposed. The worst period we had to get over was the absorption of the repudiated pork and dairy products contracts during four months, when the winter run would be over and our guarantees would expire. A hungry Europe urgently needed all this food—and more.

I informed the neutrals that the orders they had given in the United States with my approval would be filled irrespective of any blockade measures—thanks to assurances from Admiral Benson that the American Navy would not stand such nonsense.

Knowing the food situation in France and Italy, we could not believe that their Food Administrators had any serious part in this or could risk an action which might cut off all their supplies and credits from the United States. This quickly proved to be true. They repudiated the action of the "Fats Executive" and early in January placed their orders

[2] They are given in full in the publications which I have referred to in Chapter 33.

for about 120,000,000 pounds of pork and dairy products per month and requested that wheat shipments be continued.

We increased the Belgian Relief orders by $45,000,000 worth of extra food, in the knowledge that the Belgians would need this before the harvest and that it could be replaced if we wanted to sell it to Germany. I directed the Grain Corporation to buy any surplus fats and wheat and ship them on consignment to me at neutral ports in Europe. Some of these shipments were delivered directly to the liberated countries in defiance of the blockade, as the British did not dare stop American-flag ships on voyages for our Government. Thus we stopped the break.

Having overcome the first hump, I returned to the charge that the blockade on food must come down at once. I protested that it was being used to starve people. I asked the "Fats Executive" and the "Wheat Executive" to dissolve and allow the other Allies and the liberated countries to go free of control.

We did not get the blockade down on Central Europe until March. But in the meantime we transported the wheat and fats to Europe as fast as our storage in America became overcrowded. Knowing always that sometime the blockade would break—or all Central Europe would go Communist—we piled them up in Copenhagen, Amsterdam, Rotterdam and Antwerp. At one time we had over 1,200,000,000 pounds of fats and 100,000,000 bushels of wheat stored in these ports. And at one time the Grain Corporation's borrowings and my consignment obligations exceeded $550,000,000.

But during these months I had nightmares of the collapse of the American farmer and the country banking system. Not a day went by without urgent and sometimes almost hysterical cables from our Washington offices concerning the tightrope we were walking. To add to our joys, Secretary Glass got into a panic to reduce prices on food by taking off our guarantees. Secretary of Agriculture Houston held his hands until our guarantees were fulfilled.

After the glut in pork and dairy products was over in March, and our guarantee having expired, we removed all American trade restraints upon them. As the British, now out of supplies, had to buy, they, competing with others, forced prices up far above our previous levels. In the meantime we had supplied liberated and neutral countries and finally, when the blockade was relaxed, we shipped the remainder of our great stocks in neutral ports to the Germans, who paid in gold. If there is humor in these things, it is that the German population got their fat products at lower prices than did the British people.

As to wheat, the British later asked us to restore the 100,000,000 bushel contract because prices in the remote areas through speculators had risen above our prices. I did so.

THE FOOD BLOCKADE [3]

Insofar as the neutrals and the liberated countries were concerned, the food blockade by the end of January (1919) had become a fiction through American acts. Moreover, we were shipping food into Austria through Trieste, so that the remaining food problem was the blockade on Germany, Turkey, Bulgaria and Hungary. These three latter countries had enough domestic supplies to last for some months and, therefore, the practical issue was Germany alone.

Collateral to the blockade on food was the blockade on imports and exports of other materials from neutrals, liberated and enemy areas. It was impossible for the nations to export goods in payment for food and this was creating vast unemployment and economic deterioration—which our organization was supposed to cure.

The Allies made great military medicine about the necessity to maintain the blockade as the weapon to enforce peace and their economic ideas. As to the enemy states, this was nonsense. Their armies were demobilized and disarmed, while the Allies still had some 10,000,000 men subject to immediate call to service. As to the liberated countries, the blockade had no purpose except power politics. Nor was there any excuse for continuing the blockade upon neutrals.

As I have already mentioned, we had placed a provision in the Armistice agreement stating that "the Allies contemplate the provisioning of Germany during the Armistice as shall be necessary." This provision was extended to the other enemy states of Austria, Turkey and Bulgaria.

---

[3] I refer to the published documentation mentioned in the footnote on page 329, lest anyone again think this account of international conduct must be fiction rather than fact. My statements here are far milder than the documents.

Before leaving the United States, I had stated to the press:

... the watertight blockade has got to be abandoned. ... What is desired most now is for Germany to get on some sort of a stable basis. ... Unless anarchy can be put down and stability of Government can be obtained in these enemy States, there will be nobody to make peace with and nobody to pay the bill. ... Famine is the mother of anarchy.[4]

The form in which this statement appeared in the British press after the British censor had done with it is of interest:

On Saturday, Mr. Hoover sailed for Europe. Before departure he declared it to be unnecessary for the American people to deprive themselves of a single mouthful of food to feed the Germans. He was not worrying about Germany, which could take care of itself, and was not faced with starvation.

However, this idea of feeding enemy countries was unfavorably received by much of the American press. It was received with violence by the European Allied press. The hates of war are slow to cool. Starvation was now to be justified under the general head of punishment.

Sir John Beale of the British Food Ministry called upon me the day I arrived and urged that I should not discuss the food blockade further publicly, as they were opposed to relaxing it "until the Germans learn a few things." At once I repeated to him and their other officials my views, including ample denunciation of continuing the blockade on neutrals and liberated countries without even the excuses in respect to Germany.

I quickly found that the Allied officials were not in agreement with each other. They were trying to reconcile several objectives. One purpose was more adequate punishment for hideous wrongs done; the common expression was, "Germany has not really suffered." Another purpose was to establish the fantastic scheme of long post-war control of the economic world; still another was to break world prices of food and establish control of prices before the food vacuum of Europe was opened. The French did not want Germany or the other enemy states to use any assets to buy food that could otherwise be used for reparations. Neither the British nor the French wanted Germany to get

[4] *Christian Science Monitor,* November 18, 1918.

into the export business before they had recovered their own markets. Britain, France and Italy wanted to control German economic life for some years after peace. They had the blockade working. They could agree on keeping it. But from their diverse objectives they could not agree on any measure to replace it.

A month before the Armistice (October 3, 1918), the Kaiser had abdicated to a ministry headed by Prince Maximilian of Baden. On November 9th, this government was replaced by an even more liberal ministry, headed by Friedrich Ebert. The Germans had some $600,000,-000 in gold in their bank reserves and the French had posted soldiers to protect it.

The truth of these events, their effect upon the peace of the world, have been so much distorted both in the Allied countries and in Germany that it is desirable that I, who worked in the center of this whole situation, should clarify it.

Although the food blockade may have played a part in the defeat of Germany, every enemy soldier, every munitions worker, every farmer, every government official and his family had food. The rest of the people were left with less and less.

The problem was one of higher statesmanship struggling against the miasmic atmosphere of Paris. No one justified the war conduct of Germany, least of all myself, who had seen, felt, and dealt with the oppression of the Belgians. But if the world were to have peace, it had to choose one of two alternatives—either destroy the German race or set about the job of strengthening the democratic forces in Germany in the hope that they might develop a nation of peaceable membership in the family of mankind. If neither were done, there would come a Communist tyranny with aggression in its soul. The immediate hope of preserving the democracy in Germany was to strengthen the struggling liberal elements by making them masters of a food supply.

On December 10th, I gave Colonel House, who was head of the American delegation in Europe, a note on the whole subject saying in part:

1. In a broad sense, there is no longer any military or naval value attaching to the maintenance of the *blockade* of enemy territory. Its retention has

political value in the right settlement of ultimate political issues but its principal incidence is now economic in character. . . .

2. The problem of sustaining life and maintaining order in enemy and certain other territories revolves primarily around the supply of food and secondarily around the gradual reestablishment of commercial life.

3. The . . . provision of foodstuffs in the volumes necessary entails the problem of payment therefor. Under the present blockade situation payment for food supplied to enemy countries must be drawn: . . .

(*a*) in the form of gold, or of negotiable exchange of salable securities,

or

(*b*) by the provision of these foodstuffs at the cost of the associated governments,

or

(*c*) by the export of commodities.

The direct, common-sense and moral first step in view of the Armistice promise was to allow Germany at once to import food and to export such commodities as dyestuffs and potash, that were non-competitive with Allied trades. I pointed out that, if the Allies continued their procrastinating policies, sooner or later there would be a blow-up in Germany and in the ensuing rush to give her food she would have to pay in gold, which would decrease reparations for the Allies.

Soon after my arrival I sent Dr. Kellogg, Dr. Taylor, and Colonel Ryan into Germany to report. The first two men not only were food experts but in their work with the Belgian Relief frequently had been in Germany during the war. Colonel Ryan was a competent observer of public phenomena. They all spoke German.

They reported the food shortage far worse after the Armistice than before. The disturbances and the breakdown of governments interfered with transportation. The weak government could not keep the farmers from hoarding nor hold in check the bootlegging of food to the rich. Their rationing was breaking down.

They reported that the mortality of children had increased by 30 per cent, of those over seventy by 33 per cent. A third of childhood was suffering from malnutrition diseases. The effectiveness of our control of Belgian food during the war needs no more proof than comparison with Belgian children. Taylor and Kellogg stated that the entire working population was far below normal weight; that crime was rampant from the demobilized soldiers robbing farmers; that with the Armistice, industry almost stopped and unemployment was enormous. Over the whole area of central and eastern Europe the railway loadings dropped to a bare 40 per cent of normal. The countries were short of coal and exhausted of raw materials.

They reported that the liberal government of Germany was steadily becoming weaker and was in danger on one side from a military revolution, and on the other from the Communists working on the emotions of a hungry people. The Communists had staged repeated attempts to seize the government. Ebert and his supporters finally had put them down with machine guns in half a dozen cities.

A few days after President Wilson arrived in Paris on December 15th, I sent him a note outlining the dangerous political situation which was arising in Germany and urged immediate action.

Over six weeks had gone by in these fruitless discussions. Up to this time I had been fighting the blockade battle alone. But Vance McCormick, Chairman of our War Trade Board, had now arrived in Europe and proved a valiant soldier of our policies.

Hearing, on December 29th, that the small door we had opened on the 22nd was going to be banged shut, I called a meeting of principal American members of different economic organizations in Paris to agree upon united action against the continued blockade. General Tasker Bliss, then a member of the American peace delegation, who could not be present, wrote me next day:

It may offend certain governing classes, but I believe that it will rally the sentiment of the world in general to us if we now demand in the name of good business a relaxation in the blockade against the Central Powers. And in the name of common humanity I propose that we make a strong appeal to the President.

With general agreement among the Americans, we threshed out the question with the President. He asked me to give him another memorandum upon it. I did so on January 1st saying in part,

(Paris)

In a broad sense, there is no longer any military or naval value attaching to the maintenance of the blockade [of food] of enemy territory. . . . Its principal incidence is now economic in character. . . . The political values may be entirely destroyed by its present harsh action.

Mr. Wilson endorsed this in his own hand:

To these conclusions I entirely agree.

W. W.

As in the memorandum to Colonel House, I again discussed the alternative methods of action, and proposed a limited relaxation of the blockade.

The minutes of the Superior Blockade Council, the Allied Finance Committee, the Shipping Control, the Council of Ministers, the Supreme Council of Supply and Relief, the Supreme Economic Council, the Supreme War Council will be found filled with McCormick's attempts and mine to get something done. But when we had argued up and down and round again we got nowhere except to the door of some other committee. The obstruction was being directed from the top.

We finally persuaded President Wilson to raise the whole question in a meeting of the "Big Four" where we could be present. The meeting took place on January 13th. I sat in a small chair behind the President's right shoulder. Vance was behind him to the left. The Allied officials likewise sat in chairs behind their Prime Ministers. In order to coach our champions in the debate we had to poke our heads out from behind. This bobbing of heads conducting a synthetic debate, where our principals did not know the technology nor the vast intrigues behind plain issues, was a little difficult. The President made a strong presentation and we managed to get acceptance of the principle that the Germans were to have food and if nothing else could be done they could pay gold and export some limited quantities of commodities.

I thought that at least a door in the blockade was open. It wasn't. The Allied Blockade Committee refused to give the necessary orders. The British Navy refused to allow ships to go into Germany. The occupation armies refused to allow us to ship supplies across the frontiers. The Allied Committee in Berlin refused to allow the Germans to send us the gold. Every day for another two months we were given the run-around from one authority to another on some pretext.

Finally, on February 1st, President Wilson agreed to raise the whole question again with the "Big Four." He asked for another memorandum to refresh his memory on the arguments. I said in part:

Paris, 4 February 1919

Dear Mr. President:

. . . There is no right in the law of God or man that we should longer continue to starve neutrals now that we have a surplus of food. . . . I am confident that no action is possible except of a mandatory character from the top.

The President duly took up the question with the Allied Premiers and they duly agreed to my program, which included 300,000 tons of cereals and 70,000 tons of fat monthly to Germany. But there was no action, immediate or otherwise. As before, the French seemed to believe that, by properly directed pressures, they could force their own policies. Two or three new ones emerged. One was to feed Bavaria and the left bank of the Rhine under separate organizations from the rest of Germany in order to encourage separatist movements.

On February 19th, I again gave a statement on the subject to the President.

Mr. McCormick's activities on the blockade are indicated in his diary (parts of which are in the War Library) by the dates when he records his negotiations and urgings: Jan. 14, 18; Feb. 5, 11, 17, 18, 20, 25; March 1, 2, 3, 5, 8, 12, 13, 15, 19, 20, 22, 23, 24, 26, 29.

One of the objectives of British action in holding to the food blockade was made clear by Mr. Winston Churchill to the House of Commons:

We are holding in readiness all our means of coercion in full operation, or in immediate readiness for use. We are enforcing the blockade with vigour. We have strong armies ready to advance at the shortest notice. Germany is very near starvation. The evidence I have received . . . shows, first of all, the great privations which the German people are suffering, and, secondly, the great danger of a collapse of the entire structure of German social and national life under the pressure of hunger and malnutrition. Now is therefore the moment to settle.

The circumstances under which these pressures were brought to bear upon the Germans, in violation of the Armistice provisions, were scarcely those most likely to bring about a durable peace. Francesco Nitti, Italian Prime Minister at the time of the Peace Treaty, later stated:

. . . It will remain forever a terrible precedent in modern history that, against all pledges, all precedents and all traditions, the representatives of Germany were never even heard; nothing was left to them but to sign a treaty at a moment when famine and exhaustion and threat of revolution made it impossible not to sign it. . . .[6]

Finally, the situation in Germany became desperate. The Communists were making steady progress. The feeble German Government was threatened with quick collapse.

On the 7th of March Mr. Lloyd George asked me to call. With him was General Plumer, Commander of the British Occupation Army in Germany. General Plumer was in a state of emotion rare for a Briton. He announced to me in tragic tones that Germany must have food. That was no news to me. What he said later on, however, was helpful. He said that the rank and file of his army was sick and discontented and wanted to go home because they just could not stand the sight of hordes of skinny and bloated children pawing over the offal from the British cantonments. His soldiers were actually depriving themselves to feed these kids. I reinforced his arguments by mentioning the Communist governments now in possession of Munich, Hamburg and Stettin.

After Plumer left, Lloyd George demanded to know why I did not send in food. He said I had been appointed to that job. Thereupon, I turned on a torrent of expressions as to British and French officials that he ought to remember even in his grave. I reviewed their lack of co-operation since I had arrived in Europe and their universal sabotage and attempts to ruin our farmers, and made it about as clear as words

[6] *Peaceless Europe* (London, 1922), p. 114.

could convey it. I pointed out that the British Navy was preventing the Germans from even fishing in the Baltic, which they had used as a food source before the Armistice. I stated the ultimate effect in history and the immediate future, and I reviewed the grasping and trickster attitudes of his British minions—whom I named as well as the French officials engaged in obstruction.

Lloyd George was an overworked but reasonable man. His tone and attitude changed entirely. He inquired if I would deliver "parts of that speech" to the "Big Four." I said that I would be delighted, but that it would carry much more weight if it came from him. He took copious notes. I then suggested that he place Lord Robert Cecil in complete command of the British economic representation in Paris where Americans were concerned. We could work with Cecil. To this he agreed. I further asked that he have Lord Robert represent the British at this meeting instead of Lord Reading. To this he also agreed. This explosion had an unexpected result. Besides the later effect of opening the blockade, it sent the obstructive officials packing off to England.

Some days before this meeting with Lloyd George, I had redrafted a proposed agreement with the Germans covering all points of food, ships and finance in order to meet as many objections as possible. I presented it to Lord Robert as "the understanding to end all understandings" and he agreed to support it for confirmation by the "Big Four."

The meeting (March 8th) of the "Big Four" was a real occasion. The published minutes greatly soften most of the pungency of the language, particularly my own.

This time the "Big Four" sat in judgment on higher seats at one end of the room and our battalions sat in scattered national groups. Cecil read my proposed agreement and endorsed it. The French Minister of Finance, Klotz, objected to some immaterial parts, but finally disclosed his real thesis. They would not let down the blockade unless somebody, not themselves, would sell Germany food on credit. They also insisted on "month-to-month" supplies. Under such a policy I could not arrange overseas transport nor could the Germans arrange distribution. The only thing the Germans had to promptly buy food with was gold. Klotz charged the British with desertion. He charged us with being food merchants trying to sell our wares for gold, with great emphasis on the word gold. He made an appeal for this gold for France. General Foch contended that the relaxation of the blockade would disarm the Allies since with a removal of the food blockade through an agreed monthly program of imports and exports the pressure on Germany could be no longer applied. We asked him what army the Germans had left that could oppose even two Allied divisions.

The debate reached a point where Lloyd George waded in with the amplification of his notes of the day before. He recited that the "Big Four" had settled this whole principle two months before, and that he now found the functionaries of various governments were not obeying orders. Parts of his speech are worth quoting as an answer to those who later claimed the blockade had not been continued for four months after the Armistice. The official record gives Lloyd George's statement as follows:

. . . He wished to urge with all his might that steps should at once be taken to revictual Germany. The honour of the Allies was involved. Under the terms of the armistice the Allies did imply that they meant to let food into Germany. The Germans had accepted our armistice conditions, which were sufficiently severe, and they had complied with the majority of those conditions. But so far, not a single ton of food had been sent into Germany. The fishing fleet had even been prevented from going out to catch a few herrings. The Allies were now on top, but the memories of starvation might one day turn against them. The Germans were being allowed to starve whilst at the same time hundreds of thousands of tons of foods were lying at Rotterdam, waiting to be taken up the waterways into Germany. These incidents constituted far more formidable weapons for use against the Allies than any of the armaments it was sought to limit. The Allies were sowing hatred for the future: they were piling up agony, not for the Germans but for themselves. The British troops were indignant about our refusal to revictual Germany. General Plumer had said that he could not be responsible for his troops if children were allowed to wander about the streets, half starving. The British soldiers would not stand that, they were beginning to make complaints, and the most urgent demands were being received from them. Furthermore, British Officers who had been in Germany said that Bolshevism was being created, and the determining factor was going to be food. As long as the people were starving they would listen to the arguments of the Spartacists, and the Allies by their action were simply encouraging elements of disruption and anarchism. It was like stirring up an influenza puddle, just next door to one's self. The condition of Russia was well known, and it might be possible to look on at a muddle which had there been created. But, now, if Germany went, and Spain: who would feel safe? As long as order was maintained in Germany, a breakwater would exist between the countries of the Allies and the waters of Revolution beyond. But once that breakwater was swept away, he could not speak for France, but trembled for his own country. The situation was particularly serious in Munich. Bavaria, which once had been thought to represent the most solid and conservative part of Germany, had already gone. He was there that afternoon to reinforce the appeal which had come to him from the men who had helped the Allies to conquer the Germans, the soldiers, who said that they refused to continue to occupy a territory in order to maintain the population in a state of starvation. Meanwhile the Conference continued to haggle. Six weeks ago the same arguments about gold and foreign securities had been raised, and it had then been decided that Germany should be given food. He begged the Conference to reaffirm that decision in the most unequivocal terms, unless this people were fed, if as a result of a process of starvation enforced by the Allies, the people of Germany were allowed to run riot, a state of revolution among the working classes of all countries would ensue with which it would be impossible to cope.

. . . On January 13th exactly the same speeches had been made by M. Klotz [the French Minister of Finance] and he had then been overruled by the Supreme War Council. M. Klotz should . . . submit to the decisions then given by the Supreme War Council.

Nothing had, however, been done during those two months, and now the question had been brought up for discussion with all the old arguments. He would not have raised the matter, but for the fact that during the past two months, in spite of the decision reached by the Supreme War Council in January last, obstacles had continually been put in [Mr. Hoover's] way, with the result that nothing had been done. He appealed to M. Clemenceau to put a stop to these obstructive tactics, otherwise M. Klotz would rank with Lenin and Trotsky among those who had spread Bolshevism in Europe.[7]

Lloyd George's additions to my speech were effective, but his performance had a large measure of intellectual laxity. His own officials

---

[7] A few years later, Klotz was sent to jail for stealing from the French Treasury.

were as responsible as the French. And the French were very sore over this laying all the blame upon them. At any rate, the "Big Four" ordered my formula to be applied forthwith. It decided also to appoint a delegation to present the formula to the Germans which was to be headed by a British Admiral.

The Council appointed Admiral Sir Rosslyn Wemyss to head this conference to take place in Brussels. He was chosen because the British Navy managed the sea blockade. The British, French and Italians sent huge delegations of much pomp and circumstance. I headed a small American delegation including only Mr. Henry M. Robinson, Lewis Strauss, and the invaluable Hugh Gibson to plane out the rough edges. We met the Germans on March 13th and 14th. Wemyss was a stranger to international negotiations and was a very formal and precise old sailor who considered that he embodied His Majesty the King on this occasion. Meeting me in the hotel lobby, he said to me arrogantly, "Young man, I don't see why you Americans want to feed these Germans." Henry Robinson often repeated my impudent reply: "Old man, I don't understand why you British want to starve women and children after they are licked." We had no subsequent private conversations.

Some thirty Allied delegates sat on one side of a long table and eight or ten Germans on the other. The head of the German delegation was Edler von Braun, with whom we had dealings in Berlin at times during the Belgian Relief. When he came in I shook hands with him. Admiral Wemyss was shocked. One could not properly shake hands until the Peace Treaty was signed. Francqui, who represented the Belgians, and I sat together. We had the satisfaction of hearing the very Germans of whom we had so often asked concessions for the Belgians, now on the other side of the table, begging us for food. In after years he developed this incident into a great and thrilling drama.

I had no difficulty in planing out the agreement with the Germans. They wanted a larger quantity of food than we proposed. We were glad to let them have more within the limits of available shipping. We made the Admiral sign a provision in the agreement allowing the Germans to fish in the Baltic, a proceeding which he regarded with gloomy apprehension. We could not get him to agree to their fishing in the

North Sea, but he agreed they might buy fish from these waters from the neutrals. Although the German fleet was now interned at Scapa Flow, he must have thought that German fishing boats would destroy the British Navy.

One of the most utterly senseless actions of the blockade authorities after the Armistice had been this prevention of fishing by the Germans and other enemy states. That was nothing but vindictiveness. I had asked the Blockade Committee to take this restriction down early in December, but got nowhere with the civil officials. As this was a naval action, on December 25th, I asked Admiral Benson to help me out.

The Admiral reported that he had been unable to persuade the British and expressed himself verbally to me in sailor's traditional words of indignation. It was simply a stupid action, that at last, after four months, was remedied.

There was more to this fishing question than might appear.

In mid-February (1919) it had come to my knowledge that the British and French were pressing the Germans to agree to buy for $45,000,000 in gold about 45,000 tons of food—about $1,000 per ton.

I instructed our representative in Berlin to inquire of the German Food Ministry what this was all about. It appeared that the British and French had said to the Germans that they must buy the stocks of fish then in Scandinavia. These had been bought by the Allies during the war to prevent the Germans from getting them. In addition, they were to buy from the Allies stocks of several times renovated rancid fats which had been accumulated as a reserve against the submarine war. The Germans stated that they had been told that they must agree to this before the Hoover program could be allowed.

I had our representative inform the German Food Ministry that my organization had nothing to do with this transaction and that I was not a purveyor of rotten food, even to an enemy. The astonishing reply was, "The Allies will no doubt take our gold reserve for reparations, and if we can get some material for fertilizers and soap in exchange, we would be glad to have it."

It thus seemed to be all right all around: The British and French got $45,000,000 in gold, which they deserved as war damages; the Germans were satisfied to get anything back. I had cleared my skirts of selling bad food. But I refused to incorporate their transactions as "food" in our dealings with the Germans.

Under the Brussels agreements (March 14), the Germans were to hand over their commercial ships to transport food, were to pay in gold and securities, and to be allowed a limited list of exports including coal. We had lost four months' time, and the problems in Germany had been multiplied.

There were also losses to the Allies from these actions. Had the Blockade Committee stuck to the original decision of December 21st, much food would have flowed naturally into Germany through the neutrals, without cost to any of the Allies. It all came out as could be expected. Four months later when we did open the door the crisis in Germany was such that we could not wait for the slow process of creating exchange by trade but, as predicted, had to provide food quickly for gold, which made gold reparations to the British and French just so much less.

But there was a loss to the Allies far greater than this. The Germans have never ceased to use the continuation of the food blockade to poison the minds of their own people and the world.

When the door for food to Germany opened, I quickly found hate so livid on the Allied side and also in some part of America as to force me to issue a statement justifying my actions. It but represented a summary of the arguments I had been using daily for four months:

WHY WE ARE FEEDING GERMANY. From the point of view of my Western upbringing, I would say at once, because we do not kick a man in the stomach after we have licked him.

From the point of view of an economist, I would say that it is because there are seventy millions of people who must either produce or die, that their production is essential to the world's future and that they cannot produce unless they are fed.

From the point of view of a governor, I would say it is because famine breeds anarchy, anarchy is infectious, the infection of such a cesspool will jeopardize France and Britain, will yet spread to the United States.

From the point of view of a peace negotiator, it is because we must maintain order and stable government in Germany if we would have someone with whom to sign peace.

From the point of view of a reconstructionist I would say that unless the German people can have food, can maintain order and stable government and get back to production, there is no hope of their paying the damages they owe to the world.

From the point of view of a humanitarian, I would say that we have not been fighting with women and children and we are not beginning now.

From the point of view of our Secretary of War, I would say that I wish to return the American soldiers home and that it is a good bargain to give food for passenger steamers on which our boys may arrive home four months earlier than will otherwise be the case.

From the point of view of the American Treasurer, I would also say this is a good bargain, because it saves the United States enormous expenditures in Europe in the support of idle men and allows these men to return to productivity in the United States.

From the point of view of a negotiator of the Armistice, I would say that we are in honor bound to fulfill the implied terms of the Armistice that Germany shall have food.

Let us not befog our minds with the idea that we are feeding Germany out of charity. She is paying for her food. All that we have done for Germany is to lift the blockade to a degree that allows her to import her food from any market that she wishes and in the initial state, in order to effect the above, we are allowing her to purchase emergency supplies from stocks in Europe, at full prices.

Taking it by and large, our face is forward, not backward on history. We and our children must live with these seventy million Germans. No matter how deeply we may feel at the present moment, our vision must stretch over the next hundred years and we must write now into history such acts as will stand creditably in the minds of our grandchildren.

We at once started food moving from our great stocks in neutral ports, and ordered several cargoes of food then at sea into German harbors. To the utter astonishment of the Germans several of them arrived before they had sent the gold to pay for them. That America showed even so minor a mark of confidence in the liberal regime appeared in large type in their press. It gave strength to the Ebert government.

President Wilson's strong and right view was to hold together a united Germany under decent government. Otherwise in after years the world would see again the wars which would come from the explosions when the fragments came together. The French view—born of their suffering—was that we should reduce the potency of the German state by truncating it through annexing Germans to Poland and Czechoslovakia and by keeping Austria separated from Germany. Beyond this, they now began again to create separatist movements inside of Germany by a conspiracy between French and German industrialists to set up a Rhenish Republic. President Ebert ended this conspiracy by locking their industrialists up in jail. The next move was for an independent Bavaria. Whoever controlled the food would control the state. The French-Bavarian conspirators wanted to be assured of food independently from the central government. M. Clemenceau was very insistent in urging this plan on President Wilson. The President sent for me and I gave him a note on the subject which ended the idea.

Paris, France,
April 3, 1919.

Dear Mr. President:

With respect to feeding Bavaria through Switzerland, this is totally infeasible in any volume worth considering, both from a transportation, food and financial point of view.

For your confidential information, the whole of this question has been repeatedly agitated by the French Minister at Berne, who is constantly endeavoring to create a Separatist spirit in Bavaria and who wishes to send a few carloads of food into Bavaria under the French flag. The pressure from this quarter became so great in this particular about ten days ago that it was raised before the Council of Four Ministers of Foreign Affairs. . . .

Foodstuffs are moving into the ports of Germany as rapidly as we can secure transportation and the large industrial centers in the North are in far more acute distress than Bavaria. While we are insistent that some portion of shipments should be made to Bavaria, I myself consider it fundamental that we should get some American food at the earliest possible moment into the larger centers of the North and East.

As quickly as the first German passenger ship left the German harbors, and before any of the financial arrangements were completed, I diverted several cargoes intended for other quarters into German harbors. . . . I may add, however, that the situation in Germany is extremely dangerous and that I am not at all sure that our food supplies have not arrived sixty days too late.

In any event, it is a neck and neck race as to whether food will maintain stability as against the other forces that have grown out of hunger in the meantime.

We had been so delayed in opening the blockade that it was nip and tuck keeping ahead of Communist movements. On April 21st, the British sent to the President a report which urged that I increase the volume of food into Germany. Mr. Wilson passed it along to me for comment.

The relaxation of the blockade on food alone was not enough. The other parts of the blockade were stifling productive life.

I could not resist commenting to the President:

21 April, 1919

. . . You and all of us have proposed, fought and plead for the last three months that the blockade on Germany should be taken off, that these people should be allowed to return to production not only to save themselves from starvation and misery but that there should be awakened in them some resolution for continued National life. The situation in Germany today is to a large degree one of complete abandonment of hope. . . . The people are simply in a state of moral collapse and there is no resurrection from this except through the restoration of the normal processes of economic life and hope. . . .

We feel also from an American point of view that the refusal of the Allies to accept these primary considerations during the last three months leaves them with the total responsibility for what is now impending. . . .

To this, the President replied:

My dear Hoover:

Thank you warmly for your letter of yesterday enclosing your memorandum on the situation in Germany apropos of the British memorandum which I handed you. It will be very serviceable to me indeed.

Cordially and faithfully yours,

WOODROW WILSON.

In the latter part of March we got the food blockade relaxed as to Bulgaria, Turkey, and Hungary.

All of this action, of course, was merely a hole through the blockade. It did not serve the full purpose of rehabilitating Europe. We constantly urged that we must get the enemy countries back to work to produce and export goods with which to pay for food and to pay reparations. That required further relaxation of the blockade.

We saw no daylight, however, on the larger issue of the blockade in general until Lord Robert Cecil, on April 23rd, nearly six months after the Armistice, broke out with this bright idea to the Supreme Economic Council. He said:

[We should recognize] the necessity in the interest of the economic interests of the European nations as a whole of taking such steps as would publicly encourage and foster at the earliest possible date the resumption of normal trade conditions both in Germany and in other European countries.

The French representatives observed it would be a good thing after the Peace was signed and urged that it be earnestly considered after that time. All of which was amusing to the Americans. The Italians supported Cecil. I made a statement on behalf of the Americans. It was a review of what we had been saying for months.

Without French approval, we sent a recommendation from the Supreme Economic Council to the "Big Four" to take the blockade down altogether. On May 5th, the "Big Four" concluded that no action should be taken. They were hoping to give the Germans the draft treaty a day or two later and had illusions that Peace would be quickly signed. It was not to come for nearly two months—during which time untold economic harm was done.

After the draft peace treaty was sent to the Germans on May 7th, General Foch raised again the proposal to force the Germans to sign by reimposing the food blockade. I protested to President Wilson on May 14th, pointing out that under these conditions

. . . I seriously doubt whether when the world has recovered its moral equilibrium, that it would consider a peace obtained upon such a device as the starving of women and children as being binding upon the German people. . . .

I further pointed out that with Germany disarmed, a military threat would be ample if needed. As a result of our protests the "Big Four" informed Foch that if force were to be used it must be military.

The maintenance of the blockade on food during those four months from the Armistice until March was a crime in statesmanship and against civilization as a whole. But no one who reads the documents of the time, the minutes of a hundred tense meetings, will ever charge that crime against America. And yet we in America have had to suffer from the infections of revenge and bitterness which have for a generation poisoned German life. Nations can take philosophically the hardships of war; when the fighting is over they begin to bury the past as part of the fight. But when they lay down their arms and surrender upon promises and assurances that they will be no longer attacked and that they may have food for their women and children, and then find that the worst instrument of attack upon them is maintained —then hate never dies.

In after years, the mine they had planted blew up in the faces of these world peace-makers.

CHAPTER 40

THE ALLIES, THE NEUTRALS, BELGIUM AND POLAND

The fight against the famine, pestilence, economic and political disintegration on the front line was of far more interest than the dull routine of administration to which the first part of this account has been devoted.

The problems which arose in each different country teemed with interest. We could not avoid dealing with the political and economic forces in each country. Within these experiences, there are many chapters of unwritten history, interesting incidents, and some humor.

THE EUROPEAN ALLIES

From an American point of view, the British, French and Italians were, for the twelve months beginning with the Armistice, as much on relief as Poland or any other country. They had to be loaned the money to buy their imports from us, and there was no probability that they would repay the loans. The handling of their supplies to the shipside in America or from our surplus Army stocks was under my direction as United States Food Administrator. They were able to do their own transport and distribution. There was no shortage of food or suffering among them as they had a priority on the world supplies. For a period after the Armistice, they purchased food in the cheaper markets of the Southern Hemisphere and India—yet they had to draw enormous quantities from us later on. Their purchases elsewhere had to be coordinated by us with American supplies against the background of the world's narrow margins.

During the whole war and Armistice period from April, 1917 to December, 1919, under my direction America furnished France with 7,333,820 tons of a value of $1,069,205,071; Italy with 7,479,780 tons of a value of $799,608,264; and Great Britain with 8,652,688 tons of a value of $1,386,102,780; or a total of 23,466,288 tons, valued at $3,254,-916,115.

An analysis of our Treasury data and our exports shows that, included in the above totals, they drew the following amounts on credit from the United States after the Armistice—that is, during the relief period: France, 4,439,076 tons, valued at $680,428,000; Italy, 4,478,900 tons, valued at $478,210,000; and Great Britain, 4,305,300 tons, valued at $687,775,300; the totals being 13,223,276 tons, valued at $1,846,413,300.

THE NEUTRALS

The supplies to the neutral states—Norway, Sweden, Denmark, Holland, Switzerland and Spain—came into my purview from many directions. I had to concern myself with securing for these 43,000,000 people a relaxation of the blockade. We had need to co-ordinate their food supplies with those of other nations. Those that they obtained from the United States were under the supervision of the Food Administration and had to be apportioned by us along with those of all the other nations. Their inclinations took them mostly to the cheaper markets in the Southern Hemisphere. They mostly had their own ships, and paid for their food in cash or goods. They cooperated in full with me, and after the blockade was broken down, they had no suffering and needed no loans and no charity. We had a number of amiable cross transactions with them, as at times we loaned food back and forth.

From our data on the imports and exports of these countries, it would seem that all of the Neutrals together imported about 4,300,000 tons of food during this period.

BELGIUM AND NORTHERN FRANCE

I have already dealt with these two areas under the chapter on Belgian Relief.

POLAND [1]

Fortified by President Wilson's assurances, the Polish people raised the banner of independence immediately after the Armistice. They had been partitioned among Russia, Germany and Austria for 150 years. Their resurgence was proof that the spirit of a race does not die from oppression. There is more to nations than their soil, their cities, their wealth, and even their governments. There is a soul in a people. That soul is forged in the instincts of their race, their traditions, their heroic struggles, their strong men and women, and their genius in art, music and literature. It is steeled in their sufferings.

The misfortune of the Polish people was that a thousand years ago they settled on the plains between the two great military races of Germany and Russia. In their conflicts the Poles had been overrun time and again. They had been partitioned time and again. But just as often they have fought for their freedom. And the indomitable spirit of the race has time and again led them out of oppression into independence.

But once independence is won it has always been the beginning of new problems for the Poles. Under their oppressors, they had been allowed no real part or experience in government. For intellectual outlets they had been driven to art, music and literature. When they were confronted with the problems of government, they occupied themselves mostly in dialectics and disputes on almost everything. And amid it all on this occasion the Communists were planting the seed of revolution.

After the Armistice conflicting groups quickly emerged. Finally, a group under the leadership of General Pilsudski obtained control. The General was a revolutionary soldier. He was wholly without experience in civil government. He was a dictatorial person with a strange mixture of social and economic ideas. He set up a ministry mostly of military and doctrinaire character that was concerned with such matters, rather

[1] See William R. Grove, *War's Aftermath* (House of Field, Inc., New York, 1940); and H. H. Fisher and S. Brooks, *America and the New Poland* (The Macmillan Company, New York, 1928).

than with the heartbreaking and immediate job of governmental house-keeping.

I had tried at one time during the war (1915) to organize the relief of Poland but both the Germans and the British raised obstacles that could not be overcome. Dr. Vernon Kellogg had investigated the country for me at that time so I dispatched him again as head of our mission, assisted by two most able Army officers as his initial staff—Colonel William R. Grove and Captain Chauncey McCormick. And on the staff also was that most invaluable person—Maurice Pate. They arrived in Warsaw on January 4 (1919). Colonel Grove, who soon succeeded Dr. Kellogg, because he was needed by our Paris office, has since written a book of absorbing interest on the relief work.

They found a poor scene in which to establish instantly any new system of life—whether good or bad. Here were about 28,000,000 people who had for four years been ravished by four separate invasions during this one war, where battles and retreating armies had destroyed and destroyed again. In parts there had been seven invasions and seven destructive retreats. Many hundreds of thousands had died of starvation. The homes of millions had been destroyed and the people in those areas were living in hovels. Their agricultural implements were depleted, their animals had been taken by armies, their crops had been only partly planted and even then only partly harvested. Industry in the cities was dead from lack of raw materials. The people were unemployed and millions were destitute. They had been flooded with rubles and kronen, all of which were now valueless. The railroads were barely functioning. The cities were almost without food; typhus and diseases raged over whole provinces. Rats, lice, famine, pestilence—yet they were determined to build a nation.

After a few days spent in sizing up the scene, Dr. Kellogg advised me of the impossible political situation. He felt there was only one hope and that was for Pilsudski, who had the army's backing, to be put on a pedestal. To close up the factions, he recommended that Ignace Paderewski, the favorite of all Poles, should be placed at the head of a stronger cabinet as Prime Minister and take complete control of the civil government. Not only did Paderewski hold the imagination of all the people, but he was a man of superlative integrity, deeply imbued with democratic ideals. Dr. Kellogg asked that he be authorized to inform Pilsudski that unless this was done American co-operation and aid were futile. I did so and got the hint reinforced from President Wilson. As a result, Pilsudski was elevated to the position of "Chief of State," and Paderewski became Prime Minister on January 16th.

The new government set up was a sort of crossbreed of American and British systems where the Chief of State controlled the Army and the Prime Minister and his Cabinet were responsible for the civil government to a parliament subsequently convened. I arranged that the new government should be immediately "recognized" by the Allied Governments. It was the beginning of a most troubled life for the great musician.

I had known Paderewski for many years. When a college boy I had conducted with partners a sort of lecture bureau to relieve our deficient finances. We had scheduled Paderewski for an appearance, but it did not come off for some reason or other. In 1915, I again met him, when I was trying to get some relief to Poland. And while we were in the war he came frequently to discuss with me the work of the Polish Independence Committee, of which he was the head—and the main financial support.

One of Paderewski's great services to Poland was at the Peace Conference in Paris. His most important colleague at that time was Roman Dmowski, a shrewd, hard-headed negotiator. Between them they succeeded in enlarging the boundaries of Poland beyond the powers of the nation to assimilate the minorities they took in. They secured entirely too many fringes of Germans, Czechs, Russians and Lithuanians for the good of Poland.

Mr. Paderewski was not particularly strong as an administrator. At his request, we sent a whole staff of expert advisers for his governmental departments of finance, railways, and food; in fact, the American advisers practically conducted the whole food administration and the reconstruction of the railways. We secured locomotives and cars from the Armistice requisitions on Germany and from the surplus of the American Army.

On April 10th a news dispatch appeared that fifty Jews had been lined up against a wall and executed by command of a Major of the

Polish Army. A great outcry broke out in the American press. Paderewski was in Paris and I suggested that he should have an investigation made at once. In the meantime, we sent one of our staff to investigate and found there was really not much truth in the story. But it still raged in the American press and began to threaten our relief work. On June 2nd I wrote President Wilson suggesting that, with Paderewski's approval, an official American Mission be sent to look into the matter.

General Edgar Jadwin, Mr. Homer Johnson, and Mr. Henry Morgenthau were appointed as the Commission. These gentlemen did a fine service by exposing falsity and creating a generally more wholesome atmosphere.

But to return to reconstruction measures, our first food arrived in early January and continued in an increasing stream until the harvest in 1919, when it had amounted to 751,135 tons of food. We shipped second-hand and Army surplus clothing and medical supplies. We also furnished them 60,000,000 pounds of raw cotton to weave in their own mills. Of these supplies, the United States furnished 729,673 tons and the United Kingdom 21,462 tons. We received $8,523,936 in cash and gave $176,541,079 in credit and charity. The British gave them credit for their supplies, of $15,798,098.

I have elsewhere described the typhus, the railroad and the coal problems, since they involved many countries.

In addition to these, one of our universal problems was to rebuild trade between countries. The hatred of the Poles for the Germans inhibited them from trading with their western neighbor, yet they could get needed manufactured goods and fertilizers from Germany in exchange for certain Polish raw materials. I had finally to insist that this be done, and once done they liked it. Somewhere in the archives there are long and tedious documents, interviews, telegrams on this subject.

Mr. Paderewski implored Mr. Wilson to visit Poland before he left for home on June 28th. The Premier urged that despite all we had done, the people were in despair from unemployment, disease, short rations, all of which miseries were making them easy prey for the Communists. And indeed the Red Armies were actually attacking them on the Galician frontier. The Prime Minister insisted that the tide could only be stemmed by showing the Polish people that their friend America would stand by them if they persevered in support of liberal institutions. President Wilson, of course, could not go. He asked me to take his place. Paderewski joined in urging me to go and added that the Poles greatly wanted my advice upon their whole economic situation and upon a further reorganization of the government as soon as possible.

We arranged a special train from the Swiss frontier to Warsaw. In order to be as impressive as possible I was accompanied by several Generals and Admirals.

We arrived in Warsaw on the 12th of August about nine o'clock at night. The great barn of a station was filled with people and gaily decorated with Polish and American flags. The platforms were lined with soldiers with massed bands playing "The Star-Spangled Banner" —and they continued to play it. We Americans lined up alongside of our train with our silk hats clasped to our bosoms if we were civilians or our right hands frozen to our caps if we were military. The Polish officials were likewise lined up with Pilsudski, Paderewski, the Cabinet Ministers, the Mayor of Warsaw, the Polish generals and officials, likewise all frozen to salute in honor of the American national anthem. But the bands did not seem disposed to allow the salute to thaw out.

Finally, after a year of embarrassing minutes, the Mayor stepped forward and presented me with the traditional Polish welcome of bread and salt. This time it was a round loaf of bread, eighteen inches in diameter, with a great salt crystal in the dome and all of it upon a specially carved wooden platter. He spoke English but I could not hear a word. With my right hand frozen to the silk hat at my breast, I took the platter in my left hand with appropriate remarks which he in turn could not hear because the band played on. Quickly my left wrist began to wobble under the weight, and I just managed to pass it over to the left hand of the Admiral. His arm quickly began to wobble and he passed it to the left hand of the General. And I watched it go all down the line to the last doughboy. The Poles applauded this maneuver as a characteristic and appropriate American ceremony.

Hugh Gibson had now been made Ambassador to Poland and accompanied by him, Pilsudski and Paderewski, we went to the American Embassy for the night and left the enthusiastic bands still playing.

Thereafter followed a week of strenuous travel from city to city, talking with delegations from labor, industry, agriculture, universities. We attended banquets, mass meetings, reviews of troops, and we made speeches in many cities. One of the most important of the speech-makings was from Kosciusko's Tomb at Cracow. I was to speak first and Paderewski was to translate it. I had put into it the sentiments he wanted and he had a copy in advance. My speech was only about ten minutes long, as there were not a hundred out of the 30,000 massed people who understood English. After Paderewski had given about forty-five minutes to the translation, I asked my Polish aide what he was talking about. He replied: "Oh, he is making a *real* speech."

At Cracow they put on a gala performance at the opera—which was opening its doors for the first time since the Independence. The best of all Polish talent was assembled. They told me that I was not to arrive until after the play opened. I was duly escorted by the revived Kosciusko Regiment in its uniform of 150 years before and taken to Mr. Paderewski's box. He was already there with Madame Paderewska. As I entered he motioned me to the front of the box; the orchestra and the artists on the stage stopped instantly while Madame Paderewska kissed me energetically. The audience and the performers applauded—even if I did not feel that way.

The most profoundly touching incident was my reception at Warsaw by the children. They had been brought in from the soup kitchens in trainloads—50,000 of them. They were organized into a march in front of an old race course grandstand. Ranging from five up to twelve years, clad often in rags, each carried a paper banner of American and Polish colors. Some also brought banners with inscriptions addressed to me. They came by for hours—chattering, laughing, squealing, trying vainly to look sober and to maintain some sort of marching order. General Henrys, the head of the French Military Mission, stood near me with tears coursing down his face until finally, overcome, he left the stand. He said in parting, *"Il n'y a eu une revue d'honneur des soldats en toute histoire que je voudrais avoir plus que cette qu'est vous donné aujourd'hui."* [2] At one moment a rabbit jumped out of the grass and

[2] "There has never been a review of honor in all history which I would prefer for myself to that which has been given you today."

HERBERT HOOVER, PADEREWSKI, AND THE PAPAL NUNCIO (LATER POPE PIUS XI) AT THE REDEDICATION OF THE CATHEDRAL AT WARSAW, 1919

tried to run through the line of children marching. That was too much for live kids. They fell upon him in a mob of two thousand or more. The frantic efforts of the women supervisors to restore the line gave a touch of relief which we all needed. Once captured, they insisted upon bringing the rabbit to me.

The march began early in the afternoon and they had not all passed by at dark when it had to stop. I marvel yet at the capacity of those women who had thought of everything, including where every group from out of town was to sleep that night.

Premier Paderewski called a meeting of his ministers to discuss their future economic plans. I had been deluged with Polish governmental and economic problems during the previous ten months, I knew that what Poland needed was not charts and academic economics, but skilled men. At the request of this meeting I gave them on August 17th a note on their problems and organization as I saw it. I recommended the creation of a Minister of Economics with an economic council representing the different departments of government, together with a more extensive staff of foreign advisers. At Mr. Paderewski's request I replaced the temporary men we had previously furnished for the Armistice period with a more permanent American staff of seven members for different departments of railways, public health, food, mining, commerce, and finance. These advisers functioned for more than a year and contributed greatly to the reconstruction of Poland. And Hugh Gibson was a tower of strength.

Paderewski's downfall, a little later, was one of the added tragedies of Poland. When his Parliament assembled, it was divided into seventeen different groups representing every political theory on earth and doubly confused by the former divisions of the country. They were constantly engaged in battles for their favorite reform or personal power. As a governor and political leader, Paderewski had one superb quality. He was fired by a patriotism which made him one of the greatest orators of his time. His voice, his burning devotion, shamed and reconciled even the bitter and selfish factions of Poland through the dreadful year of 1919. He was resolute on representative government despite the absence of preparation in the people for liberal institutions. He knew well that the canker of Poland was the terrible subjection and poverty of the peasants under the system of great land holdings of the Polish aristocracy, which had been supported by their three oppressors. He proposed drastic land reform. He at once incurred the disfavor of the landlord class. He was already hated by Pilsudski's military clique and in time the combination not only defeated him in Parliament and drove him from the Government, but practically exiled him from the country to the independence of which he had given the best years of his life and all his earnings.

I received thousands of marks of gratitude from the Poles—a square named for me in Warsaw, streets in Cracow and other towns; a statue in the park at Warsaw [3] and degrees from all the universities. Letters, telegrams and resolutions from officials and public men and public bodies came at birthdays and Christmas for many years afterward. The most touching of these compliments were a score of elaborate bound volumes containing hundreds of thousands of signatures of children whom we had fed at schools and soup kitchens and illustrated by their own hands.

[3] Nineteen years later I visited Warsaw again. An eye-witness told me the Germans had blown off the head of the statue with a hand grenade. In any event, I found I was headless at that time—and no doubt continue so under the Communist regime.

CHAPTER 41

FINLAND AND THE OTHER
BALTIC STATES

Finland, after one hundred years of subjection to Russia, had resumed her independence at the time of the Bolshevist Revolution in 1917. Then ensued a civil war with the domestic Communists, who were supported from Moscow. The Communists were overcome with German aid, and the Finns were then required to elect the Kaiser's brother-in-law as King. When the general Armistice came, the Finns, under the leadership of General Mannerheim, shook off the German yoke and established a Republic. The German Prince disappeared from history. The Communists were still active and the repressive measures under Mannerheim were definite enough but not so inhuman as those applied by the Communists to the non-Communists in Russia. The Communist disturbances, a bad crop season, the separation from Russia whence her normal food imports had come, and the inability to make imports through the Allied blockade had all combined to reduce Finland to starvation.

Even before I left for Europe, dreadful reports had come to me as to Finland. Soon after I arrived a Finnish deputation under the leadership of Rudolf Holsti, later Minister of Foreign Affairs, called upon me. In simple terms they presented to me the plight of their people. It was a story of destroyed crops, of plundered and burned granaries, of stagnated imports and exports, a people eating bread made from a mixture of the bark of trees, a heart-breaking death roll amongst the weak and the children.

Their earnestness was so overwhelming that I replied at once we would divert certain of our first cargoes of food to their use. They had made arrangements to get some 10,000 tons of emergency supplies from Sweden and Denmark, provided I would guarantee to replace these amounts to those countries later on. I gave the guarantee. They also informed me they could pay the Swedes and Danes.

I suggested that they could instruct their people to release all reserves of food they had, to be eaten in the meantime. They wanted to know if I was sure the new supplies would arrive. I assured them that the ships were already on the seas and would be diverted at once. It is seldom that these men of the North show emotion. They broke then.

Emotional periods end best under the flash of humor. Some few minutes after they had left they returned. They wanted to know how much the operation would cost. They said they might not have money enough. I explained that I did not know what the cost would be, but that if they could not pay, I would arrange to supply it on credit. They said: "We will pay. Our people will work and pay." I explained that they could take their time to pay over years if they wished. I added further that the American people were furnishing me resources to provide extra food for their children without cost.

The Allied blockade authorities objected to my sending the ships into the Baltic. Under American naval protection we sent them, anyway. We transported the emergency supplies from Sweden and Denmark. At the same time I secured some coffee and fish products from the Norwegians, who donated them.

At this time I had no authority to make United States Treasury loans to them. I did have a promise from President Wilson of $5,000,000 from his emergency fund for cases of desperation that could not be solved otherwise. We were able to solve the problem as the Finnish banks had $5,000,000 on deposit in London under the restriction that it could not be used for exchange. They also had more than $8,000,000 of deposits in American banks which would not release it until the Government of Finland had been recognized and someone could give an authority to make the transfer. The United States Government owed them something like $5,000,000 for goods seized in the United States while they were a part of the German-dominated area. I arranged for the Grain Corporation to take a pledge of these securities. Their ships were formerly of Russian register but until their government was recognized these ships had no nationality, so they could not go to sea.

I sent a mission of American officers headed by Major Ferry Heath. The Finns are not only the most honest of peoples but they are able administrators. They had organized a capable Food Administration even before our mission arrived.

My urgent representations as to the necessity of the recognition of their independence to the Council of Foreign Ministers over months got nowhere. The French were the obstruction, as they believed Communist Russia would collapse and that the question should be kept open to settle with the expected new Russian Government. This action was such nonsense that finally I urged the President to raise it in the "Big Four" and let me do the talking. He asked for the usual memorandum to lay before his colleagues. This was sent on April 26th:

26 April, 1919

My Dear Mr. President:

I am wondering if there is not some method by which the recognition of the full independence of Finland could be expedited. They have now had a general election, they have created a responsible ministry: this ministry is of liberal character. There are many reasons why this matter should be undertaken, and at once.

1. The United States has always had a great sentiment for the suffering of the Finnish people, and their struggle over a century to gain independence.

2. By lack of recognition, they are absolutely isolated from . . . the rest of the world. They are unable to market their products. . . . They have ships without flags; have no right to sail the seas. They are totally unable to establish credits, although they have a great deal of resource, as no bank can loan money to a country of unrecognized government. They are isolated by censorship. Their citizens are not allowed to move as their passports do not run.

I then described the relief operation and their financial situation, and continued:

If ever there was a case for helping a people who are making a sturdy fight to get on a basis of liberal democracy, and are asking no charity of the world whatever, this is the case. I am convinced from our reports that unless Finland is recognized within a very short time that the present government cannot survive the difficulties with which it is faced. . . .

Nor do I see why any half measures need to be taken in this matter. They have gone through every cycle that the world could demand in political evolution, to the point of an independent people, and I feel that they would long since have been recognized had it not been for the terrible cloud of other questions that surrounds the world. . . .

Faithfully yours,

HERBERT HOOVER.

The President asked me to see Clemenceau over the matter. As always with me he was most co-operative. I did not need appear before the "Big Four" with my short but prepared oration. They sent my letter to the Council of Foreign Ministers with directions to act at once. They met on May 3rd and agreed to recognition of Finland's independence. But for some reason or other, it was agreed that the decision should be kept secret from the Finns and the public until a few days later, and then be announced simultaneously by all Governments. A few hours after their decision was made, Holsti came to see me full of emotion and gratitude. He informed me he had seen my letter, but that recognition was not to be made public yet. However, both the French and the British had communicated to him confidentially what was done, and both had said that they hoped he would appreciate their efforts. As it meant their blacklisted ships could prepare to go to sea, Colonel Logan telegraphed to Major Heath in Helsinki—confidentially over our wires—that recognition would be soon announced, and added:

The recognition of Finland has been brought about entirely by Mr. Hoover by his urgent and repeated representations to the various governments.

Heath's immediate reply makes illuminating reading:

You doubtless know that the news of England's recognition arrived three days prior to the news that we had also recognized Finland. Naturally, this resulted in a feeling of obligation towards England which was only partially dispelled by the tardy arrival of the news from the United States.

In addition to the general food supply for the population, our men set up the usual organization of devoted Finnish women to administer the free child feeding. They gave a total of 35,000,000 free meals to the youngsters. Our files are filled with thousands of letters from the Finnish organization for children. I give one example:

Three scourges, war, hunger and disease, have ravaged in Finland. They have sown sufferings and tears into many homes. But in addition to all this, the continued shortage of foodstuffs brought sufferings especially into the homes of the poor families. . . . The mother had to add bark, peat and straw when making bread. As a result of such nourishment the members of the poor families have changed into emaciated, pitiable looking human beings. Often the small ones tell their mothers, "Please, mother, give us real bread," and just as often the mothers had to reply with heavy hearts, "At present there is none, my little child, but wait, perhaps sometime we shall get it."

And then arrived the gift of the American people for the children of Finland. When the poor mothers heard this their hearts brightened and their hopes revived. Now our small ones at least shall receive of God's real food.

And then when the father or mother brought home the gift of the noble American people there was a holiday. The eyes of the children shone for joy and thankfulness toward their good benefactors. They were prepared into a meal which with glad hearts and thankful minds was eaten. Benedictions were asked for the great and noble American people living beyond the sea.

The Nurmes Committee.

The following is the statistical record:

SUPPLIES

From	Food (Tons)	Clothing, Medical, Miscellaneous (Tons)	Total (Tons)
United States	170,275	336	170,611
United Kingdom	3,467	...	3,467
Denmark	10,000	...	10,000
Norway	4,442	...	4,442
Total	188,184	336	188,520

Financed by

Cash paid to United States	$16,237,715
Charity from United States	932,780
Loans from the United States	9,872,171
Loans from United Kingdom	920,250
Exchange Commodities with:	
Denmark	1,141,700
Norway	1,177,130
Total	$30,281,746 [1]

[1] The Finns were the only nation to honor their obligations and never to fail payments on their funded debt to the United States every year until World War II.

THE OTHER BALTIC STATES

The events in Estonia, Latvia and Lithuania merit more discussion than their combined population of 4,700,000 people might indicate. Here was a heroic struggle of subjugated races of historical interest. The part we took in their struggle also has some connotations in later history.

Never has there been an instance of human emancipation occurring under such appalling difficulties. Here were three non-Slavic tribes, probably somewhat related to the Finns and Hungarians who had settled this area in some dim past. They had been subjected over centuries alternately to German, Polish and Russian oppression. There was an alien class overlordship upon them, from an aristocracy descended from the original German Baltic Barons—the "Balts"—with a sprinkling of Russians. In this top layer were the great landowners and industrialists. The mass of the people had passed through serfdom into a peasantry and city workers. Their lot was not happy. Up to the great war they were more sorely exploited than almost any other racial group in Europe. Yet over hundreds of years these races had shown extraordinary intellectual resistance to Germanization and Russification. They had maintained their languages, their racial culture and a determined resolution that freedom would come some time. There was only one large city, Riga, with such smaller ports and manufacturing towns as Reval, Libau, and Memel, which had been built up largely as the commercial outlets from Russia. Otherwise the people were farmers in rich agricultural lands.

When the political explosion in Europe came with the Armistice the resolution of these races at once asserted itself. They each broke into democratic revolutions with provisional governments. Their individualism was such that the three states could not and would not combine into one state although their racial affinities, their aspirations, their economic problems and their future defense and independence all pointed to that necessity.

They were confronted with difficulties which to any but intrepid peoples would have been too much even to contemplate. They were divided in their political ideas because there had been no opportunity for development of cohesions through experience. The great majority aspired to parliamentary government and to free economic systems. However, when their political and social ideas came to light in parliament, there were from twelve to sixteen different political groups in each legislature, stretching from Communism to rank class autocracy.

The Communist conflagration in Russia spread plenty of sparks among them—and fanned these local fires with invading Red Armies. A majority of parties agreed on two things: They would be free. They would divide the land holdings of the great Balt and Russian barons. The people therefore had on one hand to combine against the Balts who were supported from Germany, and on the other against the Communists, to say nothing of their domestic differences.

Prior to the Armistice, they had been occupied by the Germans— indeed they were practically annexed under the Brest-Litovsk Treaty between Russia and Germany. The Germans had created an army of occupation mostly of Balts and White Russians under German officers with General von der Goltz in command.

Therefore, with the Soviet spreading Communism by infection and by attacking armies, with the Balt element endeavoring to control the governments, with an uncontrolled German-commanded army in their midst, and rank starvation everywhere, these peoples were fighting on four fronts. In this almost impossible setting, however, the people of each state at once organized provisional republics.

The Allies, fearing general chaos if the German Army withdrew, had stipulated that General von der Goltz's army should stay there until the Allies settled their future. This army lived by requisition and every German and Balt common soldier had been promised a large landed estate. But everything was delayed by the French, who held that these states must remain *in statu quo* until they could be returned to Russia some time in the future when the Bolshevist Government had been abolished.

A few weeks after the Armistice I began to receive prayers imploring for food, medical supplies, clothing, and raw materials. If the liberal elements could control the food for starving peoples, they would have a powerful hold on the situation. But until some sort of order could be established we could do very little quickly.

In our preliminary organization, I first annexed Estonia to Finland for relief purposes, placing it under Major Ferry Heath at Helsinki. I annexed Latvia and Lithuania to Poland under Colonel Grove at Warsaw. But as the situation became more strenuous I set up a separate mission for the three Baltic states under Colonel John C. Groome and a staff of thirty-six American officers.

With this sort of background, we can move into their individual and hitherto unwritten histories—and behind each was the question of food and freedom.

ESTONIA

In Estonia, four days after the Armistice a council of various groups erected a provisional government at Reval. This council had indeed been born at the time of the Russian Revolution (April, 1917) but had been snuffed out by the German occupation. In December, 1918 the Russian Red Army invaded them. With an improvised force of Finnish, Swedish, White Russian, and Latvian volunteers, but mainly Estonian peasants, they held the Communists off. Our men reported that George Washington's army at Valley Forge was better clothed, better fed and better armed. There can be no doubt of their courage. One division lost 50 per cent in a single action against the Communists but held its ground.

The food situation was horrible enough but our staff soon overcame the worst conditions. In some of the towns the mortality of children had been as high as 35 per cent during the past year. From the Finns we secured in January 1919 an advance of 2,000 tons of flour by undertaking to replace it later on. With another shipment from Copenhagen and a small transshipment from England, we managed to keep things going until we could get regular shipments in motion. In due time we established the free feeding of children from which a lasting impression of America has remained in the Estonian mind.

The Estonians more formally organized a Constitutional Assembly on April 13th (1919) and discovered there were twelve different political parties with no one in majority. Anyway they were united in their determination to be free. Having beaten the Communists, their volunteer contingents joined in an attempt to capture Petrograd, which I relate elsewhere. Otherwise, Estonia offered little more than the usual routine of fighting famine and disease. Being an agricultural state, they were finally comfortable after the arrival of the harvest of 1919.

A human note of true Americanism sounds in one of Lieutenant John Thors' reports. He had charge in Reval and related that upon the arrival of the S.S. *Lake Dancey* the captain asked for a baseball field for his crew to determine whether they or the firemen had the better team. Thors found a field and decided that he would charge the Estonians admission to this strange performance. He borrowed a band from the town and inserted full publicity into the press. Our sailors and firemen gave cigarettes to be sold for 1.50 marks a pack—say 25 cents— a reduction of about 80% of the current price. The brass band, cigarettes and baseball game proved to be a huge success. After the performance was over, he found that the receipts amounted to 3,200 marks for the Children's Relief.

Our Estonian statistical record was:

SUPPLIES

From	Food (Tons)	Clothing, Medical, Miscellaneous (Tons)	Total (Tons)
United States	53,554	4,179	57,733
United Kingdom	8,224	400	8,624
Denmark	462	....	462
Total	62,240	4,579	66,819

Financed by

Cash paid to the United States	$ 414,815
Loans from United States	16,764,071
Charity from United States (Child Feeding)	1,460,796
Loans from United Kingdom	2,342,360
Denmark Exchange Commodities	35,207
Total	$21,017,249

In looking over the musty statistics one item of charity catches the eye—"230,000 children's garments, 35,000 needles and 139,000 buttons."

LATVIA

The new Republic of Latvia had a more troubled infancy than Estonia. Five days after the Armistice, a council of leading Letts, under the leadership of Karlis Ulmanis, proclaimed a Republic at Riga. Ulmanis was provisional President. He was one of the unique figures to emerge in the war years. He had been brought to Nebraska by an uncle when ten years old, had been educated at a mid-West University and had taught economics. Shortly before the war he had returned to Latvia to minister to his mother and was caught in the draft of the Russian Army. Probably more than any one other man he was responsible for the independence movement of these three Baltic races. His devotion to freedom gave direction to all of them.[2]

His frail government was at once opposed by the Balts. Due to refusal of their support he was unable to overcome a Communist rising in Riga early in January (1919) supported by an invasion of the Russian Bolshevist Army.

We were about to land food supplies when Ulmanis and his government were forced to retreat underground. Later (on April 2), he pulled his government together and established a headquarters for it at Libau. He then renewed his appeals to me to stop starvation. Through Colonel Grove, I sent Major Frank Ross and Captain John B. Hollister from our staff in Warsaw. We ordered a cargo into Libau which arrived on April 9th in charge of Major DuBois Brookings and Lieutenant George P. Harrington. In a week they had kitchens operating and were feeding some 20,000 of the most distressed people. But at the end of that week a Balt uprising, led by large land owners and surreptitiously supported by von der Goltz's army, seized Libau. Von der Goltz's action was part of a general conspiracy to establish Balt control of all three Baltic states under a Baron von Stryck. Ulmanis had to flee again, this time to Sweden. Our men, therefore, suspended food distribution for a

---

[2] Twenty years later, at his invitation, I visited the prosperous Latvian Republic. Still later, as a captive, he was executed by the Communists at Leningrad.

few days to see what would happen next. On April 20th a squadron of Allied destroyers appeared and von der Goltz issued a proclamation announcing that he had nothing to do with the overthrow of the Latvian Government; whereupon our men resumed distribution.

Ulmanis again began to organize. Things in Libau rocked along under uncertain control with von der Goltz's army in and out of the situation. In the meantime, I received the most terrible reports about the conduct of the Communist Government in Riga. On May 7th I sent a memorandum to the "Big Four":

The situation at Riga has developed into a most distressing form. From advices received from different quarters, it appears that the Bolshevik Government being unable to provide foodstuffs was mobbed by the populace and had withdrawn its army from the city, which was given over to complete anarchy of wholesale massacre and murder. It appears that a large number of women and children of the so-called "bourgeois" were transported to an island in the bay and have been slowly starving under the guardianship of a lot of female harpies.

We are endeavoring to arrange for a shipload of food, but the question arises at once as to any form of guardianship by which the food could be discharged and distributed. It seems almost impossible to contemplate sending any merchant ship in without naval escort and to secure anything like a reasonable distribution without some kind of military protection.

My information was incorrect in the detail of the withdrawal of the Russian Communist army from Riga. They were still on the job and doing their worst.

As nothing happened, from this appeal, I followed on the 9th with a more urgent letter to Mr. Wilson going into more details, and asking for naval protection to our ships and the port cities.

Mr. Wilson replied:

Paris, 21 May, 1919

My dear Hoover:

I read with deep interest and concern your letter of the ninth of May about the situation in the Baltic Provinces, and yesterday had an opportunity to read it to the other members of the "Council of Four." Mr. Lloyd George suggested that I request you to have a conference with Admiral Hope, or anyone else who represents the British Admiralty here, in order to ascertain whether it was feasible from a naval point of view to carry out the programme you suggest. If the programme were adopted, it would, I suppose, necessarily be the British Navy that executed it, and we would very much appreciate a memorandum from you as to the result of your conference with the British Admiralty.

Cordially and sincerely yours,

WOODROW WILSON.

At a session of the Council of Foreign Ministers on May 13th, they appointed a committee including me, to make a recommendation. We reported promptly, but the military seemed to think it would require weeks to organize action.

In view of what was going on in Riga, this was slower than I could bear. In desperation I sent a telegram to General von der Goltz (whose duty under the Armistice was to preserve order in that region) asking him to occupy Riga. On receiving his agreement, I instructed our men to prepare food for immediate delivery to the city. On May 21st, Major Brookings loaded a train of 40 carloads at Libau and started it for Riga under Lieutenant Harrington following von der Goltz's army. The train reached a point ten miles from the city. Beyond that the tracks were destroyed. Von der Goltz, assisted by the ragged Latvian Army, made a quick movement and occupied parts of the city on May 22nd. In the meantime, I had ordered one of our cargoes afloat into Riga and Admiral Benson sent a destroyer to protect it. Lieutenant Harrington, like the real American he was, set his doughboys to recruiting labor and repairing tracks while he went ahead into Riga, and by using wagons and hand-carts was able to get some food into the city on the 24th.

From one of Lieutenant Harrington's sergeants, there came to me a story of which America should be proud. When Harrington arrived at Riga, fighting in the suburbs between von der Goltz and the Communists was still going on. There were many dead from starvation and battle in the streets. Harrington did not quite know how to get hold of the situation. He inquired if there was an American Consulate. There was. He sent the sergeant who found a small American flag nailed to the door and a typewritten notice in Lettish and vigorous

English warning all comers to stay away—signed by the "Acting Consul of the United States of America." The sergeant had some difficulty in raising anybody, but finally a girl peeked through a crack and, seeing his uniform, threw the door wide open—and broke into tears. She was the stenographer, an American of Lettish birth, who had stayed by the ship when the Consul had been withdrawn in advance of the German occupation a year before. She pulled herself together quickly when told that they had a trainload of food on the edge of the city and wanted to find somebody in authority. She knew whom to get and managed it as if she had been the very mother of Riga itself. She was very thin and hungry and the sergeant assumed the duty of caring for her needs.

Three days after Harrington's arrival, our ship *Lake Mary* arrived amid rejoicing. By this time, however, Harrington was giving one meal a day from his meagre supplies to 200,000 people.

The history of the Communist doings in Riga from January to May, 1919, had never been adequately told in English. A Latvian Soviet Republic had been set up mostly under Lettish and Finnish Communists. The prisons were opened and the dregs of Riga—once a city of a million people—were turned loose on the people. Together with the Communists, they looted every store, every house. The people were left without food except at exorbitant prices from the Communists. The banks and public institutions were plundered. Literally hundreds of innocent people were daily executed without trials in a sadistic orgy of blood, of which the world has known few equals. Clergymen, doc-tors, teachers, young girls, were taken to prison and mowed down by machine guns. On many days as many as 1000 were executed. The deaths from starvation and other causes were so many that coffins could not be provided and bodies by the hundreds were dumped into trenches.

But we were soon to experience another kind of trouble. A German colonel, placed in charge of the city by von der Goltz, set up a military court made up mostly of Balts to find and try those guilty of assassination and execution under the Red regime. There were men on the court whose wives, sons and daughters were among the executed. At once a White Terror replaced a Red Terror with its round of executions. Our ~~men~~ not only protested, but asked me to protest.

I had no particular authority in the matter but sent a telegram to Colonel Groome:

> . . . The Germans alone are responsible for this white terror which succeeded the red terror in this particular instance. . . . As soon as you get to Reval see the various military commanders, communicate to them my views and secure from them a definite assurance that the Riga incidents will not be repeated. Tell them plainly that you are directed by me to see that these unlawful and inhumane acts do not occur. . . . The American people will not lend their support for an instant to any movement which would countenance such actions. Show this telegram to Admiral Cowan and General Gough.
>
> HOOVER.

The Germans reduced their executions mostly to proved criminals.

Ulmanis now returned to Riga and, with food behind him, set up a provisional government again. But another fight which lasted a month developed between the Balts and the Letts. Colonel Groome with Lieutenant Harrington took a distinguished part in making an armistice and bringing various elements together into a temporary coalition under Ulmanis against the Communists. Ultimately, when Ulmanis got his legislative body together, it outdid Estonia, for it had sixteen different political parties—but he managed it somehow.

On June 28th, the day peace was signed at Versailles, the citizens of Riga, Libau and other towns came, with their children, in parades of thousands to the offices of our organization bearing flowers, with bands playing "Yankee Doodle," their view of our national anthem—but they brought also tears and prayers of thanksgiving.

The Allied mission under British and French officers appointed from Paris arrived a month after Riga was relieved. However, before this exhibit of power arrived on the scene of action, we had the adults fed and in addition had set up free feeding of 50,000 stunted children, under the direction of Captain Thomas J. Orbison and with the co-operation of Latvian women. It performed a healing service not only to bodies but to spirits.[3] Our statistical balance sheet for Latvia shows:

[3] An interesting book has been written by Captain Orbison: *Children, Inc.* (Boston, 1933).

SUPPLIES

From	Food (Tons)	Clothing, Medical, Miscellaneous (Tons)	Total (Tons)
United States	25,390	976	26,366

Financed by

Charity from the United States (Child Feeding)	$1,588,170
Loans from the United States	5,880,931
Loans from the United Kingdom	80,920
Total	$7,550,021

And among the details as to the $1,588,170 of charity I find "meals served to undernourished children, 41,200,000. . . . Two thousand Latvian women took part in this work."

LITHUANIA

Lithuania had suffered as the others. The ebb and flow of plundering armies had left even an agricultural people starving. They, too, had declared independence at the time of the Bolshevist Revolution in Russia in 1917 and had seen their new nation snuffed out by the German annexation. After the Armistice they followed the lead of the other Baltic states and, in January, 1919, called a national assembly which set up a provisional government. At once they were invaded by the Soviet armies. Again a ragged army of 25,000 peasants repelled the invaders.

Captain Hollister was originally in charge and was succeeded by Captain John T. Scott, who, being needed by our work elsewhere, was succeeded by Major W. A. Burbank and later by Lieutenant Harrington. The usual free child feeding was organized alongside the general relief and 45,000 children nursed back to health.

The Lithuanian balance sheet is not extensive:

SUPPLIES

From	Food (Tons)	Clothing, Medical, Miscellaneous (Tons)	Total (Tons)
United States	9,244	3,633	12,877

Financed by

Charity from the United States (Child Feeding)	$ 463,817
Loans from the United States	5,459,884
Loans from the United Kingdom	57,120
Total	$5,980,821

One last service I performed for all three Baltic states was to arrange with the Danes for the supply of several thousand tons of seed grain, we to replace it from the United States with other grains. Thus it arrived in time for the planting. And the Danes themselves made a very substantial donation.

CHAPTER 42

CZECHOSLOVAKIA, YUGOSLAVIA AND ARMENIA

I had seen a good deal of the Czechoslovakian leader, Dr. Masaryk, in Washington prior to the Armistice. I believe I secured him, through Secretary Houston, his original introduction to President Wilson. He was a noble figure—scholarly, wide-visioned, tolerant, yet with an iron determination. He had an honest, philosophical mind and was a deep student of the arts of government. At that time, Eduard Beneš was a sort of Man Friday to Masaryk. Beneš was a scholarly man evolved into a statesman. He was a great master of diplomatic formula and devices—and rather intolerant. But when I think of intolerance in these men who had lived under the Austrian heel all their lives, struggling to bring freedom and release to their people, I cannot think of it in terms of unreserved condemnation.

The Sudeten German minority in Bohemia plus the Austrian Germans had dominated the state for most of the past three hundred years. All this time they had, with the utmost brutality, tried to break the Czechs' racial aspirations. Only by sheer intellectual resistance had this intelligent and plucky people been able to preserve their language, their culture and their moral independence. The Czech race is one of superb courage. No greater odyssey lives in history than the retreat of the Czech army which during the war revolted from Austria and ultimately found its way across the whole of Bolshevist Russia and Siberia to join the Allies on the Western Front.

The original setup of Czechoslovakia agreed upon by both Masaryk and Beneš in writing was to be a cantonal, non-military state like

Switzerland.[1] In Paris, Masaryk came to see me over his doubt about the inclusion of a part of western Bohemia in the new state. It was the center of the Sudeten German strength. He asked me to suggest to President Wilson that the President oppose the inclusion of this area, as it would place him in a difficult position with his colleagues to do so himself. Mr. Wilson soon found that the French were insistent on including as many Germans as possible in Czechoslovakia in order to weaken Germany and to provide a stronger military frontier against them. He was able to do very little.

The abilities of Masaryk brought about a quick and effective organization of the new nation. Its difficulties were great, for all finance, transportation, communication and commerce had centered in Vienna. A new economic center had to be built.

Our food relations got off with a bad start because Beneš telegraphed me immediately after the Armistice as to Czech needs:

> "Foodstuffs. Thanks to the productive wealth of our soil . . . there is no need to consider this important question."

I did not, therefore, take them into account in our original set-ups. But by January frantic appeals came from the Czech people.

I set up Dr. Lincoln Hutchinson as head of a mission, with Captain R. S. Beifeld as his assistant. They arrived in Prague in mid-February; later we had to stiffen the mission with some thirty Americans, including railway, finance, coal and child-feeding experts.

Our food problems presented all the usual difficulties except one. The Czechs were capable, honest administrators, but they were ignorant of food administration.

[1] Masaryk had the tolerance and vision required to overcome a hate centuries deep, to weld and to lead the Sudeten Germans to accept the new republic and co-operation with the Czechs. After Masaryk died, Beneš did not have it. Masaryk had the confidence and co-operation of the Slovaks. Beneš lost it. After the Peace, and under the encouragement and finance of the French, the color of Czechoslovakia as a non-military state quickly disappeared. They constructed the nation into a dagger pointed at the German flank. Under Beneš the cantonal equality of races disappeared. Even the names of the streets and roads through the German areas, which had been there 400 years, were changed. When the opportunity came for Germany to remove the dagger, the Sudeten Germans were ripe for revolt. The Slovaks were glad of a chance for delivery from the Czech domination. But they made a bad exchange when they got the Germans under Hitler instead of the Czechs.

One of our difficulties with them was over coal. They held the coal mines which normally supplied Vienna and other Austrian cities. Their dislike of the Austrians and the usefulness of coal for political trading resulted in a thousand reasons why the Czech production could move only in a small intermittent stream. But it was our job to keep the gas works going in Vienna and other Austrian cities just the same. I have described this operation elsewhere.

I visited Prague in August when en route to Poland. The Czechs gave me a most vociferous reception—cheering crowds, dinners, speeches, university degrees and domicile in the ancient castle, where nobody served me breakfast. One of the great streets leading to Wilson Square bears—or did bear—my name.

Our Czech balance sheet of food tonnage is an incomplete record, as it does not include all the "barter" commodities which we arranged from other parts of Eastern Europe in exchange for coal and the small Czech surplus of sugar. Aside from this the statistical record is:

SUPPLIES

From	Food (Tons)	Clothing, Medical, Miscellaneous (Tons)	Total (Tons)
United States	388,890	7,120	396,010
United Kingdom	6,012	1,120	7,132
France	16,571	....	16,571
Italy	75,861	....	75,861
Austria	50,000	....	50,000
Others	560	....	560
Total	537,894	8,240	546,134

Financed by

Cash to the United States	$ 922,607
Charity from United States (Child Feeding)	5,353,171
Loans by United States	80,540,827
Loans from United Kingdom	2,552,198
Loans from France	7,540,918
Exchange Commodities with:	
Italy	16,653,920
Yugoslavia	587,050
Poland	1,000,000
Others	287,660
Total	$115,438,351

YUGOSLAVIA

With the Armistice, Yugoslavia either occupied with its armies or acquired by Allied orders large slices of Austria and Hungary and the whole of Montenegro, making about a 15,000,000 population for the new state. However, the sections taken from the old Austrian Empire were more advanced in the arts of living than the Serbs and aspired to liberal government. Serbia had been a pastoral and agricultural country with honest and rugged officials, but devoted to a monarchical system. The combination did not move smoothly. Moreover, the Serbs soon came into conflict with Italy over Dalmatia, and a month after the Armistice the Italians blockaded them. Which we had to undo.

The leaders of the new state were of course ignorant of all such modern organizations as food administration. I sent Colonel Atwood as chief of our mission and Dr. Alonzo Taylor to assist him at the start.

When it was announced at the Armistice that food would be sent to "enemy" countries the Serbians bestirred themselves. They sent us the most impressive statements of starvation and need, with the suggestion that their people would never understand it if food were sent to the enemy first.

However, Dr. Taylor reported that there was a considerable food surplus in the Serbian areas and a real famine among the Adriatic provinces. We decided that for transportation reasons the eastern surplus should be used to help provision Hungary, Austria and Czechoslovakia and that we would import supplies from America into the western parts which were easily accessible from the seaboard. We had some difficulties in inducing the Serbs to accept this idea, as they did not like the kind of money which the other states initially offered. And they certainly remembered that Austria and Hungary had been enemies for a hundred years, whose armies had repeatedly ravaged and defeated them. Old hates were vivid and vocal. However, our men solved it all by exchanges of coal, oil and goods which Serbia needed, together with gold from Hungary. Only once did I have to appeal to the "Big Four" to direct them to carry out these trades.

We had great difficulties with their dismembered railways but I pro vided a capable railway staff under Colonel Atwood and Col. W. B

Causey to disentangle and rehabilitate them. As I have related elsewhere, we furnished considerable rolling stock from the Armistice surrenders by the Germans and from American Army surplus.

The repeated invasion and plunder of many sections during the war had left the children in a desperate condition. We built up the usual child feeding on American charity.

We had only one unusual incident. In January a civil war broke out in Dalmatia, one side at least inspired by Italians. Sometime later one of the junior American Army officers on our Serbian staff asked special leave to come up to our Paris office on an urgent matter. Lewis Strauss, that invaluable secretary, came in to me, urging that I listen to the lieutenant with a straight face.

The officer—a splendid type of effective, earnest American—told me that he, with two trucks of food and two American doughboys, had come under fire on the mountain road above Cattaro. He had stopped; investigated; made contact with the general of the immediate army and expressed wonder and indignation that they did not know that an Armistice was on and the war over. He found that the general of the army liked neither his war nor his immediate situation. Our American offered to negotiate an armistice. It was promptly accepted.

With a guide, he made his way around the mountain trails to the headquarters of the opposing army. He found the same attitude in the commanding general there and a welcome acceptance of his offer to negotiate an armistice. All that was easy, but neither side would surrender to the other, or admit defeat. Being of a direct mind, the lieutenant concluded to draw up in writing a surrender of each general and his army to the United States of America. But when he came to put it down on paper he became fearful that he was taking responsibilities on behalf of his Government that were far beyond his powers. He did not want to involve our Government in possible political consequences. He had finally solved it by making out the surrender to me as the United States Food Administrator. He demanded a formal surrender of the generals' swords and, remembering General Grant, allowed the men to keep everything else except machine guns and artillery.

He was short of labor to unload a ship in the harbor, so it occurred to him to offer a wage in flour and bacon if one of the armies would unload for him. This was promptly accepted, and he marched them down the mountains to the harbor under command of one of his dough-boys. Then the other army, hearing of this, also wanted a job. So he put one army on the night shift and one on the day shift, and they got along all right. There were about 300 on each side.

But when he thought it all over he became greatly worried for fear he had used my name wrongly. It worried him for weeks, so he concluded to come to Paris to explain it all and take whatever was coming to him. He was plainly anxious. Without even a smile, I asked him what became of the two swords. He said he had brought them along. I told him that if he would give me one and keep the other for himself I would tell nobody in Paris. He was relieved. Lewis got him a week's leave and I wrote him a note to say that he was of the stuff that had made America a great country.

Our statistical balance sheet shows:

SUPPLIES

From	Food (Tons)	Clothing, Medical, Miscellaneous (Tons)	Total (Tons)
United States	77,038	16,665	93,703
United Kingdom	19,561	14,089	33,650
Total	96,599	30,754	127,353

Financed by

Cash paid to United States........................	$ 533,677
Charity from United States (Child Feeding)	2,074,343
Loans from the United States	33,655,437
Loans from the United Kingdom	9,635,192
Total	$45,898,649

These statistics do not show about 150,000 tons of food we exported from the eastern provinces which were fully paid for in goods or gold from the receiving countries. The abundant new harvest ended all troubles.

Colonel Atwood made so great an impression as to his railway abilities that the Serbian Government engaged his services as a technical adviser for some years after the peace.

GEORGIA AND AZERBAIJAN

These two races had been a part of Russia for hundreds of years. After the Communist Revolution they had declared their independence. They had been occupied by German armies to secure the Caspian oil supplies and the pipeline to the Black Sea. The British took over from the Germans, after the Armistice, probably for the same reasons. Our Constantinople staff, under Howard Heinz, soon determined that neither of them needed much food, but some minor supplies were furnished as part of a larger operation in Armenia.

The three new Republics of Armenia, Georgia and Azerbaijan sharply differed in race and religion. Their hates against each other dated back to the time the Ark landed and the sons of Noah started into religious and governmental competition. In modern times the Czarist Russians had kept them from each other's throats.

A White Russian Army, under Denikin, was fighting the Bolshevists north of these Republics; and this gave them a temporary shield against the Red Armies. But Georgia and Azerbaijan were shivering for fear that the White Russians would take them over—and they played with the Communists.

ARMENIA

Probably Armenia was known to the American school child in 1919 only a little less than England. The association of Mount Ararat and Noah, the staunch Christians who were massacred periodically by the Mohammedan Turks, and the Sunday School collections over fifty years for alleviating their miseries—all cumulate to impress the name Armenia on the front of the American mind. Added to that is a very considerable group of good American citizens of the Armenian race, who, under our stimulus of freedom, have shown great qualities in literature, art, and public persuasion.

To give the political background of Armenia at the time of the Armistice is beyond any space available here. Roughly stated, the Armenians were partly settled in old Russia where, at odd times, they were protected, and partly in old Turkey where they were regularly massacred.

The American Near East Relief Committee under the leadership of Mr. Arthur Curtiss James and Mr. Cleveland Dodge of New York, with large funds raised by the American churches, announced they would look after Armenia. I welcomed anybody who would help. We assisted that Committee by looking after their shipping and diverting to them some cargoes en route. Their sailings began early in January (1919). Five or six weeks later, Mr. Heinz at Constantinople informed me of rumors that "things had gone to pieces" in Armenia and that the Near East Committee's work had broken down.

He sent Major E. R. Stoever to investigate. Stoever's report led Mr. Heinz to go over himself, with other officers. Their report to me pictured an incredible state of affairs both as to the Near East Committee staff and the condition of the Armenians. Although some thousands of tons of food, clothing and medicine had been landed at Batum on the Black Sea for the Committee, only a part had ever reached the Armenians. Thousands of tons had been sold in Georgia and Azerbaijan, where there was no need of relief. The corruption and thievery were beyond belief. I instantly demanded the removal of the local American Director of the Committee and subsequently we had nearly every member of their business staff arrested. Some were convicted and others required to disgorge. The Committee replaced the Director with Mr. Yarrow, an able and devoted man, and for the sake of America's good name, I made no public remark on the episode. Aside from this, the Near East Committee did heroic work throughout other parts of Turkey and Greece and I can bear witness to the devotion, honesty and the many acts of great heroism by both women and men of their American staff.

As to the Armenian people themselves, our reports were shocking enough. A few sentences from these reports are indicative.

In the larger towns the dead and dying were everywhere in the streets, children wandering about like dogs looking through the offal.

I have seen women stripping flesh from dead horses with their bare hands. There is abundant evidence of cannibalism.

Typhus is rampant.

In this town of 20,000 people the deaths are at the rate of 3,000 a month

The estimates were that there were about 1,500,000 people in the Armenian Republic including about 500,000 Armenian refugees who had been driven in from Turkey. At least 250,000 were at the absolute point of death and all would be out of food in twenty days.

Mr. Heinz recommended that we take charge of Armenia ourselves with our own men, directly from Paris. As Heinz was shortly leaving for home, I at once sent Major Joseph C. Green, then in Roumania, to move in with a staff of officers. We immediately diverted more cargoes to Batum. Green quickly got things going. In addition, he sent his officers into Azerbaijan and the Kuban province of Russia where additional supplies were obtained.

The Armenian Republic was hardly even a shadow of a government. President Khodissian was an honest man whose sole governmental experience had been gained as mayor of Tiflis. The so-called ministers had never had an atom of administrative experience. They were either incompetent or corrupt and moved by a variety of politics that produced a new cabinet every few weeks. They were all, including the President, simply stunned and helpless in the face of their problems. If anyone wants material for a treatise on human woe, intrigue, war, massacre, incompetence and dishonesty, he can find ample source material in the mass of reports from our American officers.

The British gave us guards for our trains, but away from the railway there was complete anarchy. Several of our officers were held up and robbed in broad daylight in the Armenian capital of Erivan.

Armenia had only 41 locomotives, mostly broken down, for its whole railway system. It had always been operated by Russians and as the Russians had long since left, our men had to organize that job also. One of our troubles was the Georgian Government. The railway to Armenia ran from Batum through Georgian territory. That government held up our trains, demanding that we pay huge sums in food or money for tolls. One demand was for 2,000 tons. Finally, I secured from Prime Minister Clemenceau (July 19th) a sharp dispatch to the Georgians implying that if they did not behave the whole Allied power would be visited upon them. I did not myself know where that power was but the threat of it worked. We reinforced Green's staff and poured in 50,000 tons of food from overseas in 90 days, including 3,300 tons of milk for children and 500 tons of soap and medical supplies to fight typhus.

Under the law our American governmental operations had to end July 1st. Major Green and his associates, all ill and worn, urged that they be relieved. As the situation was certain to be desperate for another year I proposed to the "Big Four" that Colonel William N. Haskell, who was then head of our organization in Roumania, be appointed High Commissioner for Armenia to represent all the power of Allied and Associated Governments and be given backing to preserve order, protect the country, find food and do everything else that could be done. My note to the President on the subject was adopted by the "Big Four" as their directive.

The period which followed partially belongs after our organization came to an end, but I include it here to clean up the Armenian account.

The British decided to withdraw their troops a few weeks after Haskell began; but we secured that they remain for some months and give aid to the Colonel in organizing a small Armenian army. The Azerbaijanese under Turkish officers started invasions and massacres of border villages. When this vigorous tribe was not busy attacking someone else, it put in its time satisfying a thousand-year-old hate by massacring Armenians. In one village on June 7th the Azerbaijanese killed 640 Armenian women and girls.

Colonel Haskell then established a neutral zone between Armenia and Azerbaijan under American officers, which lasted for a while. His mission stayed for a year, until July 1, 1920. During this time we arranged that the Grain Corporation should support him; also the Near East Committee contributed. Further, I gave him support from the private relief agencies that we had created for extended work for children.

The Colonel found himself in probably the most hideous human and political mess in all the world. He certainly faced unparalleled difficulties with a courage and capacity that is an eternal credit to the American Army. Soon after his arrival, he telegraphed me: "The Ministry has resigned. We have no government." I replied: "Refuse to accept their resignations," and they continued, with variations.

One day in June 1920 the Azerbaijanese went Communist; the Georgians followed, and the British withdrew their troops. Haskell's organization, having brought in a good harvest, came home. The Armenians, now having food and a small army, concluded to right their wrongs by invading Azerbaijan, which had few arms. While the Armenians were busy massacring the Azerbaijanese, the Turks invaded Armenia from the south and carried away their crops. The Near East Committee had to return again. But later on Armenia was absorbed by Communist Russia.

The following is our statistical balance sheet with Armenia:

SUPPLIES

From	Food (Tons)	Clothing, Medical, Miscellaneous (Tons)	Total (Tons)
United States	119,149	16,614	135,763

Financed by

Charity from the United States....................	$12,671,722
Loans from the United States	15,492,304
Loans from the United Kingdom (Transportation) ...	631,400
Total	$28,795,426

CHAPTER 43

GERMANY, AUSTRIA, BULGARIA
AND TURKEY

GERMANY [1]

The opening of a door through the blockade on food to Germany (March 14th) was only the beginning of an enormous administrative problem. I appointed Mr. Edwin Sherman to take charge with our main office at Rotterdam. As I have mentioned, we established free child feeding on a charitable basis through the administration of the Quakers. We spent $9,237,788.00 on food and clothing for this purpose.

The Germans paid us for their major food supply altogether about $320,000,000 in gold, and some salable neutral securities. We credited them with about $18,700,000 for the use of their ships and other means of transportation.

The gold arrived by the carload in boxes and bags. We had it deposited in bank vaults in Amsterdam, Rotterdam and Brussels. We had no way of knowing whether it was gold coin or iron washers. We had some sample boxes and bags opened, and found a considerable part was American gold coins. It included also the French gold coins paid by the French on the indemnity of the Franco-Prussian War of 1871. Finally I arranged that the New York Federal Reserve Bank should take possession of the gold and advance us 92 per cent of the estimated value at once and the balance when it was melted at the American mints.

The Brussels Agreement provided that the gold and securities handed to me by the Germans should be used to purchase food. But the mints

[1] Aside from publications already mentioned, see *America and Germany, 1918–1919*, by Sidney Brooks (The Macmillan Company, New York, 1925).

would require months to melt it all. I did not want to hang around Europe or the United States with unsettled accounts. I therefore proposed to the Germans at the end of August, after the Peace Treaty had been signed, that if they would accept our auditors' statement at once as final, based upon the estimated 92 per cent of the gold value, I would later on pay the residue, when realized, into some American bank which should be authorized to expend it upon food for them, as originally contemplated. I had agreed that if we found on examination of our books that we had made any profit on this food we would pay it over to the children's fund in which they would participate.

I informed them that if I could not secure release from all future claims or arguments over accounts, which I requested, I would hand the whole business over to the Reparations Commission to settle, and no doubt the Commission would keep the 8 per cent gold residue. They accepted my proposal with alacrity, and I received a complete acceptance of our accounts and a quittance of all future claims.

The residue payments were made and in fact the gold realized more than anticipated. I never had any thanks from Germany. Neither did Mr. Wilson, who saved them from being torn to shreds.

The food operations with Germany under my direction were as follows:

SUPPLIES

From	Food (Tons)	Clothing, Medical, Miscellaneous (Tons)	Total (Tons)
United States	810,708	124	810,832
United Kingdom	270,684	28,496	299,180
France	14,404	55,000	69,404
Argentina	135,000	20,000	155,000
Netherlands	38,343	6,303	44,646
Switzerland	28,886	.....	28,886
Total	1,298,025	109,923	1,407,978

Financed by

Gold and services paid to the United States	$205,214,850
Charity from the United States	9,208,101
Gold to United Kingdom	75,653,861

Financed by (*cont'd*)

Gold to France 16,262,889
Gold to Argentina 16,774,000
Gold to the Netherlands 9,784,989
Gold to Switzerland 5,825,812

Total $338,724,502

The payments to the United States included $44,350,810 of food through the Belgian Relief Commission.

The food listed here from the British and French included the Scandinavian fish and the rancid fats amounting to about 45,000 tons and $40,000,000 in gold.

AUSTRIA

Austria—for her sins—had been shorn down to 7,500,000 people, of whom over 2,500,000 lived in Vienna. The peacemakers had done about their best to make it a foodless nation. Even had she not started at the Armistice with a famine, it would have been bad enough. But add to this the fact that she had for a few hundred years subjected the Croats, Serbians, Slovenes, Czechs, Slovaks and Poles to cruel tyranny and it was hardly to be expected that they would give her enthusiastic co-operation. Her neighbors at the beginning cut off all the natural flow of food and coal by way of reminder of past sufferings. Austria's sudden conversion to liberal government did not wipe out the hates overnight.

The day after my arrival in Europe the prayers for help from Vienna began to pour in upon me with vivid and pathetic details. I appointed Captain T. T. C. Gregory as the head of our mission with a staff. The first problem was to get Allied embargoes and blockades down. Then we must find the food and get it transported. As Austria was an enemy state, that was not easy, for under our relief law we could not give any credit to such states and she was penniless. There was a national bank gold reserve of about $40,000,000 or so, of which 80 per cent was claimed by the other succession states. There was $2,000,000 or $3,000,000 of gold exchange in the private banks, but this constituted about all the assets except the pictures in the galleries.

At my suggestion the Austrians tried to raise a loan in Switzerland, but were refused even $3,000,000. And they needed $100,000,000 worth of food to get through to the next harvest. We concluded this was the place where the Allies should help. In order to face them with the realities, I arranged for an Austrian delegation to meet an Allied delegation in Berne on December 24, 1918, and sent Captain Gregory and Dr. Taylor to represent the United States. The conference sat for several days and wrote up the minutes with thousands of words after each meeting. They mailed them to all the committees in Paris. On December 30th, Dr. Taylor advised me laconically that "(a) everybody was sympathetic; (b) the British had refused to allow the Austrians to sell any ships to pay for food; (c) the French wanted it understood that Austria must not join Germany; (d) the Italians would not allow the gold reserve to be touched, as they expected to receive it as reparations; and (e) the Austrians must have food."

To meet the immediate emergency, I secured $3,000,000 from their banks and $5,000,000 from the President's Fund, with which to send in that amount of food and thus to carry along until something could be arranged. The Italians in mid-January agreed to send a thousand tons of food a day for 30 days and take their own securities or some certain goods in exchange. Knowing both the Italians and their food resources, I accepted the idea as more power politics than food. The arrivals from Italy were only 4,000 tons in the thirty days.

However, Captain Gregory completed some food transactions with Serbia and Hungary and kept things going. Finally, early in February, we arranged that the British, French and Italians should borrow $45,-000,000 from the United States and lend it to Austria, who gave it to us to buy food. As it worked out, this was really a gift from the United States, for the Allies never paid us. As shown later on in the "balance sheet," we arranged some further source of supply.

So great was the famine in Austria that we poured more food into her territory in proportion to the population than into any other country in Europe—Belgium alone excepted.

My first act for the Austrians within a week of my arrival in Europe was to ask President Masaryk of Czechoslovakia to raise his embargo on coal against Austria. He did so because we asked it, but did not fail to mention their former wickedness.

Early in the winter, I set up feeding of the children as a matter of charity. It was organized by three invaluable C.R.B. men—C. M. Torrey, Dorsey Stephens, and Gilchrist Stockton.

As I pore over the thousands of telegrams, letters and reports in the Austrian file I find the words, "Hate," "Communist" and "Bolshevism" always forming the background of discussion. The food operation was indeed a race against both death and Communism. Doing the best we could we never had ten days' supply of food on hand in Vienna. It was expected that the Communists would try to seize the government on May Day 1919. I authorized the authorities to post the city walls with a proclamation containing a statement signed by me that "Any disturbance of public order will render food shipments impossible and bring Vienna face to face with absolute famine." Things passed off quietly. Again, a Communist crisis arose when Hungary went Bolshevist. But fear of starvation held the Austrian people from revolution.

The Austrians wanted to express their gratitude. In the middle of the famine, their astronomers discovered a new planet and named it *Hooveria*. That ought to have placed me among the Greek Gods, for names of planets had been, I understand, previously reserved for them. However, some member of a world astronomical committee on nomenclature subsequently protested, and I was put off Olympus.

The highly skilled physicians of Vienna not only gave great aid to the organization of the Austrian women for our child-feeding operations, but they developed a series of easy tests of whether a child was undernourished and when it was reasonably restored. We adopted these tests in all our European child-feeding operations.

My final note to the "Big Four" before I left for the United States sums up my view of Austria's future:

It is obvious to the most superficial observer that the present economic resources of . . . Austria are incapable of supporting the population of seven and one-half million people . . . A large part of this population has for generations lived on Empire with its centralization of political life, finance, economic and educational institutions, and a population has been thereby created totally incapable of supporting itself when denuded of its hinterland. Its future lies not only in full production of such resources as exist, but also in . . . migration. To restart the established industries involves credits, reorganized currency, raw material, etc. . . . the very insistent fact stands out that to prevent sheer starvation the population will need to be fed and furnished raw materials on credit continuously. The food production of this year's harvest in Austria (1919) would not, even if it could be uniformly distributed, last the population more than three months. As the peasant population will undoubtedly retain its twelve months' supply, it means that the probable food intake to the city populations from the state itself does not exceed six or eight weeks . . .[2]

Our Austrian statistical balance sheet was:

SUPPLIES

From	Food (Tons)	Clothing, Medical, Miscellaneous (Tons)	Total (Tons)
United States	612,952	2,609	615,561
United Kingdom	11,500	6,500	18,000
Italy	65,061	....	65,061
Yugoslavia	33,886	....	33,886
Czechoslovakia	39,873	23,025	62,898
Switzerland	11,723	....	11,723
Hungary	8,878	....	8,878
Poland	105	3,921	4,026
Netherlands	2,810	....	2,810
Others	357	....	357
Total	787,145	36,055	823,200

Financed by

Charity from the United States (Child Feeding).....	$10,787,537
Loans from the United States (in effect)	71,903,600
Cash paid the United States	4,642,723
Loans from the United Kingdom	15,709,631
Loans from France	5,500,000
Loans from Italy	1,000,000
Exchange of Commodities with:	
Italy	20,878,122
Czechoslovakia	9,914,858
Hungary	805,063
Yugoslavia	2,464,561
Switzerland	1,529,537
Others	345,577
Total	$145,481,209

[2] And Europe found this to be true. And found that, despite their props of continued loans, Austria was so unstable a state that it was a constant threat to the peace and prosperity of Europe.

BULGARIA AND TURKEY

Bulgaria also organized a "democratic" government three days after the Armistice. Decreased production due to war and a bad season had left a normally food-surplus-producing country short of food. On March 28th, Mr. Heinz, our Constantinople director, signed a contract for food, to be paid for by a deposit of gold from the Bulgarian National Bank reserve. A total of 22,862 tons of flour and fats was delivered for $4,856,649. We had the gold placed upon an American destroyer at Constantinople. In due time the destroyer was ordered home and I arranged that she should take the gold along. The gold realized $5,210,357; the balance we returned to the Bulgarian Government.

Some months later I was astonished to find that we were being sued for a percentage of this gold in the name of the Captain and crew of the American warship under a law some hundred years old, which provided that "valuables" could be transported upon American war vessels only for a toll payable to its human complement. Robert Taft defended us and won judgment in the lower courts and finally in the Supreme Court on the ground that the law did not apply to government "valuables." In any event, the food had long been delivered and was sufficient to get the Bulgarians through the winter and spring.

Constantinople suffered the only serious food shortage in Turkey. Here Mr. Heintz arranged to sell 20,278 tons of American flour for $2,369,404 in cash to a group of responsible merchants who resold it upon a ration with an agreed small margin of profit. It was sufficient to meet this situation. The price of bread dropped 50 per cent overnight.

CHAPTER 44

HUNGARY AND ROUMANIA

Although Hungary was an "enemy" state and Roumania was an "ally," their histories and our relief activities became so mixed that they need to be recounted together.

Hungary in the year 1919 presented a sort of unending, formless procession of tragedies, with occasional comic relief. Across our reconstruction stage there marched liberalism, revolution, socialism, communism, imperialism, terror, wanton executions, murder, suicide, falling ministries, invading armies, looted hospitals, conspirators, soldiers, kings and queens—all with a constant background of starving women and children. Defeat in modern war means much more than surrender of a general's sword.

The Hungarians needed food. But they also needed something no one could bring. They needed revival from despair. The relief organization contributed something to their spiritual recovery. But had there not been a magnificent toughness in the Magyar spirit, the race would have collapsed.

There had been the usual revolution at the Armistice which proclaimed a liberal government. The Hapsburgs were dethroned and a parliamentary government established under the Presidency of Count Michael Karolyi. He was not a strong man. He had been a liberal thinker, but not a man of action.

As Hungary was an "enemy" state, I had no financial resources with which to finance imports of supplies. We found they had substantial gold reserves in the National Bank. With this resource we arranged for a shipment of food from Trieste. As outlined in my discussion of Yugoslavia, we arranged to move food from the surpluses in the eastern part of that country into Hungary for goods and gold while I imported food from the United States into the seaboard areas of Yugoslavia. These arrangements served to get by for a time.

In February (1919) the Peace Conference announced preliminary boundaries for Hungary which gave Slovakia, Serbia and Roumania chunks of undoubtedly Hungarian population and denuded her of industrial and agricultural areas vital to national existence. This at once gave impulse to Communist agitation and greatly weakened the Karolyi regime. I forwarded to the "Big Four" the urgent reports from Captain Gregory, Chief of our mission to Austria and Hungary, that the government was in precarious condition and a Communist revolution imminent. About this time, Karolyi apparently got the notion that if the country went Bolshevik it would frighten the Peace Conference into supporting Hungary's claims more strongly. The second revolution came on March 22nd.

Bela Kun, a Hungarian, as a prisoner of war in Russia, had been indoctrinated by Lenin and had been sent back to Hungary to agitate. He seized power and installed the usual Soviet form of government. He inaugurated a red terror with typical sadistic liquidations and executions without a semblance of trial. He decreed the seizure of all private property. At the outbreak of the revolution we had a train of twenty-five carloads of food on its way to Budapest. It was held up by the French military at the Serbian frontier. I was in a good deal of a quandary as to what to do, as it had been paid for by the Hungarian National Bank and was mostly special food for children. However, I protested to the "Big Four," and Premier Clemenceau (April 3rd) ordered release of the train. We arranged with the Communists that the supplies should be distributed under American control. We continued supplies for children during most of Bela Kun's regime under great difficulties, owing to arrests and some executions of our Hungarian Committee members.

Bela Kun had a busy time. He secured the support of some of the old military elements by remobilizing an army and occupying a piece of Hungary ceded to Czechoslovakia. He threatened to do the same to Roumania. Seeming to have some time left over, he organized a Communist movement in Austria.

The Allied military representatives in Hungary urged that Allied armies should occupy Budapest to stop the executions and the spread of Communism to surrounding areas. However, on May 2nd, the Roumanian Army took the matter in hand and began a small advance into Hungarian territory, undoubtedly with French encouragement.

We had found, incidentally, that the Italian military officers were selling Bela Kun arms for the remaining gold reserves which he had seized from the National Bank. We traced a large shipment of arms and reported it and the location of the gold to the Peace Conference (June 4th). The Italian representatives (men of integrity) later settled the matter by having the gold turned over to us for the purpose of food, mostly from Serbia for the Hungarians.

On July 5th the "Big Four," where Frank Polk now represented President Wilson, asked me to state my views on the then "confused" situation. I recommended that they so define Allied policies for the future of Hungary that it would raise opposition to Kun inside of the country. Instead the Peace Conference announced (June 14th) further reduced boundaries of Hungary and ordered Roumanian and Hungarian armies to move back into these limits. The Roumanians did not respond. The "Big Four" (July 10th) asked Foch to advise whether they should occupy Hungary and what would be required. He took a week and then recommended the kind of army required. It included mostly an American contingent. I advised Mr. Polk that American soldiers should not take on such activities, but that my previous alternative of offering decent treatment to Hungary, if she would throw off the Communist regime, should be tried out.

On July 16th General Boehn, an old regime general, now Commander of Bela Kun's Hungarian Army, resigned and came to Vienna, where he got in touch with Captain Gregory, offering to organize a counter-revolution to Bela Kun if he were made the new "head of state." I reported the facts to the "Big Four" and on July 26th informed Gregory that we had no part in such conspiracies. At the same time again I urged the "Big Four" to make a declaration of policy which would stimulate the anti-Kun forces in Hungary. At their request I submitted a draft which without substantial alteration was issued on July 26th:

The Allied and Associated Governments are most anxious to arrange a Peace with the Hungarian People and thus bring to an end a condition of things which makes the economic revival of Central Europe impossible, and defeats any attempt to secure supplies for its population. These tasks cannot even be attempted until there is in Hungary a Government which represents its people, and carries out in the letter and the spirit the engagements into which it has entered with the Associated Governments. None of these conditions are fulfilled by the administration of Bela Kun: which has not only broken the Armistice to which Hungary was pledged but is at this moment actually attacking a friendly and Allied Power. With this particular aspect of the question it is for the Associated Governments to deal on their own responsibility. If food and supplies are to be made available, if the blockade is to be removed, if economic reconstruction is to be attempted, if peace is to be settled it can only be done with a Government which represents the Hungarian people and not with one that rests its authority upon terrorism.

On August 1st after 100 days of government, Bela Kun was overthrown by the trades union leaders who brought about a revolt in his army. Kun fled by plane; some of his assistants committed suicide. A government largely of trades union leaders assumed power with the usual liberal proclamations. This was Hungary's third revolution. Immediately I ordered (August 2nd) large food shipments in accord with the Allied promise.

As Bela Kun's army had been dissolved, there was now no possible resistance to the Roumanians by the Hungarians. The Roumanian Government at once decided to occupy Budapest. The "Big Four" on August 2nd issued orders to the Roumanians to stop. They issued them again August 4th. On that day I appeared before the "Big Four" to protest at the Serbians' holding up food we had arranged for Hungary from the Banat. On August 5th the Roumanian Army occupied Budapest in defiance of direct orders of the "Big Four." There was more evidence that they were encouraged by French army officers.

Then began a regime equally horrible with Bela Kun's. The Roumanian army looted the city in good old medieval style. They even took our supplies from the children's hospitals. Many children died.

They looted art galleries, private houses, banks, railway rolling stock, machinery, farm animals—in fact, everything movable which Bela Kun had collected.

The Roumanians finally gave an ultimatum to the Hungarians, ordering them to deliver at once 20,000 carloads of food. That is where I came in again. On August 6th the Allied representatives, at the insistence of Captain Gregory in Budapest, made a strong joint protest. The same day I sent a vigorous protest to the members of the "Big Four." There was no such an amount of food.

Also that same day, with the undoubted help of the Roumanian Army, the Archduke Joseph (a Hapsburg) threw out the trades union government and seized power—thus bringing about by *coup d'état* the fourth Hungarian revolution. I always suspected the influence of the Roumanian Royal House who were part of the "trades union" of kings.

Now we were confronted with three problems: the looting by the Roumanian Army, the return of the Hapsburgs to power, and food supply. It seemed an ironic consequence of a war which had been directed to the job of putting the Hohenzollerns and Hapsburgs out of power. All the surrounding new states began to shiver in their boots. They raised a cry to Paris of "No Return of the Hapsburgs."

Upon receiving news of all these events, the "Big Four" appointed four generals of the four nationalities to proceed to Budapest "to examine and report."

The "Big Four" (August 7th) again asked the Roumanians if they intended to defy the Allies. Then they rested for some days from further exertion. And while the secretariat was filing documents, the 1,000,000 people in Budapest were desperate for food. Children were dying. The Roumanians continued to seize all food coming to the city from the countryside. My men brought in 250 tons which Captain Leach distributed to 25,000 children (August 10th). The four generals discussed, reported, and examined, discussed and reported—finally issued ultimatums, cautions, reprimands and indignations to the Roumanians. Daily they sent records and details of Roumanian plunder and killings. They recited train-loads of food and machinery, hundreds of locomotives, thousands of cars seized or destroyed in sickening repetition.

The Roumanians (August 11th) again plundered the children's hospitals. They continued to plunder the city. In the meantime I had gone to Poland at President Wilson's orders; from there I fired volleys of protests at our American officials in Paris. Upon my return to that city on August 19th I found that Mr. Polk was acting vigorously enough. On August 22nd the four generals in Budapest reported that they were impotent to stop plundering or anything else. On the morning of August 21st, at the request of the "Big Four," I appeared before them to advise again. Their minutes show that I said:

Up to 10 a. m. on the previous Monday, the Roumanians were still requisitioning food all over the country and in Budapest they were taking supplies even from the Children's Hospitals. Trains carrying the requisitioned supplies were passing out of the country as fast as possible. . . . None of the members of the Relief Organization believed for a moment that the Roumanians intended to accede to the desires of the Council. . . . Two of his [Hoover's] officials, Captains in the American Army, had themselves seen the Roumanians take sixteen wagon loads of supplies from the Children's Hospitals and eleven deaths had resulted therefrom within twenty-four hours, for there was no way of replacing these supplies. He did not think that any action by the Roumanians could be secured unless the military Mission were instructed to send agents to frontier points to stop the Roumanians from shipping out any more of the requisitioned material until its disposal could be decided by the Council. In his own opinion the supplies requisitioned should be turned back to Budapest to feed the population of that city. . . .

[As to the Archduke's usurpation,] he would like to call attention to . . . a sidelight on the situation. The *coup d'état* by which the Archduke Joseph's Government had been installed was not entirely a Hungarian affair, Roumanian troops had surrounded the meeting place of the Ministry and had turned their machine guns on the building in which they were sitting. This event had had an immediate repercussion throughout Poland and Eastern Europe and the Bolshevists were making much of it and claiming that the Alliance was trying to re-establish reactionary government in its worst form. This had done more to rehabilitate the Bolshevist cause than anything that had happened for a long time. . . . If things were allowed to continue as they were, the old reactionary party would be well established in ten days and the Allied and Associated Powers would have to be prepared to see the House of Hapsburg begin to re-establish itself throughout all its former dominions. He [Hoover] could only suggest that the Council should instruct its representatives in Budapest to call the Archduke before them and say that his Government could never be accepted or recognized. Such action might induce the Archduke to step aside and invite the social democrats to form a coalition government.[1]

I was asked to draft such an instruction, which I did with zest. I presented it at the afternoon session. There was some hesitation in adopting it for fear that it was too direct and that the Archduke would defy the "Big Four." I suggested that he was probably still under the impression that the Allies had armies of ten or fifteen million men and that his Roumanian military support was a weak reed. Finally, rather than acting through the Commission of four generals, I was directed to send the telegram over our wires to Captain Gregory for delivery in person. The telegram in important parts read:

The Allied and Associated governments . . . are most anxious to conclude a durable peace with the Hungarian people, but they feel that this cannot be done while the present Hungarian Government is in power. That Government has been brought into existence, not by the will of the people but by a *coup d'état* carried out by a small body of police, under the protection of a foreign army. It has at its head a member of the house of Hapsburg, whose policy and ambitions were largely responsible for the calamities under which the world is suffering, and will long suffer. A peace negotiated by such a Government is not likely to be lasting, nor can the Allied and Associated Governments give it the economic support which Hungary so sorely needs. . . .

In the interests, therefore, of European peace the Allied and Associated Governments must insist that the present claimant to the headship of the Hungarian State should resign, and that a Government in which all parties are represented should be elected by the Hungarian people. The Allied and Associated Powers would be prepared to negotiate with any Government which possessed the confidence of an Assembly so elected.

On the following day (August 23rd) I received over our wires a reply from Captain Gregory, expressed in the effective slang code which our men had adopted in amplification of *en clair* language:

[1] Minutes of the Meeting of the Heads of Delegations. 21 August 1919. H. D. 35.

Archie on the carpet 7 p.m. Went through the hoop at 7:05 p.m.

I had this code message translated into more formal language and sent to Prime Minister Clemenceau. Our messenger showed the old Tiger the original, commenting that this was the decline and fall of the last of the Hapsburgs. The Prime Minister, having been a reporter on a New York newspaper, needed no translation but seized the original as a "memento" of the war.

A new and representative ministry was set up. This was Hungarian revolution number five in a period of eight months.

As the 1919 harvest was now available, our mission in Hungary was finished. When we recalled our staff, the four generals were still arguing with the Roumanians over continued plundering.

There were two subsequent echoes. On September 23rd, the "Big Four" ordered a blockade of Roumania until its army withdrew from Hungary and accounted for their plunder. They withdrew, but the accounting for plunder was mostly words. In any event, as will be related later on, they had, in Eastern European morals, some justification for it.

And now comes a Queen across this stage. After I reached New York a 1200 word letter reached me from the Queen of Roumania. The letter was written wholly in longhand and the ink itself sputtered her indignation. She accused me of being a traitor to the Allied cause as siding with Hungary against Roumania; she was long in her explanations of her own righteous conduct and my evil mind. The letter may some day become a collector's item.

The method of reprisal by plunder by a supposed civilized nation, the deaths that flowed from it, the weakening of that decency which we so hoped would be the reward for America's sacrifice was not indicated in the lady's views.

Out of it all came a Hungarian hate of all Roumanians which festered unceasingly and only awaited the first war opportunity for vengeance.[2]

---

[2] Some time in the twenties when the Queen of Roumania visited Washington on an advertising tour with the hope of raising a loan for Roumania, she did not invite me to call. Thus I did not have to refuse. That journey, however, had some high lights. She paid few of the bills for her special train and for hotels; she laid a wreath on Buffalc

Our statistical balance sheet for Hungary showed:

SUPPLIES

From	Food (Tons)	Clothing, Medical, Miscellaneous (Tons)	Total (Tons)
United States	21,152	241	21,393

Financed by

Cash payments to the United States	$ 511,327
Charity from the United States (Child Feeding)	1,845,416
Loans from the United Kingdom (Transport)........	564,561
Total	$4,607,139

This does not include the major supplies that were bought from Serbia as they were not included in our accounts.

ROUMANIA

Immediately after the Armistice the exiled Roumanian Government returned and started to regain possession of the promised land. This included parts of her neighbors, that is Transylvania, Bukovina and Bessarabia, and the Dobruja promised to her in 1916 as the reward of her joining the Allied cause. At the Armistice she promptly occupied them with a hastily organized army to make sure that she got them. This move doubled her area and her population to more than 16,000,000.

As usual, at once upon my arrival in Europe, reports of a desperate food situation poured upon me. It was difficult to believe because Roumania had always been a food surplus state. I dispatched Major

---

Bill's grave in tribute to American heroes. Her advance agents implanted the idea in each visited city that it was customary for visiting Queens to receive some memento of the visit. She received many watches, rings and solitaire stones. At Philadelphia at the gala reception of the best dress suits and gowns in the city the Mayor with great feeling presented her with a beautifully beribboned box. With girl-like enthusiasm she untied its wrappings, only to discover that it contained a smaller and beautifully beribboned box. Again a smaller box, and so on until a final and very small box. That contained a splinter of the floor of Independence Hall. The Mayor glowed and expounded his conviction of how she would value it above all jew-ells because of the tie of liberty, freedom and humanity which bound our two countries. I have never heard that she blamed this on me.

Joseph C. Green, an old C.R.B. man, to Roumania under the general direction of Howard Heinz, who was chief of our Near East Division with headquarters at Constantinople. Pending their report I ordered two preliminary cargoes, then en route, into the Black Sea ports for immediate relief.

Our men found the Germans, assisted by the Hungarians, had ravaged and plundered the country beyond belief. Just a few scraps from the dispatches of these men are poignant enough:

> . . . the most starved looking lot of people I have seen in Europe. The women and children for the most part are without shoes and stockings, everyone had patched ragged clothes. . . . All of them complained that their children had died for lack of food. . . . I visited many homes or hovels. . . . I found no food. . . . Cattle, pigs, even dogs are about half their normal weight. . . . Eggs $1.80 per dozen, butter $3.00 per pound, ham $2.20 per pound.
>
> In the areas occupied by the Germans and Hungarians the country was pillaged, all manner of commodities extorted from the inhabitants. . . . It is difficult to describe the minuteness of the German despoliation. Every town house and farm was visited. . . . removed table linen, silver, kitchen utensils, furniture, blankets, clocks, metal articles, wagons, work animals, livestock. They gave not even a receipt or a requisition . . . packed and sent to Germany. . . . An examination showed in one area alone the horses reduced from 745,000 to 149,000. Cattle from 3,445,000 to 1,125,000. Sheep from 5,550,000 to 445,000.

I felt that here was a country where the British and French must take a real part in the relief burden. Both these nations had large commercial interests in Roumania, especially oil and railways. They could spare something from their colonial supplies which were daily coming through the Suez Canal. It was nonsense for these supplies to go all the way through the Mediterranean to England and France and at the same time for us to send American supplies backward over the same 2,000 mile route.

In order to secure their co-operation in the Roumanian problem, I had on January 7th asked them to send delegates to Roumania to examine the situation and set up co-operation with us. They sent the delegates, but at once demanded more commercial concessions from the Roumanians, which caused Minister Constantinescu to exclaim to Mr. Heinz, "We would rather starve than accept the conditions that the French and British propose." The British and French delegates daily telegraphed their governments asking for instructions and for food—and gave us copies for our files. However, the British did ultimately co-operate and they did it right. They diverted cargoes en route from Australia and surplus Army stores from their base at Salonika. The French sent Army equipment and a large amount of cosmetics for sale, but no food. I have related how the newly equipped Army became a terrible embarrassment to the Allies in Hungary later on.

The destruction and the looting of the railways by the Germans and Hungarians was heartbreaking. At the Armistice there were only 62 live locomotives and a few thousand fit cars to serve 16,000,000 people. Repeatedly I raised questions concerning Roumanian railway rehabilitation in the "Big Four," as France and Britain were financially interested in those railways. Early in the year I had assigned from the American Army 150 locomotives out of those given us by the Germans under the Armistice. The French also ultimately made an allotment from the same source. However, as I have related, the Roumanians got their real railway relief by taking it from Hungary. This part of their seizures from Hungary certainly had real justification, for the Hungarians had stripped the Roumanian railways in their retreat.

We found Roumania had a weak and often a corrupt government. It was faced with the huge tasks not only of famine, pestilence and reconstruction, but of administering the huge new areas. They were ignorant of the first principles of effective food distribution.

Some specimens out of dozens of reports are indicative. On March 6th, Major Green advised me that the Roumanian Government was

wholly incapable of devising any scheme of its own to meet the present situation.

On April 1st he telegraphed:

There is no inspection by the Government of the distribution of the foodstuffs. . . . The Minister in charge insists such inspection by Roumanians is impossible. He is anxious for us to do it.

He telegraphed again on March 29th:

This is a curious government. The [all-embracing] Minister of Commerce, Industry, Labor, Economic Reconstruction, Public Works and Food has fallen ill again. All government work is at a standstill. He keeps everything in his own hands and personally decided. . . . This is paternalism with a vengeance. And inefficient paternalism at that. . . .

With great reluctance I finally took larger responsibilities of administration and dispatched Colonel William N. Haskell with forty-three Americans to take charge, sending Major Green on to organize Armenia. They established some sort of order and justice in distribution. But they were unable to get adequate co-operation inside Roumania. The Roumanian officials in Paris were even worse. We wanted to start the exchange of their oil for food from other parts of Southeast Europe. We had to have their lubricants to keep the Central European railways alive. They seemed stunned, confused or unable to act. On April 25th Mr. Taft wrote Colonel Haskell as to their Paris delegation:

. . . Their whole attitude has been that of doing us a favor . . . they care very little whether food reaches their country or not.

Finally, I took the bull by the horns and wrote a stiff letter directly to the head of the Roumanian delegation in Paris on April 24th.

I sent a copy to Colonel Haskell. On May 4th the Colonel wrote back:

Your statement that the Roumanian officials in Paris show a lack of co-operation with you. That is exactly the attitude that I find in Bucharest. . . . They have no inclination to exert themselves and in all matters large and small we have to beg them over and over to do those things which are evidently essential for the relief of the country. . . .

I showed Mr. Hoover's letter to Premier Bratiano with inclosures to Minister Constantinescu and it had the effect of dropping a bomb shell on him.

I think it will help us considerably out here and no doubt will react in Paris. . . .

Things went partly better after that. But not fully. Haskell found that a whole cargo of food had been divided among Roumanian officials for them to resell in the bootleg market for their own benefit— a profit of over $300,000. Their pleasant justification was that they simply had to have some money. That was too much—I demanded that the entire lot be got back and put under the control of our men for distribution to the people. Under threat of exposing to the world this piece of graft and stopping all further effort, we recovered 90 per cent of it.

It is easy to condemn weakness in such governments as Roumania; it is easy to denounce corruption; it is not difficult to illuminate the all-consuming hates and vengeances. But I sometimes wonder what Americans would have done if they had gone through what Roumania suffered at the hands of the combined Germans and Hungarians.

By the end of April matters began to clear up. Haskell was able to advise that they were getting better results in distribution, that the crisis of the famine was rapidly passing, and that

the dangers of Bolshevist insurrection have been greatly lessened if not entirely obviated by the arrival of our food cargoes. . . . It is, however, still the chief topic of conversation.

Their plunder of Hungary soon began to help in their recovery. We built up the usual child feeding on American charity to 200,000 children, providing over 25,000,000 meals for them during our period. The arrival of the new harvest solved their problems, for Roumania was inherently a food-surplus country.

Our Roumanian balance sheet was as follows:

SUPPLIES

From	Food (Tons)	Clothing, Medical, Miscellaneous (Tons)	Total (Tons)
The United States	124,687	4,817	129,504
British Empire	88,688	11,100	99,788
Total	213,375	15,917	229,292

Financed by

Cash paid to the United States	$ 1,024,322
Charity from United States (Child Feeding)	733,272
Loans from United States	36,451,028
Loans from British Empire	15,428,688
Total	$53,637,310

CHAPTER 45

RUSSIA

Russia was probably among the worst problems before the Peace Conference or the "Big Four" or the Supreme Economic Council or any of the other multitudinous Allied agencies. It was the Banquo's ghost sitting at every Council table. The British and particularly the French were obsessed with making war on Red Russia.

The Allies, including the United States, had placed troops at Murmansk and Archangel to keep the munitions which had been sent to the Czarist and Kerensky Governments from falling into the hands of the Communists. They soon got into a small war with the Red armies in those quarters. And they had to feed the civilian population. The Allies had sent troops into Siberia to support Kolchak's White Russian Army. The Americans had joined in this adventure to prevent the Japanese from doing it alone. The British and French had furnished arms and munitions to Generals Denikin and Wrangel, who were attacking the Red armies from the south. The British furnished arms to General Yudenich for an attack upon Petrograd from the Baltic States. The French sent troops to support Wrangel at Odessa. The Red armies were trying to invade Poland and the Baltic States. The Communists were spreading their agents, and their gold was stirring up trouble everywhere.

The Peace Conference wanted Russia at peace, and was badly divided on what to do. Finally they invited the Soviet Government to a conference at Prinkipo. The Bolshevists toyed with the idea, but the conference did not take place.

Winston Churchill appeared (February 14, 1919) before the "Big

Four" on behalf of the British Cabinet, protesting at any peace action and demanding united invasion of Russia by the Allies. I did not want the United States involved. Obviously, the major financial and military burden with its loss of life would fall upon us in a long war. Restoration of the old regime seemed likely to be the result of White Russian and Western European Allied collaboration.

President Wilson on many occasions asked my advice, not alone because of the information that flowed into my organization all along Russian frontiers, but perhaps because of my pre-war knowledge of Russia. He was absolutely determined that the United States would not send another man to Russia—and that we would withdraw the Americans already there as quickly as they could get out.

I concluded that, in view of the desperate food situation in Petrograd, Moscow and the other large Communist cities, there might be a remote chance to stop fighting everywhere and at the same time to save millions from starvation. On March 28th I wrote to the President a letter of which the essential paragraphs were:

Dear Mr. President:

As the result of Bolshevik economic conceptions, the people of Russia are dying of hunger and disease at the rate of some hundreds of thousands monthly in a country that formerly supplied food to a large part of the world.

I feel it is my duty to lay before you in just as few words as possible my views as to the American relation to Bolshevism and its manifestations. These views at least have the merit of being an analysis of information and thought gleaned from my own experience and the independent sources which I now have over the whole of Europe, through our widespread relief organization.

It simply cannot be denied that this swinging of the social pendulum from the tyranny of the extreme right to the tyranny of the extreme left is based on a foundation of real social grievance. . . . This situation was thrown into bold relief by the war and the breakdown . . .

The Bolshevik ascendency or even their strong attempts so far are confined to areas of former reactionary tyranny. Their courses represent the not unnatural violence of a mass of ignorant humanity, who themselves have learned in grief of tyranny and violence over generations. Our people, who enjoy so great liberty and general comfort, cannot fail to sympathize to some degree with these blind gropings for better social conditions. . . .

I expressed the hope that in time the pendulum would swing back from these insane ideas and actions, and continued:

Politically, the Bolsheviki most certainly represent a minority in every country where they are in control. The Bolsheviki has resorted to terror, bloodshed and murder to a degree long since abandoned even amongst reactionary tyrannies. . . . [They have] embraced a large degree of emotionalism and has thereby given an impulse to his propaganda comparable only to the impulse of large spiritual movements. . . .

. . . [There is danger] the Bolshevik centers now stirred by great emotional hopes will undertake large military crusades in an attempt to impose their doctrines on other defenseless people.

I expressed the fear that it might breed more wars but that must wait. I had the most serious doubt that outside forces can do other than infinite harm, for any great wave of emotion must ferment and spread under repression, and continued:

We have also to contemplate what would actually happen if we undertook military intervention. We should probably be involved in years of police duty, and our first act would probably in the nature of things make us a party to the Allies to re-establishing the reactionary classes. It also requires consideration as to whether or not our people at home would stand for our providing power by which such reactionaries held their position. Furthermore, we become a junior in this partnership of four. It is therefore inevitable that we would find ourselves subordinated and even committed to policies against our convictions.

In all these lights, I have the following three suggestions:

First: We cannot even remotely recognize this murderous tyranny without stimulating actionist radicalism in every country in Europe and without transgressing on every National ideal of our own.

Second: That some Neutral of international reputation for probity and ability should be allowed to create a second Belgian Relief Commission for Russia. He should ask the Northern Neutrals, who are especially interested both politically and financially in the restoration of better conditions in Russia, to give to him diplomatic, financial and transportation support; . . . He should be told that we will raise no obstructions and would even help his humanitarian task if he gets assurances that the Bolsheviki will cease all militant action across certain defined boundaries and cease their subsidizing of disturbances abroad; . . . This plan does not involve any recognition or

relationship by the Allies of the Bolshevik murderers now in control. . . .
It would appear to me that such a proposal would at least test out whether
this is a militant force engrossed upon world domination. If such an arrangement could be accomplished it might at least give a period of rest along the
frontiers of Europe and would give some hope of stabilization. Time can
thus be taken to determine whether or not this whole system is a world
danger, and whether the Russian people will not themselves swing back to
moderation and themselves bankrupt these ideas. This plan, if successful,
would save an immensity of helpless human life and would save our country
from further entanglements which today threaten to pull us from our national
ideals. . . .

Faithfully yours,

HERBERT HOOVER

The President welcomed my plan because it would keep the Allied
debating organizations in Paris busy talking for some time, and while
it was pending it would keep Churchill's and the militarists' pressures
on the United States in the background.

My plan was a faint hope. To carry it out, I needed some neutral person with a well-known name to head it. I telegraphed to Fridtjof
Nansen, the Polar explorer, asking him to come to Paris from Norway.

Nansen had come to the United States during the war seeking food
for his country and I had arranged it as well as it could be done in
those difficult times. We had become friends. Nansen was a fine, rugged
character, a man of great moral and physical courage. But when it came
to going outside of his sphere of life and mixing with international
politics, he was paradoxically timid and hesitant. Nor did he have any
affection for the British. When he was in America I had found him
very resentful of the British blockade. It was from him I learned that
the depth of his feeling lay not only in the immediate difficulties but in
the starvation suffered by Norway through the British blockade of her
food during the Napoleonic wars. The fire of resentment has been kept
hot all these long years by Ibsen's epic tragedy which has burned into
the mind of every Norwegian school child.

Through the Norwegian Prime Minister, I induced Nansen to at least
come to Paris. When he arrived I had the whole program ready, including the exact text of the documents to be exchanged.

But Nansen was frightened by the task. He reiterated that he had never handled such large amounts of food; that he had no experience with such negotiations; that he did not like the Bolsheviks. He suspected that every paragraph held some insidious trap. I did not blame him for that, as I had experienced the worst in our Allied documents. I wasted some days in trying to persuade him that we would start him off by furnishing initial ships, buying the food, that we would get him expert neutral staff and so on. It was not until we got the Norwegian Prime Minister to press him again that he consented. Finally he signed, and as hitherto the documents have been published only in part, I give them here. The first was a letter addressed to President Wilson:

My dear Mr. President: Paris, April 3, 1919

The present food situation in Russia, where hundreds of thousands of people are dying monthly from sheer starvation and disease, is one of the problems now uppermost in all men's minds. As it appears that no solution of this food and disease question has so far been reached in any direction, I would like to make a suggestion from a neutral point of view for the alleviation of this gigantic misery, on purely humanitarian grounds.

It would appear to me possible to organize a purely humanitarian commission for the provisioning of Russia, the foodstuffs and medical supplies to be paid for perhaps to some considerable extent by Russia itself, the justice of distribution to be guaranteed by such a commission, the membership of the commission to be comprised of Norwegian, Swedish and possibly Dutch, Danish and Swiss nationalities. It does not appear that the existing authorities in Russia would refuse the intervention of such a commission of wholly non-political order, devoted solely to the humanitarian purpose of saving life. If thus organized upon the lines of the Belgian Relief Commission, it would raise no question of political recognition or negotiations between the Allies with the existing authorities in Russia.

I recognize keenly the large political issues involved, and I would be glad to know under what conditions you would approve such an enterprise and whether such commission could look for actual support in finance, shipping and food and medical supplies from the United States Government.

I am addressing a similar note to Messrs. Orlando, Clemenceau and Lloyd George.

Believe me, my dear Mr. President,
Yours most respectfully,
(Signed) FRIDTJOF NANSEN

Their letter in reply to Nansen (which I also drafted) ran as follows:

Dear Sir: Paris, 9 April, 1919

The misery and suffering in Russia described in your letter of April 3rd appeals to the sympathies of all peoples. It is shocking to humanity that millions of men, women and children lack the food and the necessities which make life endurable.

The Governments and peoples whom we represent would be glad to co-operate, without thought of political, military or financial advantage, in any proposal which would relieve this situation in Russia. It seems to us that such a Commission as you propose would offer a practical means of achieving the beneficent results you have in view, and could not, either in its conception or its operation, be considered as having any other aim than the "humanitarian purpose of saving life."

There are great difficulties to be overcome, political difficulties, owing to the existing situation in Russia, and difficulties of supply and transport. But if the existing local governments of Russia are as willing as the governments and peoples whom we represent to see succor and relief given to the stricken peoples of Russia, no political obstacle will remain. There will remain, however, the difficulties of supply, finance and transport which we have mentioned, and also the problem of distribution in Russia itself. The problem of supply we can ourselves hope to solve, in connection with the advice and cooperation of such a Commission as you propose. The problem of finance would seem to us to fall upon the Russian authorities. The problem of transport of supplies to Russia we can hope to meet with the assistance of your own and other Neutral Governments whose interest should be as great as our own and whose losses have been far less. The problems of transport in Russia and of distribution can be solved only by the people of Russia themselves, with the assistance, advice and supervision of your Commission.

Subject to such supervision, the problem of distribution should be solely under the control of the people of Russia themselves. The people in each locality should be given, as under the regime of the Belgian Relief Commission, the fullest opportunity to advise your Commission upon the methods and the personnel by which their community is to be relieved. In no other circumstances could it be believed that the purpose of this Relief was humanitarian, and not political, under no other conditions could it be certain that the hungry would be fed.

That such a course would involve cessation of all hostilities within definitive lines in the territory of Russia is obvious. And the cessation of hostilities would, necessarily, involve a complete suspension of the transfer of troops and military material of all sorts to and within Russian territory. Indeed, relief to Russia which did not mean a return to a state of peace would be futile, and would be impossible to consider.

Under such conditions as we have outlined, we believe that your plan could be successfully carried into effect, and we should be prepared to give it our full support.

> Signed: V. E. ORLANDO
> Signed: D. LLOYD GEORGE
> Signed: WOODROW WILSON
> Signed: G. CLEMENCEAU

Doctor Fridtjof Nansen
    Paris

We then sent this dispatch from Nansen to Lenin by wireless:

Paris, 17 April, 1919

Mr. Nikolai Lenin,
President Russian Soviet Government, Moscow
Sir:

On April third I sent the following letter to President Wilson, Clemenceau, Lloyd George and Orlando [quoted above]:

Today, April seventeenth, I have received the following answer [quoted above]:

I would be glad to hear from you in this matter at your earliest convenience.

I may add that the neutral organization which I propose offers its services in this cause without any remuneration whatever, but of course its expenditures in the purchase and transportation of supplies must be met by the Soviet Government.

Believe me, Sir,

Yours most respectfully,

(Signed) FRIDTJOF NANSEN

I had arranged, or thought I had arranged, with the French to have this message sent from the Eiffel Tower Radio Station on April 17th. However, in the meantime the French concluded that Kolchak, Denikin, Wrangel or someone would defeat the Reds, and although Clemenceau had agreed to our proceeding, his Minister of Foreign Affairs

Pichon protested violently. After ten days with no reply from Moscow, I became suspicious and sent Nansen's dispatch to Lenin to our representative in Holland with instructions to send it again from the Dutch Radio Station. The Russians acknowledged having received it on May 3rd through that station. The French had apparently never sent it.

The Bolshevists made full reply by radio on May 14th. The message was picked up by the Denmark Station and sent to me by them. It developed that the Eiffel Tower had received this dispatch but the French did not transmit it to me. The Russian reply was a warm acceptance of relief, but a violent refusal to stop fighting until they had won their objectives either by war or negotiation. They added a long essay on the wickedness of capitalism. I believed the reply left a crack open and that the many words were for internal consumption. I wanted to pursue the question further, but the French in the meantime emitted vociferous denunciations of the whole business and so the effort died at no cost but words. The reply of the Soviet certainly contained much comment upon the undesirable way of life of the Allied and Associated Powers. However, by this time, the Allied military proposals in Paris had cooled off.

NORTHWEST RUSSIA

In March and April, 1919, a group of White Russian officers and men gathered in Finland and the Baltic States under General Yudenich. He proposed to take Petrograd from the Communists. The nucleus of his army was White Russians who had fought the Communists alongside the Finns, the Estonians, and the Letts. Yudenich secured the support of some arms and munitions from the British and French Governments. The British General Gough was assigned by the Allies as his advisor, and his advance on Petrograd began on May 13th.

Our State Department requested me to extend the relief we were giving the civilian population in Estonia into the area captured by this army as it advanced, and to be prepared to provision Petrograd. I did not particularly like the looks of the expedition and insisted that my organization would feed only civilians and that the British would have to get food for the White Russian troops. They solved that problem by the Yudenich Army's buying some of our food from the

Finns with British money. As Yudenich advanced, a provisional White Russian Government was established at Narva inside the Russian frontier. He finally advanced over an area which included about 400,000 people. Captain Miller, of our staff, reported on the reclaimed territory. It was a terrifying document. The Communists on their retreat had plundered the district of what little food and livestock the people had, and machine-gunned the resisting peasants.

To be ready for Petrograd, I had increased the cargoes en route for the Baltic States, but our men never had confidence that Yudenich would succeed and, therefore, were very cautious as to where they landed them. Incidentally, a cargo of food bought by the State Department for the civilian population at Murmansk was diverted to us to be turned over to Yudenich. But he lost out before it arrived, and I used it for other relief.

We received very authentic reports showing that 100,000 people a month were dying of starvation in Petrograd. Yudenich got within a few miles of the city when his army went to pieces. They plundered some of our storehouses in their retreat. Nevertheless we had fed some 400,000 starving people and left them enough food to get through until the next harvest. The affair dallied along until early July when I directed Colonel Groome to use elsewhere the stocks we had built up in preparation for the fall of Petrograd.

SOUTH RUSSIA

In March (1919) the French demanded that we provision the civil population of Odessa, which they were holding with French troops as a support for Wrangel's White Russian Army. They threatened to withdraw from Russia if we did not do it. Mr. Heinz, of our organization in Constantinople, telegraphed me that there was a surplus of food in the Kuban which the French could get if the Denikin White Army, who occupied it, would co-operate. I offered our cargo ships returning from Batum to transport it. And in any event the British had food at Suez. The fact was that the French army was mutinous and the government wanted an excuse to get it home. When the French General in command tried to blame the withdrawal on me in a press statement, I made appropriate remarks and he kept still thereafter.

All of which ended any effort to relieve starvation in Russia until a year later—which is another chapter.

If we include, for convenience, the supplies we furnished after peace (described later on) we get the following balance sheet from dealings of my organizations with Russia:

SUPPLIES FROM THE UNITED STATES

	Food (Tons)	Clothing, Medical, Miscellaneous (Tons)	Total (Tons)
To White Russia	19,693	7,895	27,588
To Soviet Russia	729,091	11,480	740,571
Total	748,784	19,375	768,159

FINANCING OF SUPPLIES

To White Russia

Cash paid to United States	$ 444,718	
Charity from United States	332,508	
Loans from the United States	14,353,244	
		$15,130,470

To Soviet Russia

Cash paid to United States	$ 7,064,900	
Charity from United States	55,994,588	
Gold from Soviet Russia	20,000,000	
Charity from Estonia, Latvia, and Poland.	115,360	
		83,174,848
Total		$98,305,318

CHAPTER 46

APPROACHING THE END

Under the law, our organization officially ceased either with the date of peace or on the first of July. Despite this there were many movements on foot, in both Europe and the United States, for continuation of relief and rehabilitation over another year.

To prepare for our possible withdrawal, I sent out in April a recommendation to each of the weaker governments that they should set up an economic committee to study their needs and resources for the following year. I recommended that they should establish commercial agencies abroad through which they could negotiate for export sales, credit and purchase of supplies.

Before taking final decision on our course of action, we waited until we could be certain of the harvest prospects (the 1919 crop). When the evidences of a good crop came, we determined to withdraw.

On June 1st, I presented to the "Big Four" a detailed review of the whole economic situation in Europe. On June 2nd, I gave a summary in a press release, including these passages.

. . . From the initiation of relief measures in Europe, I have held steadily in view that the indefinite continuation of such widespread measures was not only a physical and financial impossibility, but that its continuance beyond peace and harvest would undermine the very initiative and the economic structure of the states concerned. Therefore, every step in administration has been dominated by the necessity to so create local institutions that each state could at the proper moment take over its own food measures.

Official food departments in each relieved government have been created or reorganized, with the help of our experts, to the point where practically all can control their own internal food distribution. River and rail transport have been greatly improved, and within a few weeks after peace the normal flow of transport will serve these ends without further control from the outside. With peace, communications will open and blockade will cease. With peace, exports and credits should begin to revolve. Of more importance than all, however, with the arrival of harvest every state will possess its supplies of major staples varying in quantities from five months' supply in some states to a surplus for export after reserving its entire year's supply in others. . . .

I stated that all but two or three states could now secure private credits, or with exports pay for their staple commodities.

But I stated as to special food for children:

The matter of systematic feeding of sub-normal children, which has been in progress for some months, is one that should proceed over some months to come, and the American Relief Administration is now creating the necessary organizations in the United States and providing the necessary funds from various quarters by which this enterprise, involving the fate of some three or four millions of children, can be continued. . . .

On June 10th, I sent the Supreme Economic Council a note describing the steps I had taken to wind up the whole of our economic operations. As related later I also prepared a memorandum for Mr. Wilson on our whole relation to the continuation of American participation in Allied controls in Europe.

The Allied Governments did not take kindly to the trend of these recommendations, and the old ideas of continued economic pools, joint action and the like after peace were by no means dead. Lloyd George tried to revive them with President Wilson, and Lord Robert Cecil urged continued measures to me. Vance McCormick and I advised the President against these ideas. I likewise refused to entertain Lord Robert's proposals. The pool idea never really died until we went home.

A vast amount of discussion and documentation passed on all these economic subjects. The discussions usually wound up with the question, "What will the United States do?"

However, on June 25th the "Big Four," as the result of Allied pressures, passed a pious resolution providing for a continuance of the Supreme Economic Council or a substitute. The real question—what kind of substitute and what its powers were to be—they did not mention. I did wish to see broad co-operation in remedying the world's ills, provided the United States could be free to decide every question on its merits. With the approval of the President I informed the Supreme Economic Council on June 27th of the views of the United States:

The American delegates on the Supreme Economic Council, being as they are, officials for the period of war only, have felt that the establishment of some form of international conference on economic matters must rest for decision, so far as the United States is concerned, with the permanent departments of the Government. In conference with the President on this matter, he has taken the same view and feels that on his own authority alone he could not establish such an American representation in a body of this character as would make it an effective organ from the American point of view. The matter, therefore, requires to be laid before the leading officials in the Government at Washington and their views obtained. It is my understanding that this will be undertaken. I also understand that the present Council in any event continues until the end of July pending the signature of peace with the Governments with whom the Entente have been at war. It seems to the American delegates undesirable that the present Council should continue after such a date lest it should give the impression to the world of an economic block of the Governments who have been aligned in war.

The President left Paris on June 28th. As all the governments kept raising the subject of further loans from the United States and as our bankers at home were agitating credit schemes I ended up a statement to the American people:

If we undertake to give credits, we should undertake it in a definite and organized manner. We should have a consolidated and organized control of the assistance that we give in such a way that it should be used only if economy in [European] imports is maintained, that definite rehabilitation of industry is undertaken, that people return to work, that orderly government is preserved, that fighting is stopped and that disarmament is undertaken, that no discrimination is made against the United States in favor of other countries. If these things are done, the matter is of nothing like such enormous figures as we have been handling during the war, and generally I look upon the third stage of our intervention in the assistance of Europe as infinitely less difficult and less expensive than the two previous stages in our intervention. . . .

If these things [return of Europe to productivity] are not done, Europe will starve in spite of all we can do. The surplus of our productivity could not support a Europe of today's idleness if every man of us worked fifteen hours daily.

At the request of the Supreme Economic Council, I again (July 3) wrote a review of the whole economic situation on the Continent, the major thesis of which was that we should forget artificial controls, government manipulation and support; that it was time for Europeans to get to work and produce, and if they did they could secure private credits.

Later (July 10th), Vance McCormick and I proposed that, subject to the approval of the President, an economic conference composed of members of the British, French, Belgian and Italian Cabinets should meet similar officers of our government in Washington, about September 15th, to consider what steps should be taken toward further international economic co-operation.

But when the matter was followed up by our State Department, the Allies said they would send only delegates and not Cabinet members if the meeting were held in Washington. President Wilson decided that a meeting of this sort would be useless, and the matter was dropped.

In September, I recalled all our men from the field, except those whom the governments themselves retained. We appointed Colonel Logan to take over the winding up of the Paris office, Edward Flesh to wind up the London office and the accounts, with Walter Lyman Brown to take charge of the continued child feeding.

CHAPTER 47

—————— ❧❀❧❀❧ ——————

SOME RESULTS

The Third and Fourth Horsemen of the Apocalypse—Famine and Pestilence—were experienced and hard riders.

Complete and detailed statistics of our operations have been published.[1] They can be quickly summarized. In the 12 months after the Armistice, my organizations directed 19,346,821 tons of food, seed, clothing, medical and miscellaneous supplies from overseas to 22 nations.

The sources and finance were:

	Tons	Cash or Goods	Credit or Charity
United States	18,143,411	$305,000,100	$3,380,010,000
British Empire	497,936	75,653,361	67,961,985
France	85,975	....	31,803,807
Italy	139,922	22,532,150	....
Others	434,215	51,788,502	2,300,001
Totals	19,301,459	$454,974,113	$3,482,075,793

But this is not the complete picture. These amounts do not include the food imported by the Allies from countries other than the United States during the armistice period, nor the imports of food of neutrals in Europe co-ordinated under my direction during the period. They do not include clothing and medical supplies furnished to Britain, France and Italy from the stores of United States Army. They do not record our internal movement of several hundred thousand tons of supplies in Europe, which we arranged by barter or sale between nations in Middle and Eastern Europe. Nor do they embrace tens of millions of tons of coal, much oil, and railway reconstruction materials, or antityphus

[1] Frank M. Surface and Raymond L. Bland, *American Food in the World War and Reconstruction Period* (Stanford University Press, 1931).

equipment and supplies. All of which were co-ordinated by my administration but were not passed through our books.

From a study of the amount of these statistical deficiencies I conclude that the total import of overseas food into Europe in the twelve months following the Armistice was about 27,000,000 tons, of which four to five million tons were meats and fats—the balance being cereals. The size of the American effort of over 18,000,000 tons can be better appreciated if we remember that our three-year prewar average export of food was about 6,350,000 tons. In other words, we increased our supplies by almost 200%.

It may be noted that in the total credits extended for supplies from all quarters, the United States carried over 96% and furnished 93% of the supplies. All of which confirmed my insistence in setting up the organization in such fashion that the United States, carrying the burden, should direct its operations.

The total amount of overseas food and other supplies handled by the organizations which I directed during the First World War was 33,841,307 tons, of a value of $5,234,000,000. This does not include "co-ordinated" supplies.

It was, of course, American credits and loans which saved Europe during the Armistice. But it was a very thin line between charity and loans or credit. At the time I was convinced that the recipients did not intend to repay much. In fact, as payment must be made by shipping goods to us, I saw no way such sums could be transferred. The total we had advanced the Allies during and after the war on all counts was $11,000,000,000. However, the insistence upon obligations to repay served to keep down demands and produce economy in distribution.

(Years later I was to serve on the Commission under a Congressional direction to settle all war debts from other nations "within their capacity to pay." I proposed at that time we should differentiate between the pre-Armistice and post-Armistice debts. I suggested we should abandon all claims to loans made during the war and settle the post-Armistice loans on a strictly business basis. The post-Armistice loans or credits were not part of winning the war. They were aids to reconstruction. Practically all these nations had resources by which this lesser amount could be met over a long term of years. The British had settled their loans and credits practically on this basis, plus their share of German reparations, and rigidly collected the money.

The effect of my proposals would have reduced the total debts to us by about 60 per cent. Our moral position in attempting to collect a substantial part of the remaining debts would have been much stronger. The Congressional members of the Debt Commission decided they could not secure Congressional approval of such settlements and that the gross sums must be maintained in appearance. By giving annual payments over 65 years for repayment of capital with absurdly low interest rates the appearance was preserved, and the total debt reduced about 40% with variations in different cases. In 1933, all the nations, except Finland, repudiated their debts to the United States.

Some payments were made upon principal of our loans and credits, and minor amounts of interest, prior to repudiation. Applying a proportion of these payments to post-Armistice supplies, the amounts paid to us came to about 5%. Thus, in fact, of the post-Armistice credit supplies, about $3,000,000,000 was charity.

However, great as the loss was, this operation saved the Allies millions of human lives; it saved the peace-making; it saved large parts of Europe from Communism; it saved millions from starvation, and restored at least 15,000,000 children to health.)

CHAPTER 48

THERE WAS IDEALISM

In preparation of this description of our operations I have refreshed my mind by search among the dusty files of those days—thousands of dossiers on different subjects, different incidents, reports, telegrams, letters, figures, memoranda—a medley of dead and dry information.

It has come over me again and again that Americans have never seen real famine in their homeland. Not even during our Civil War did famine in any town or city reach anywhere near the heights that it had reached in Europe. It is impossible for one who has never seen real famine to picture it—the pallid faces; the unsmiling eyes; the thin, anemic and bloated children; the dead pall over towns where the children no longer play in the streets; the empty shops; the dull, listless movements and dumb grief of the women; the sweep of contagious diseases and the unending procession of funerals.

Surrounded by all the ancient and dry records, my tendrils of memory began to clothe them with life. I could see again the Paris office—fifty rooms full of men, mostly in Army or Navy uniform, the clatter of typewriters, adding machines, telegraph instruments, the voices of direction and instruction; the walls covered with ocean maps upon which every morning little flags showed where our hundreds of ships were and where they were going; charts of twenty-five countries showing what their stocks of food were at the last date and what they would need in the next month. There were no photographs of starving children, no evidences that all this machinery had to do with human suffering; the hopes of freedom, the future of nations; and the prayer for peace. Somehow the office always seemed inhuman and mechanical.

But as I go through these frayed papers from the working front they throb with messages of human emotion. They portray vividly the courage, sympathy, tenderness, indignation, horror, determination, pride of accomplishment, and hope. But I fear that such a response can come only to me. For I alone can today draw emotion from a dry telegram from Harrington saying, "This special train of food has encountered blown-up tracks and bridges. Will be delayed some days." That is all that the record shows but I see that long delayed train en route to save a half million lives in Riga. I see Harrington, with two American sergeants, urging it along. I see the flat car which they were pushing ahead of the slow moving train for safety jumping the rails. I see Harrington and his men rushing for help to repair the track. I see them and their crew shove the pilot car over the embankment. I see them hurrying to gather carts from the villages and farms; passing through the actual fire of a raging battle. And I see Harrington in an empty box car slowly picking out with one finger by the light of a guttering candle that telegram—this very original—on his typewriter.

And from dry words of many men—"I visited," "I called upon," "I suggested"—I know that the way Goodyear, Grove, McCormick, Haskell, Groome stopped renewed fighting in Europe was not by politeness. For, knowing the men, I know that when they "suggested" there was no mistake in somebody's mind as to what was what. I know the language they really used.

Somehow, when Americans get into Army uniform, the spark of life is extinguished in their written reports. Yet, even then at times they break over the peculiarly stilted style of the services. Major Miller's longhand says: "Hell has been to this place. It is still here. Twenty-five per cent of the children in this town have died in the last two months." Gregory summarizes, "Anybody who likes Communists, Germans or war in general ought to come here," and Colonel Groome remarks, "It makes me sick to go on the streets and see these kids." And there is this from Peden: "We can count food in calories but we have no way to measure human misery." But perhaps all this means little to anyone else.

And why do civilians in Army clothes get the habit of numbering paragraphs made of such laconic words? Here is Major Ferry Heath reporting, whose feeling I interpret in parentheses: "Events of the month: (1) the Prince did not seem to think the outlook very favorable in Finland" (which refers to the abandonment by the Kaiser's brother-in-law of his high office as King of Finland). "(2) The Minister changed this week" (good riddance). "(3) Yudenich Army withdraws on Northwest Front" (it was licked). "(4) SS Lake Mary turning round in three days discharged 800 tons of condensed milk, according to B.L." (it meant food of full quality, urgently needed for ten-thousand children).

I could relate such incidents from many of our grim military men and our civilian staff—Taylor, Kellogg, Taft, Strauss, Flesh, and a score of others.

And as I go through these old papers one thing stands out with great vividness. Our major job was economic reconstruction, a part of which was food supply to their people as a whole. But parallel to it ran an operation quite minor in volume, but far greater in sentiment—our free feeding of the millions of undernourished children. And that was American. We ran it. European governments had nothing to do with it. This special work constituted but a small part of our effort but comprises also a wholly undue proportion of the papers. No man can read them without knowing that these Americans were vicariously caring for their children at home. The papers still breathe the awakening of the kids from lethargy to chatter.

And within all this mass of paper, there are the thousands of little items daily giving evidence that we were succeeding, that starving people had not held out their hands in vain—these made those old yellowing papers live.

The American Crusade
and the
Halls of Peace

CHAPTER 49

THE AMERICAN CRUSADE
AND THE HALLS OF PEACE

During the Armistice I was destined to have some relations to the peace making. In this topical treatment of autobiographical matters, I have separated my relation to this question during the Armistice from the coincident work of relief and reconstruction so as not to confuse the two different worlds in which I worked. The present chapters were originally written in the years from 1922 to 1926 when the treaty making was fresh in my mind. A few years later I added some subsequent disclosures from statements of European statesmen as to what happened during this period.[1]

I realize fully that in a recital, after years, of one's own part in historical action there is always a danger of coloring what one's views were at the time from the subsequent events. That the views on American relations to the Treaty of Versailles and to Europe recited here were held by me at the time can be proved by the current documents which I refer to. Those documents have some merit in their appraisal of the forces at work and their implacable consequences.

I was not a member of the five-man American Peace Mission. I dealt with the gaunt realities which prowled outside. I had rooms with the American delegates at their chartered hotel—the Crillon. I talked with them daily. I served on several committees of the peace delegation. I and my staff were called on constantly and sometimes hourly for infor-

[1] A summary of these chapters was published in *The Saturday Evening Post* in November, 1941 (copyright, 1941, by The Curtis Publishing Company), before we entered upon the Second Crusade. I would write them more pungently in the light of this second experience, but I have thought that without revision they better illustrate my own experiences and the backgrounds of the time.

mation not only by the Americans but by the Allied councils and committees engaged in formulating the peace. As shown in this narrative, I was frequently called before the "Big Four"—Wilson, Clemenceau, Lloyd George and Orlando—for information and advice.

The American Peace Mission was in its subsidiary divisions commanded by men of mostly academic background. They were good men, but few men with experience existed in America. My organization of necessity had more contact with what was currently taking place over Europe than any of the peace delegations. I also had ideas as to the nature of what the peace ought to be.

My mission had large political implications, besides the transcendent purpose to stop floods of human misery, to save millions of lives from starvation; to prevent a dwarfed and mentally impaired generation of children, and to bring about measures of reconstruction. My job was to shield the frail plants of democracy in Europe against the withering blasts of the time and their possible aftermaths of unemployment, anarchy, or Communism. If there was to be peace in the world, the one hope was support to representative government. Then their social and political systems would more probably be geared to peace than to war. And Communism was the pit into which all governments were in danger of falling when their frantic peoples were driven by the Horsemen of Famine and Pestilence.

I was one of the few men around President Wilson in Washington who had replied adversely to his inquiry for opinion on whether he should go to Europe and personally lead the American delegation. Colonel House who had experienced the intimate picture of Europe also advised against going as did Secretary Lansing and Bernard Baruch. Without knowing each other's views, we had all counselled that from the thunderous and free pulpit of the White House he could be far more effective. He, however, believed, and continued to believe, that he could bring a "new order" from the New to the Old World. The words "new order," "justice," "right," "reason" were constantly upon his lips. He conceived that he had the moral power to impose this new order upon a receptive Europe and that it would remove the major causes of incessant wars. He felt that only on the ground itself could he make sure of this mission.

Mr. Wilson had little knowledge of the men he would need to deal with and the forces which controlled them. He was a gentleman and when he became tied in the confidences of personal discussion his public voice was stilled.

With the Armistice the whole American people were filled with high hopes that the time had now come when a lasting peace would be made, that it would end all war, and, by establishing representative governments over the earth, would insure that peace. We had fought far less to defeat Germany than to bring an end to aggression and war. To Americans it was a crusade for freedom of mankind.

Indeed, these ideas of representative government and free men were the purposes for which we were led to violate the 140 years of American tradition by a military intervention outside our hemisphere. It was for these purposes that Americans died.

President Wilson represented this idealism of the American people. His peace aims were set out in the Fourteen Points of January 8, 1918. These points were added to and expanded in addresses he delivered on the succeeding February 11th, July 4th, and September 27th, until they became in fact twenty-five points.

The Fourteen Points are so well known and the text so generally available that they require only titles here. Those are: 1. Open covenants openly arrived at. 2. Freedom of the seas. 3. Removal of trade barriers, equality of trade conditions. 4. Reduction of armaments. 5. Colonial settlements in interest of peoples concerned. 6. Russia to be unhampered and unembarrassed. 7. Restoration of Belgium. 8. Restoration of Alsace-Lorraine to France. 9. Readjustment of Italian boundaries on lines of nationality. 10. More autonomy in Austro-Hungarian Empire (subsequently amended to provide independence of Czechoslovakia, additions to Serbia and Poland). 11. Restoration of Roumania, Serbia and Montenegro on lines of nationality. 12. Nationalities under Turkish rule to have autonomous development and security of life. 13. Polish state to be erected of indisputably Polish populations. 14. League of Nations.

The additions to the Fourteen Points he gave in his subsequent addresses were a vital part of his program, as evidenced by his insistence on their incorporation in the Armistice negotiations with the

Germans as the basis for peace. I have summarized these further ideas in Mr. Wilson's phrases, titling and numbering them for convenience of discussion.

15. (THE NEW ORDER) "A new international order . . . based upon principles of right and justice." "A new international order under which reason and justice and common interest of mankind shall prevail."

16. (DESTRUCTION OF AGGRESSION) "Destruction of arbitrary power anywhere." "The day of conquest is gone by."

17. (INTERNATIONAL COMBINATIONS) "Abolition of all military alliances . . . and balances of power." "The great game, now forever discredited, of the balance of power." "No selfish economic combinations." "Economic policies equal for all nations." "There can be no leagues or alliances or special covenants within the common family of the League of Nations."

18. (EQUALITY OF NATIONS) "Equality of all nations in rights and privileges."

19. (SELF-DETERMINATION) "The right of self-determination." "Self-determination is not a mere phrase . . . it is an imperative principle of action." "No people to be forced to live under a sovereignty which it does not wish to live under." "Dominated and governed only by their own consent."

20. (SAFE FOR DEMOCRACY) "The world must be made safe for democracy." "Peace must be planted upon the tested foundations of democracy."

21. (UNIVERSAL DEMOCRACY) "We are fighting for democracy . . . free and self-governed peoples." "Governments derive their just powers from the consent of the governed . . . no others will be supported." "Governed only by their own consent."

22. (No ANNEXATIONS) "There shall be no annexations." "Peoples and provinces not to be bartered about." "Every territorial settlement involved in this war must be made in the interest and for the benefit of the people concerned." "German colonies should be the common property of the world, and through the League should be administered through small nations."

23. (A NEGOTIATED PEACE) "All parties in this war must join in the settlement of every issue anywhere involved in it." "Settlement of every question . . . by free acceptance of the people concerned."

24. (JUST PEACE) "Impartial justice in every item of the settlements." "Each part in final settlement must be based . . . upon justice." "No discrimination . . . against those to whom we do not wish to be just."

25. (INDEMNITIES) "There shall be . . . no contributions, no punitive damages."

In the months before the Armistice the European Allied leaders in public addresses had eulogized the President's proposals and had accepted them in full. And this American program was at once acclaimed by the peoples of Europe as a new era for mankind. Hope inspired by these ideas caused weakening and division among the people of enemy countries.

Lloyd George at a review of the American Army near Paris, on July 5, 1918, said:

President Wilson yesterday made it clear what we are fighting for. If the Kaiser and his advisers will accept the conditions voiced by the President, they can have peace with America, peace with France, peace with Great Britain, tomorrow. But he has given no indication of an intention to do so. Because he will not do so is the very reason we all are fighting. What are we fighting for? Not because we covet a single yard of German soil, not because we desire to deprive the German people of their legitimate rights. We are fighting for the great principles laid down by President Wilson.

Discussing peace terms in an address at Manchester, September 12, 1918, Lloyd George said:

There have been other terms indicated. I have stated them repeatedly on behalf of the British nation. They were so moderate that they commanded even the support of the whole of the Labour representatives of this country. President Wilson has stated them from time to time and we stand by them.

The Germans proposed an Armistice on October 6, 1918; the basis of peace was stated by Mr. Wilson in his dispatch to them of October 23rd:

The explicit assurances of the German Government that it unreservedly accepts the terms of peace laid down in his address to the Congress of the United States of the 8th of January, 1918, and the principles of settlement enunciated in his subsequent addresses, particularly the address of the 27th of September. . . .

These were the twenty-five points. Having submitted them to the Germans and secured their acceptance, the President formally submitted this basis of peace to the Allied Governments. The Allies accepted the whole of the twenty-five points except the second—"freedom of the seas." And Wilson so advised the Germans. The Germans thereupon signed the Armistice. The various things that happened to each of these twenty-five points appear later on.

When I arrived in Paris soon after the Armistice I learned from Colonel House that he had proposed to Mr. Wilson that a preliminary peace should be made; that the enemy be disarmed; that temporary boundaries be announced, the blockade removed and all other questions, including colonial annexations, reparations, and the League of Nations, should be referred to Commissions which could take all the time necessary to settle these problems adequately. Mr. Wilson could then return home quickly. That would give time for hate to cool and reasoned statesmanship to emerge. It would have given time for American pressures. He was probably right. But except for myself he was apparently alone in this idea.

When Mr. Wilson arrived in Europe, he was sincerely acclaimed as the Second Messiah by the common people of every nation. But soon after the Armistice, forces inherent in Europe began to take over the control of human fate, and they presented stupendous obstacles to Mr. Wilson.

Destructive forces sat at the Peace Table. The future of twenty-six jealous European races was there. The genes of a thousand years of inbred hate and fear of every generation were in their blood. Revenge for past wrongs rose every hour of the day. It was not alone the delegates that were thus inspired. These emotions of hate, revenge, desire for reparations, and a righteous sense of wrong were at fever heat in their peoples at home. England after the Armistice had just re-elected Lloyd George on a platform of "Hang the Kaiser" and wringing from the enemy fantastic indemnities for Britain. Clemenceau had secured a vote of confidence from the French National Assembly with a blood-thirsty program to render Germany innocuous for all time, and collect every centime of French losses. The oppressed races were there, with their recollection of infinite wrong. Every warring nation in Europe was exhausted, economically desperate, and most of them hungry.

Their officials naturally wanted every atom of advantage for their people that could be secured. Their delegations at Paris had to go home to governments still in these fevers and get subsequent parliamentary approval of their actions. Moreover, every Allied official had a high regard for his future political life.

Their statesmen were shackled by these malign forces. None of them were free to make peace on the twenty-five points even if they had wanted to. Moreover, the governments of the Allies were committed to a maze of secret treaties dividing the spoils of victory.

Americans had been more detached from the war, and had the least degree of hate. Our statesmen were free to rise above it. We had no ideas of acquiring territory or reparations or profit. What we wanted was for Europe to so order itself as to end wars.

The attitude of Allied statesmen toward America changed at once with the armistice. They immediately became jealous and fearful of the part America might play in the peace. Prime Ministers Lloyd George, Clemenceau and Orlando were determined that they were going to dominate the peace, and not President Wilson.

As a matter of fact, the Allies never took the Fourteen Points and the eleven points from "the subsequent addresses" more seriously than any other of their eulogies of American idealism and flattery of the President.

That this was a definite attitude by dominant European statesmen disclosed itself quickly. In general they considered that we had really had but a little part in the war; that the American people had made no comparable blood sacrifices; that Americans were a foolish people, pliable to ingenuous Allied propaganda; that President Wilson was a visionary idealist wholly out of tune with European realities; that having won the war they were going to have the spoils of victory; that they were going to establish their power over Europe against the Germans or any other combination once for all. Their objective was power to protect themselves and their Empires, much less noble than the salvation of mankind.

The impoverishment by the war of their countries drove them to seek every economic advantage, every scrap of exploitable territory that might bring relief to their own people. They thought further economic benefits could be gotten out of the United States, and therefore continued lip-service and flattery. They set up various lines of action, determinedly to avoid any American foolish idealism.

To those who do not believe these assertions, I commend the preceding chapters on relief and reconstruction and the chapters which follow.

Those of us who gave warnings of these attitudes from our long experience with these men and their intricate national purposes and necessities were not readily believed by many of our American colleagues. But no one can peruse the records of the Peace Conference, or read the subsequent publications of Lloyd George, Balfour, Churchill, Clemenceau, Orlando and others, or review the actions of their governments at the time and after the peace, without finding ample confirmation of all this.

To prove the above summation of the attitude of Allied statesmen, I may quote a few of many statements by these gentlemen themselves. Mr. Lloyd George in his *War Memoirs* says:

A few days later President Wilson gave utterance to his famous Fourteen Points. This declaration, which subsequently played such an important part at the Armistice and the Peace Conference, was not regarded by any of the Allies as being at variance on vital matters, except in respect of Freedom of the Seas, with their own declarations—*although we never formally accepted them, and they constituted no part of the official policy of the Alliance.*[2]

As for Wilson's Fourteen Points, they might be, and in the main were, in harmony with our desired terms, but they were in places phrased in the language of vague idealism which, in the absence of practical application, made them capable of more than one interpretation. It was not sufficient for Germany to express readiness to negotiate on the basis of the Fourteen Points, unless we were in a position to insist on her accepting our exegesis of the sacred text.[3]

Lloyd George in his *Memoirs of the Peace Conference* says:

Clemenceau followed his movements [Wilson's] like an old watchdog keeping an eye on a strange and unwelcome dog who has visited the farmyard and of whose intentions he is more than doubtful. . . .

I really think that at first the idealistic President regarded himself as a missionary whose function it was to rescue the poor European heathen from their age-long worship of false and fiery gods. He was apt to address us in

[2] Vol. V, p. 47. All quotations from Lloyd George's *War Memoirs* are used by permission of Curtis Brown, Ltd.

[3] Vol. VI, p. 256.

that vein, beginning with a few simple and elementary truths about right being more important than might, and justice being more eternal than force. . . .

. . . They [the Allies] were therefore impatient at having little sermonettes delivered to them, full of rudimentary sentences about things which they had fought for years to vindicate when the President was proclaiming that he was too proud to fight for them. . . .[4]

He was the most extraordinary compound I have ever encountered of the noble visionary, the implacable and unscrupulous partisan, the exalted idealist and the man of rather petty personal rancours. . . .[5]

Mr. Balfour asked the Delegation to remember how it came about that the Fourteen Points were accepted. The Prime Minister and he suddenly found themselves faced with the Fourteen Points, and the time was then too short to discuss them [11 months had elapsed]. There was really no question whether there should be an Armistice or not. There had to be an Armistice. Time was the essence of the matter. They had no option but to take the Fourteen Points. They made some corrections in them, and they were supplemented by some perorations. He agreed that if the Fourteen Points were pressed from a legal point of view, it was possible to make out an awkward case, but it was only necessary to read the Fourteen Points to see that they were incapable of being treated in that strictly legal manner. For example, one point dealt with Russia, and by it all the Allies pledged themselves to welcome her into the League of Free Nations and to give her assistance of any kind which she might need or desire. It was impossible to interpret those words literally and to make a contract out of them. The point dealing with Italy afforded another example. It provided that a readjustment of the frontiers of Italy should be effected along recognisable lines of nationality.[6]

Winston Churchill's views were even more explicit. At a meeting of the British Cabinet and the Dominions' Premiers held after the Armistice, at the end of December, 1918, to consider the twenty-five points and the terms of peace, according to Lloyd George:

[Mr. Churchill] considered that the only point of substance was to induce the United States to let us off the debt we had contracted with them, and return us the bullion and scrip we had paid over, on the understanding we

---

[4] Vol. I, pp. 140–141. All quotations from Lloyd George's *Memoirs of the Peace Conference* are used by permission of Yale University Press.

[5] Vol. I, p. 145.   [6] Vol. I, p. 467.

should do the same to the Allies to whom we had made advances. If President Wilson were prepared to do that, we might go some way towards meeting his views. . . . For the rest, we should be civil and insist on our essential points. . . .[7]

In his book, *The Aftermath,* Mr. Churchill says:

The adhesion by the United States to these profoundly important war-objectives [the Fourteen Points], involving as it did a fight to the finish with Germany, was very satisfactory to the Allies. . . .[8]

The American peace argosy wended on across the waters bearing a man who had not only to encounter the moral obloquy of Europe, but to produce world salvation in a form acceptable to political enemies whom he had deeply and newly offended. Before him lay the naughty entanglements of Paris; and behind him, the sullen veto of the Senate. . . .[9]

If Mr. Wilson had been either simply an idealist or a caucus politician, he might have succeeded. His attempt to run the two in double harness was the cause of his undoing. The spacious philanthropy which he exhaled upon Europe stopped quite sharply at the coasts of his own country. . . .[10]

He [Wilson] did not wish to come to speedy terms with the European Allies; he did not wish to meet their leading men around a table; he saw himself for a prolonged period at the summit of the world, chastening the Allies, chastising the Germans and generally giving laws to mankind. He believed himself capable of appealing to peoples and parliaments over the heads of their own governments. . . .[11]

. . . In the Peace Conference—to European eyes—President Wilson sought to play a part out of all proportion to any stake which his country had contributed or intended to contribute to European affairs . . . he sought to bend the world—no doubt for its own good—to his personal views. . . . If President Wilson had set himself from the beginning to make common cause with Lloyd George and Clemenceau, the whole force of these three great men, the heads of the dominant nations, might have played with plenary and beneficent power over the wide scene of European tragedy. He consumed his own strength and theirs in conflicts in which he was always worsted.[12]

---

[7] *Memoirs of the Peace Conference*, Vol. I, p. 122.

[8] p. 99. All quotations from Winston Churchill's *The World Crisis, 1918–1928: The Aftermath* are used by permission of Charles Scribner's Sons.

[9] p. 121.   [10] p. 125.   [11] p. 112.   [12] p. 478.

Lloyd George in his *Memoirs of the Peace Conference* gives an account of a meeting of the British Cabinet with the Dominion Prime Ministers after the Armistice and prior to the Peace Conference. Mr. Hughes (the Australian delegate to Paris) said, according to Lloyd George:

. . . That if we were not very careful, we should find ourselves dragged quite unnecessarily behind the wheels of President Wilson's chariot. He readily acknowledged the part which America had played in the war. But it was not such as to entitle President Wilson to be the god in the machine at the peace settlement, and to lay down the terms on which the world would have to live in the future. The United States had made no money sacrifice at all. They had not even exhausted the profits which they had made in the first two and a half years of the war. In men, their sacrifices were not even equal to those of Australia. . . . America had neither given the material nor the moral help which entitled her to come before France. . . . He hoped that Great Britain and France, which had both sacrificed so much, would defend their own interests, and not let their future be decided for them by one who had no claim to speak even for his own country. Mr. Lloyd George had received an overwhelming vote from his fellow-countrymen . . . He and M. Clemenceau could settle the peace of the world as they liked. They could give America the respect due to a great nation which had entered the war somewhat late, but had rendered great service. It was intolerable, however, for President Wilson to dictate to us how the world was to be governed. If the saving of civilisation had depended on the United States, it would have been in tears and chains today. As regards the League of Nations, Mr. Hughes considered that a League of Nations which was to endure and weather the storms of time would have to be a thing like the British Empire, framed in accordance with historical associations and practical needs. President Wilson, however, had no practical scheme at all, and no proposals that would bear the test of experience. The League of Nations was to him what a toy was to a child—he would not be happy till he got it. His one idea was to go back to America and say that he had achieved it, and that everything else could then be left to the League of Nations to complete. . . . Speaking for Australia, [Mr. Hughes] wanted to know what Australia was to get for the sacrifices she had made. When he had secured what he wanted . . . and reparations and indemnities, then he would have no objection to handing over other matters to a League of Nations. . . . He insisted that in any case

we should not commit ourselves to the League of Nations until the Conference had completed its labours.

Lloyd George continues:

Lord Curzon considered that Mr. Hughes' views were shared by many
members of the Imperial War Cabinet. . . .

Mr. Long agreed cordially with the views expressed by Lord Curzon.[13]

M. Clemenceau in his book *Grandeur and Misery of Victory,* says:

Mr. Wilson, when he sent us the American Army, had put to us the
famous Fourteen Points. Were we prepared to cease fighting on the day
when the Germans accepted these various points? If I had refused to reply
in the affirmative it would have been nothing less than a breach of faith, and
the country would have denounced me with one voice, while our soldiers
would have disowned me, and with good reason. . . .[14]

Later there comes on the scene President Woodrow Wilson, armoured in
his Fourteen Points, symbolized in as many pointed wisdom teeth that never
let themselves be turned aside from their duty. . . . Doubtless he [President
Wilson] had too much confidence in all the talky-talk and super talky-talk
of his "League of Nations." . . .[15]

England in various guises has gone back to her old policy of strife on the
Continent, and America, *prodigiously enriched by the War,* is presenting us
with a tradesman's account that does more honour to her greed than to her
self-respect. . . .[16]

Whatever the number and the form of the Wilson proposals, it was a purely
American idea to fix the organic conditions of future peace beforehand,
while the battle was in full swing. In those conditions each of the "Allied"
and "Associated" Powers found guarantees against all excesses of ambitious
militarism, while German opinion had the benefit of learning from them how
far it might find itself committed by weakening its own resistance. . . .

President Wilson, the inspired prophet of a whole ideological venture, . . .
had insufficient knowledge of . . . Europe . . . It became incumbent on
him to settle the destiny of nations by mixtures of empiricism and idealism.

[13] Vol. I, pp. 120ff (Charles Scribner's Sons). Lord Curzon and Mr. Long were members of the British Cabinet.

[14] p. 119. All quotations from M. Clemenceau's *Grandeur and Misery of Victory* are
used by permission of Librairie Plon.

[15] p. 148.   [16] p. 25.

. . . He acted to the very best of his abilities in circumstances the origins of which had escaped him and whose ulterior developments lay beyond his ken.[17]

Mr. Wilson had produced a marvellous effort of ideology when he proposed, systematically, and in accordance with their interdependence, to solve a mass of European problems which had long been the source of disturbance in the civilized world. At the word of the President saviour the old injustices were to be redressed. . . .[18]

. . . A "League of Nations," which was nothing more than an epitome of the Parliaments of all nations, to which all historic disagreements, all diplomatic intrigues, all coalitions of national, or even private, egoisms were to come and concentrate, multiply, intensify, and perhaps sometimes even find some momentary mitigation. . . .

Six months after the proclamation of the Fourteen Points Mr. Wilson, following up his idea without worrying about ways and means, submitted to American public opinion, in a speech at the Independence Day celebrations at Mount Vernon the notions for a general peace on which his mind was centred. This time it was a question of four new points forming a sort of mystical creed defining the objects to be attained through the League of Nations. . . .

And to realize this work of pure ideology, in which the orator imperturbably entrenches himself, he concludes confidently that a simple "organization of peace" will "make this result certain." . . .

There are probably few examples of such a misreading and disregarding of political experience in the maelstrom of abstract thought.[19]

On the question of the twenty-five points Mr. Churchill gives an account of a meeting at the Quai d'Orsay in the afternoon of October 29th, thirteen days before the Armistice and months after the points had been pronounced, and months after they had been accepted by Lloyd George. This meeting was between the representatives of France, Great Britain, Italy and the United States. The principals were M. Clemenceau, Mr. Lloyd George, Mr. Balfour, Baron Sonnino and Colonel House. The question was how the Allies should reply to President Wilson's note, asking them to formally confirm his proposals of the basis of peace with Germany. Churchill says:

[17] pp. 166–167.   [18] p. 170.   [19] pp. 171–173.

Mr. Lloyd George said that there were two closely connected questions. First there were the actual terms of an armistice. With this was closely related the question of terms of peace. If the notes which had passed between President Wilson and Germany were closely studied, it would be found that an armistice was proposed on the assumption that the peace would be based on the terms in President Wilson's speeches. The Germans had actually demanded an armistice on these conditions; consequently, unless something definite was said to the contrary, the Allies would be committed to President Wilson's peace terms. Hence, the first thing to consider was whether these terms were acceptable. He asked Colonel House directly whether the German Government were counting on peace being concluded on the basis of President Wilson's Fourteen Points and his other speeches. Colonel House said this was undoubtedly so. Mr. Lloyd George said that unless the Allies made their attitude clear, they would in accepting the armistice be bound to these terms.

M. Clemenceau asked whether the British Government had ever been consulted about President Wilson's terms. France had not been. If he had never been consulted, he did not see how he could be committed. He asked if the British Government considered themselves committed. Mr. Lloyd George replied that they were not committed yet, but if he accepted an armistice without saying anything to the contrary, he would undoubtedly regard the British Government as committed to President Wilson's terms. Mr. Balfour confirmed this. Then said Clemenceau, "I want to hear the Fourteen Points." [20]

Mr. Wilson's points included no annexations. Yet in a joint memorandum of Lloyd George and Clemenceau, this passage appears:

Surely the victors if they want it are entitled to some more solid reward than the theoretical map-makers working in the void may on abstract principles feel disposed to give them.

[20] Churchill, *The Aftermath* (Charles Scribner's Sons), p. 102.

CHAPTER 50

DIFFICULTIES CONFRONTING WILSON— AND SOME PERSONALITIES *

Aside from this attitude of European statesmen, other difficulties confronted the President. Representative government had proved its strength as the victor in war. It held out the only hope of peace and prosperity to the people of Europe. There were nine pre-war democracies. Within a few weeks of the Armistice thirteen liberated nations and four enemy nations went through democratic revolutions. They set up national independence, and guarantees of personal liberty under provisional governments.

Within a month every one of the "liberated" nations had mobilized an army and was busy grabbing the utmost boundaries that either ethnological, economic, historical or military power could hold or in any way justify. Half a dozen small wars took place among them in the first six months.

No doubt the acceptance of representative government by the enemy states was stimulated by the hope that it would placate the Allies. But, on the other hand, it was genuine with the men who had led the revolutions in those countries. Upon their groups and the building of representative governments rested a real possibility of a stable structure for peace. The hope of the world rested upon their sustained strength.

In addition to these political *faits accomplis* each new state had at once set up tariffs and trade obstructions to protect its own people or further to cut the ties with formerly dominant governments. And European nations were busy already creating power blocs to strengthen themselves in the negotiations at Paris. Power politics and balances of power were alive before Mr. Wilson arrived in Paris.

Beyond these obstacles to establishing his twenty-five points President Wilson was confronted with the secret treaties. They were based upon a continued imperialistic and militaristic system for the world. He naturally insisted that the acclaim and acceptance of his basis of peace by the Allies had dissolved these treaties for they violated many of his "points." Not so. Every beneficiary insisted upon his pound of flesh.

These treaties must never be forgotten because of their evidence that the acceptance of the twenty-five points was simply lip-service; their effect upon the treaty-making; and their proof of the implacable forces which dominated Europe.

In the main they consisted of

(a) An Allied treaty with Roumania in 1916 by which she was to receive large masses of Hungarians and Russians; she was even to have part of Serbia, then fighting on the Allied side. Serbia was not informed until the war was over.

(b) Various treaties among Britain, Russia, France and Italy, from 1916 to 1917, for the division of Persia, a neutral state, as well as of Turkey. Out of Turkey, Russia was to have the Dardanelles and the Northeast provinces; France was to have Syria; Italy was to have Smyrna and its hinterland; Britain was to have most of the rest, which included the oil.

(c) A treaty of Britain and France with Italy in 1915 by which she was to have slices of Dalmatia, of Turkey, of Africa and a multitude of islands.

(d) A treaty between Britain, France and Japan in 1917, by which Shantung, an integral part of China, went to Japan, while Germany's Pacific Islands were divided between Japan and Britain. A little later when China joined the war, she was not informed of this.

(e) A treaty between France and Russia giving the left bank of the Rhine to France and a part of Poland to Russia. The British apparently did not know of this one.

(f) A treaty between the British and the Arabs of which the French claimed ignorance.

Anyone who looks at the map of the world after the Peace Conference will find that, except for modifications arising from the disappearance of Russia from the war, and the shrinkage in Italy's share, this secret division of the world mostly all came about under the name of "mandates" or other disguises.

Americans, however, must soften their critical views by remembering that alliances and agreements of these kinds are part of European wars and were the natural consequence of desperation and European tradition.

Still another weakness of the President's position was the vanishing military importance of the United States after the Armistice. The defeat of the Allies was prevented by the military intervention of the United States. When the Armistice came, America had 2,000,000 men in Europe. She was a dominant military power. But at home we were spending unprecedented sums. We were undergoing unprecedented taxation. We were faced with unemployment and all the problems of demobilization of a country regimented to war. Our people clamored to have it over and to get out of Europe and stop the expense. The native common sense of the American citizens who composed the Army saw after victory no continued use for military operation in Europe and demanded that they be allowed to return home. The members of their families wanted them home to get into their ordinary work. Thus with victory won, we could not resume war—we could not even threaten to resume war. The military potency of the United States was gone.

Students of the peace-making, to understand its processes and its incidents, must constantly keep in mind that the British, French, and Italians had determined to bring about a peace treaty by which they would dominate Europe politically and economically. They were going to divide the German colonies and large parts of Turkey among themselves. Their intention was to reduce Germany to economic as well as military impotence and to secure large indemnities. With these resolutions they were jealous and suspicious of each other.

For all these purposes, the necessary preoccupations of the Allied statesmen were to asphyxiate whatever of the Fourteen Points and the "subsequent addresses" with their eleven more points might stand in their way.

The declarations of independence of submerged races at and after the Armistice were no doubt greatly inspired by Mr. Wilson's points.

The men who would conduct these eighteen new governments were already in power. The map of Europe for good or ill to all practical purposes was already fixed before Mr. Wilson's arrival in Paris.

The Allies befogged and delayed the Conference by quarrels among themselves over many questions—quarrels not over justice but over "interests" and setting-up of "balanced power." The preoccupation with detailed boundaries and annexations dissipated much of the force of peace-making.

LLOYD GEORGE

I had scores of sessions with David Lloyd George extending from 1915 to 1919. His official and unofficial character has been amply discussed and will no doubt continue to be discussed by historians. I may say at once that he gave great weight to my views at all times on matters in which I was concerned. He had a quick, adroit mind and was instinctively sympathetic to human suffering. He had full moral courage and a driving physical energy. He was possessed of great administrative ability. He was a man of great oratorical powers, a magnificent leader of the mob. Instinctively he adopted any cause that led up the political ladder of the day. When the interest of Britain was at stake the end always justified the means. He was as nimble as the pea in a shell-game. His major principle was expediency. He had two fine qualities in that he was not personally malicious or vindictive.

President Wilson's passionate devotion to truth in international relations made him an easy prey for such adroitness. Lloyd George had the delicate job of modifying the twenty-five points and establishing the secret treaties and the harvesting of the victory. And making it all look nice and idealistic to Mr. Wilson.

CLEMENCEAU

Clemenceau was the most utterly realistic, blunt statesman at the Peace Table. His soul contained to his dying day all the bitterness of the sufferings of the French people. The widows, orphans, and ruined homes of France were the lenses he looked through. To him the turn of Germany to democracy was a fraud; the only way to deal with Germans was to make them impotent forever. As the sole victor in the

war he would have taken Carthage as the only adequate historic precedent for action. He treated the "New Order" and the twenty-five points
as a joke on history. His essential creed as far as he may have had one
was that force always triumphed over abstract justice. He in fact believed
that the strong ought to direct the weak. He had no belief that right
would prevail without plenty of force. Personally he had a fine sense
of humor, a biting wit and little regard for the feelings of other men.
The consideration with which he treated me at all times, however,
leaves only a grateful memory of this rugged son of France. He never
did understand Mr. Wilson. I don't think he tried to.

ORLANDO

Orlando was a polished Italian gentleman with just one mission. He
had to secure the territorial and other concessions which had been
promised to Italy in 1915 as a consideration for her joining the Allied
side of the war. Those concessions in that secret document were set out
with metes and bounds. They were great slices of the earth and some
little islands. As I have stated, Mr. Wilson had either never known of
this treaty or not appreciated its meaning. He was greatly outraged.
The French and British had no objection to his indignation. He possibly unconsciously aided them. In any event, the other Allies got the
important mandates and Italy the little islands. Thus Orlando was at
times a difficult member of the Supreme Council.

THE SUBSIDIARY PEACE-MAKING

There was a strong minority of European broadminded liberal[1]
thinking men in each of the peace delegations who looked with hope
on the American "new order" in Europe. They held that whatever the
wickedness of the past may have been, the world must live in the
future; that while Germany must pay, revenge must be put into the
background; that there were 70,000,000 Germans and 30,000,000 other
enemy peoples who could not be swept off the earth; that we must live
with them. They believed that civilization was one body; that their

---

[1] I may remind the reader that at this period—1919—we still used the term "liberal"
in its Nineteenth Century connotation. That connotation is far different from the pseudo
liberalism of later years. That is a collectivist mixture of socialism, fascism, and a
dictatorial state.

tender plant of liberty must be encouraged and nurtured as the only hope. The majority of the men in Paris, however, were tied to the European order.

Mr. Wilson was the hope of these groups of right-thinking men. One of the cynical things in history, however, is that while he fought their battle manfully and with every weight he could decently bring to bear, yet they became his major critics. The British writers blamed him because he did not overcome Lloyd George, instead of blaming themselves and their own leader. The French liberals called him a deserter for not overcoming Clemenceau.

An American leader more given to European intrigue and diplomacy than Mr. Wilson might have dictated the peace at least temporarily. The President could have demanded our share of territorial spoils and of German reparations, and could have traded it for concessions to his views. He could have stopped all vital American financial advances —over two-fifths of our loans were after the Armistice. He could have even threatened their food supply. He could have taken up the Italian cause and won support from Italy.

But the President was too great a man to employ European methods, and American idealism was wholly unfitted to such a scene.

CHAPTER 51

⟨०⟩⟨३⟩⟨०⟩⟨३⟩⟨०⟩

SOME INCIDENTS OF PEACE-MAKING*

One day soon after the President arrived (December 15, 1918), we had a discussion of my immediate problems. He asked me what I thought of the situation in Paris. I remarked that the whole air had suddenly become charged with currents of indescribable malignity. There had been a let-down in the whole *élan* of the war. All Europe was faced with desperation. I said if they were persons, I could describe their attitudes as dominated by greed, power, hate and revenge. But I could think of no equivalent expressions applicable to nations. In any event, he would meet with fevered nationalism, imperialism, militarism, balances of power, reaction, determination to get there first. I said that certainly the bonds of private integrity, generosity or sportsmanship would not count in the forthcoming battle of national ambitions and national fears. I said that these things were not attitudes toward the enemies alone—that they would embrace advantages over one's partners. I said the deference to American views and wishes was already pretty weak. I was convinced America was accepted in Europe as the golden-egged goose—as such our life would be safe, but not the eggs. He was shocked and expressed a disagreement that such terms should be used in respect to men who had led these glorious triumphs of democracy. About two months later he recalled that conversation and remarked: "I have often agreed with you."

ECONOMIC ADVICE

Believing that the President was not being fully advised on economic questions, I sent to him the following note a month after he had arrived in Paris:

* Copyright, 1941, by the Curtis Publishing Company.

As you are aware, our government has been represented in Europe upon various Inter-Allied Councils, relating to finances, food, shipping and raw materials, War Trade measures, etc. The purpose of these councils is rapidly changing and the American attitude toward them and the problems they represent must change. The matters involved are much interlocked and up to the time of the armistice were co-ordinated through the Council sitting under your chairmanship. Its members, Hurley, Baruch, McCormick and Hoover, are, or will soon be, in Europe. The working of these bodies still needs co-ordination by the heads of the departments concerned, who will be in Europe together with the chief representatives here of the departments whose heads are still in Washington.

This same group are essential in determination of policies to be pursued by our government in the Peace negotiations.

It is recommended that a council be set up, comprising Messrs. Hurley, Baruch, McCormick and Davis, with a Treasury representative to be appointed by Mr. Glass, and possibly myself, under your chairmanship, to discuss and decide such joint policies as are necessary in both these phases.

To co-ordinate it with the Peace Commission I proposed the inclusion of General Bliss. This memo was returned marked "Approved W. W."

I had been a member of the War Council in Washington with Baruch, McCormick and Hurley. America has never had more intelligent and devoted public servants than these three men. Henry Robinson and Norman Davis likewise contributed greatly to the solutions of the many problems with which we had to deal. We incorporated General Tasker Bliss in our discussions just because of his abundant wisdom. The committee served helpfully to keep the American delegation in tune among themselves on economic questions and warn them as to purposes malign to America.

WAR DEBTS

The British, French and Italian governments never weakened in the idea of casting off their war debts to the United States or, alternatively, of making the amounts dependent on German reparations. In April, the British delegates proposed a scheme of League of Nations' bonds to be issued after the peace. They were to be used for the general finance of

Europe and to be secured by German reparations and to be guaranteed by the various governments, including the United States. The Allied Governments proposed to pay off their war loans by selling them over the world, including the United States. The scheme had as tinsel wrapping that it would provide a method by which they could also pay for our surplus commodities in the future. By gentle opposition this idea faded out.

As late as June Mr. McCormick told me the President had informed him that Lloyd George wanted to pool the total expenses of the war. The President was much exercised and wanted our Committee to oppose it. We did.

THE MANDATES

Mr. Wilson had developed the idea of world trusteeships of peoples incapable of immediate self-government who were separated from Germany and Turkey. It was to be "solely for the good of the inhabitants." He proposed administration of these trusteeships by the small nations in order to avoid more imperialism in the world. The idea presented a difficult question to the annexationists. General Smuts found the key for them, however, by proposing that this trusteeship should be administered by mandates nominally from the League of Nations. Then it was all neatly managed through a prior agreement as to who was to be the "mandatory" for what. It was all well wrapped up in the tinsel of the "White Man's Burden."

Under Smuts' euphemism, the "mandate" was one of the most monumental attainments of old diplomacy in history. No one has yet been able to find any practical difference between these mandated areas and British, French, or Japanese possessions or colonies. And no power on earth could take the mandates away without war. The total territory annexed as "mandates," including Shantung, was about as large as continental United States.

Under the mandate system the British Empire grew by 1,607,053 square miles with 33,000,000 inhabitants. The French Empire grew by 420,392 square miles with 4,000,000 inhabitants. The Belgian Empire got 53,000 square miles with 3,387,000 inhabitants. The Japanese Empire, including Shantung, grew by 30,000 square miles with 20,000,000 inhabitants. Italy got a few islands and seized from Turkey her provinces in North Africa of 680,000 square miles with 880,000 inhabitants. The mandates have been highly profitable for colonization, raw materials and military controls. The United States wanted nothing and got nothing.

AN AMERICAN ADVENTURE IN MANDATES

The British and French in mid-May set forth their ideas of partitioning Turkey and developed the idea of America taking a "mandate." This mandate was to include both Turkish and Russian Armenia with all the old historic Armenian kingdom which included an area of other races in Northern Turkey. It was also to include Constantinople and the Dardanelles. The oil-bearing and other profitable extractions from the Arabian areas were to go to the Allies as mandates or to the creation of new states under their control.

President Wilson was attracted by this mandate idea. I learned of it a few days later when Colonel House suggested that I should be appointed Governor of the mandate. I was greatly distressed at this whole notion and argued at some length with the President that we should not undertake it. I thought, aside from its other disqualifications, it was wrong because it would involve America in the whole power politics of Europe.

I had had some experience in that quarter of the world and I was sure that if he had a picture of it he would not be led into it. It seemed certain to me that among many other objections we would find that combined pressures of Russia and Turkey would necessitate our having to keep an American army of 150,000 in garrison, and that we would be at war with either Turkey or Russia sooner or later. I finally suggested to the President that he send a competent mission to examine the whole project. He agreed, and asked that I suggest the personnel of such a mission. I proposed General Harbord as Chairman, but the matter was still unsettled when the President left Paris. A few days later we cabled to him urging that it be sent (July 3).

The President agreed, and I secured for the General as member his mission William B. Poland, James McKnight and Harold of my staff as engineering and economic experts. Th on the spot August 15th, and in September reported very adversely. The subject was dropped.

EUROPEAN COMMISSIONS UNLIMITED

During the war and the Armistice, the United States was a member of almost a score of control commissions in the economic and military fields. It was proposed that most of them be continued after the peace, and more be added. This was another form of the pool idea. It seemed to me the United States should terminate all such relations except the League. Many of the American staff favored continuing on these commissions, no doubt for good reasons and perhaps with hopes of good jobs in the international field. On April 11th I sent a memorandum to the President and the members of the peace delegation expressing my views, the subject having come before our economic group. The essential paragraphs were:

Dear Mr. President:

Your economic group has had before it the question of whether the United States should continue membership in the various commissions.

I feel strongly that any continuation of the United States in such Allied relationship can only lead to vast difficulty and would militate against the efficiency of the League of Nations.

These commissions would appear to be for one of the following purposes.

a) To give moral and political support to the Allied Governments in measures generally for their benefit. It cannot be conceived that in the prostrate condition of the enemy that the Allies will require any physical assistance to the enforcement of their demands.

b) Another objective might be that we should remain in these commissions with a view to securing justice and moderation in the demands of the Allies against the Central Empires. We would thus be thrust into the repulsive position of the defender of our late enemy. Our experience during the last four months has shown us bitterly that we thus subject ourselves to complaint and attack from the Allied Governments and such a continued relationship would only breed the most acute international friction.

The continuation of this relationship will bind us for a long period of years to a succession of compromises fundamentally at variance with our national convictions. I am not attempting to dispute the righteousness of any Allied demand, but merely to set up the fact that our viewpoint is so essentially different. One other practical result of our experience already is that the

Americans who sit on such commissions, if they don't acquiesce and assist in enforcing any propositions from various government officials, become immediately and personally subject to attack as being inimical to their interests and with the powerful engines of the propaganda which they employ in Europe and our own country no such man can endure for long. . . .

This whole matter has a very practical relationship to the League of Nations. If we can again secure our independence, we can make of the League that strong and independent Court of Appeals that will have authority.

I am convinced that there has grown up since the Armistice the policy, perhaps unconscious but nevertheless effective, of dragging the United States into every political and economic question in Europe where we have no interest. For instance, I don't see how we can remain in these enforcement commissions unless we participate in the military enforcement with its enormous cost and risk, and the tendency will always be to exact the political objectives with the military strength of the United States as a background.

Revolution in Europe is by no means over. The social wrongs in these countries are far from solution and the tempest must blow itself out, probably with enormous violence. . . .

The United States is the one great moral reserve in the world today. . . . We cannot maintain the independence of action through which this reserve is to be made effective if we allow ourselves to be dragged into detailed European entanglements over a period of years.

In my view, if the Allies cannot be brought to adopt peace on the basis of the 14 points, we should retire from Europe lock, stock and barrel, but we should lend to the whole world our economic and moral strength, or the world will swim in a sea of misery and disaster worse than the dark ages. If they cannot be brought to accept peace on this basis, our national honor is at stake and we should have to make peace independently and retire.

I know of nothing in letter or spirit of any statement of your own or in the 14 points that directly or indirectly ties the United States to carry on this war through the phase of enforcement or the multitudinous demands and intrigues of a great number of other governments. . . .

Faithfully yours,

HERBERT HOOVER.

Paris, 15 April, 1919.

My dear Mr. Hoover:

I am very much impressed by your objection to the United tinuing to supply members to the various commissions up under the Peace Treaty and am ready to say at once that I agree with you.

I am afraid that we cannot escape membership on the Financial Commission on Reparation because that commission will undoubtedly need an umpire, and I am afraid we must take the necessary risks in that matter. But with regard to most of the others, you may be sure I shall fight shy.

With warm appreciation of your letter,

Cordially and sincerely yours,

(Signed) Woodrow Wilson.

SIDE-LIGHTS ON THE LEAGUE

On February 15, 1919, President Wilson sailed for the United States for a month. Before his departure he had secured agreement to a preliminary draft of the League. Some time before this semi-final draft was settled, he asked me if I had read the various proposed organization set-ups of the League. I had. I expressed my view by reminding him of the ill-fated Supreme Council of Supply and Relief, which attempted to make an over-elaborate charter; and although we never agreed to it, the organization had died from interminable debate among the other Allies. It was subsequently replaced by the Supreme Economic Council, which had no elaborate covenant but merely a declaration of purpose to deal as best it could with economic problems together with a simple statement of its membership. I suggested to the President that this episode gave a little experience which was worth while. It indicated that if an international body had too elaborate a contract, and too precise powers, the organization would exhaust itself disputing over the extent of its powers and the application of them. Having the powers, if it fell short of performance, it would be damned. Without such powers it was far more effective, for then its efforts would be devoted to finding solutions for immediate problems, and through the building of precedents from successful solutions it could create the greatest of all powers—moral power and prestige. And failure to perform would not be an irreparable injury. I was bold enough to remind him that even with the nebular "Concert of Europe" the powers had so dealt with major jeopardies as to prevent general war over 100 years after the Congress of Vienna.

In that light I suggested he set up the League Council and Assembly, its place of residence and its working machinery including the World Court. That he then give it no powers but the right to enquire into facts and to state the facts. That it should have broad purposes to promote, negotiate and arbitrate peace in the world, and to call the nations concerned into session in times of jeopardy. But the President's mind was on a great detailed political document such as the Constitution of the United States to be applied to the whole earth.

He may have been right, but if it had to be done over again, the light of subsequent experience shows that my line was the only practical one for the time. It would have avoided a thousand pitfalls, and would assuredly have secured American membership and support. And I believe it would have been of infinite service. It might cure the festering cancers to future peace. However, he believed the League would readjust everything, including the appalling economic provisions which the Allies demanded in the peace treaty. The League would bring about disarmament. It would establish liberty under law. It would substitute goodwill for hate.

But in the creation of the League itself, the Allied Powers made sure that they would surrender nothing, change nothing. They did it by securing effective control of the Council by certain permanent members from the Great Powers and the requirement of unanimous vote on major issues. The Allies, knowing Mr. Wilson's fixity of purpose for the League, certainly gave the appearance of holding the President's desires in the offing while they ploughed the immediate field.

One of the stumbling blocks to the President's ideas of the League (which purported not to be a military alliance) was Clemenceau and the French. He sought to secure Clemenceau's support through the provision in Article 10 which in effect guaranteed the boundaries of Europe, as set up in the treaties. Even this did not satisfy the old Tiger and, to get the Covenant approved by the French Prime Minister, Wilson signed a separate and full treaty of alliance. I was disturbed not only by this but by Article 10 itself.

On Mr. Wilson's return to Paris from a month in the United States in mid-March, he found the whole peace-making going badly. The peace-makers were revelling in the ancient practices of diplomacy. The spirit of the twenty-five points was not even receiving lip-service. He started valiantly to restore the solution of the multitude of problems to "fundamentals of justice" and the "New Order" for Europe. He battled manfully but finally they began to wear him down physically and mentally. Early in April he became ill and for some days was helpless. The American peace delegation had no real authority during his illness. When he got about again he seemed to have changed. And at the same time the whole economic and social situation in Europe was dangerously degenerating with the delays in treaty making.

Soon afterwards the President sent for the passenger ship *George Washington*. My belief is that he really intended to break off and go home. However, he received advices from the United States that it would not be understood or well-received. This was natural, because the American people had no way of knowing what was really going on. The "covenants" had not been "openly arrived at" or, to be more exact, openly departed from. With that situation confronting him, I gained the impression that he relaxed in his battle, except on the League, and thus Lloyd George and Clemenceau had much their own way. He apparently came to the conclusion that the only hope lay in the League.

CHAPTER 52

THE PEACE TREATIES *

It must be understood by readers that the treaties with enemy states were elaborate documents apart from the League Covenant. The formulation of the treaty with Germany (and with other enemy states) was done by a host of committees of representatives of the different governments subject to the top council of the "Big Four." The committees each cut out a piece of a mosaic. The document was to be presented to the Germans and they were to be allowed a short time to formulate and present their objections to its terms. Then with such amendments as the "Allied and Associated Powers" concluded to give, they would be shown the dotted line. There were interminable postponements in the final fitting of this compound into one document. It finally comprised 75,000 words, of which only a small minority is devoted to the League Covenant.

I was awakened at four o'clock on the morning of the 7th of May, 1919, by a troubled servant who explained that there was a messenger waiting with a very important document which he would give to no one else than myself. It was the printed draft of the Peace Treaty which was to be handed to the Germans that day. I at once read it. While I had known many of the ideas, agreed upon by committees, I had not before envisaged it as a whole. I was greatly disturbed. In it hate and revenge ran through the political and economic passages. Many provisions had been settled without consideration of how they affected other parts. Conditions were set up upon which Europe could never be rebuilt or peace come to mankind. It seemed to me the economic consequences alone would pull down all Europe and thus injure the United States. I arose and went for a walk in the deserted streets at early daylight. In a few blocks I met General Smuts and John Maynard Keynes. If ever there was something telepathic it was in that meeting. It flashed in all our minds why the others were walking about at that time of day. In comparing notes, I found Smuts and Keynes especially interested in the political pattern, while I had given more thought to the economic side. We agreed that it was terrible and we would do what we could among our own nationals to make the dangers clear.

Keynes at that time was a young economist connected with the British delegation. Lloyd George did not like him, referring to him as the "Puck of Economics." He had a brilliant mind, powerful in analysis and expression. Like most modern intellectuals, he was constantly groping for new shapes and forms for the world rather than for wisdom in what to do next. That sort of mind has a high place in the world, although it sometimes gets on the nerves of the fellow who has to keep the machinery of civilization operating in the meantime. However, Keynes and I agreed fully on the economic consequences of the treaty. I at least won his commendation, for in a book he published later he remarked:

Mr. Hoover was the only man who emerged from the ordeal of Paris with an enhanced reputation. This complex personality, with his habitual air of weary Titan (or, as others might put it, of exhausted prize fighter), his eyes steadily fixed on the true and essential facts of the European situation, imported into the Councils of Paris, when he took part in them, precisely that atmosphere of reality, knowledge, magnanimity and disinterestedness which, if they had been found in other quarters, also, would have given us the Good Peace.[1]

I called together the thinking men of my own organization for breakfast. These men knew every economic and political back alley of Europe better than any group in Paris. And they were men of objective minds, free of hate and violence. We sat for some hours digesting the social, political and economic consequences of the provisional treaty. The Germans would no doubt point out every pinhole with

[1] John Maynard Keynes, *The Economic Consequences of the Peace,* New York, 1919, p. 257. Reprinted by permission of Charles Scribner's Sons.

vigor when they had their say upon it. They would no doubt ask for more than they deserved. In the meantime, we would move on the peace-makers and explain some other things to them. There might be opportunity on our side to get some sense into it through the reply to the Germans.

General Smuts and Keynes met with Vance McCormick and myself to discuss the Treaty. Vance probably had more personal influence with the President than any other American in Paris, as Colonel House had left in a huff over a difference with Wilson concerning the Italian claims.

Smuts was a most able and farseeing man. He became very active for correction of the Treaty. He and other British officials in Paris communicated their views to the Cabinet in London. Their leading men came to Paris to discuss Lloyd George's handiwork in shocked terms. Lloyd George was easily adaptable. As time went on, the British shifted sensibly. But the Englishmen complained that Mr. Wilson was very difficult. It was at this time that Keynes coined his famous phrase that Lloyd George, having bamboozled Wilson, could not debamboozle him.

McCormick, myself and some others called upon the President and urged that we take advantage of the British recantation. He did not seem very enthusiastic about doing it and was obviously tired and on the defensive. We urged him to call the American leaders in Paris into conference, which he agreed to do when the Germans made reply.

The question arose of the method by which the Germans would be compelled to sign on the dotted line. Mr. Wilson's "point" "on the basis of a free acceptance of that settlement" had been forgotten. Foch proposed that the food blockade be re-imposed. At that spot he was in my province. I protested to the President on May 14th:

Dear Mr. President:

. . . I . . . express to you my strong view that we should not be led into joining with the Allies in a food blockade against Germany as a method of forcing peace. The margins on which the German people must live from now until next harvest are so small that any cessation of the stream of food, even for a short time, will bring the most wholesale loss of life. It might be that the imposition of a blockade would be effectual in securing the German signature to the peace. I seriously doubt when the world has recovered its moral equilibrium that it would consider a peace obtained upon such a device as the starving of women and children as being binding upon the German people. If the Germans did resist, it is my impression that it would throw Germany into complete chaos and military occupation would need to follow in order to save Europe. . . .

HERBERT HOOVER.

The Supreme Council informed Foch that if force were to be used it must be military. He mobilized his armies ostentatiously for invasion about June 19th.

On May 30th the Germans gave their expected answer and asked for more amendment than they deserved. But some of their criticism was sound. They pointed out the entire failure to adhere to the Fourteen Points and the "Particulars" upon which they claimed to have surrendered. In the meantime the reports of my organization showed a most serious degeneration in Germany. It looked as if their newly elected Parliament would blow up and leave the country without a responsible body to make peace. Renewed Communist riots and disturbances took place over the Reich which were put down with much bloodshed.

The meeting of the American group with the President took place upon the 3rd of June. It did not get much of anywhere except to point out the major weakness in the Treaty. My remarks upon the subject irritated the President, and he made sharp replies.

On June 5th I drew up a memorandum on the whole subject at the request of Secretary Lansing who sent a copy of it to the President.

In any discussion of the draft treaty, I think it must be accepted as a premise that real justice can never be meted out, for no adequate punishment of German crimes is conceivable or even compassed in the present draft treaty. Therefore, if we strip the subject of questions of punishment and also of all humanitarian views toward the Germans the impression I get from a study of the situation is as follows:

A

The objectives desired appear to me to be:

I. To take all the economic surplus of Germany for a generation. This premise necessarily assumes that it is not desired to claim more than the surplus, for in such case the population will either (*a*) die, (*b*) migrate, or (*c*) plunge into economic chaos that will engulf Europe, and in either case yield no surplus.

II. To effect such regime and control as will strip Germany of the power of political and military offensive. This premise assumes that it is desired to establish stable democracy in Germany, for otherwise she will turn either to Communism or to reaction, and will thereby become either militarily or politically on the offensive.

III. To secure signature to and acquiescence in the treaty by the German people. This premise necessitates that the signature should be obtained without either (*a*) blockade, (*b*) bombing of towns, or (*c*) military occupation. I assume that a treaty signed under either blockade or bombing would be revised within twelve months under the recoil of the moral shock to the world, and I also assume that military occupation means not only further enormous sacrifices to the Allies but also developing political entanglements amongst themselves. Furthermore, it is not at all certain that it would be unwelcomed by a very large part of Germany as a guarantee of food, industrial recuperation and protection of private property, for under any occupation the population must be fed and put to production, and this will be at least at the initial expense of the Allies.

B

As I weigh the draft treaty on these premises, and alternatives, I am convinced that: (*a*) the demands made are greater than the economic surplus; (*b*) that the regime and controls are such as endanger stable democracy in Germany; and (*c*) that the Germans will never sign the treaty in its present form. The present Government in Germany is the only alternative to either Reactionary or Communistic Government, and if it fails we have political debacle in any event. . . .

C

I am not unaware that criticism is easy, nor am I unaware that the problem involved is the most difficult that statesmen have been confronted with, because it resolves itself into the degree with which all the objectives above can be imposed and still not create the adverse currents to which I have referred. Nor am I unaware of the fact that every statesman will have a different view as to the degree with which these demands can be imposed with success.

The point I would like to make is, however, that many of the demands in the draft treaty are impossible either of acceptance or, if accepted, will not obtain the results expected. They have been included against the protests of the President and his colleagues, but yielded by them because of their belief that the very survival of 200 million people revolved around the immediate conclusion of these negotiations and the return of these populations to production. . . .

D

I see in the present British change of heart a tendency to the recognition of the President's original propositions, and it appears to me that it offers an opportunity for the President now to definitely insist from an American point of view that these modifications should be carried out.

E

I am not sure how far we ought to sacrifice the United States to the objectives of the European Allies. To me, from an American point of view, we have been fighting autocracy and militarism and it has been destroyed. I feel that the paramount issues are now to secure stability of government in Europe; to secure the establishment of democracy in Germany; to secure a League of Nations that may be able to further correct the international wrongs which have been accumulated over centuries and deter the repetition of such wrongs in the future; to give security to the many nations that have been re-created and to secure to the Allies any practicable reparation.

If tested by this touchstone alone, modifications in the proposed treaty will not involve or jeopardize these points, whereas the failure to make immediate stable peace does jeopardize them. These are the high objectives which the President has held constantly before him as in the interest of the world as a whole, and I feel that the opportunity is arriving for the President to absolutely insist on his original contentions, even at the risk of disruption of the Conference. I believe this disruption is the least of evils; I do not believe it will happen. . . .

(Signed) HERBERT HOOVER.

A few days after the President had received my memorandum on the subject, I had what proved to be my last important discussion with him. He had sent for me as he wished to discuss the memorandum. He said that we could not go on and on in this negotiation in the face of European degeneration. I pointed out the certainty of disastrous financial repercussions over the huge indeterminate amount of reparations, and at the same time the hobbling of productivity in Germany, which would make it impossible for her to pay any reparations. Among the examples of totally impossible confusions, I cited that the coal to be furnished to the Allies for reparations and lost to Germany by separations of coal territory such as the Saar, Silesia, and Teschen would in total reduce Germany's supply to little more than the household consumption, leaving nothing for railways, utilities, and manufacture.

As to the other proposed treaties I objected that the failure to secure some sort of economic unity in the Danube states would bring trouble to the world; that Vienna with all its trade cut off, would never be self-supporting and in consequence would always be a center of instability. I objected to the transfers of large blocks of German, Hungarian and Russian nationals to the "liberated" states, as only fuel for another war. I complained that there was no disarmament of the powers, other than Germany.

I had, perhaps, used over-vigorous words. He flashed angrily at these expressions as being personal accusations against him—which I, least of all persons, intended. But his nerves, like those of all of us, were taut. Colonel House had already broken with him over the Treaty and left Paris. Other than a formal goodbye at the railway platform at Paris, I never saw him again while he was in the Presidency.

Mr. Wilson has been much blamed that he did not secure more revision of the Peace Treaty at this opportunity of the British recantation. That view, I hold, is not just, although I urged more action.

It should be said for him that he profoundly distrusted Lloyd George and considered much of that statesman's action was part gesture and part secretive power politics. He had for months fought many of the provisions which Lloyd George now wanted changed. I suspect he got satisfaction from witnessing the fullness of his intellectual somersaults in the sudden reversal under pressures from London. In these matters, Mr. Wilson rightly wanted Lloyd George to fight it out with Clemenceau. The President had made up his mind that the men and forces that dominated the situation were not to be surmounted at this time. He had given way on many points because of his belief that in the League he had the remedy. Moreover, he had in him a strain of the

Scotch Covenanter who, having once concluded he was right, saw only evil in any other course.

In the end, Mr. Wilson did accept some modifications. However, even those proposed by Lloyd George did not take the dragon's teeth out of the Treaty.

The real problem facing the President was, should he break off and go home? A few months earlier, he could have done so and Europe would have made its own treaty. Now it was too late. The deterioration in Europe was such that a break now would have been a world catastrophe. With all my forebodings about the Treaty, I decided for myself to support its ratification by the United States as a lesser evil.

There is another element in this episode which only history will verify. During the Peace Conference, the President was absent for some time, because, it was said, of an attack of influenza. When he returned he was drawn, exhausted, and haggard. He sometimes groped for ideas. His mind constantly strove for previous decisions and precedents in even minor matters. He clung to them.[2]

Prior to that time in all matters with which I had to deal, he was incisive, quick to grasp essentials, unhesitating in conclusions, and most willing to take advice. After the time I mention, McCormick and Davis and I found that we had to push against an unwilling mind. And at times, when I just had to get decisions, our constant resort was to find a "precedent."

On Saturday, June 28th, we all went to the Hall of Mirrors at Versailles to witness the signing. General Smuts signed the Treaty as a British delegate and at the same time issued a press statement denouncing it and demanding revision.

I took satisfaction in the great spiritual lift given to the French people by this ceremony at Versailles in the spot where they had been ruthlessly humiliated nearly fifty years before. But I had difficulty in keeping my mind on the ceremony. It was constantly traveling along the fearful consequences of many paragraphs which these men were signing with such pomp, and then it moved back to the high hopes with which I had landed in Europe eight months before. I did not come away exultant.

[2] Years afterward his servant told me it was a mild thrombosis.

CHAPTER 53

WHAT HAPPENED
TO THE FOURTEEN POINTS
AND THE ADDITIONAL ELEVEN POINTS*

It is important to consider the results of this gigantic crusade to impose American ideas and ideals upon Europe. To illuminate the subject,
the fate of the Fourteen Points and the further eleven points from the
"supplementary addresses" may be first reviewed and mourned.

The fate of each point can be stated briefly.

Point 1, "open covenants openly arrived at—diplomacy . . . frankly
in public . . .," died before the President reached Paris, through
private understandings among the Allies, and the secret treaties. Its
funeral was attended in the limousines which bore the statesmen to
every day's secret conference.

Point 2, that is, "freedom of the seas," was dear to Mr. Wilson's concept of freedom at large. His definition of freedom of the seas was:
"Absolute freedom of navigation upon the seas outside territorial waters
alike in peace and in war," except as the seas may be closed by "international agreement." It was not objected to by the Allies when promul-
gated, but was flatly rejected fifteen days before the Armistice. Wilson
was helpless, as the war was already won. He was compelled to agree
to the feeble compromise that the "freedom of the seas would be discussed at the Peace Table." It was feebly discussed.

Point 3, the removal of international barriers to commerce, was violated in individual action by every one of the twenty-six governments
in Europe. Without consulting the peace conference, new tariffs, trans-

portation and other trade barriers were erected. And the Treaty itself in effect prohibited Austria from a tariff union with Germany.

Point 4, on universal disarmament, was applied only against the enemy. The provisions in the League amounted only to agreement to discuss.

Point 5, amplified by "later addresses" on "no annexations," "no barter of peoples," and "self-determination," was asphyxiated under the word "mandates." It was unblushingly rejected by the cession of Shantung to Japan. The huge blocks of aliens included in the liberated states did not feel that "self-determination" was a very lively reality.

Point 6, on "non-interference with" and "aid to Russia," was executed by subsidizing futile White armies to attack her. British, French, Americans and Japanese were engaged in this operation for months after the "point." When the British army got tired and the French mutinied at Odessa, Mr. Churchill proposed a whole new campaign to be participated in by the American Army. But President Wilson had the power to and did stop any American participation in this idea.

Point 9, on Italian boundaries that should include only Italians, was fulfilled, but groups of Austrians, Germans, and Slavs were put in as good measure. Their right of "self-determination" and "not to be bandied about" was not hinted at.

Points 7, 8, 10, 11, and 13, relating to independence and restoration of specific oppressed peoples, were largely carried out. This was the President's real success, and I shall expand on this later.

Point 14, the League of Nations, was largely as Mr. Wilson wanted it.

The further eleven points in the "subsequent addresses" mostly met disaster. We can list them with their fates.

Point 15 (the New Order) became a slogan of derision.

Point 16 (ending of aggression) failed because the League members subsequently were not able to agree on the use of its powers in such emergencies.

Point 17 (abolition of military alliances, balance of power, etc.) had died long before Mr. Wilson left Paris. Already the French were building their alliances to encircle Germany. An alliance was at once entered into between Britain and France. Even before peace was signed

France by furnishing arms to various nations were preparing military alliances.

The "balance of power" concept sprung quickly to life. Mr. Wilson made a great speech in Manchester, England, denouncing the balance of power as a root of evil. Two days later, Clemenceau made a speech in the French Assembly rejecting the President's idea *in toto*.

Point 18, on equality of nations, was dead the moment the permanent seats on the Council of the League were created.

Point 19, "self-determination—an imperative principle of action"— was not applied to Austria or Danzig, nor to the border populations, who were "bandied about."

Point 20, the "world safe for democracy," was indeed transitory.

Point 21, universal democracy, was somewhat launched except in Russia, Japan, Hungary, Turkey, Bulgaria and Roumania. And under treaty and other war aftermaths, it died successively in a dozen other nations.

Point 22, on German colonies and other backward people being the wards of the world, has already been discussed under Point 5.

Point 23, negotiated peace with "settlement of every question . . . on the basis of free acceptance of that settlement," was blunted by the massing of armies to force signature of the enemy states on the dotted line.

Point 24, that it was to be a "just peace," and Point 25, that there were to be no indemnities or "punitive damages," certainly were not permitted to function.

In general, twenty out of twenty-five points were variously violated or distorted by the time they came out from under the millstones of the best European diplomatic thought. Europe said the United States ran out on them after the Peace. The fact is, Europe ran out on the United States in the Peace.

Mr. Wilson's expression of American ideals was the only spiritual expression in the Conference. At every step he fought the forces of hate. It was Mr. Wilson's force that carried through the League Covenant. But the League was shackled to enforcement of the Treaty and, through the permanent members, was placed in control of the Imperial Powers. Wilson's concept that it should be an independent and reviewing agency was lost. Nevertheless, the League idea re-enforced the idea of international co-operation to preserve peace, which will not die if civilization is to endure.

There can be no doubt that Mr. Wilson made the major contribution to lifting oppression from millions of people and setting them upon the road to hope. His inspiration made certain the independence and freedom of the Finns, the Poles, the Latvians, the Estonians, the Lithuanians, the Czechs, the Slovaks, the Slovenes, the Croatians, after hundreds of years of oppression. These millions of people will forever hold Wilson's name in grateful memory. And it is Wilson's name that stands out in their monuments and the names of their streets and parks.

A further service of America under his leadership was the generosity unparalleled in the history of mankind, which saved hundreds of millions of lives in Europe from famine, pestilence, and revolutionary chaos. We thereby gave the tender plants of representative government a chance. In war and peace, Mr. Wilson went down into the pit of chaos and came out with something that expanded liberty and lessened the suffering of the world.

CHAPTER 54

WHY AMERICA CANNOT MAKE PEACE IN EUROPE

I came out of all these experiences with one absolute conviction, which was: America, with its skill in organization and the valor of its sons, could win great wars. But it could not make lasting peace. I was convinced we must keep out of Old World wars, lend ourselves to measures preventing war, maintaining peace and healing the wounds of war.

I came to this conclusion because of irreconcilable conflicts in concepts and historic experience between the New World and the Old World. They reached into depths of our international relations, government, social and economic life. They confronted me daily during the war, the Armistice, and in the confusion of making peace. The two worlds were indeed strangers to each other. We had drifted farther and farther apart over 300 years. Indeed, the departure was greater than this number of years, for our ancestors had fled from Europe because they already opposed its ideas on religion and freedom.

During the war and Armistice years I had made many notes on the fundamental separation and its consequences, with a multitude of examples. Again I may repeat, this statement as to events at Versailles and the discussion of our relations to Europe were written in 1922–26. They reflect somewhat the world setting and the climate of American international policies and actions in this period.

IMPERIALISM

Prior to the war, every one of the European states (except Sweden and Switzerland) was an Empire, holding colonies, or to some degree

[473]

dominating and exploiting other races and their resources. The standards of living of the people in the "Mother Country" in each Empire
had been built up and their economies geared to returns from these possessions. This Imperial concept was also induced, in part, by the pressures on the home population.

European countries had been afflicted for hundreds of years by
rivalries and conflicts over their holdings and their expansions. They
had relied, and inevitably must continue to rely, upon military strength,
military alliances, "balances of power," and power politics for the protection of their possessions.

The World War and the peace stripped the enemy nations—Germany, Austria, Turkey, and Bulgaria—of all their possessions and the
victors either liberated or annexed these through "mandates" or otherwise. The peace partly stripped the Russian Empire, liberating some
races, and the victors annexed others. The victor states all profited in
Empire. Therefore, the theory and practice of Empire was by no
means uprooted by the war. It was expanded by the peace.

The New World nations had no Empires or spirit of Empire. With
abundant resources, a paucity of population, there was no population
pressure or inspiration to Imperialism. Indeed, through the Monroe
Doctrine, we had stopped the expansion of European Empires in the
Western Hemisphere. By the Spanish-American War, we had freed
Cuba and the Philippines from Spain. We had established the independence of Cuba and were in process of doing so for the Philippines.
But the conflict of these concepts reached to the very base of our ideas
of freedom.

RACIAL INDEPENDENCE

In 160 years of national life, we had learned the values of independence of nations. We were proud of the blessings of freedom which
sprang from it. We naturally wished them for all other peoples. We
instinctively sympathized with every race struggling for these ideals.
Ours was a concept of the "self-determination" and freedom of states
built on racial boundaries. All of which was a far departure from Old
World ideas in this field and brought constant conflict in approach to
its problems of peace.

The borders of mixed populations in Europe—the "irredentas"—have been the scene of constant agitation and conflict for centuries. In every one of them some nationals are separated from their fatherlands. The dominating government unceasingly sought to impose its national language and customs upon these minorities. Their cries to the sympathies of their racial brothers across the borders were an unceasing stimulant to friction. These boundaries shifted with every war and the conflicts flamed up in new areas. The "irredentas" were awarded from expediency or often upon favor to some ally. In many of these assignments our ideas of "self-determination" came into sharp conflict and the American people were constantly stirred by the appeals of these minorities.

DICTATORS

The continent of Europe has another constant experience strange to the United States. Out of the political pressures, miseries, revolutions and ambitions of men, it has had to bear the periodic rise of militant dictators who at once endanger the peace. Its history, from the foundation of our Republic to 1926, has seen the succession of Napoleon, Kaiser Wilhelm, Lenin and Stalin, and Mussolini. The processes which give rise to these disasters involve forces from which we have departed for centuries.

COMMUNISM, SOCIALISM, FASCISM

With the First World War new explosives were planted in Europe. Communism and Socialism, stimulated by Hegel, Karl Marx, and others, had become a living force.

These infections with their propaganda and actual militant organizations added to the disintegrating forces from the war itself. These European infections, born of miseries, spread into the United States. I published a little book upon our relations with them and tried to express the ideals of our American system in contrast with European social and economic systems generally.[1]

HATES

We in the New World were strangers to the Old World's inherited hates, its jealousies, and constant fears of military invasion. We had never been subject to the fear of military attack. There had been no

[1] *American Indiviaualism,* Doubleday, Doran & Co., New York, 1922.

continued national wrongs and consequently, no national hates on this side of the ocean. We had a peace-time Army of only police size, and that without conscription. We had a modest Navy mostly to create respect for our citizens engaged in peaceful purposes abroad. Ours had been a security from aggression the nations in Europe had never experienced, and in consequence we had no conception of their needs for military protection.

METHODS OF DIPLOMACY

The practice of Imperialism, its expansion and protection, together with the constantly disquieting "irredentas," fears of aggression, dictators and frictions generally, made "power politics," "balances of power," and military alliances a national necessity to the major nations of Europe.

The duty of European statesmen of good-will is to engage incessantly in adroit power politics, by which aggression is checked and the malign forces allayed, in hopes that a tenuous peace can be extended a little longer. It is a delicate job in which national honor and loyalties to agreement by any of them are continuously sacrificed to expediencies and self-preservation.

We were ill-adapted or prepared to engage successfully in these practices or even to understand them. Our form of representative government gives neither opportunity to learn the skills of power politics and balances of power, nor to practice them if we did. Our government, with its shifting administrations and policies, prevents us from developing the experienced personnel which could know. With our changing elections we can never have the continuity in foreign policies upon which such men could act with assurance in these fields, if they did know. Moreover, we are made up from these many races of Europe, each retaining a subcurrent of sympathy with its origins which exerts a clouding influence on objective action. To participate successfully in foreign power politics, we must become something other than a free people as we conceive it.

If anyone wants confirmation of all this, he needs only to analyze our group of peacemakers who, with little experience in foreign affairs, worked in a sort of daze over the forces they met at Paris.

REPRESENTATIVE GOVERNMENT

Beyond these immediate currents, our concepts of government were far different from Europe. Our founding fathers perhaps owed more of their initial ideas to Ancient Greece and Rome than to Europe of their time. Few and only minor republics then existed and the Divine Right of Kings was almost universal. In setting the pattern of representative government, the fathers no doubt adopted some ideas from the British but even here we grew up on entirely different lines.

Where representative governments had developed on the Continent, they were widely different from ours. They were all of parliamentary form, where administration was carried on in fact by a committee of the legislative arm reinforced by a long-trained and skilled bureaucracy, as contrasted with our single executive for a fixed term of years with changing public servants. In ours, we rigidly separated the executive, the legislative and the judicial branches. In theirs, there was no separation of executive from the legislature, and less separation of the judiciary. Ours was a Federal government of limited powers, based primarily on local responsibilities; theirs were centralized governments. Their Prime Ministers and Cabinets could speak for the legislative arm. Our President could not. And therefore our government representatives could not speak for, or bind, the nation in complicated peace negotiations.

SOCIAL STRUCTURE

Our departure from the social concepts of Western Europe spanned the full distance of three hundred years. We separated from them because we did not like them. A separation of thought was inevitable, and the breach constantly widened. Their class stratifications clogged the free rise of particles in the social solution. Opportunity, even in Britain, was mostly confined to a semi-oligarchy of about 20 per cent of the people. France was somewhat better. Broad concepts of individual right and true individual dignity of the American type more nearly existed in some of the small countries. But even there it was fenced in by a mass of aristocratic survivals and barriers. The signs of equal opportunity were rare indeed. In our widespread opportunities, and at least an ideal of equal opportunity, there had developed a genuine fellowship among our people that contributed a deep sense of equality for which there was little European counterpart.

ECONOMIC CONCEPTS

Our departures on the economic side are equally vivid. We have not only been free from need to exploit other nations as a part of economic support to our daily living, but in the eighties we brought about a revolution in our economic system which has been a major departure from the *laissez faire* economies of Europe. At that time we passed the Interstate Commerce Act establishing the public regulation of natural monopolies. Of much greater importance, we enacted the Anti-Trust laws. Europe never had adopted this Anti-Trust concept. Its economies were honeycombed with cartels, trusts and agreements in restraint of trade, the object of which was to make profits by control of price and distribution. By maintaining competition, we compelled profits to come from improved technology, new inventions, labor-saving devices, and more skilled labor. Thus costs and prices were steadily diminished. With these dynamic forces, we had lifted our standards of living far beyond anything known to European masses. In consequence our economic relations in treaty-making brought sharp conflicts.

CROSS CURRENTS

Too many Americans do not realize to what extent our ideas and our way of life have grown apart from Europe in these three hundred years of separation. American Society with a capital S, and many of our Intellectuals with a capital I, have made a sort of fetish of their spiritual home in Europe. They fail to recognize that ours is a setting three centuries distant.

They are much influenced by its magnificent cities, historic cathedrals, art, music, literature, great universities, monuments of human heroism and progress. They meet peoples of fine hospitality, of the widest cultivation and attainments. It is easy to recall that in Europe ever since the Renaissance men have fought and died to build the structure of personal liberty, to lift the dignity of men, to bring security and peace. And that from every country—England, Germany, France, Russia and all the others—we have received magnificent inheritances of human thought.

But these Americans too often see little of the gigantic explosive forces that are constant among these peoples. The reality is that there are twenty-six races of 400,000,000 people, cheek by jowl in an area two-thirds the size of the United States. Through them surge the deep-seated tribal instincts of nationalism, imperialism, age-old hates, memories of deep wrongs, fierce distrusts and impellent fears. There are the conflicts of religion and racial persecution. And even before the World War these forces received added ferment from new and fierce ideologies.

These conflicts in concepts, this experience of the treaty-making should indicate how impossible it is for America to resolve the problems of Europe.

In sum, the forces which lay behind the rejection of American ideas at Paris were far deeper than the intrigues of diplomacy or the foibles of European statesmen. Here was the collision of civilizations that had grown three hundred years apart. The idealism of the Western World was in clash with deep forces in Europe with its racial *mores* and the grim necessities of these twenty-six races.

CHAPTER 55

LIVING IN PARIS—
AND LEAVING FOR HOME

During the eleven months which I spent mostly in Paris, I saw practically no one except officials. Very rarely did I accept invitations to dinners; I did not go to a single theatre; I visited no museums or galleries and, except for an occasional Sunday hour at Notre Dame, I saw no cathedrals or "sights." I never went into a shop; when my clothes ran short, some one secured them for me. Only twice did I take time for a short motor trip to the countryside. Had I not already known France rather intimately, I would have learned nothing of her greatness, nor of her abundant intellectual and social life from this eleven months' visit. I worked from twelve to eighteen hours daily and on Sundays. I used breakfast, lunch and dinner as times to do business with my own staff and officials of other Governments.

The Crillon Hotel had been leased for the American Delegation, and I kept an apartment there as a meeting place with the American officials and sometimes to sleep. As I wished to live with my staff, we secured a large furnished residence on Rue de Lübeck in which I stopped most of the time and where most of our important staff members stayed when they were at headquarters. The expense was borne by us and not by the American Government. How the staff lived, I never quite knew, for there were only four bathrooms for thirty men.

Soon after arriving in Paris, I received word from Kosta Boris, a former servant of one of our neighbors, but now a private in the Army, that he would "like dreadfully" to come to Paris. I brought him in just for general purposes, for he could do anything about a house. Gradually I noticed new privates and even sergeants about the place. Finally on consulting Boris, I found he had brought in sixteen of them, all friends whom he had saved from village drill and for whom he had inveigled jobs in our house on the ground that Mr. Hoover wanted them. He had selected them with a certain wisdom, for among them were a professional tailor, a clothes cleaner, a bootblack stand operator, four or five chauffeurs, several assistant cooks, and plenty of watchmen. The French lady cook, who ran the house, took them all in amiably, taught them some French, and they really worked—when on duty.

Usually thirty of our men sat at the table. They arrived from every part of Europe with all their troubles, the adventures and the humor they gathered, and in addition many specimens of curious foods and drinks. Hugh Gibson and Will Irwin furnished the never-failing rays of sunshine. These occasions forged a rare *esprit de corps* and hundreds of friendships were formed which endured over the rest of our lives.

A few weeks before the end, Mrs. Hoover came to Paris with Allan to be with me for a little while and to accompany me home. She brought about a union of Allan and General Pershing's son, Warren, both of whom were then about twelve years old. She attached to them a French lady to improve their French and the General contributed a sergeant who served as enforcement officer and tourist agent. They roamed the old battlefields and Paris generally. Allan undertook an important collection of arms from the spots where they had been used. Among them was an aerial torpedo which he had picked up on the Chemin des Dames. His enforcement agency had carefully unloaded it, and Allan prized it highly. One night a group of generals dined with us, and one of them inspected Allan's collection. When he came to the aerial torpedo he expressed vivid alarm. He insisted on taking it at once from the hotel. He had it dropped carefully into the Seine. No explanation that we could give satisfied Allan as to the General's character as a gentleman or his competence as a military man.

When the date of my departure from Europe in September was announced, I received a deluge of letters and telegrams of appreciation. They came from Presidents and Prime Ministers of Britain, France, Italy, Belgium, and all the other countries we had served. They came from my colleagues in every country. They came from His Holiness the Pope, the heads of the Greek, Armenian, and Lutheran Churches. An especially affectionate message was from my old friend, Cardinal Mercier. But the most touching of all were the volumes which arrived over the years containing literally millions of signatures of children, with their own illustrations.

My last call before leaving was upon Prime Minister Clemenceau to express my appreciation for his undeviating support. He was in a gloomy mood, saying, "There will be another world war in your time and you will be needed back in Europe." [1] We would not have agreed on the methods of preventing it, so I did not pursue the subject. But to lighten the parting, I said, "Do you remember Captain Gregory's report on the decline and fall of the Hapsburgs?" He laughed, pulled out a drawer in his desk and produced the original telegram, saying, "I keep it close by, for that episode was one of the few flashes of humor that came into our attempts to make over the world." He was still chuckling when we parted.

[1] The Prime Minister was fairly accurate on both counts. The Second World War began twenty-one years after the end of the first one. I was back in Europe in 1946 to co-ordinate world food supplies to meet the terrible famine arising from the Second World War.

INDEX

Abyssinia, 97–98

Adams, Prof. E. D., 327

Adelante Villa (Stanford), 16

Agnew, John A., mining engineer, 34 and n., 36, 45, 51–52, 57, 78 n., 81; H. H.'s chief of staff, 100, 110 n., 139

Agricola, *De Re Metallica,* 117–119, 129; on miner's calling, 134

Agricultural Advisory Committee, 243

Albany (Western Australia), 30

Albert, King of the Belgians, 185–187, 232, 235

Alcohol, trials by, 43, 45

Allen, Ben S., 156, 209, 253

Allied Blockade Committee, 331, 339, 346, 347

Allied Food Council, 259

Allied Maritime Council, 311–312

Altai Mountains, 107

Amalgamated Zinc Co., 89

American Committee in London, and the war-stranded Americans, 141–148

American Communists, 108 n.

American Marines at Tientsin, 52, 53

American missionaries in China, 42–44

American Peace Mission, 312, 432–433

American Red Cross, 321, 325, 327

American Refugee Committee in Brussels, 152–153

American Relief Administration (Child Feeding), brief account of, 322–324; in Estonia, 371; in Latvia, 377; in Lithuania, 378; in Czechoslovakia, 381; in Yugoslavia, 384; in Austria, 394, 395; in Hungary, 401, 405; in Roumania, 409; continuance of, 422, 424; children restored to health, 427; significance of its work, 428, 430

American Woman's Hospital (Paignton), 210, 211–212

American Women's Committee for Economic Relief, 211

Americans, in Russia, 105, 105 n., 106, 107, 108; war-stranded, in London, 141–148

Amsterdam, 333

Anderson, Frank, 112–113

Angell, Frank, 209

Angell, Norman, 138

Antonio López, ship, N.Y. to Cadiz, 219, 220–222

Antwerp, 153, 229, 233, 333

Argentina, 158, 241, 391–392

Arkansas, vacation job on State Geological Survey, 17–18

Armenia (Republic), 385–389

Armistice (1918), and the C.R.B., 227–228; negotiation for, 275–276; world food problems at, 276–280; shipping problems at, 310; rail facilities at, 313, 383; American hopes at, 434; change of Allied attitude toward U.S., at, 438

Asquith, Herbert H., Prime Minister, 162, 234

Associated Press, 153, 156

Atwood, Colonel W. G., 313, 315, 382, 384

Australia, mine engineering in, 28, 29–34, 36; and Commission for Relief in Belgium, 158; at Paris Peace Conference, 442

Austria, famine in, 304–305, 392, 393, 394, 395; hatred of, 317, 381, 382, 392, 394; and coal, 317, 318, 392, 393; barter with other states, 320, 393, 395; and food blockade, 334, 392; relief of, 392–395

Austria-Hungary, ultimatum to Serbia, 137; effect of Armistice on railways of, 312, 314

Automobiles, use of, 85–86

Azerbaijan (Republic), 385–389 *passim*

70
71
72
74
75
76
77
79
83
88